PENGUIN BOOKS

1914

Over the past twenty years Lyn Macdonald has established a popular reputation as an author and historian of the First World War. Her books are *They Called it Passchendaele*, an account of the Passchendaele campaign in 1917; *The Roses of No Man's Land*, a chronicle of the war from the neglected viewpoint of the casualties and the medical teams who struggled to save them; *Somme*, a history of the legendary and horrifying battle that has haunted the minds of succeeding generations; *1914*, a vivid account of the first months of the war and winner of the 1987 *Yorkshire Post* Book of the Year Award; *1914–1918: Voices and Images of the Great War*, an illuminating account of the many different aspects of the war; and *1915, The Death of Innocence*. All are based on the accounts of eyewitnesses and survivors, told in their own words, and cast a unique light on the First World War. They are all published by Penguin.

Lyn Macdonald is married and lives in London.

D0167172

LYN MACDONALD

1914

THE DAYS OF HOPE

PENGUIN BOOKS

PENGUIN BOOKS

Published by the Penguin Group
Penguin Books Ltd, 27 Wrights Lane, London w8 5tz, England
Penguin Books USA Inc., 375 Hudson Street, New York, New York 10014, USA
Penguin Books Australia Ltd, Ringwood, Victoria, Australia
Penguin Books Canada Ltd, 10 Alcorn Avenue, Toronto, Ontario, Canada m4v 3b2
Penguin Books (NZ) Ltd, 182–190 Wairau Road, Auckland 10, New Zealand

Penguin Books Ltd, Registered Offices: Harmondsworth, Middlesex, England

First published in Great Britain by Michael Joseph 1987
Published in Penguin Books 1989
7 9 10 8 6

Set in 9.5/11pt Monotype Bembo
Typeset by Rowland Phototypesetting Ltd,
Bury St Edmunds, Suffolk
Printed in England by Clays Ltd, St Ives plc

For the Chums
for old times' sake.

Contents

List of Illustrations

Consultation at a crossroads in Ghent. (*Imperial War Museum*)
One of Commander Sampson's armoured cars on the Menin road.
   (*Imperial War Museum*)
The lush and leafy countryside provided useful cover, soon to vanish as
   the land was devastated. (*Imperial War Museum*)

First Battle of Ypres
Devastation in Ypres. (*Imperial War Museum*)
The Queen's Own Oxfordshire Hussars leaving St-Omer.
Father Camille Delaere. (*Imperial War Museum*)
Charles Worsley with his wife.
The temporary cross that marked Worsley's grave at Zandvoorde.
The west wing of Hooge Château. (*Imperial War Museum*)
Transport retiring down the Menin road, October 1914. (*Imperial War
   Museum*)
Troops on reconnaissance near Zandvoorde. (*Imperial War Museum*)
The 2nd Scots Guards entrenched at Zandvoorde. (*Imperial War Museum*)
The Cloth Hall still smouldering two days after it was set alight. (*Imperial
   War Museum*)
Remnants of the London Scottish after their blooding at Messines.
   (*Imperial War Museum*)
The French 75mm gun – the famous Soixante Quinze. (*Imperial War
   Museum*)
The troopship *Afric*.
Ralph Langley, a newly enlisted soldier of the King's Royal Rifle Corps.

Copyright owners are indicated in brackets; all photographs not credited are from private sources.

List of Maps

Author's Foreword and Acknowledgements

The history of 1914 is not so much the story of a war as of an army.

It is hard to pin down the spirit of 1914, for the spirit and attitudes of the men who were actually doing the fighting were strikingly different from the attitudes of the civilians and those who were flocking to the colours at home and around the Empire. Their War, their blooding and their disillusionment were yet to come. Brooke, Grenfell, Owen, Sassoon, Hodgson, made no secret of their idealism (and how soon it changed with the experience of war!) and it is difficult for succeeding generations to identify with their extraordinary view of war as a purification, their strange resignation to dying, their passive embracement of fate, their unquestioning acceptance. The questioning and the bitterness were born later, in the stultifying horrors of trench warfare.

For the soldiers of 1914 it was different. Kitchener's Army was proud of its amateurism, but the regular soldiers of the old British Army took pride in their bold professional skills – and they were professionals to the marrow. The nickname 'Old Contemptibles' which they so good-humouredly adopted does not appear in these pages. (In any event, the Kaiser was referring to the size of the British Expeditionary Force, and not to its quality.) If Kitchener's Army of volunteers was prepared to fight and possibly die because it was their duty, the officers and men of 1914 were prepared to fight and die simply because it was their job.

My thanks as always must go first and foremost to the old soldiers who have taken the trouble to recall those times and to talk and write about their experiences. Only some of them are directly quoted; the recollections of many, many more are incorporated in the text and they will recognise the tales and the details they have supplied which have helped so enormously in the task not only of writing about their war and their experiences, but also of setting them in the context of their world and the times they lived in 'the day before yesterday'. It is almost – but not quite yet – part of history, for many people who were young at the beginning of this momentous twentieth century are still alive. Some centuries from now, in purely historical terms, we will all be seen as contemporaries, and their history will come to be regarded as part of ours, as indeed it is.

Only yesterday (at the time of writing) one old soldier* (a volunteer) remarked to me: 'We thought we were fighting the War to end Wars.' Well, perhaps, in a sense, they were, for the profound effect of their experiences on succeeding generations has surely been a powerful force for peace, even if it has not precisely been 'Peace in our time' so much as peace *some* time. Of course, that can only be a matter of opinion. What is undeniable is the continuing and, indeed, growing interest in the First World War. People – and especially young people – still flock to those old battlefields of the Western Front, visit the cemeteries, tramp the trenchlines, ponder, remember and, in a sense, still mourn – long after the generation of parents and grandparents, and even brothers and sisters, who had first-hand reasons for mourning has itself 'faded away'. And they still ask 'Why?'

I would be the last to try to claim that this book comes anywhere near supplying an answer to a question which has exercised the minds of countless historians of infinitely greater skill and profundity than I. But I hope that it goes some way towards telling 'How'. Inevitably, it has had to be concerned with politics to a far greater degree than anything I have previously written, but I make no apologies for that. The war that sent the British Army to France in 1914 was the sequel and the consequence of all that went before and a knowledge of the background and the run-up to it is necessary to an understanding and appreciation of what happened next . . . and next . . . and next . . . to the people who endured the four black years of war and returned, if they were lucky, to take up the threads of life in societies that were shaken to their roots, and a world in which the Old Order had disappeared forever – not always to their disadvantage. *1914* has not been an easy book to write and has taken a long, long time. But I hope it will be easy to read.

With every book the list of those to be thanked becomes longer and it is difficult to know where to start. As always, the Commonwealth War Graves Commission has dealt with enquiries with courtesy and enthusiasm, as have various regiments. Tony Spagnoly has, as always, been ever-willing to discuss points which have arisen and has also worked extremely hard on drawing the original drafts of the numerous maps which appear in the book. John Woodroff, with his usual indefatigable industry, has burrowed deep to supply the answers to many queries and has checked all the military details. Although Alma Woodroff, much to my regret, has not been able to put in the mammoth amount of work she has done on previous books,

---

* Gunner Bert Stokes, of the New Zealand Field Artillery, still hale and hearty enough at 91 to have made the 12,000-mile trip from Auckland for the 70th Anniversary ceremonies at Ypres, and whose story appears in *They Called it Passchendaele*.

she has always been ready to bail me out when the going got rough and I am immensely grateful to her.

As always, several people have helped in tracking down and interviewing old soldiers, notably Barbara Taylor, John Woodroff, Guy Francis, Colin Butler and Stan Taylor and I am, as always, in their debt.

Yves de Cock in Belgium has supplied much useful information and I am also grateful to the Elfnovembergroep for valuable material on the First Battle of Ypres contained in their private publication *Van Den Grooten Oorlog*.

My French friends have, as usual, entered enthusiastically into the project and I am indebted to Jean Verdel (whose mother, before her marriage, was Flora Dignoire) and to Gaston Degardin for kindly making available his assiduous research on Bapaume before and during the German occupation. This has enabled me to do far greater justice to the French side (and in particular to the experiences of French civilians) than I would otherwise have been able to do. Guy and Jeannine Danquigny have also untiringly assisted with this project, as with many others, and Dr Marechal, the present-day owner of Miss Mildred Aldrich's house on the Marne (and whose uncles remember playing in her garden as children in the twenties), has been most kind and helpful. I am deeply grateful to them all.

I should also like to express my gratitude to the many people, too numerous to name, who so kindly, and often out of the blue, made available family letters, diaries and written accounts (and in particular for the diaries of Sergeant Packham and Corporal Letyford which occupy an important place in this book) or who took the trouble to put their own recollections on paper and to expand on reams of 'matters arising'. Many who did so will find that they are not included in this book. The reason is simple. It was originally planned and researched to cover a longer period and to carry the story from the beginning of the war through 1915 to the Battle of Loos. But 1914 turned out to be a book-length story in itself. My apologies to those who are disappointed – and my assurance that all will be revealed in the next volume!

Lastly, and by no means least, my thanks to my long-suffering family who, if they are not precisely the last casualties of the Great War, from time to time have a lot to put up with – in particular my husband, Ian Ross, who very often puts himself out in the midst of his own demanding professional commitments to accommodate the exigencies of mine. I don't always tell him how much I appreciate it. But I do.

Lyn Macdonald,
London, July 1987.

THE WESTERN FRONT
— August 1914 —

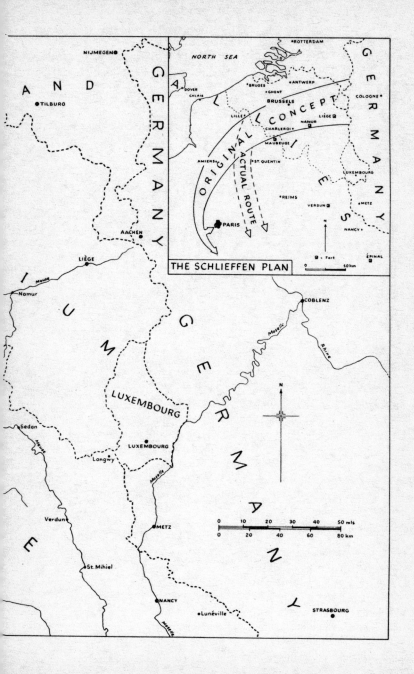

THE SCHLIEFFEN PLAN

Part One
All in the Day's Work

The great Duke of Wellington stood on the path which runs round the ramparts of Walmer Castle on a sunny day in July 1843. Near him, standing at attention, was a young Staff Officer of the Adjutant-General's Department. He had just asked a question on a small matter of detail which the War Office thought should, as a courtesy, be referred to the Commander of the Forces. A name typical of the British private soldier was required, for use on the model sheet of the soldiers' accounts to show where the men should sign.

The Duke stood gazing out to sea while the young officer waited, searching in a long memory stored with recollections for a man who typified the character of Britain's soldiers. He thought back to his first campaign in the Low Countries where he had fought his first action with his old Regiment, the 33rd Foot.

When the battle was over and won, Wellesley rode back to where little groups of wounded men were lying on the ground. At the place where the right of his line had been lay the right-hand man of the Grenadier Company. Thomas Atkins. He stood six foot three in his stockinged feet, he had served for twenty years, he could neither read nor write and he was the best man at arms in the Regiment. One of the bandsmen had bound up his head where a sabre had slashed it, he had a bayonet wound in the chest, and a bullet through the lungs. He had begged the bearers not to move him, but to let him die in peace. Wellesley looked down on him and the man must have seen his concern. 'It's all right, Sir,' he gasped. 'It's all in the day's work.' They were his last words.

The Old Duke turned to the waiting Staff Officer. 'Thomas Atkins,' he said.

From *The Ypres Times*,
April 1929.

Chapter 1

In August on the golden plains of Picardy and Flanders, the grind of giant combines smothers the sounds of summer. Travelling in swathes across the fields, they peel the harvest from the land as a thumb peels the skin from an orange. Then the land comes into its own. Scrawled across it, after almost seventy years and more than sixty harvests, are the traces of old trenchlines. You see them in a zigzag patch of weed, a line of soil unnaturally discoloured, an undulating billow on the flat surface of a field. Here and there a rampaging thicket of nettles marks the entrance to a long-sealed tunnel or hints at a deep dugout long buried in the damp dark below. Even the lush summer grass, swaying tall on a bank or an incline, hardly blurs the outlines of deep-gouged crevices that once sheltered a battery of guns.

As the summer vegetation dies back, laying bare the bones of the earth, uglier shapes emerge. The mangled iron and brick of a ruined machine-gun post. The concrete emplacements of a formidable redoubt and, along dusty farm-tracks churned up by heavy tractors, a sprinkling of shrapnel and some rusted shards of shell. In the lowlands of Belgium, across the face of Artois, on the downlands of the Somme, and across the breadth of France, all along the line of the old Western Front, three generations of farmers have lived among the debris and the dangers of war.

With the advent of the technological age accidents and casualties have diminished, and the modern farmer who sets his hand to the plough or who grubs up beets or potatoes without first passing a metal detector across his field is a rare and reckless bird. Each season of the farming year still yields a lethal harvest of unexploded shells. The locals are used to them. They are a routine nuisance easily dealt with by Munitions Disposal Squads. Only strangers stop with cautious curiosity to examine them, stacked neatly according to calibre on the verges of country roads as far apart as Ypres in the north and Verdun a long way to the south-east. The shell-heaps stand like milestones along the path of the wind that tore through Europe, laid waste a generation and blew up into a hurricane that swept away their safe and ordered world. In the awesome stillness of its aftermath they marvelled to think that it had begun as the merest zephyr, so distant, so inconsequent, that it would hardly have rippled a field of corn growing ripe under untroubled skies in that long, hot summer of 1914.

It was something of a novelty for British troops to arrive as allies on the soil of their old enemy France. The names of Malplaquet, Corunna, Waterloo, Quebec, rang like battle-cries through Regimental Histories, were emblazoned in gold on Regimental Colours and were linked with a host of the Regimental traditions that cemented *esprit de corps*.

Memories in the north of France were equally long. It was a mere ten years since the two nations had signed the *Entente Cordiale* under the beneficent eye of the francophile King, Edward VII, and, as the first of the boats that would carry her soldiers to France gathered in Southampton Water and prepared to set course for the French ports of Le Havre, Rouen and Boulogne, the Mayor of Boulogne gave some thought to the circumstances of their arrival.

It was from Boulogne after all (and less than a hundred years ago) that Napoleon, Emperor of the French, had planned to invade England, and his statue, perched on a pillar a hundred feet high, still gazed implacably across the Channel from the hills where he had poised his army. It was the dominating feature of the town, and it was hardly likely that the British troops could miss it, since some of them would be encamped at Napoleon's very feet in the tents which, for some days now, their advance parties had been busily erecting.

There had already been one unfortunate incident early on Sunday afternoon. Some elderly reservists, in charge of a coastal defence gun on the cliffs above an isolated beach, waking abruptly from a light doze after a heavy lunch, fell under the delusion that a force of naked Germans was assaulting the shores of France from the sea, and fired off several rounds at a party of British soldiers cooling off with an afternoon swim.

All things considered, the Mayor had concluded that it would be prudent to issue a Public Notice to remind the people of Boulogne that times had changed.

> My dear Citizens. This day arrive in our town the valiant British troops, who come to co-operate with our brave soldiers to repel the abominable aggression of Germany . . . Boulogne, which is one of the homes of the *Entente Cordiale*, will give to the sons of the United Kingdom an enthusiastic and brotherly welcome. The citizens are requested on this occasion to decorate the fronts of their houses with the colours of the two countries.

The citizens enthusiastically obliged.

★

The soldiers of the 8th Brigade, arriving in a hastily commandeered cattle-boat, had not enjoyed a pleasant voyage. They were packed so closely together that, once settled, it was hardly possible to move, even to allow the few who were seasick to struggle to the ship's rail. That had given rise to more ill-feeling than could be put down to the slight swell which had marred an otherwise calm crossing. But ill-feeling and ill-temper, like the stiff aching of cramped limbs, were soon forgotten in the warmth of a welcome so tumultuous that some well-travelled Tommies, accustomed to less cordial receptions in ports round the British Empire, could hardly believe the evidence of their eyes and ears.

Boulogne had turned out *en masse*. Even the long harbour wall was packed with cheering crowds and as the ship inched towards its berth, they waved and cheered in such a frenzy that one old gentleman, more frenzied than the rest, was propelled by his enthusiasm over the edge of the pier into the water. Happily, he was promptly fished out again and delighted the crowd and the Tommies alike by coming to a watery salute on the quayside.

The harbour was full of boats – motor torpedoes that dashed busily up and down the estuary, two cruisers of the French Navy, fishing smacks unloading the night's catch on the town quay, and steam whistles and horns and sirens hooted and screeched and boomed a deafening welcome.

It was all a delightful experience, if somewhat harassing for the NCOs and officers in charge of disembarkation who had the task of clearing a space through the multitude on the pier and marching the troops off in some kind of order which would not entirely discredit the British Army.

The French army (or those of its representatives who formed the guard of honour, holding its ragged ranks with some difficulty against the pushing of the crowd) were glorious in gaudy uniforms of red and blue, looking, to the irreverent Tommies, like a male chorus-line in an operetta. But there the glory ended. Their coats of sky blue were buttoned uncomfortably over elderly paunches. Their eyes, though alight with patriotic fervour, were unmistakably rheumy. Their beards and the hair beneath their red-peaked caps were distinctly grizzled and, despite the businesslike appearance of their long rifles and bayonets, the most casual inspection would hardly have passed them as fighting fit.

But these all-too-ancient warriors, hastily recalled to the colours, were all that was left. France had mobilised on 1 August, three days before Great Britain. The young and the fit were already in the field, and the French command was anxiously awaiting the arrival of their British allies to swell their numbers. It was not that France lacked manpower – she had already called up more than a million men – but, with the rapid and unexpected advance of the German army, the French already had an uneasy feeling that large numbers of their troops were in the wrong place. There were all too few on the left of their long line, close to the Belgian border where it was becoming increasingly clear that the brunt of the German advance would fall. The British Force, small though it was, was badly needed to extend their vulnerable line and it was with some relief that news of the first arrivals was received at the headquarters of General Lanrezac whose Fifth Army stood directly in the path of the German thrust and was in serious danger of being outflanked.

So far, the only British soldier they had clapped eyes on was a certain Lieutenant Spears, a Junior Staff Officer who, by an accident of fate, had been the first British soldier in France. Several months earlier, when there had been no hint of war on the horizon, it had been arranged by the War Office that this young Intelligence officer should spend some weeks during the summer on attachment to the Ministère de Guerre in Paris. As the date approached and there was a real threat of war in Europe – a war, moreover, in which France was likely to be embroiled – the War Office saw no reason to revise the plan. It would be no bad thing to have an observer on the spot in a strictly unofficial capacity, for France was an unofficial ally and, despite the existence of the much-lauded *Entente Cordiale*, Great Britain was bound by no treaty or obligation to support her in any military emergency or adventure.

So, according to plan and on the designated date (discreetly clad in mufti, but having taken the last-minute precaution of packing his uniform) Spears had crossed to France on a holiday steamer. It was Monday 27 July 1914. On the 28th he reported for duty in Paris – a month to the day since the Archduke Franz Ferdinand had been assassinated in Sarajevo. By nightfall Austria had declared war on Serbia, and in Britain the Admiralty had ordered the First Fleet to set sail for the north to its war station at Scapa Flow.

The population of the British Isles, peacefully going about the daily business of unruffled life, paid little attention to reports of 'Trouble in the Balkans' which flared up so regularly that it seemed to be almost a fixture in the less prominent headlines of serious newspapers. But it required a far greater knowledge of history, geography and politics than the average reader possessed to begin to understand the course of the tortuous quarrels over the Slav states between the rival powers who wished to order their destinies. They had been going on for generations.

Serbia, in particular, had been a bone of contention, first between Turkey and Bulgaria, then between Turkey and Russia, and latterly, between Russia and the vast Austro-Hungarian Empire that sprawled across Europe from Vienna to the doorstep of Asia. Serbia now enjoyed a recent and precarious independence – although in a somewhat truncated form. The Serbs had been reluctantly forced to hand over their provinces of Bosnia and Herzegovina whose Slav population now lay uneasily under the Austrian yoke – still a bone of contention and the cause of deep resentment in their Serbian 'homeland'. Russia was resentful too. Until recently, Serbia had been her protectorate and rightly belonged, in the Russian view, within the Slavic territories of the Russian Empire.

But, by the end of 1913, Serbia was on the up and up. She had done well out of the Balkan War which had finally booted Turkey out of Europe and shared out the conquered territories between the independent Balkan states. National pride was running high. It spilled over into Bosnia and Herzegovina, and the Slav nationalism that was always simmering just beneath the surface boiled up in a series of guerrilla and terrorist attacks.

The disturbances were hailed in Serbia with ill-concealed glee. They were watched with interest by Moscow. From the viewpoint of Vienna they meant trouble, and the Austrian authorities were not slow to lay the trouble at Serbia's door. Agents of the Austrian secret service with an ear to the ground in Serbia's capital city, Belgrade, were feeding Vienna with suggestions that dark plots were afoot, that Serbia was backing the guerrillas by providing funds and that, when things got too hot, they could count on a safe haven in Serbia. Belgrade, they hinted, was a nest of intrigue aimed directly at undermining the suzerainty of the Austrian Empire over her Slav states. In Vienna the feeling grew that, at the first opportunity, Serbia must be taught a lesson. Austria was now on the look-out for a pretext to go to war.

It came a few months later, in the summer of 1914, at Sarajevo, capital of the annexed Serbian province of Bosnia. Sarajevo was a hotbed of Slav nationalism that showed signs of erupting into open insurrection, and it was not by coincidence that the city had been chosen as the site for the annual manoeuvres of the 15th and 16th Corps of the Austrian army. It would do no harm to favour the fiery Slavs with a demonstration of military might, and to drive home the message with a visit by a royal personage, who was not only Inspector-General of the Austrian army, but heir to the Austrian crown.

It was a fine summer Sunday morning. The troops had been preparing since dawn and by ten minutes to ten, when the royal train drew into Sarajevo station, they were already drawn up in burnished columns, glistening in the sunshine, on the Filipovitch parade ground. The inspection was hardly more than a formality, for the Archduke and his wife arrived from the station in an open motor car, drove at a spanking pace along the ranks and in less than twenty minutes were on their way again to the Town Hall where, according to plan, they were to receive an official welcome.

But things did not go according to plan. The couple arrived shocked and flustered. A bomb had been thrown at their motor car and, although the Archduke and the Duchess were unharmed, one of their aides had been hurt by a flying fragment. The efforts of the mayor, desperately trying to restore the situation by launching into his prepared speech of welcome, were brushed angrily aside by the Archduke. 'What is the good of your speeches? I come to Sarajevo on a visit, and I get bombs thrown at me. It is outrageous!'

It was some small consolation that the culprit had been caught and arrested. It came as no surprise to learn that he was a Serb. It did not occur to the police that he had not been acting alone. It did not occur to them to drag-net the crowded streets for other suspects, nor did there seem to be any reason why the royal visit should not go ahead as planned. The suspicion that the abortive assassination had been part of a nationalist plot came later. But by then it was too late to take precautions. The royal visitors were already dead. They had been killed in the streets of Sarajevo, shot by another Serb just half an hour after his accomplice had been arrested.

It was the excuse that Austria needed. After the first shock, over the coming weeks it was gradually realised in the corridors of power that she need look no further for a pretext on which to go to war with Serbia and settle the Slav question once and for all.

It was evening before the news filtered through to the rest of Europe. Almost everywhere it had been a perfect summer's day.

The sun had shone in London where it took an army of cleaners half the morning to clean up Hyde Park after Saturday's display by the London Fire Brigade, which had exhibited its dash and daring to five thousand eager spectators before galloping past the King in a rousing finale. Up-river at Henley, preparations were well under way for the annual regatta, and the Thames was bright with boating parties and rowdy groups of youths trying their skill as oarsmen between the marker flags. At Wimbledon, halfway through the All-England Championships, groundsmen sweated in the Sunday sunshine rolling the grass courts to velvet smoothness ready for the next week's matches. At the seaside, summer visitors strolled on the promenades, listened to the band, and congratulated themselves on the fine weather which looked set fair for their holidays.

The sun had blazed down on Paris where the Grand Prix was run that afternoon at Longchamps and the *beau monde* of Europe saw Baron de Rothschild's Sardanapale win by a neck. It was the most dazzling event of the season. The couturiers had sent the most elegant and beautiful of their mannequins to mingle with the crowds and stun them with the most exquisite of their latest creations. Sharp-eyed fashion journalists, scribbling discreetly, noted that 'dead black, unrelieved by any touch of colour' was what the well-dressed woman would be obliged to wear to be *à la mode* in 1914. Next week, when they gushed into print in British newspapers and magazines, aristocratic England was delighted to hear it. In the wake of the tragic death of the Archduke Franz Ferdinand in far-off Sarajevo, Buckingham Palace had ordered a week's court mourning. Fashionable London was happy to learn that it could don respectful black in the certainty that, according to Paris, it was the last word in chic. Black-garbed Austrian ladies, scanning the social notes in the *Wiener Tageblatt*, were similarly gratified.

28 June, the day of the assassination at Sarajevo, was a significant date for the people of Great Britain. It was the anniversary of the coronation of Queen Victoria. Seventy-seven years later, and thirteen years after her death, the accession of the old Queen was still looked on by the British as the curtain-raiser to their golden age. The Queen's Birthday on 24 May continued to be held as a public holiday in celebration of the great Victorian Empire that spanned the globe. 'Empire Day' was the happy inspiration of the Earl of Meath and it had rapidly caught on. Every village was decked with flags, every church had its special service, every school its ceremony. For the children it was a day of treats and high jinks, of picnics and outings – but they were left in no doubt as to the object of the celebrations nor of the links of pride and responsibility which bound the youngest of them to the far-flung countries and islands and continents where the British flag flapped above government offices, above barracks and residencies as a symbol of Britain's benevolent rule.

> *England, Home and Beauty.*
> *Empire, Pride and Duty.*

In a hundred stirring tales and popular poems Rudyard Kipling had underlined the maxim that precisely summed up the popular feeling that to have been born an inhabitant of the British Isles was to have drawn first prize in the lottery of life. No Empire Day celebration was considered to be complete without a choir of schoolchildren to enliven the proceedings with a fluting rendition of Kipling's 'Children's Song':

> *Land of our Birth, we pledge to thee*
> *Our love and toil in the years to be,*
> *When we are grown and take our place*
> *As men and women with our race.*

Nothing could have been more appropriate, and the lines were eagerly embraced by patriotic schoolteachers. They did not, however, find favour with Kipling's own son Jack, aged twelve, and a pupil at St Aubyn's Preparatory School at Rottingdean. His schoolfellows held him personally responsible for the tedium of being forced to learn all eight verses of the new song in honour of Empire Day in 1910, and Jack Kipling, sick to the teeth of being so unjustly baited, wrote a disgruntled letter home and laid the blame squarely on the shoulders of his father. Kipling apologised gracefully: 'Sorry about the "Children's Song". *You* know that I didn't write the darn thing with the faintest idea it would be so cruelly used against the young.'

For the song itself there was no need to apologise. Kipling had merely voiced sentiments that were universally held to be part of the national heritage.

> *Teach us to rule ourselves alway,*
> *Controlled and cleanly night and day,*
> *That we may bring, if need arise,*
> *No maimed or worthless sacrifice . . .*

Later he was to speak again for his bewildered generation, sick with self-reproach.

> *If any question why we died,*
> *Tell them, because our fathers lied.*

But that was far in the future and in another world. Now the fortunes of the British Empire were at their zenith, patriotism was its watchword and nobody was questioning anything.

> *Land of our Birth, our faith, our pride,*
> *For whose dear sake our fathers died;*
> *O Motherland, we pledge to thee,*
> *Head, heart and hand through the years to be.*

The Empire was growing all the time – and the British Army was scattered round the globe to prove it. Since the death of the old Queen the Empire had acquired new territories larger than the whole of the United States of America.

The 2nd Battalion, The Rifle Brigade, had left for overseas in 1897, the year of Queen Victoria's Diamond Jubilee. Now, in 1914, in the reign of her grandson, King George V, they were preparing to go home. They had missed the reign of his father, Edward VII, altogether.

It had been quite a tour. In its seventeen years of foreign duty, the Battalion had served in Malta and in Crete. It had done two stints in the Sudan and three in Egypt. During the Boer War it had been shipped to South Africa, had fought in the Transvaal and the Orange Free State and, after the uneasy peace, had been posted for a tour of duty to Natal. For the last seven of their seventeen years abroad, the RBs had been in India. Although they had covered some 40,000 miles by sea or river, by road or by rail, and half as many again on their feet, in all their wanderings they had seen perhaps a hundredth part of the British Empire. More than 4,000 men and 120 officers had come and gone as time-expired men had gone home and new drafts had replaced them, but there were still thirteen of the original Battalion which had sailed from Southampton seventeen years before. One of them was Quartermaster J. H. Alldridge.

Alldridge had served under seven separate generals (including the great Sir Redvers Buller) and five Commanding Officers. There was nothing he did not know about the Battalion and no one in the Battalion who did not know it. Alldridge could produce statistics at the drop of a hat. He could name the eleven troopships in which they had travelled. He could name the men who had won medals in their tour of foreign service, from the single Victoria Cross to the sixteen Distinguished Conduct Medals and the thirty-three for Long Service and Good Conduct. Without reference to roll books he could reel off the casualties – 75 killed, 167 wounded and 191 dead of typhoid or cholera or of one of the virulent nameless fevers that struck without warning in the tropics. If pressed he would reveal, with reluctance, that, over the seventeen years, two men had deserted.

In the weeks before their departure, despite his manifold activities as quartermaster, Alldridge had amused himself by compiling the statistics from his voluminous records. Not that there had been much time to spare. By July the heavy baggage, the mess silver and linen, the officers' furniture, the household effects of the families on the strength, was already being packed ready to be shipped in advance and that, for the Quartermaster's department, was a full-time job in itself. They were due to sail at the start of the Trooping Season, on 29 October. In the meantime, life continued as usual. It had been a fairly typical year, starting as it always did with the New Year's Day Proclamation Parade which, thirty-eight years on, still celebrated annually Queen Victoria's assumption of the title 'Empress of India' in 1876.

But, like all units serving in India, the soldiers' year was regulated by the seasons rather than the calendar, by the Cool Weather from November to February, and the Hot Weather when temperatures rose from reasonable discomfort in the month of March to blistering, unendurable heat in June, when the weather broke and the monsoons began. To keep the Battalion at the peak of efficiency, it had to be kept on the move. The cool weather was spent round Lahore in a rigid timetable of battalion training, culminating in Brigade Manoeuvres and mock battles with other units of the Division. For the hot weather and the monsoon season, the Battalion marched some two hundred miles, up the Great Trunk Road to Rawalpindi and on to the north-east to the barracks at Kuldana in the Murree Hills to skirmish and manoeuvre in the rough country of the uplands and to carry out a stiff programme of signalling and musketry practice in the clear, crisp air, where the flash of a heliograph lamp could be seen for fifty miles.

The long and dusty route marches between camps and bivouacs toughened the feet, strengthened the muscles, built up stamina and scorched the soldiers' skins to leather.

When no marauding tribesmen disturbed the peace of the frontiers, when no unruly natives claimed their attention on the plains, in the intervals between the exigencies of training and exercises there was plenty of sport to be had. The army was generous in the matter of local leave for elephant shooting, for pigsticking, for shooting sand-grouse in the Bikanir Desert, for hunting bear and ibex in Kashmir. The trophies from the current season, having been stuffed, mounted and duly displayed and admired in the Officers' Mess, were already crated up ready to be shipped home with the Battalion's heavy baggage.

The polo season had been disappointing, but largely because most far-seeing officers had already sold their best ponies in anticipation of their early departure. The cricket season, when officers and men formed a single and singular democratic team, had been more than satisfactory, and in the inter-Brigade competitions the men had acquitted themselves well in the economical, less exclusive sports, cross-country running, boxing, football, which were encouraged in the interests of fitness and of keeping boredom at bay. Taken as a whole, the 2nd RB had had a satisfactory year. It culminated in the annual event which was devised to test to the limit their skill and efficiency in soldiering – the Divisional competition known as the Grand Assault at Arms.

The RBs were not displeased with their performance. They had taken both first and second places in Individual Bayonet Fighting, and come first in the Bayonet team event. They had been first in the tough obstacle race, designed to reproduce conditions in which soldiers might have to advance in actual warfare. Despite rigorous training they had failed miserably in the Tug-of-War, but the Battalion had come second in the Officers' Revolver Competition and in hand-to-hand sword fighting their officers had not disgraced themselves. Overall, the Rifle Brigade had been narrowly beaten into second place by the Yorkshire Regiment who had carried off the coveted cup for the best Regiment at Arms, but there had been some brilliant individual performances. The Battalion was of the unanimous opinion that, if they were able to hold on to the best of the men when they got back to Blighty and the barracks at Colchester, they would have an excellent chance of putting a team into the arena at Olympia for the Royal Tournament in the summer of 1915.

The Grand Assault at Arms ended on 27 June. Next day, after the obligatory church parades, the Battalion enjoyed a well-earned rest. It was a Sunday like any other. They had no inkling that in Europe it had been a fateful day nor how profoundly its events would affect their future. It was three weeks before the mail brought newspapers from Home with reports of the shooting at Sarajevo. Avid though they were for news, no one read them with particular attention.

The bulk of the British Army was spread around the Empire, and in India alone there were more serving soldiers than there were in the British Isles. Unlike the land-locked nations on the Continent, ever snapping and yapping across their easily breached frontiers, often separated by as little as a range of hills, a river or a road, Great Britain had no need of a large standing army. Her natural frontier was her coastline, her backyard the seas that lapped her shores, and the first line of her defence the mighty ships that sailed them. Encircled by the protective power of the world's largest navy, enriched by the voyaging of a great merchant fleet that carried her trade to the four corners of the earth, Great Britain could afford to stand aloof from European quarrels and the tangle of enmities and alliances that maintained Europe's balance of power.

But recently, that delicate balance of power had shifted and the events of the past ten years had made it increasingly obvious that she could not remain aloof for ever.

Not that Britain, as a paramount power, had ever been averse to poking a finger into the European pie when it had suited her to do so. Palmerston had been a prime architect of the plan to relandscape Europe which released Belgium from Holland, made her an independent kingdom and guaranteed her neutrality in perpetuity. Lord Salisbury had played a major role in the Congress of Berlin which had placed Bosnia and Herzegovina under the suzerainty of Austria and thus lit the slow-burning fuse of resentment in the Slavs which was to spark off the conflagration that would engulf Europe in 1914.

It had also balked Russia of her ambitions in the Balkans, made her fearful of the growing power of the German and Austrian Empires, once her allies, and sent her looking for a new ally. She had found one in France, still aggrieved, still brooding, still nursing passionate hatred for Germany after her crushing defeat in the Franco-Prussian War. And, recently, Great Britain's own attitude to Germany had changed.

Twenty years earlier, the idea of war between Great Britain and Germany would have been unthinkable. Queen Victoria was on the throne and her influence extended by intimate family connection into every major court on the Continent. Queen Victoria, although she prided herself on her Englishness, was the daughter of a German mother and the widow of a German husband. German philosophy, German music, German literature, German sentiments were the keystones of the private life of the Royal Family and, on a domestic level, the Victorian virtues which permeated downwards to humbler households had a good deal in common with German notions of respectability. The dearest wish of the Prince Consort had been to see a liberal, united, democratic Germany, wrested from autocratic political hands, a strong and benign force for peace at the centre of chaotic Europe. If Great Britain, powerfully ensconced at the head of her far-flung Empire, was Mother Country to half the world, Germany should be her 'Brother Country', her staunchest friend in Europe.

His eldest daughter, the Princess Royal, had been married to a Hohenzollern prince and now, although Albert had not lived to see it, his grandson was the German Emperor. He was also a thorn in the flesh of Great Britain and regarded by the Royal Family with, to say the least, mixed feelings. There was no avoiding the fact that Kaiser Wilhelm was an awkward and a complicated character.

Undoubtedly much of the explanation lay far back in the circumstances of his birth. The Kaiser's left arm had been damaged so badly that it was useless and withered for life. It was a traumatic disability for an emperor traditionally acclaimed as the 'All Powerful' and 'All Highest', who must take his place in a line of soldier kings whose legendary prowess and bravery went back to Frederick the Great. All his life, the Kaiser was driven by the need to prove himself better and stronger than the next man. This desire crystallised into a determination to make Germany better and stronger than Great Britain. It was a schizophrenic obsession, which had grown out of love and of hate.

In his boyhood, long visits to the court of his grandmother the Queen and Empress, enthroned metaphorically at the centre of the sun that never set on her great Empire, had bred in the Kaiser an admiration and enthusiasm for England and all things English.

In Berlin, by contrast, he was held deliberately under the influence of the Emperor, his autocratic grandfather (who disliked and suspected his mother for her liberal 'English' ideas), and was brought up in the rigid discipline of a military education, surrounded by flattering toadies at his grandfather's militaristic court.

It was hardly surprising that the mixed loyalties of his heritage as a boy had set up warring traits in the character of the man. 'Please remind William,' remarked King Edward VII testily, on the eve of a visit by his nephew, the Kaiser, to Sandringham, 'that it is *not* the custom to wear uniform in the country in England.'

The Kaiser adored uniforms, and none in his extensive collection gave him more pleasure and satisfaction than the uniforms he was entitled to wear as an honorary field marshal of the British Army and honorary admiral of the Royal Navy. There were some in the British royal family who believed that the latter honour, awarded to him by his grandmother Queen Victoria, had gone to his head. His heartfelt desire was to build up the German navy until it was a battle fleet as glorious, as prestigious and as powerful as the Royal Navy itself. Freed from the restraining hand of Bismarck, from whom he had cut loose in 1891, too blinkered and egocentric to see that he was being used as a tool by Bismarck's political successors, the Kaiser, with single-minded enthusiasm, had set about achieving his ambition and embarked on a mammoth programme of ship-building, which had sent a shiver of apprehension through the body politic of Europe, not least in Great Britain. Even the man in the street had regarded it as a piece of infernal cheek.

In July 1914 a combination of chance and foresight brought the ships of the British Navy together, fully mobilised, at maximum efficiency, and at the very moment they were needed. It was the most extravagant display of sea-power ever assembled and, ironically, it was the result of an economy measure. As long ago as October of the previous year, the Lords of the Admiralty had decreed that, in the summer of 1914, the expensive exercise of Test Mobilisation should be combined with the annual summer exercises.

Twenty thousand regular sailors who had completed their time on active service but were required by the terms of their enlistment to rejoin in an emergency, had been called up and every destroyer, every cruiser, every battle squadron, every shore establishment was at full strength. The coal-mines had worked overtime to fulfil the demand for fuel – unprecedented even by the lavish standards of Admiralty contracts – and the matelots, filthy, sweating and swearing, had toiled day and night to coal the ships in record time, and toiled on again to clean and polish and scrub away the resulting dust and grime. When all the tasks had been accomplished, every ship that could reasonably be spared from the seas of the British Empire sailed from its Home Port to join the Fleet riding at anchor off Spithead.

It was the sight of the summer, and holidaymakers by the thousand flocked to the south coast to see it.

Even the names were enough to strike terror into the heart of any upstart nation who dared to challenge the might of Great Britain and her Empire: *Colossus, Hercules, Centaur, Ajax, Superb, Monarch, Marlborough, Audacious, Conquerer, Thunderer, Dreadnought*. Fifty-nine great battleships led the Fleet. There were one hundred and eighty-seven destroyers, twelve squadrons of cruisers, and fifty-nine submarines. At the head of them all rode the mighty *Iron Duke*, 25,000 tons, the pride of the British Navy and the flagship of the officer in command of the Fleet, Admiral Sir George Callaghan. It was the proudest day of his life.

By the time the last ship had weighed anchor and steamed into position, the ships of the vanguard had long since sailed over the horizon. Far out in the Channel stood the Royal Yacht at anchor, the King at the salute as his Royal Navy steamed past at precisely fifteen knots, ship after ship streamered with flags, ships' companies drawn up on white-scrubbed decks, ships' bands playing the National Anthem again and again. And again and again, faintly heard across the water, came the orders 'Off caps' and 'Three cheers for the King!' 'Hip hip HOORAY! HOORAY Hoor-a-a-a-y . . .' tailing off into the wind as one great ship ploughed on and the next rode up astern. It took six hours for the whole fleet to sail past. Nothing like it had been seen since the glorious days of Victoria. Nothing remotely like it would ever be seen again.

It was a salutary reminder to certain irascible European nations that Great Britain was not to be trifled with, and that a war in which she might possibly intervene was not something to be undertaken without careful consideration of the consequences. It was hoped that the Kaiser in particular would take the hint. He had held a naval occasion of his own the previous month when he had formally opened the newly deepened Kiel canal. It had not escaped the notice of British naval officers among the guests that, through this new channel, large German warships could now move speedily from the Baltic into the North Sea. They hoped that this greatest naval review in history would serve to draw the Kaiser's attention to the fact that, should they do so with belligerent intent, the Royal Navy would be waiting for them.

Until recently, a Europe in which a strong Germany held the central position had posed no threat to the interests of Great Britain either at home or abroad. Seen from this British viewpoint it had seemed more to her advantage than otherwise that strong Prussia had gathered a scattering of weak German states under her wing to make a united Germany, and an emperor of the Prussian King. But certain unfortunate circumstances, offensive in their brashness, far-reaching in their consequences, had attended the birth of the new Germany. It had been proclaimed at the end of the Franco-Prussian War – not in Berlin but, with arrogant flamboyance, in the Hall of Mirrors at Versailles. Thus Prussia, having scooped in the long-disputed French provinces of Alsace and Lorraine to swell the territory of the new German Empire, stamped her jackboot hard on the neck of defeated France.

The Kaiser at the time had been twelve years old. Seventeen years later, in 1889, he had become Emperor of a very different Germany. The German Empire, formed by the unification of small states, had been rendered indivisible by the explosive growth of their combined industrial power. The coal of Westphalia and Silesia, the iron ore of sequestered Lorraine, the timber resources of the vast forests, the mineral deposits of the Harz mountains, the great ports of Hamburg and Bremen, were now at the disposition of one centralised Reich. Investment capital poured in to develop them, cities doubled and redoubled in size and population as factories, foundries, mills, chemical plants, engineering works, sprang up and a vast labour force poured in from the rural areas to man them. In the space of seventeen years Germany became an industrial force to be reckoned with, and by the turn of the century the Kaiser was beginning to throw his weight about in earnest.

1904 was the first year of the decade of fateful events which would come to an inexorable climax. It was the year in which Great Britain and France were brought together by the *Entente Cordiale* and the year when the Kaiser began to make a series of bombastic gaffes which might have attracted less attention had they not so clearly demonstrated Germany's intentions of aggrandisement.

It was not just that he gloated so publicly over the growing strength of the German navy, going so far as to refer to himself (to his cousin the Tsar of Russia) as 'The Admiral of the Atlantic'. It was not just that he publicly (at a banquet for three hundred people) referred to his uncle, King Edward VII, in virulent terms, 'He is a devil. You cannot believe what a devil he is!' It was not even that he proclaimed in an official speech (when refusing a placatory invitation to visit France), 'The Order of the Day is, keep your powder dry – keep your sword sharp – and keep your fist on the hilt!' In a series of ill-considered, injudicious outpourings, the Kaiser postured and strutted on the delicate tightrope of European politics – now rushing forward with apparent abandon that drew gasps from the watching nations; now drawing back with cat-like cunning; now teetering with windmilling arms in calculated exhibitionism intended to test the nerve of the countries allied against Germany, and intended in particular to test the nerve of Great Britain. Just how far would she be prepared to go in support of France?

Three years earlier Germany had put that question to the test at Agadir. In one clause of the loose agreement between France and Great Britain, two old rivalries had been resolved. France had agreed to withdraw her interest in Egypt and the Suez Canal, that vital highway to the British Empire, while Great Britain pledged herself to support the claims of France in the Sultanate of Morocco. It was the latter to which Germany took exception, for France could claim little more than squatter's rights to parts of the coastline and the Germans themselves were anxious for a toehold in Morocco. They had already tried to stir up trouble shortly after the signing of the *Entente Cordiale* but Britain had then made no bones about supporting French interests; the matter had been put to international arbitration and the Germans had reluctantly backed down.

In 1911 Germany tried again. The Germans wanted a naval base and they sent a gunboat to Morocco to stake a claim at Agadir. It was only an insignificant town on the edge of a remote sandy bay, but Agadir lay on the coastline of the Atlantic Ocean and far too close for comfort to the sea-lanes plied by the Royal Navy and the British Merchant fleet. The possibility of a German base in this sensitive position was not to be thought of.

For the first time since the Napoleonic Wars, the British Government ordered the concentration of the Fleet. It was no more than a token gesture – the merest warning growl, as a dozing bulldog might grumble at a cheeky kitten playing between its outstretched paws. But, in a routine speech to Britain's bankers, the Chancellor of the Exchequer, David Lloyd George, made it crystal clear that the British Government would stand no nonsense and that the growl might easily turn into a snarl.

It was a carefully planted allusion, officially inspired, that was largely lost on an audience more concerned with the Chancellor's economic views and intentions, but it was widely reported in Europe, and in Germany the point was not missed. Again the Germans climbed down. But the Agadir adventure had enabled her to make a deal with France and, in return for waiving all territorial claims in Morocco, Germany was given a substantial slice of the Congo to swell her African empire. Berlin saw Agadir as a victory for the politics of power. London saw it as the moment when the prospect of war with Germany changed from remote possibility to near-certainty. Discreetly but painstakingly Great Britain began to prepare for war.

Chapter 2

Although the events in the Balkans caused brows to furrow at the Foreign Office, despite the fact that Britain's potential enemy was Austria's ally, bound by treaty to support her if she went to war, regardless of the fact that a European war was now felt to be inevitable, no one expected it to come in the summer of 1914. The last to suspect that there was war in the air was the Army.

The only event that loomed on the horizon of the 1st Battalion, The Rifle Brigade, was the start of the Trooping Season. They were bound for India to replace their 2nd Battalion and already their heavy baggage was piling up near the Guard Room at the barracks at Colchester where sentries could keep an eye on it. For some weeks batches of men had been going off on a rota of Embarkation Leave, and the ranks were thinner than usual. Only the bandsmen, contemplating the packed programme of events at which their services were required, gloomily speculated on their chances of getting leave at all.

The band had been much in demand for local events. They had performed at the Colchester Rose and Agricultural Show where the Battalion had put on a military display. They had performed at the local Polo Championships, a three-day event outstanding for the appalling meals dished out to the musicians by a local caterer less interested in their nourishment than in making a profit at the expense of the Army. In mid-July, as the Fleet was gathering for its rendezvous with the King, the band was on the move again, this time to Winchester to provide the music for Greenjacket Week. Bandsman Victor Shawyer had looked on his engagement as a bonus, for he was a Winchester boy, and, since his home was only ten minutes away from the barracks, he had been anticipating some pleasant hours off duty and the chance to tuck into some home cooking. After three years in the Army he had just reached the age of nineteen and graduated from Boy Service to fully fledged soldier. He had also grown to the height of six foot and could never get enough to eat.

But Greenjacket Week was turning out to be something of a disappointment. It was a gruelling schedule of marching and performing by day and, after the briefest of rests, playing during the officers' dinner and providing

dance music afterwards in the Mess. The programme was so packed, so
exhaustive, that Shawyer had only twice been able to sprint the short
distance home, swallow a hasty cup of tea and double back again for
the next parade. At least they were spared the soldiering on the parade
ground, on route march, on rifle range which, in addition to their band
duties, fell to their lot at Colchester. Not that there would have been time
for it.

All in all, 1914 had so far proved to be an average summer. But there
would be one difference. In view of the fact that they would be off to
India in October, General Sir James Grierson had been persuaded that it
would be pointless for the Battalion to take part in the September
manoeuvres of Eastern Command. This the regiment collectively regarded
as a stroke of luck. The quid pro quo was that, during the manoeuvres,
they were to mount a fortnight's guard at Buckingham Palace in order to
release the Grenadier Guards. This stint of duty would require an inordinate
amount of spit and polish, but the men were no strangers to that and there
was a certain glamour in the job. There was also a distinct consolation in
the thought that it would be the Guards who were slogging on thirty-mile
marches, fighting mock battles and bivouacking in the open, while the
RBs took their place – if not under the eye of the Sovereign whom they
would theoretically be guarding during his absence at Balmoral, at least
under the admiring gaze of his subjects who remained in London. The
memory of last year's manoeuvres was still fresh in their mind and their
feet ached at the very thought.

Although the bandsmen were trained as soldiers of the line, and despite
the fact that many sleeves bore the crossed rifles of the prized marksman's
badge, in manoeuvres they were assigned to their wartime role as stretcher
bearers. In the absence of genuine casualties, this amounted to a great
amount of time spent hiding in woods before the bands met up with their
exhausted battalions for the essential task of lifting the spirits of the troops
by playing at the head of the Battalion as they lifted their feet over the long
road home. It was the best moment of the day and, for many soldiers like
Shawyer, a thrilling one. With all the units marching together it seemed
as if the Home Army itself was on the march.

Bandsman H. V. Shawyer, No. 4142, 1st Bttn., The Rifle Brigade,
B.E.F.

Often from some such vantage point as the top of a steep gradient I
have looked both forward and back and seen the long column of
troops snaking away into the distance in both directions, the long
khaki columns broken here and there by the twinkle of brass band

instruments reflecting the sun. Village folk used to turn out in force at the closing of the day to watch the Army go by – a long drab sequence of thousands of khaki uniforms, unit following unit with bands playing, some like ourselves with buglers and silver bugles, country regiments with drum and fife and the Scots with their droning pipes. Tired though I was at the end of many a long day, the sight of those swinging columns never failed to rouse me.

By the middle of July it was beginning to dawn on a few people with an eye to events in Europe that war was in the air and that it was not impossible that the Army might soon be marching in earnest.

To those who chose to read between the lines, the Austrian newspapers were carrying reports of far greater significance than the latest dictates of fashion so convenient to stylish ladies who were forced into mourning black by the death of the Archduke Franz Ferdinand. Many black-bordered pages were devoted to the lying-in-state of the victim and his consort, to the sorrow of the chief mourner, the aged Emperor Franz Josef, to the universal grief of the crowds who lined the streets to see the cortège pass, to the great state funeral and to long lists of dignitaries who had travelled to Vienna to attend it. Only the Kaiser was absent and he had made a lame excuse. He was waiting to see which way the wind would blow.

He had not long to wait. The Archduke had hardly been laid to rest when the 'confessions' of the two assassins arrested in Sarajevo were splashed across the newspapers and, as the examination of the prisoners continued, day after day, the lurid details were released in an avalanche, less calculated to whip up indignation on the domestic front as to impress the world with the righteousness of Austria's case. Cabrinovic, the Serb who made the first attempt on the Archduke's life, was said to have admitted that he had been acting under orders from Belgrade and had been given the bomb by an unnamed member of an anti-Austrian society. Then (in shock-horror headlines) the man was named as an officer in the Serbian army. 'Revelation' followed 'revelation'. The Serbian major was no small fry. He had been acting on behalf of the Chief of the Serbian General Staff and the bombs, far from being the crude home-made devices of amateurs, had (according to the Austrians) been supplied, along with army-issue pistols, from the Serbian arsenal at Kragujevac.

Princip, the actual murderer of the Archduke, had held out for rather longer in his claim to have been acting alone 'to save the Serbian nation from oppression'. Under repeated interrogations (at which no independent witnesses were present however) he finally admitted conspiracy. Then the ball began to roll. The police had found a suspicious hoard of gold in Princip's lodgings at Sarajevo. The assassination plot had been concocted at a high level in Belgrade where it had been common knowledge that the Archduke would not leave Sarajevo alive.

The *coup de grâce* came with the 'verbatim' report of Princip's statement. 'I hope', he was alleged to have said (with unlikely rhetoric), 'that the fatal revolver shots will open the way to the Serbian army to march and occupy Bosnia, for this land is destined by its inclinations and traditions to belong to Greater Serbia.'

Within three weeks, on the basis of her own investigations, Austria had succeeded in proving, at least to her own satisfaction, that a vile conspiracy engineered from Belgrade was not only responsible for the death of the Archduke, but, with the connivance of the Serbian government, was threatening the peace and security of her empire. It was obviously a farrago of nonsense, but, although no shred of evidence ever emerged to support this fiction, Austria was on the war path. On 23 July, she sent a note of protest to Serbia. It amounted to an ultimatum and Serbia was given forty-eight hours to reply.

The chilling implications of the text raised goose-pimples of dismay in every capital in Europe. Austria accused Serbia of perfidy, of fomenting insurrection against the Austro-Hungarian Empire, of tolerating anti-Austrian propaganda in her press and in her schools, of plotting to overthrow the governance of the Empire in the Slav provinces. The note set out the results of Austria's 'magisterial investigation' of recent weeks and quoted from 'the depositions and confessions of the criminal perpetrators of the outrage of 28 June'. It formally accused Serbia of planning the assassination through its secret service and of instructing the 'Chiefs of the Serbian frontier services' to smuggle a posse of armed assassins across the border. Eleven were named, besides the two arrested.

Then came the demands. There were ten in all, beginning with the publication of a formal condemnation by the Serbian government of all anti-Austrian propaganda and 'interference' in the affairs of any of the inhabitants, including the Slav inhabitants, of the Austrian Empire. Special laws were to be introduced by which 'rigorous action' would be taken against anyone 'inciting hatred' against Austria. Newspapers were to be suppressed. The teaching of history in schools was to be revised. The Serbs must undertake to sack, and to sack without question whenever the Austrians demanded it, any officers of the administration or the army who might now, or at any time in the future, be considered 'guilty of propaganda against the Austro-Hungarian Monarchy'.

They wanted heads too. The 'officials of the frontier services' who had allowed the assassins to pass must be 'severely punished'. High-ranking officers who had been shown by the Austrian investigation to be 'implicated' must be immediately arrested, and 'accessories to the plot of 28 June' who were still on Serbian soil must be hunted down and brought to justice. They wanted a pogrom.

But that was not all. Ingeniously, and with cynical deliberation, the Austrians had inserted the clause which, in the unlikely event of Serbia accepting all the rest, would be guaranteed to stick in her throat. The Austrians demanded the right to enter Serbia, the right to undertake investigations herself and a free hand to suppress 'subversive movements' by whatever means she chose. It amounted to an abrogation of Serbia's hard-won independence, a demand so outrageous that no country could possibly have been expected to comply.

But Serbia's reply was phrased in words of sweet reason that completely took the wind out of Austria's sails. Serbia agreed to seven of the ten demands, was prepared to discuss modifications of the remainder and suggested that the whole dispute should be put to international arbitration.

Europe breathed again.

The respite lasted for twenty-four hours. In London, the Foreign Secretary, Sir Edward Grey, busying himself with the arrangements to convene the conference of four disinterested powers which would settle the troublesome Balkan squabble was astounded to receive a note from the Austrian Ambassador.

> In order to bring to an end the subversive intrigues originating from Belgrade and aimed at the territorial integrity of the Austro-Hungarian Monarchy, the Imperial and Royal Government has delivered to the Royal Serbian Government a Note in which a series of demands were formulated. The Royal Serbian Government not having answered this Note in a satisfactory manner, the Imperial and Royal Government are themselves compelled to see to the safeguarding of their rights and interests, and, with this object, to have recourse to force of arms . . .

Austria had already declared war on Serbia, and nothing could now stop the march of events moving forward, it seemed, by their own momentum.

Chapter 3

It was entirely by coincidence that the Aldershot Command had arranged for a test mobilisation of the 2nd Division to start on 27 July. It was simply common practice towards the end of the month's Divisional Training. Most peacetime battalions operated at little more than half their nominal strength. In an emergency they would augment their numbers by calling up the men of the Reserve and, since it was the job of the Army to be constantly in a state of readiness for an emergency, the exercise of speedily integrating hundreds of men into the Battalion had to be practised at least once a year. This year it was the turn of the 1st Division to supply the personnel and animals to bring the 2nd Division up to strength. Next summer their roles would be reversed.

No one enjoyed mobilisation, least of all the NCOs and orderlies snowed under with sheaves of paperwork, forever counting heads and checking and re-checking long lists of men and supplies. Quartermasters, inundated with desperate pleas to supply improvident soldiers with missing items of kit, made them sweat for it. Cooks grumbled and cursed as they tackled the extra workload and prayed for defaulters to peel the mountains of potatoes. But defaulters were few. No officer in the throes of gathering in the full complement of men necessary to put his platoon or his company on a 'war footing' was in the least anxious to incur the Colonel's wrath if even a single man was missing on the final parade. Short of murder, it was wisest to turn a blind eye to minor misdemeanours – and Heaven might help the overzealous NCO who reported one.

After forty-eight frenetic hours, all was completed in time to put on a reasonable show for inspection by the Divisional Commander and the following morning the 1st Battalion, The Oxfordshire and Buckingham-shire Light Infantry, in the happy knowledge that the worst was over, marched out with the 5th Infantry Brigade to bivouac for the last two days of the exercise. On the return journey some were destined to march back again, and in considerable disgust, for they were more accustomed to ride.

Certain young officers with limited personal resources and an eye for a bargain had taken advantage of the Army's 'boarding-out scheme' which gave them the use of a mount worth hundreds of guineas, which they could use for hunting and hacking, for the modest outlay of a small insurance premium and the cost of the horse's feed. This was not disinterested philanthropy on the part of the Army. It was a practical method of maintaining a reserve of trained cavalry horses for an emergency but, in the meantime, at no cost to the taxpayer. The agreement gave the Army the right to call in the animals for a short period every year, but the Army undertook to give a month's warning of this inconvenience. No one could remember an instance of any horse having been recalled, and the officers looked on their mounts as their own.

The Ox and Bucks were about to have a nasty surprise. It happened in the middle of their field exercises. In retrospect, it amazed them that the agents of the Army had had no difficulty in tracking some half dozen subalterns across the wilds of Hampshire to the very fields where they were on manoeuvres and, with neither warning or by-your-leave, slapping requisition notices into their reluctant hands and as good as leading their horses away from beneath them. It was the first hint that active service might be in the wind – or, at least, in the wind for the cavalry. Their second shock came with their return to barracks and the unwelcome news that Bank Holiday leave which had been granted earlier in the week was now cancelled.

The Royal Navy had already been on standby for two days. After the Review at Spithead, the Fleet went steaming off for ten days of sea exercises. They were due to finish on 27 July and, in normal circumstances, the ships would then have dispersed to their home ports, to land their reservists and to give their regular crews the traditional reward of Manoeuvre Leave for a job well done. But, by 27 July, it was becoming increasingly apparent that the circumstances were not normal, that the situation in Europe was blowing up to a crisis and that the giants of the European nations were flexing their muscles for war, among them Germany.

It seemed to Churchill, who was First Lord of the Admiralty, as it did to his First Sea Lord, Prince Louis of Battenberg, that the happy chance which had concentrated the power of the world's strongest navy on the very doorstep of its Empire at a moment of incipient danger, should not be thrown away. In a spirit of 'safety first', they decided, on their own authority, to issue the order that would keep the Fleet where it was and in a state of readiness. Now another order had sent the First Fleet northwards to take up its War Station off Scapa Flow.

On the parade ground of Colchester Barracks, the music issuing from the open windows of the band rehearsal room was unusually harmonious for a Wednesday evening. According to the band's timetable, the hour between six and seven was a tuition session rather than a full practice, and normally only the boys of the band of the 1st Battalion, The Rifle Brigade, would have been suffering under the baton of the Bandmaster. Charles Barry was a bully and a martinet, as handy with his fists as he was with his baton, which served a dual role as an instrument of punishment. Barry made use of it almost as often to rap the knuckles of hapless apprentice musicians as he used it to beat time to their playing and most of them had, more than once, had a swollen, bleeding hand to prove it. Barry was loathed by every member of the band, from his own band-sergeant to the newest recruit. And tonight his popularity, never high, was at its lowest ebb, for he was also a perfectionist and, with three days to go before the Bank Holiday weekend, he had called a rehearsal of the full band of sixty soldiers to put a final gloss on some items of the repertoire they were to play for the entertainment of holidaymakers at Ramsgate during Bank Holiday week.

The bandsmen, known by long brass band tradition in the Army as 'the Windjammers', were not delighted to be indoors at the mercy of the irascible Barry on a fine evening after a long day of duty and music and drill. Most of them had other plans. There was a dance in Colchester and, with Barry's grudging permission, more than half the bandsmen were in civilian clothes ready for a quick getaway. A man in civvies had a better chance of clicking with a girl, for soldiers, whether attired in smart walking-out dress or glorious in full-dress uniform, were looked on by toffee-nosed Colchester as the rag, tag and bobtail of society. They were even barred from drinking in the better class of pub, so civilian clothes were obligatory for the full enjoyment of an evening off. They were looking forward to it. Meanwhile, they concentrated hard on the music. It was best to avoid the ire of the Bandmaster who, on a whim, could keep them at it for hours.

At twenty minutes past six the band had just begun a selection from the opera *Maritana*, when the door crashed open and an orderly sergeant appeared.

'All men of B Company to parade in full marching order.'

Barry glared, scowled and barked back, 'I only take orders like that from Battalion Orderly Room!' He added with masterly sarcasm, 'And *may* I remind you that Band practice is a Commanding Officer's Parade?'

He was quite within his rights. Band Practice took priority over all other duties and over the demands of any officer of the Battalion other than the Colonel himself. And the Colonel, well aware that, but for this rule, the Bandmaster would rarely have a full band to command, respected it scrupulously. Barry raised his baton again. The band had played perhaps five bars when the door was thrown open again.

'All men of C company to parade in full marching order.'

'Get OUT!'

Barry was enraged. The unfortunate sergeant retired smartly, and the Windjammers waited with interest for further developments. Within moments the same thing happened again.

When the sergeant of D Company had been seen off in short order, Barry snapped at Sergeant Farley, 'Go to the Orderly Room and find out why the hell my band rehearsal keeps being interrupted. This is ridiculous! Who the devil wants a parade at six o'clock in the evening?'

The answer came back that the War Office wanted one. An alert had been flashed from Whitehall to Army Commands throughout Great Britain and Ireland, warning the Army to prepare for war. They called it the 'Precautionary Period' and, under provisions laid down long before, every serving soldier was ordered to stand to arms. The 1st Battalion, The Rifle Brigade, was ordered to the Suffolk coast to protect it against invasion and also to guard the tanks that held the Navy's oil.

The Band Practice came to an abrupt end. It would be five years before there was another. They were not dispirited. It was something at least to have escaped, even temporarily, from Barry's clutches. Paddy Doyle was especially gratified. It was largely due to Barry's attentions that he had deserted the year before. He had been caught in the spring. Now he was back with the Battalion and, after his spell in military prison, glad of it.

The Battalion marched off at eight o'clock, and for once they marched in silence. The trumpets, the cornets, the tubas, the clarinets, the drums, had been left behind, packed away with the dashing full-dress uniforms of green and black. Clad in sober service dress, the long khaki column marched to Colchester station without the benefit of music to cheer them on, and the Windjammers, tramping in the ranks of their parent companies, were indistinguishable from anyone else.

It was the evening of 29 June. For almost twenty-four hours Austria had been at war with Serbia. Earlier that day the great guns of the Austro-Hungarian Empire had fired the first shells of the war on Belgrade. And all Europe was jumping.

The Tsar sent a personal message to his cousin the Kaiser, begging him to restrain the Austrians before it was too late, but Germany, teetering on the sidelines, was in a dilemma. Perhaps as a sop for his non-appearance at Franz Ferdinand's funeral, the Kaiser had sent a series of unctuous friendly messages assuring Austria of Germany's support if she should be forced to take up arms against Serbia. But that had been weeks ago when the risk seemed small.

On the other hand, as the Kaiser was quick to assure his Cousin Nicky, Germany was not anxious to go to war with Russia. He was even more reluctant to take on the country of Cousin George, and the German Ambassador in London had already been instructed to sound out British intentions. Would she be content to sit on the fence if France went to war? The non-committal diplomatic reply gave him reason to hope that she might. As for the war itself, there seemed no possibility of avoiding it. The best that could be hoped for, from the Kaiser's point of view, was that it might be contained within bounds that would be to Germany's advantage. Nor did the Kaiser wish to lose face by appearing to be the instigator, though he was not blind to the advantage to be gained by getting in first. Germany had not officially mobilised, but all officers on leave had been recalled. Bavarian soldiers, recruited almost without exception from the peasantry, learned with dismay that their usual harvest leave had been cancelled. Reservists had been warned to stand by.

The temperature was rising in France. Lieutenant Spears, who was combining his attachment to the French War Office with a visit to friends at Passy, was surprised on the night of his arrival to find them packing boxes of groceries into their attic. People still remembered the siege of Paris forty years earlier, when the Prussians had encircled the city, and no one had any intention of being reduced for a second time to a diet of cats.

By chance the President and the Prime Minister of the French Republic had been on an official visit to Russia and had returned with all speed when the crisis began to blow up. It was 29 July. That morning Austria had declared war on Serbia and the astute French had not been slow to assess the possible consequences to themselves. President Poincaré and Prime Minister Viviani were astonished to find a vast crowd waiting to yell a welcome at the Gare du Nord. They cheered, they whooped, they threw their hats in the air. They sang the 'Marseillaise'.

Each nation believed that it had something to gain by going to war. Austria and Hungary, by soundly defeating Serbia, could bolster the stability of their crumbling empire, subdue the unruly Slavs and, with the aid of Germany, deliver such a rap to the paw of the Russian bear, whose greedy eyes were fixed on the honeypots of the Balkans, that it would howl for mercy.

Germany, less interested in the Balkans, would have no objection to augmenting her empire by the addition of the Russian territory that would fall to her share when the spoils of victory were parcelled out. But, first and foremost, she could put France decisively in her place and advance the power and the glory of the new Germany by confiscating French territories overseas.

Russia and France, although not anxious to instigate a war, might each turn a successful outcome to some advantage. France could get back Alsace and Lorraine and avenge her humiliation at the hands of the Prussians forty years before. Russia could 'rescue' the Slavonic states and bring them into the sphere of the Russian Empire.

Even Great Britain, unwilling to break the golden chain of peace and prosperous expansion which, give or take some far-off conflicts, had endured unbroken for a hundred years, was forced to conclude that, sooner or later, a trial of strength was unavoidable. Only by curbing the upstart aspirations of the German Empire could peace be assured in Europe and the influence and power of its own empire continue undisturbed.

Tiny Serbia alone had nothing to gain but eventual oblivion and a spurious immortality based on the accident of fate by which a Serb fired the shot that gave Austria the excuse she needed to take up arms against her and, by doing so, plunged Europe headlong into the Great War.

It was by a fatal accident that the situation jolted forward from unease to tension. Someone had tipped off a Berlin newspaper, but it had jumped the gun and at lunchtime on Thursday the *Berlin Lokalanzeiger* rushed out a special edition announcing that the German army had mobilised. The statement was indignantly denied, but it was too late. It had already been picked up by the press agencies and wired around the world. They were slower to pass on the news of the contradiction. Before it reached Moscow, some hours after the original statement had thrown the Tsar and his General Staff into a panic, Russia had ordered mobilisation. It was the afternoon of 30 July.

In London it was speechday at St Olave's Grammar School in Bermondsey, and the guest of honour was Sir Henry Newbolt, poet and patriot. The highlight of the afternoon was to have been the presentation to the retiring headmaster, Mr Rushworth, of his portrait in oils. He had already prepared the courteous speech in which, in accordance with long-established custom, he would hand it back to the school so that it could hang beside those of his predecessors in the Great Hall. But there had been a last-minute hitch. The portrait had been sent to Germany for prints to be made. Unfortunately the Berlin firm, specialists in the technique of photogravure, had had an unexpected rush of work. The painting was still in Germany and the presentation must, therefore, be postponed.

Despite the growing seriousness of the international situation none of the audience of boys, parents and masters dreamed that the postponement would last for five long years. They could hardly have guessed that by the time the portrait was hung three of St Olave's masters and a hundred and ninety-one of their past and present pupils would have died in the Great War.

On the eve of the long holidays stretching enticingly ahead, the boys were in high spirits. Only the guest of honour cast a gloom. His address, hastily revised in the light of the crisis whose gravity had been pointed out for the first time to the general public in the leading article of that morning's *Times*, was remarkable for its lack of the platitudes which were the normal ingredients of prize-giving ceremonies. There were the sketchiest of congratulations to the winners, little or nothing in the way of commiseration to the losers, no allegorical allusions to the example set by the tortoise and the hare, little or no sermonising on the satisfaction of a job well done and the worthiness of effort for its own sake. Sir Henry addressed himself directly to the scrubbed and shining schoolboys.

'When you are engaged – as we may be in a few days – in a great world-shaking war, your prizes will appear very little things.'

It was the first that most of the Olavians had heard of it.

Earlier that morning, some six hundred miles to the north, another party of young men, little older than the sixth-formers of St Olave's, had enjoyed a riotous hour of bathing and horseplay in the bracing waters of the Dornoch Firth. They were Territorial soldiers of the 4th (Reserve) Battalion of the Gordon Highlanders and they enjoyed a unique alphabetical distinction. The four companies of the Battalion were known as A, B, C and U. 'U' stood for university and its members were, without exception, undergraduates of Aberdeen University where, for fifty weeks of the year, they applied themselves with varying degrees of conscientiousness to their studies in the Faculties of the Arts, of the Law, of Divinity and of Medicine. As pranksters the Divinity students were generally conceded to hold the palm but during the annual camp there were no holds barred.

For twelve days now, U Company had been camping on the hills above Tain and a good time had been had by all. The examinations were over and even those who were convinced that they had failed philosophically resigned themselves to re-sitting in September and settled down to enjoy themselves as soon as they had boarded the special train at Aberdeen. They had sung all the way to Tain and the journey was long enough to allow them to run through the entire repertoire of the well-thumbed students' song-book at least five times from cover to cover. Their favourite song was the mildly risqué 'Riding down to Bangor', and they never tired of it.

> Riding down from Bangor, on an eastern train,
> After weeks of hunting in the woods of Maine,
> Quite extensive whiskers, beard, moustache as well,
> Sat a student fellow, tall and slim and swell.

> *Enter aged couple, take the hindmost seat,*
> *Enter village maiden, beautiful, petite . . .*

and so on, in a dozen raucous choruses.

It was a glorious beginning and U Company, wallowing in the pleasure of having exchanged stiff collars and red gowns for the delightful freedom of the kilt, made the most of it.

> *Blushingly she falters, 'Is this seat engaged?',*
> *See the aged couple properly enraged!*
> *Student quite ecstatic, sees her ticket through,*
> *Thinks of the long tunnel, thinks what he will do.*

They had roared it out when the train stopped at Inverness, to the delight of an appreciative audience on the station platform, and a few stalwarts were still croaking the song, after a fashion, when they tumbled out of the train in the evening and formed up for the march to the campsite on the hills above Tain.

> *. . . Whizz, slap, bang — into tunnel quite,*
> *Into glorious darkness black as Egypt's night.*
> *Out into the daylight glides the eastern train,*
> *Student's hair is ruffled, just the merest grain,*
> *Maiden seen all blushes, for then and there appeared,*
> *A tiny little ear-ring in that horrid student's beard.*

It had been an idyllic fortnight, despite the fact that training had started at six o'clock of a chilly highland morning and had continued all day with drilling and route-marching, manoeuvres and mock battles and eventually a demonstration of field operations in front of a real, serving general.

There had been plenty of opportunity for fun. Some men of mighty stamina who had enough energy left after the rigours of the day had even ventured out after lights out, bribed a fisherman for the hire of a boat and rowed across to Dornoch village in order, as they put it, to 'give the girls a treat'. Now, on the eve of their departure, the programme of training had eased off and U Company, tanned to mahogany by the warm sun and the salt seawinds, had spent most of the day gathering driftwood for the mammoth bonfire that would be the centrepiece of their farewell evening. After their last swim they lined up on the beach for the benefit of a photographer who had been commissioned to take the farewell photograph. Their soldiering was over. It had been time out of life. No one had seen a newspaper. No one had the faintest idea what had been happening in the cockpit of Europe. When they got back to camp, they were thunderstruck. New orders had arrived.

That night, Alex Rule, who had expected to spend the evening round the convivial bonfire, found himself with a group of twenty others who had volunteered for 'special duties' marching up and down a chilly headland above the Dornoch Firth guarding a coastal battery. The rain fell in a steady northern drizzle. It soaked the soldiers on guard, fell steadily down on the camp above, turning the white bell-tents to soggy grey, and dripped relentlessly into the heart of the piled-up wood that, even now, should have been burning merrily to speed them on their way. Pending further orders, the special train which should have taken the Gordons back to Aberdeen on Saturday morning had been cancelled.

By Saturday the European crisis was spinning downhill so fast, the pace of events was accelerating so rapidly, the miasma of rumour was so thick and speculation so rife, that it was impossible to tell the difference between fact and hysteria. Even in Whitehall, the foreign telegrams bringing news and often contradictory reports from foreign governments, from British embassies and consulates, were arriving in such erratic profusion that it was difficult to make either sense or order of the situation, except to see that it was grave and growing more serious with every hour that passed.

Sir Ernest Shackleton was to sail from the West India Dock that Saturday morning on the first leg of his third voyage to the Antarctic. In the light of the worsening situation, Sir Ernest had contemplated cancelling the project and offered his services to the Admiralty. The King pressed him to stick to his plans. He himself had been forced to change his. He had intended to be on the quayside and to wave farewell as *Endurance* cast off, to present Shackleton with a Union Jack to carry across Antarctica. But the flag had to be handed over privately in the course of a brief audience at Buckingham Palace an hour before *Endurance* set sail on her ill-fated voyage.

All week, as the shadows gathered, the bevy of European royalty who had come to London for the Season, instead of travelling to Cowes as guests of some exclusive house-party, or even of the King and Queen, had been hurriedly leaving for home. The King himself was staying put. On Saturday morning the Royal Navy was officially mobilised and Cowes Week, due to start on Monday, was cancelled.

Despite the confusion of rumour and conflicting reports, by Saturday evening there were certain inescapable truths. The most important development was that Germany, whose demand that Russia should cease mobilising had been refused out of hand, had ordered the mobilisation of her own forces and declared war on Russia. On receiving this news, the French had mobilised too, but they had also issued a solemn order. No French troops were in any circumstances whatever to move within ten kilometres of the frontier with Germany. If war came, it would come with no provocation on the part of the French. But France, like Russia, was prepared to fight and the Germans had evolved a plan to defeat them both.

It had been made long ago in 1892. That was the year in which republican France and autocratic Russia, setting aside their political differences for more practical considerations, had signed their pact of mutual support. The Germans were distinctly rattled, for now it became clear that if Germany went to war with one she would also have to take on the other, and that such a war would therefore have to be fought and won on two separate fronts.

The plan was drawn up by the German Chief of Staff, Field Marshal Count von Schlieffen, with such precise attention to detail, with such clarity of logic, and it seemed such an infallible blueprint for success that no attempt was ever made to revise it or even to alter it in the smallest particular.

Following the maxim that attack is the best method of defence, the nub of the Schlieffen Plan was to knock out France in a swift, decisive action before the huge, unwieldy war machine of the Russian Empire could grind into action. Russia could call on millions of men but, with only a sparse and primitive railway system to transport them and huge tracts of wild territory to cover, it would take weeks to gather her forces together and move them into position. Russia could safely be left until France had been crushed. Then, having reduced one enemy to impotence, Germany could turn her attention eastward and concentrate all her resources of men and materials on defeating the other. And the plan had an added attraction. A crippling war levy imposed on France would nicely fill Germany's coffers and enable her to fight the war at the expense of the French.

But everything hinged on speed, and since Germany had sequestered Alsace and Lorraine, France had strengthened her new shortened frontier with a chain of fortresses and fortifications. It would take weeks, perhaps months, of siege warfare to smash through them, but the success of the Schlieffen Plan depended on striking so quickly, so powerfully, so deeply into the heart of France and so overwhelming her army, that she would be forced to sue for peace in a matter of days.

There was only one way of achieving it. They must lure the French to the east by sending an army to attack them precisely where they expected an attack to fall – along their fortified border with Germany. Meanwhile a far stronger force would be poised to hammer into France through her back door further west, where the frontier was weak and undefended.

Then, as the Germans marched towards the south-east in a vast encircling movement, the French army could be neatly caught like a ferret in a sack. There was just one snag. Tiny, neutral Belgium barred the way.

Unless the Belgians could be intimidated or persuaded into allowing the German army to pass through unmolested, the fat would be in the fire. The difficulty was that France, Great Britain and Germany herself were solemnly bound to protect Belgian neutrality, and to protect it if necessary by force of arms.

As far back as 1898, during a state visit by King Leopold II of Belgium, the Kaiser had seized the opportunity to approach the King and to ask him if, in the event of Germany going to war with France, he would agree to open his frontier to the German army and guarantee its passage through Belgium to France. It was an ill-chosen moment. Leopold was an unpredictable character, addicted to sensuous living and the flesh-pots of southern climes. He did not like Berlin. He had not enjoyed the obligatory review of the Kaiser's troops drawn up in review order on a windswept parade ground and he had been chilled to the bone while taking the salute at the interminable march past. To add injury to insult, a careless servant had filled his hip bath with near-boiling water, the King had been badly scalded and was eating his dinner standing up. He was in a furious temper and in no mood to look kindly on the Kaiser's proposal which, even in the best of humours, he would have refused. He rewarded the Kaiser with a flea in his imperial ear, returned thankfully to Brussels and lost no time in reporting this interesting conversation to the British Government.

It had been duly noted by the Foreign Office but, with the passage of time and the intervening changes of staff and of government, the information had been filed away and forgotten. Even if it had been remembered, no one could seriously have thought that this tiny snippet of ancient gossip was a significant clue, sixteen years later, to Germany's immediate intentions. But it was. Germany, now embarking on the Great War of the twentieth century, was about to place her faith in and entrust her fortunes to the plan drawn up by Schlieffen twenty-two years before.

The last thing that Schlieffen had wished to provoke was a war with Great Britain and, now that his plan was to be implemented and Germany had no other, the Kaiser was no more anxious than Schlieffen had been to bring Britain into the conflict if it could be avoided. King Leopold was dead and his nephew King Albert was now on the throne of Belgium. The first move was to cajole or, if necessary, to threaten him into giving the German army full and free permission to use Belgium as a highway to France. It hardly met the conditions of 'neutrality' which Belgium was required to uphold, and the Germans knew it, but it was an area just grey enough to allow Germany and Belgium to argue the technicalities and, the

Kaiser believed, to deter Britain from entering the lists on the issue of Belgian neutrality.

A note had been prepared on 26 July, two days before Austria had gone to war with Serbia. It warned the Belgians that their neighbours the French were about to breach their frontier and march on the Meuse through Namur. In view of this 'intelligence', the Germans requested free and unrestricted entry into Belgium in order to repel the attack. The demand had been sent to Germany's ambassador in Brussels but with instructions that he was not to hand it to the Belgian government until he received further orders. Now the order had been sent. It was Sunday, 2 August.

The British and American passengers who had embarked on the Dutch vessel *Hollandia* for a leisurely summer cruise down the Rhine were finding the journey a good deal more exciting than they had anticipated, and the excitement had been building up since Thursday at Cologne when they heard the first hint that Germany was on the brink of war. On Friday night, at Biebrich, they found the streets crowded with people queueing to buy newspapers whose headlines were proclaiming Germany's ultimatum to Russia.

The captain assured them that there was no need to worry. Russia was a long way off, the *Hollandia* was a neutral ship, they were perfectly safe on board and would be far better to stay there and leave as planned at Mannheim. From there, frequent trains crossed the French border to Strasbourg. All the same, it might be wiser to spend the evening on board and not to venture into the town. As dusk fell the passengers gathered on deck to enjoy the cool evening air. They were astonished to find the sky aglow with searchlights. They were sweeping the sky for foreign aeroplanes. From the ship, anchored at the quiet dockside, they could hear excited shouting and singing. They were singing 'The Watch on the Rhine'.

> *Lieb Vaterland kann ruhig sein!*
> *Lieb Vaterland kann ruhig sein!*
> *Fest Steht und treu die Wacht,*
> *Die Wacht am Rhein.*

Hollandia cast off early in the morning for the final stretch of her cruise. The journey took many hours for she was stopped every few miles by military police in armoured patrol boats searching for French or Russian officers. At Mannheim her passengers learned that Germany and Russia were at war, that France had mobilised and that the trains had stopped running to Strasbourg.

★

The first battle of the war was fought in Trafalgar Square on Sunday afternoon. A peace meeting was arranged and the main speakers were to be Keir Hardie, Socialist Member of Parliament, and the trade union leader Ben Tillett, who had organised marches to converge on the square at four o'clock.

But the national crisis had drawn others to the centre of London. There was an air of expectancy in the crowded streets. With every fresh speculation or development, Fleet Street was rushing out newspapers, and swarms of delivery vans, even hastily hired motor-cabs, piled high with late editions still damp from the press, sped honking through the streets to deliver them to the newsboys strategically positioned on every corner. If anything happened, the streets of London would be the first to know it. And now that the Kaiser was on the march and war was brewing, the crowds were waiting for something definite to happen. Since their latest information was that the Kaiser had ordered the seizure of British ships in the German port of Kiel, they were waiting, in particular, for the news that Britain was ready to slap the Kaiser down.

They waited outside Buckingham Palace in the hope of seeing the King and Queen. They waited in Downing Street, watching grave-faced ministers come and go, and under the stony gaze of Lord Nelson hundreds of people were milling round Trafalgar Square where the very air seemed to breathe 'England expects . . .' The more excitable elements had provided themselves with Union Jacks and, when the peace marchers arrived, they were not disposed to tolerate the Red Flag. Nor were they prepared to tolerate another point of view.

> . . . I speak as a man in the street. Doubtless I am an abnormally dense one, because I cannot for the life of me see why on earth this country should be dragged into war. How can it possibly matter to us whether or not a strong Serbia is a menace to Austria, or whether Russia feels compelled to intervene and Germany to follow suit? It is not worth the life of a single British Grenadier! And what earthly . . .

But the speakers trying to make themselves heard from the plinth of Nelson's Column were shouted down with boos and jeers, counter-cheering from their own supporters, fervent chanting of the National Anthem, roaring counter-attacks of 'The Red Flag'. Tempers flared, fights broke out and police reinforcements arrived to restore order.

A mile away, a packed congregation in Westminster Abbey was listening to the Archbishop of Canterbury preaching the sermon he had already delivered that morning at a private service for the Royal Family at the Chapel Royal. His theme was the National Crisis.

This thing which is now astir in Europe is not the work of God but of the Devil . . . God has given us in our land an incomparable heritage . . . It is for us at all times, and especially at such a time as this, to make and keep our home life worthy of such a trust . . . It is, I suppose, just conceivable that, for us in England, the storm-clouds will roll by unbroken. God grant it . . . So far as the Nation in its corporate life is concerned, responsibility must rest with those to whom in the providence of God it has fallen to hold the trust for Britain's well-being, and for Britain's honour . . . We look outward among wars and rumours of wars, uncertain in the most literal sense what an hour may bring forth. And therefore? After this manner pray ye, 'Our Father which art in Heaven . . .'

They prayed. They sang the National Anthem. Many, reluctant to leave the atmosphere of high emotion, so tangible in the Abbey, so heady in the crowded Sunday streets, wandered down Whitehall past government buildings where those entrusted with 'Britain's well-being and Britain's honour' were awaiting developments and deliberating on the possible implications they would have for Great Britain when they came.

In Brussels, at about this time, the German Ambassador von Below-Saleske, was handed a coded telegram from Berlin. Shortly after, he unlocked the safe where, for the four days since he had received it, Germany's ultimatum to Belgium had been ticking like a time-bomb. Von Below removed the sealed envelope and a little before seven o'clock he drove off to the Belgian Foreign Office to deliver it. His instructions were to inform the Belgians verbally that they had twelve hours in which to reply. The note itself would leave them in no doubt of what they might expect if the reply were unfavourable.

At nine o'clock that evening, at a Council of State chaired by King Albert, the Belgian government formally and unanimously decided on their reply, but it took until dawn to hammer out the details and formulate the wording. They also speculated sadly on what would be the Germans' next move. None of them was under any illusions. At precisely seven in the morning a messenger rapped on the door of the German Embassy and delivered the Belgian reply. It said 'No'. It said it in unequivocal terms. And it said that Belgium would fight to repel any invader and to preserve the neutrality that Germany herself was bound by treaty to protect.

In London it was the morning of Bank Holiday Monday. The situation was brought home more forcibly by a small notice in the personal columns

of the morning newspapers than by the tens of thousands of words that
had filled the news and the leader columns in the previous weeks.

GERMAN MOBILISATION

Germans who have served, or are liable to serve, are requested to
return to Germany without delay, as best they can. For information
they can apply to the German Consulate, Russell Square, London
WC

R. L. VON RANKE. Consul.

The papers also carried the news that Germany had declared war on
Russia. That Germany had invaded Luxembourg. That Germany was now
on the brink of invading Belgium. The evening newspapers would inform
the public that Germany had declared war on France.

For Londoners, Bank Holiday Monday was the traditional day out and,
after two changeable, muggy days on Saturday and Sunday, the weather
obliged with traditional unclouded sunshine. Crisis or not, the usual crowds
began arriving at railway stations as early as seven in the morning, intent
on making a day of it.

Noisy family parties attired for the seaside, weighed down with buckets
and spades and with baskets knobbly with apples and ginger beer bottles
wedged between packets of buns and sandwiches, were annoyed to discover
that all holiday excursion trains had been cancelled. The more prosperous
took the regular trains and paid the full fare, but many changed their plans
and decided to make the most of it in London instead.

At Waterloo, disappointed holidaymakers were in no hurry to move on,
for the Royal Navy had now officially mobilised and the station was
teeming with Naval Reservists. They stayed to give them a send-off, and
Waterloo, more accustomed at eight o'clock on a Monday morning to a
sedate stream of bowler-hatted gentlemen *en route* to the city from the
suburbs, rang with the sound of a huge crowd singing, more or less in
unison, 'All the Nice Girls Love a Sailor' and, loudly enthusiastic, 'Rule
Britannia', as the special trains, which should have been packed with
trippers off to Southsea, pulled out packed with cheering sailors bound for
Portsmouth.

There was no singing at Victoria, and the people who stayed to gawp
were less enthusiastic than curious as they gathered round the boat train
barriers to watch passengers departing for the Continent. They were
third-class passengers for the most part, and a shabby bunch, wearing
anxious expressions and lugging cheap fibre suitcases. They lugged them
with difficulty for they contained all their worldly possessions and most
were also struggling with unwieldy paper parcels that clearly contained

the overflow. They were cooks and waiters from London's hotels and restaurants; they were butchers and barbers from London's East End; they were itinerant musicians who had earned a living in London's streets. They were German. A few, leaving English wives and children at the barrier, were in tears.

For those thwarted of their day at the seaside, London held alternative attractions. A flying display at Hendon drew considerable crowds. There was the Anglo-American Exhibition at the White City with thrilling scenes of the Wild West. There was 'Sunny Spain' recreated at Earl's Court, complete with flamenco dancers. But by far the most popular entertainment was a visit to Madame Tussaud's. With topical acumen the management had rearranged the wax models of royal and political personalities into a single display and sent men with sandwich boards round the streets to advertise it.

THE EUROPEAN CRISIS.

Lifelike portrait models of

THEIR MAJESTIES KING GEORGE AND QUEEN MARY

H.I.M. THE EMPEROR OF AUSTRIA

H.M. KING PETER OF SERBIA

and other

REIGNING SOVEREIGNS OF EUROPE.

NAVAL AND MILITARY TABLEAUX.

Delightful music.

Refreshments at popular prices.

Madame Tussaud's opened as early as eight o'clock in the morning and was packed out all day. The zoo did good business and by noon every square yard of grass in the London parks was covered with picnic parties, doubtless consoling themselves with the thought that at least there was no sand in the sandwiches.

For Post Office shift-workers, Bank Holiday counted as a normal working day. Private telephones were a rare, new-fangled luxury and the public depended on the postal service for all its social and domestic needs. There were five deliveries a day, and every day of the year the Post Office delivered millions of halfpenny postcards and thousands of sixpenny telegrams. An army of telegraph boys, cheeky in pillbox hats, pedalling red Post Office bicycles through city streets and country lanes, were the public's guarantee that a telegram would be delivered to any part of the country within an hour. On Monday the Post Office handled more than 100,000 for the Government alone.

The cost of a telegram was sixpence for twelve words. But on 3 August the Army required only one. '*Mobilise*'. The decision had been taken the previous evening, within an hour of Germany's ultimatum to Belgium. At four o'clock on the afternoon of Bank Holiday Monday it was officially announced. The machinery had been ready for years and now it swung smoothly into action. All night, behind the lighted windows of the War Office, thousands of envelopes, already addressed, were stuffed with printed mobilisation notices. Telegram forms, already completed, were checked against long lists of reservists, kept constantly updated for such an emergency. They went to every man on the Army Reserve, to every Territorial Unit in the country, to every police station and to the headquarters of every Army command, division and brigade in the British Isles. It was still not certain that Britain would be drawn into the war, but it was better to play safe.

The Government had also sent a stern note to Germany demanding an assurance that they would not violate Belgian neutrality. All day on Bank Holiday Monday they waited for a reply. It was many hours before one came. When it did it amounted to little more than an hysterical plea that Germany was 'fighting for her life', and an attempt to shift the blame on to the shoulders of the French by citing yet again the 'hostile acts of aggression' which the Germans had fabricated for home consumption and used as an excuse to go to war with France.

But the French had been careful to ensure that no hostile act could be laid at their door. The French army stood braced for the first blow – but it was standing well within the borders of France. The fact was that the French needed the British, and they knew very well that Britain was far more likely to come to the aid of an ally who was the victim of an unprovoked attack than to rush to her side to assist her in the role of aggressor. A little patience now, a stance of moral rectitude, could just tip the balance and convince Great Britain of her moral obligation.

Now, belatedly, the Germans realised that too, and the British note had given them a bad attack of nerves. It particularly upset the Kaiser. He had hoped, and he hoped even now at this last minute, that the British would refuse to be dragged into the war. The Kaiser had banked in the last resort on family loyalty. Now Russia, ruled by his cousin the Tsar, and Great Britain, ruled by his cousin King George, were moving against him. 'How could Nicky and George have deceived me so?' he raged. 'My grandmother would never have allowed it!'

But Queen Victoria was long dead, the German army was already on the move, and it was too late to stop it.

All Bank Holiday Monday the question hung in the air. Will Britain go to war for France? Next morning there was a new development, and a new question. Will Britain rescue Belgium?

The German army had crossed the neutral border at half past eight in the morning. The Belgians resisted their advance as best they could, and appealed to France, to Russia and to Great Britain for assistance. In Berlin the British Ambassador presented Britain's ultimatum to the German government. Unless Germany undertook by midnight to withdraw her troops from Belgium, she might consider herself to be at war with Great Britain and her Empire.

The terms of the ultimatum were icy and uncompromising. They were intended to leave the Germans in no doubt that Honour was at stake. The Allies had been drawn into war on a pretext. Now Germany had given them a Cause.

Chapter 4

The miracle was that, thanks to the War Book, everyone knew precisely what to do now. They called it the War Book, but it was more accurately an encyclopaedia. It ran to several million words of detailed instructions and arrangements compiled to provide a blueprint for action in 'certain eventualities'. It had been in the making for three years, ever since the 'eventuality' which had now come about had cast a foreboding shadow over Europe from as far away as Agadir. Every government department had a section to itself and a Central Co-ordinating Committee made sure that the War Book was constantly updated and dovetailed, that nothing was forgotten and that new ideas were incorporated as they came to mind. The section devoted to railways alone amounted to eighty-seven pages of print, plus eighty-two pages of typewritten additions and amendments.

The War Book was the product of many minds and it was a work of pure imagination. Its authors had hatched a dozen different plots of hypothetical villainy that might conceivably plunge the nation into war, and with infinite pains had gone through them step by step, detail by detail, until they were satisfied that no circumstance could arise which had not been envisaged, no question could be asked which the War Book had not already answered and few problems could be encountered which its authors had not solved in advance.

The answers were at hand in the close-printed sheafs of instructions kept under lock and key in the safes of army depots, police headquarters, mayoral parlours, of postmasters, railway managers and shipping lines and of the civil authorities in every region of the British Isles, the Colonies and Dominions. It only required the despatch of the long-prepared War Telegrams to put them into effect.

> IN THE CIRCUMSTANCE THAT GREAT BRITAIN IS
> AT WAR WITH ———, ACT UPON INSTRUCTIONS.

All day Tuesday, through the hours of mounting tension, even the most senior of Whitehall's civil servants had busied themselves with the task of rubber-stamping *GERMANY* into the gap.

No sea captain setting sail from any port between Hull and Hong Kong need hesitate or wait for instructions from the owners. Emergency War Insurance of merchant shipping had automatically come into effect. A firm in a quandary over a consignment of goods packed for despatch to Hamburg or Vienna need only apply to the Board of Trade whose guidelines on Trading with the Enemy would instantly resolve its dilemma. The Turkish navy, anxiously awaiting delivery of two warships ordered from British shipyards, were doomed to disappointment for, under these provisions, their ships had already been confiscated, renamed and assigned to the Royal Navy.

No impecunious soldier of the Army Reserve, suddenly recalled to the colours, needed to beg or borrow the fare to his distant regiment. His identity document told him exactly what to do. Produce it at the counter of any post office and the clerk would hand over five shillings for his travelling expenses; show it at any station and the ticket office would promptly hand him a rail warrant to his destination. And he would not have to spend the journey wondering how his wife would contrive to stretch a few coppers across the gap between the last wage packet and the first Army Allotment. The Soldiers' Families Emergency Fund, administered by the local town hall, would see her through until it came.

The judiciary had its own instructions, and some thousands of local magistrates would spend the best part of a day signing a host of measures to empower the police and the military to swear in recruits, to requisition billets, to control the movement of all transport, to prevent aliens from leaving the country, to arrest suspected spies.

No adjutant of a battalion whose strength had suddenly doubled would be driven frantic by the problem of whistling up the extra transport required to carry the men, the stores, and their munitions to war. The War Book contained a census of all horses and commercial vehicles in the country and a proportion had already been earmarked for the use of the Army. No quartermaster would wonder where the extra kit and stores were to come from. No brigadier or colonel would have to decide what orders to issue to his command. They had already been drafted with such care that not a single serving soldier, down to the humblest private, would be left in the least doubt as how to prepare himself for active service. It was all laid down, from the method of packing his dress uniform for storage to a stern reminder that the book he was reading must be returned forthwith to the garrison library.

The War Book had thought of everything and hardly a detail had been overlooked. It had considered morale too. Envisaging extreme circumstances in which half the King's subjects might conceivably be separated from the other half, it had seen to it that the Postmaster-General had evolved a system to cope with the burgeoning of the Royal Mail. It would work in tandem with the Army postal service to ensure that letters and parcels from home would follow swiftly on the heels of the soldiers wherever the war might send them. It was further decreed that the Tommy's mail would travel to the war-zone with his daily rations and that it would share the same priority status. Later they took justifiable pride in this system. Although it had been worked out in the years before the war to meet the imagined needs of a tiny Expeditionary Force of eighty thousand men, it was able to expand with no modification to meet the needs of several millions. In another August, two years hence, one astonished soldier in a listening sap far out in No Man's Land was cheered up by receiving a parcel of gooseberries from his garden at home in Woking. It had come up with the rations.

But that was a long way in the future. For the moment, now that ten thousand theoretical flights of fancy were about to be tested in the reality of full mobilisation, the question in the minds of the nervous authors of the War Book was, 'Will it work'?

The Precautionary Period at least had gone off without a hitch and, in a sense, the most difficult part of the mammoth task had been to envisage circumstances which would put Great Britain on guard but not necessarily in a state of war. The most obvious threat to the security of the British Isles was the threat of invasion so the keynote of the Precautionary Plan had been defence and it had made provision to put part of the Army on standby, ready to move to wherever trouble might be. Others, like the 1st Battalion, The Rifle Brigade, had been posted to sensitive parts of the coast to guard it, to look out for danger and to be on the alert to repulse any raiders who might slip through a chink in the iron-clad wall of the ships at sea.

The activity round the cruiser *Amphion* riding at anchor off the coast near Felixstowe was the only diversion in sight for the fed-up sentries on their monotonous patrols. Fortunately, the weather was fine and off duty the soldiers could swim or laze on the beach. Victor Shawyer preferred to stretch out in the long grass that reached down to the edge of the sands and catch up on some badly needed sleep.

Sentry duty did not normally fall within the scope of a bandsman's duties and Shawyer had not taken kindly to it. Four years of peacetime discipline had taught him that it was not the role of the private soldier to question the whims of the Army but, until now, that Army had dutifully seen to it that he got his quota of sleep, and Victor loved his bed. He failed to see why a sentry should be on duty around the clock, two hours on and two hours off. It was not that there was any shortage of men. Half of C Company had been sent to guard this short stretch of isolated coastline whose only distinguishing features were empty, windswept beaches, a huge container that held the oil for the Navy's submarines, a scattering of buildings that held the Navy's stores, and a short refuelling wharf for the Navy's smaller ships. Not content with posting double sentries, the Army had even brought in a contingent of Territorials to augment them and the fact that this reduced each sentry's patrol to fifty yards merely made the job more tedious.

The nights were the worst. Apart from some desultory chat with a neighbouring sentry when their leaden tramping brought them to the end of their respective beats, there was nothing but the lap of the sea to disturb the silence.

In the six days since their hasty departure from Colchester, the R Bs had not enjoyed a full night's sleep. They had received no news and were still under the impression that the whole exercise was a practice mobilisation. If the officers knew any better they were not letting on, though Captain Prettie had lectured Shawyer on the heavy responsibilities of a sentry with an earnestness that left him distinctly uneasy. So far the only party he had had occasion to challenge was his own relief. Someone else along the coast had challenged a grey seal. Its corpse had been found on the beach, shot neatly through the head, but no sharp-shooting marksman had been willing to run the risk of ridicule by claiming the kill. It had been the only event of passing interest in a week of total boredom. Only the Navy seemed to be busy.

Bandsman H. V. Shawyer, No. 4142, 1st Bttn., The Rifle Brigade, B.E.F.

The *Amphion* was the flagship of a flotilla of small destroyers. She was anchored a little way out to sea and there were always two or three of these fast little ships anchored around her. Often we'd see one of them come tearing home and after a while another one would up anchor and sail off. We knew they were on North Sea patrol because sometimes one would come in and tie up alongside the wharf to refuel and we got a chance to talk to the crews. That was our only entertainment. The day after August Bank Holiday I was on sentry from ten o'clock to midnight, on the seaward side of the oil tanks. It was a still, still night with no wind at all and the sea was like plate glass – the sort of night when sound travels for miles. Eerie, really, just you and the stars and the sea and the sound of your own feet, soft on the grass. Suddenly, I heard this tremendous roaring noise coming from across the water – cheering and shouting. I couldn't work it out at all. Then I decided that it must be the crew of the big ship cheering at the end of a deck concert. It was ages before it died away.

My relief was late that night. I had my ears cocked to hear if they were coming, but what I actually heard was the sound of a boat being rowed ashore. I was absolutely nonplussed. I had no idea what to do, because I wasn't prepared for anything to come at me from the seaward side. But I knelt down among the coarse grass and the reeds and raised my rifle and shouted as loud as I could yell, 'Halt. Who goes there?'

I could hear the boat grounding on the beach and I could make out a figure standing up in it. He shouted, 'Naval officer with urgent orders for the Military Commander of this post.' I shouted back to them to stay where they were and I yelled for the guard. They came running and the Corporal, Harry Warren, went closer to the water and covered the crew while they landed. There was an officer and two ratings. They spoke for a minute and then Corporal Warren shouted to me (because my relief had turned up by this time), 'Shawyer, take this officer to Captain Prettie.'

I walked with them back to the little campsite a few hundred yards back from the beach and the Captain came out of his tent and the naval officer saluted him. He said, 'Sir, I have the honour to report that as from eleven o'clock, a state of War exists between Great Britain and Germany.'

As long as I live I'll never forget those words. While the officers were talking one of the ratings told me that the noise I'd heard earlier was the sailors cheering the order to clear the decks for action.

The message had been radioed from the Admiralty to all ships at one minute past eleven. Its exact words were *Commence hostilities against Germany*. The war telegrams took a little longer to reach military commands but, by early morning, the R Bs were ready to march off, leaving the Territorials to keep guard over the beaches. It was time for the Army to be on the move. As the morning mist lifted, a last glance over the empty sea showed them that the Navy had gone too.

The *Amphion*, at the head of the flotilla of destroyers, was already steaming seventy miles away to the north-east. She had been ordered to patrol the sea-route from Harwich to Antwerp, to keep it open and clear of any ships with hostile intentions. But the Germans had got there first. Since midnight the *Königin Luise* had been laying a deadly pattern of mines across the shipping lanes of the North Sea. She was sighted at nine o'clock in the morning. The *Amphion* and her destroyers gave chase and by ten o'clock the *Königin Luise* had been sunk in the first naval engagement of the war.

The bedraggled survivors of the *Königin Luise* were packed into the roomy messdecks of the *Amphion*. After he had sent off the signal to report the sinking and set his flotilla back on course to resume its interrupted sweep to the north, Captain Fox went below to look at the first prisoners of the war. Naked but for borrowed coats and blankets, still shivering despite their steaming mugs of cocoa, they looked a miserable bunch. The Captain was sorry for them and ordered an issue of rum. The Germans were doubtless equally sorry for themselves and fervently hoping for a short war. But it was to be the best part of six years before some of them saw Germany again – and they were the lucky ones. By this time tomorrow, 130 British sailors and twenty of their German prisoners would be dead, lost when the *Amphion* struck one of the mines laid by the *Königin Luise*. She was the first British vessel for almost a century to be destroyed by enemy action and the first vessel in naval history to have been sunk by a magnetic mine.

As the second of two mighty explosions sent the crippled *Amphion* to the bottom, another ship of the Royal Navy sailed over the horizon. She was bound for neutral Rotterdam and she carried the German Ambassador, his family and his staff on their way back to Berlin. Its captain was struck by the irony that, had the mines not been hit by the *Amphion*, they might have homed in on his own vessel and sent the German contingent to kingdom come.

Chapter 5

Before the loss of the *Amphion* caused dismay, the news of the sinking of the mine-layer *Königin Luise*, released late in the afternoon of 5 August, reinforced Great Britain's almost religious faith in the Navy. In the high-charged elation of this first day of the Great War, the British public was only too happy to demonstrate its approbation of the Army too.

The progress of the RBs, marching through Felixstowe to entrain for Colchester, was seriously impeded by the attentions of an enthusiastic mob. After the boredom and frustration of the past few days, most of the soldiers were revelling in it. Bandsman Shawyer, still smarting at the ignominy of marching in the ranks, was acutely embarrassed.

Bandsman H. V. Shawyer, No. 4142, 1st Bttn., The Rifle Brigade, B.E.F.

The place was full of holidaymakers lining the pavements to see us go by and come war, hell or high water they seemed determined to get a laugh out of things. Of course none of us could foresee the four terrible years that lay ahead of us, but I didn't feel too generously disposed to some of them. There were bunches of men in the doorways of the public houses holding up their foaming tankards at us as we slogged along – mocking us! And there were we under the weight of all our equipment and not a wink of sleep had we had the night before. Of course a lot of them were young – young enough to be feeling the weight of a full pack on their own backs before long. I often wondered if they were laughing then!

But most of the people couldn't do enough for us, and they were pretty loud in the doing of it. Cheering, shouting, singing, waving their handkerchiefs, and showering us with sweets and packets of cigarettes. Some of the young girls were even pelting us with flowers as if we were blooming Spaniards or something. One man rushed out of a newsagent's with his arms full of copies of the morning papers – he must have bought up the shop! He was running alongside us and the lads were grabbing the papers as fast as he could hand them out. And the cheering and yelling!

I was on the outside of a flank of four. I turned up my head and found myself inches away from a woman who was staring straight into my face. Being nineteen and bashful I was terrified that she was going to kiss me – some fellows were *surrounded* by women kissing them! – but she didn't. She just put her hand up to her mouth and as I went by I could see that she had tears in her eyes. All the same, being a bit of a Kipling fan, I couldn't help thinking of his lines. *It's Tommy this and Tommy that, and Tommy get outside, but it's 'Thank you Mr Atkins', when the troopship's on the tide.*

The troopships were not precisely on the tide but the Army was up to its neck in preparations for the move. Exactly where they were to move to no one had, as yet, decided.

In Germany, troop trains carrying reinforcements to follow up the thrust into Belgium puffed incessantly towards the frontiers. The trains were decked with flowers and German civilians, no less enthusiastic than civilians in Britain, lined the railway tracks to cheer them on their way.

Now the focus of enmity in Germany had shifted to Britain, and British perfidy was roundly condemned by the morning newspapers beneath the headlines that blazoned the news that Britain 'had declared war on Germany'. Technically, this information was correct, but there was no mention of the British ultimatum or its terms. Rather, in a natural desire to recruit patriotic feeling to the colours now nailed irrevocably to Germany's masthead, the German press put forward the theory that Great Britain had jumped on the bandwagon in the hope of capturing German trade and German markets. It was equally natural that the German public should accept this version of events and that indignation was running high in the streets of Berlin.

Feelings were running equally high in government circles and, when the British Ambassador called on the German Chancellor to take leave, Herr von Bethmann-Hollweg reproached him bitterly. It was more than a courtesy visit, for the two men had got on well together and the Chancellor had been more concerned than any other German statesman about the morality of Germany's actions. He had done his utmost to curb impetuosity, to delay the decision to mobilise. Only a few hours earlier – to the consternation of less scrupulous colleagues – he had publicly admitted that Germany's invasion of Belgium was a violation of international law. As a patriot, he sincerely believed that the means justified the end, but von Bethmann was a sophisticated and cosmopolitan man, and he suspected that world opinion might take quite a different view. He believed in German decency and German honour. He simply could not believe that Germany and Great Britain were now at war.

The interview with the British Ambassador was a painful one. Von Bethmann all but wrung his hands. What the British Government had done was terrible. The consequences would be appalling and Britain would be entirely to blame. And all for one word – 'neutrality'! All for 'a scrap of paper' Great Britain was going to war with a kindred nation who desired nothing more than her friendship. It was like striking a man from behind when he was already being attacked by two assailants. The two men parted sadly. All Sir Edward Goschen's protestations could not mollify the Chancellor nor reduce the temperature of his fevered indignation.★

A hostile mob who apparently shared the Chancellor's opinion besieged the British Embassy with volleys of stones and missiles. Deeply embarrassed, profoundly apologetic, the German Foreign Office ordered mounted police to be sent to restore order and to protect the Ambassador and his staff from further disturbance. In the morning the Ambassador received an apology of sorts from the Kaiser, and he received it with mixed feelings. It was delivered verbally by an *aide-de-camp* whose chilly arrogance and exaggerated courtesy conveyed beyond any shadow of doubt that it was intended to be a slap in the face.

The Emperor has charged me to express to your Excellency his regret for the occurrences of last night, but to tell you at the same time that you will gather from those occurrences an idea of the feelings of his people respecting the action of Great Britain in joining with other nations against her old allies of Waterloo. His Majesty also begs that you will tell the King that he has been proud of the titles of British Field Marshal and British Admiral, but that in consequence of what has occurred he must now at once divest himself of those titles.

Next morning the Ambassador and his staff left the Lehrter Station by special train for the Hook of Holland. The German Foreign Office had gone to considerable trouble to ensure that their journey would be comfortable and that the Ambassador would not be harassed. Other British subjects caught by the war in Germany were not so fortunate.

The Bayreuth Festival had ended on Saturday and a number of affluent British, and a few rich American music-lovers had travelled adventurously by motor car, intending to follow a feast of Wagner by a leisurely tour of Wagner's Germany. There were some ugly incidents in country villages whose inhabitants merely recognised them as foreigners. No amount of

★ Quoted from the official report of the British Ambassador: Sir Edward Goschen.

argument would convince them that the travellers were not also spies. In the spa resorts of Carlsbad and Baden-Baden where wealthy Europe 'took the cure', hundreds of people who had been caught unawares by the war were the victims of hysteria whipped up by the 'foreign air raid' scare. Everyone was trying to get out. Perhaps the only person who was positively enjoying the adventure was Margaret Foote from Hayling Island. She was fourteen years old and had come to Germany on holiday with her mother. They cruised down the Rhine on the *Hollandia* and, like their fellow passengers, were stranded when the riverboat docked at Mannheim.

Margaret Foote

We travelled to Heidelberg in the evening and stayed there the weekend. All the shops were left open by order on the Sunday and everywhere one heard men's voices singing, 'Der Wacht am Rhein'. We were stopped on a bridge by an officer, who enquired (in German, of course) what nationality we were. Some Americans with us told him theirs, whereupon he asked, 'Do you speak English?' We all five burst out laughing and said, 'Don't you know what language they speak in America? Did you think it was Red Indian?' He had thought we were Russian spies!

On 3 August we went to Stuttgart. The journey took seven and a half hours instead of two! We saw several troop trains, crowded with men cheering and singing. After them came open trucks, on each of which was a cannon with a soldier upon it. It was a wonderful sight. On arriving at Stuttgart we heard that a Serbian spy had just been caught. Crowds were waiting to see him – but it was really a German workman who had been sent by the police to do something to the telegraph wires. The people, thinking that he was cutting them, shot him dead!

There was a great fall of shooting stars that night and everyone began to fire at them, mistaking them for the lights on a French aeroplane. On August 7th, three days after England declared war, the English were ordered to leave the country and were given a safe conduct into Switzerland. We were treated well in Germany, but the spy mania made it unsafe to go out alone.

War fever was sweeping Europe like an epidemic and people could hardly wait to get to grips with the enemy. So far, of the Allies, the only people to have had a taste of the fighting were the Serbs and the Belgians. They were at the wrong end of it and they were fighting for their lives.

★

Now that Britain was officially at war with Germany, Lieutenant Spears in Paris was able to cast off his discreet civilian garb and appear in the uniform of British officer. Paris was already like a ghost town. The French system of a compulsory military service meant that almost every able-bodied man was a member of the Army Reserve, obliged to join the colours in the event of war. Overnight, men had disappeared from the streets. Shops were shuttered and hastily affixed notices informed would-be customers that the *patron* had gone to fight for France. Taxis disappeared, motor buses were few and far between and the only form of transport for those not fortunate enough to possess bicycles were some ancient horse-drawn carriages driven by equally ancient coachmen. It was impossible for a civilian to travel by train, for the trains were running to military timetables and to military destinations. Rumour was in the air and by nightfall on the 5th, most citizens were convinced that a string of barges carrying British soldiers had been seen travelling down the Seine towards Rouen. They were pleased with this news. It seemed to indicate (as Lieutenant Spears reflected with amusement) that the British Army, if not numerous, was at least prompt.

They were not quite as prompt as all that. But before the war was twenty-four hours old, most of the Reservists were back in the fold of their regiments. The crisis had even alarmed some of them into turning up, off their own bat and uninvited, as early as Bank Holiday Saturday. Most of the soldiers on the strength were young soldiers of less than six years' service. The Reservists were the experienced men, the veterans, the men the army badly needed in case of trouble, but not all the young soldiers stood agape with admiration as they marched in. By the time the 1st RB arrived back at Colchester after a tedious roundabout journey, their Reservists had moved in and had virtually taken over their quarters. They were none too pleased.

Bandsman H. V. Shawyer, No. 4142, 1st Bttn., The Rifle Brigade, B.E.F.

We found the barracks full of Reservists – many still in civilian dress – and more were flocking in by almost every train. Fitting them out with uniform, boots and equipment was proceeding rapidly, but in some cases it was no easy job. Quite a few men had lost the soldierly figure they had taken with them into civil life. I remember one man in particular who must have weighed all of eighteen stone. In fact, the Quartermaster's staff simply couldn't fit him out, and he had to stay behind in England for several weeks until the training and the exercise – not to mention less sumptuous feeding! – tore about four stone off him.

It was hard on the Reservists, leaving good jobs and comfortable homes to come back to coarse uniforms and heavy boots. Even so, I found it hard to forgive them. Our Band Rooms were the showpiece of the Battalion, but after *they* took them over they looked like an old clothes shop down Petticoat Lane. All our review order tunics had been tossed into heaps in corners and our carefully creased black trousers were just lying around wholesale. All our spare kit, our grey shirts and our socks and pants, had been pinched – we'd left in such a hurry that there was no time to put things away securely.

Even so, we'd left our barrack rooms spick and span – hand-scrubbed floors, kit precisely folded and everything neat and tidy. I could hardly believe it was less than a week ago. I just stood inside the door with all my full kit still on and stared at it. I don't know what expression was on my face – disgust I suppose! – but one man who was stretched out smoking on *my* bed-cot had the cheek to say to me 'Never mind, kid. The war won't last long enough for *you* to get hurt. You're too young to worry.'

I had a fair idea that he could have told where my kit had gone if he'd had a mind to! We were all furious, and there was more than hot words exchanged, I can tell you. We had to break up quite a few fights!

My kit – or what was left of it – was strewn all over the floor for me to choose from. I salvaged what I could, packed it into a small suitcase I had and sent it home by rail. As it turned out, I needn't have bothered. But I wasn't to know then that I'd worn that lovely dark green review order tunic for the last time in my life. And it was the last I ever saw of those barrack rooms where the Band had lived for nearly three years.

After I'd rescued what was left of my belongings, I went straight off to the barrack quarters of C Company as a dutyman. And that was that!

Shawyer's sarcastic comrade had been partly right. The Army had spared a thought for its young soldiers and, for the moment at any rate, they would not be needed. As their battalions prepared to move off, the boys were given railway warrants and orders to proceed to the home depots of their regiments to join the tamer ranks of Reserve battalions. They went with varying degrees of reluctance.

With a thousand and one details to attend to, the Commanding Officer of the Royal Artillery Depot at Woolwich could have done without the deputation of boy trumpeters who had, respectfully but purposefully, exercised their right to a personal interview. Twelve of them marched in, escorted by the trumpet major, and came to attention in front of the Colonel's desk. Once a week, one or two of the trumpeters ostentatiously went through the motions of shaving a suspicion of fluff from their cheeks. Most did not, for the oldest was not yet eighteen and the youngest a mere sixteen and a half. Nevertheless, Jimmy Naylor had been in the Army for more than two years and, like the others, he was absolutely determined not to be left behind when the guns went to France. He had been elected to plead the trumpeters' case.

The Colonel listened carefully, but he shook his head.

'It's against all the rules.'

'But, Sir . . .' Jimmy launched into another argument. He was a persuasive speaker. He knew, too, that the Royal Artillery, if not precisely a private army as some of its members liked to think, was an élite body which, by and large, made its own rules and got away with it.

While the trumpeters stood stiffly at attention and endeavoured to read his thoughts, their Commanding Officer reflected. The youngsters were keen. They could make themselves useful. It would be good for the lads to test their stamina and too bad to do them out of what would, in all probability, be a bit of a lark.

'Very well. *If* your parents will give permission. I know you won't let me down.'

He was rewarded with an ecstatic chorus of '*No*, Sir!' The boys were cock-a-hoop and rushed back to their quarters to write the required letters home. A few looked slightly worried. Jimmy Naylor, knowing that it would take his parents in India some six weeks to answer, decided that it was pointless to trouble them and unblushingly forged his father's signature. He couldn't afford to wait. Everyone knew that it would take far less than six weeks to sort out the Kaiser. By the time a letter of permission could possibly arrive from India the war would certainly be over.

Trumpeter was a 'boy's' rank and it went back to the earliest days of the Army. The duties of a trumpeter were not onerous but they carried a high degree of responsibility. It was the trumpeter's task to sound the bugle-calls that governed his unit's every move, from reveillé to lights out. On field days and in manoeuvres, his place was at the elbow of the officer in command of his battery, ready to transmit his orders, to send the guns forward into action, to halt, to cease fire, to trot, or to limber up and gallop to the rear. Only the high, clear notes of a trumpet could pierce the noise of battle and reach the scattered sections of a battery of guns. Trumpeters, at least in action, were almost obsolete in the Regular Army but in the Royal Horse Artillery they still played a vital role. They were the obvious people to carry urgent messages to and from the gun-line and they acted, in effect, as private orderlies and personal messengers to the battery commanders. The pay of a trumpeter and of all boy soldiers was one shilling a week.

As a boy piper with the 2nd Battalion, The Highland Light Infantry, Dan Bonar's duties were similar, if less exclusive than those of a trumpeter in the Royal Horse Artillery. Bonar was no mean musician. Although he was only fourteen he had been playing the bagpipes for years, and even Pipe Major William Young had been sufficiently impressed to put him under the personal charge of Corporal John Smith. Smith hailed from Lochboisdale and was easily the best piper in the Battalion. He had listened keenly to Dan's playing. Then he said, 'Boy, I'll make you a great piper.' That had been two months ago when Dan had first joined the Battalion at Aldershot, and in his short time under Smith's tuition his prowess had already earned him promotion to Orderly Piper of the Battalion. Like all Scottish regiments, the HLI ordered its day to the call of the pìpes. Dan had to be up at half-past five to rouse the Battalion at six with the duty tune that traditionally woke the Jocks from slumber – 'Hey Johnny Cope are ye waukin' yet?' His last duty of the day was to send them to sleep at a quarter past ten to the strains of 'Johnny lie doon on yer wee pickle straw'. Notwithstanding his tender years, Dan was the first man up and the last man in the battalion to go to bed. The question of extra pay did not arise.

On the eve of the Battalion's departure for France, Boy Bonar was about to be packed off to the Regimental Depot at Hamilton. Late in the afternoon Corporal MacKinnon called to him across the barrack room.

Boy D. Bonar, No. 12302, 2nd Bttn., Highland Light Infantry,
2nd Division, B.E.F.

He said, 'Right, Boy, we're off to the war and I've got some money belonging to you. Come and we'll count it out.' In those days soldiers got no benefits at all – and my princely shilling a week didn't go very far. MacKinnon was a fatherly chap and he'd got hold of me a day or so after I joined the Battalion. We got a month's furlough once a year in the wintertime, and he pointed out to me that when furlough time came round I would have my fare to pay to Scotland. What was I doing about it, he wanted to know. I said, 'Nothing.' I hadn't given it a thought! He said, 'Well you'd *better* do something about it. Any money you have to save, you give it to me.'

In those days there were no dining rooms where the soldiers could eat. They ate where they slept, and every evening the mess duty orderly went to the ration store and drew the following day's ration of bread – a pound per man. The soldier put it in his locker and when breakfast came he cut off what he needed and the same at dinner time at twelve o'clock. At tea-time nothing was issued except the urn of tea and there was nothing to put on the bread that was left. But you could buy pennyworths of jam and butter and cheese in the canteen, and this is where we boys used to earn the odd copper, going to the canteen to fetch these tit-bits for the soldiers. As often as not we got a halfpenny or a penny for ourselves. Sure enough, I gave all these coppers to Corporal MacKinnon – and it had mounted up to a good few shillings!

We counted it out on the top of his kit box. Then I put it in my sporran and he went with me to the post office and I opened a savings account. He showed me the benefit of saving, old Corporal MacKinnon, and from then on I put a bit away every time I got paid. The number of my post office book was 24317A and, as time went on and I got promoted, my bank book became well worth admiring!

But Bonar's unexpected affluence was small consolation for the indignity of being left behind. Naylor was more fortunate. He was already on his way to join a battery attached to the 2nd Division and it was on the point of leaving to embark for France.

From the point of view of regimental officers on the staff of the Army's depots, the departure of the Expeditionary Force could not come too soon and they would be only too happy to see the back of them. The Victorian architects who had planned the spacious barracks as model quarters for the soldiers of the Queen had never envisaged such an influx of men. On top of housing their resident battalions whose numbers had been suddenly doubled by the embodiment of Reservists, they were obliged to squeeze in entire Reserve battalions. Somehow it had been managed, but only by doubling up accommodation (in extreme cases, even trebling up) and by staggering mealtimes so that there was hardly a decent interval between 'Last Breakfasts' and 'First Dinners'. The latecomers were lucky if they got more than scraps of bully beef and slops from the bottom of the tea urn.

By the weekend most barracks were a shambles. Even the holiest of holies, the barrack squares that in normal times were models of good order and discipline, began to look more like market squares on an auction day. Long lines of men queued up to get into the mess halls. They queued outside the sick bay to be medically examined. They queued for extra kit at the Quartermaster's stores. They queued outside the armoury, where relays of NCOs worked overtime inspecting rifles and humping heavy boxes of ammunition, and where the whetstone whined interminably as it sharpened the officers' swords. In the stables and in the fields where the

Army had set up temporary horse lines the transport men were busy with whitewash brushes and buckets of permanganate darkening the coats of light-coloured horses to camouflage them for active service in France. The War Book had thought of that too.

The War Book had also provided for 120,000 horses to be 'called up' in the first two weeks of the war. All week and all over the country, the authorities had been going about the business of collecting the animals and vehicles needed to bring the Army's transport up to strength. Some of the Army's representatives had gone about this task with more enthusiasm than commonsense. The powerful horses that pulled heavy tram-cars were now required by the Army to pull its guns and supply wagons, and zealous officials in Morecambe had commandeered so many that the trams stopped running altogether. Some protesting farmers, more anxious about getting in the harvest than sending the Expeditionary Force on its way, almost came to blows with requisitioning officers who came to enlist their work-horses. And country gentlemen, chagrined to see their fine-bred steeds departing on War Service as 'officers' chargers', were not much consoled by the comparatively generous payment of £75 in exchange for a favourite mount.

The arm of the military was long. By the end of the week it had reached as far as the island of Arran on the west coast of Scotland. Eighty horses had been requisitioned and on Sunday morning the Caledonian steamer *Duchess of Argyle* arrived to take the first batch to the mainland.

Although it was just half an hour's sail by Clyde steamer from Gourock, Arran was a quiet island that had more in common with highland Argyll across the Firth to the north than with lowland Ayrshire a stone's throw away on the southern coast.

Even in August when the population was swelled by holidaymakers, there was little amusement to be found in Arran except when the weekday boats came in from Glasgow and Gourock. Young men in the Territorials, caught on the hop by the war during their annual holidays, had left the island earlier in the week. Their elders, hungry for news which only reached Arran when the midday steamer brought the early editions of the Glasgow papers, had clubbed together to subscribe to a telegraph service offered by the *Glasgow Herald* and besieged the post office in Brodick as soon as it opened in the mornings. On Sunday there were no steamers and no news and although Wartime Regulations kept the postmaster on the alert for emergencies, the post office itself remained firmly shut.

The *Duchess of Argyle* steamed in early in the morning and the work began right away. Even on market days when occasionally a horse, or a cow, or a coop of clucking chickens was loaded on to the steamer to be sold on the mainland, Arran had never seen anything like it. All Brodick gravitated to the pier-head to watch as the reluctant horses were urged up the gangway and persuaded into the railed enclosures that had been knocked up on the deck. The whinnying, the shouting, the bustle would have been unusual even for a weekday, and groups of curious locals stopped briefly on their way to church. Not all of them were diverted by the entertainment. One elder of the Kirk, dour in his Sunday black, exclaimed in a voice that was meant to be heard, 'This is not the Sabbath we are accustomed to in Arran!' He had spoken in Gaelic but in case any stranger should be left in doubt of Arran's disapproval, he said it again in English.

It was Sunday 9 August, and the fifth day of mobilisation. Yesterday the advance parties of the Expeditionary Force had landed secretly in France. Tomorrow the first contingents of the main force would set out on their way to join them.

On Tuesday, within hours of the Declaration of War, Lieutenant Spears had been ordered to attach himself immediately to the French army. He was supposed to be engaged on intelligence work but in the absence of anyone else he found himself acting, willy nilly, as liaison officer.

Since Spears knew as little as the French did of Great Britain's intentions and of the progress of her newly mobilised Army towards the Front, he was in a far from enviable position. At General Lanrezac's headquarters he was welcomed with all the cordiality due to a comrade-in-arms and invited at once to join the Junior Officers' Mess where he was favoured with lavish meals but also with much ribbing at the expense of the so-far-invisible British Army. 'How,' demanded the French in tones of honeyed sympathy, 'could the poor creatures be expected to arrive on time, when war had so inconveniently broken out on their Bank Holiday weekend?' The Tommies were probably indulging in a last paddle in the sea or in a last blow-out of roast beef. Perhaps, since the *banks* were on holiday (this with heavy irony) they had no money for the fare! But doubtless, with their well-known respect for the principle of 'le fair play' the British expected the Kaiser to suspend hostilities until they were ready to meet him.

Despite the sneering of the French, it was no mean achievement in little more than a week to mobilise, to equip and to ship an expeditionary force of some 80,000 men across the English Channel.

Civilian trains were commandeered to carry reserves to their units and battalions to the ports, and civilian ships were pressed into service to take them across the Channel. A mountain of stores and forage, field-guns, shells and munitions went with them. There were 80,000 rifles to inspect, 80,000 bandoliers and pouches to fill with small-arms ammunition, 80,000 iron rations to issue, and none of it could have been achieved at short notice had it not been for the meticulous plans prepared long ago for just such a contingency. One afterthought had caused a minor headache, at least to the Army's printers already overwhelmed by a torrent of military orders and notices. The Secretary of State for War, Lord Kitchener, had taken the trouble to compose a personal message to the troops. Somehow 80,000 copies had been produced. They were distributed on the very eve of departure, and every soldier of the Expeditionary Force was given a copy of Lord Kitchener's farewell words to carry with him in his paybook.

You are ordered abroad as a soldier of the King to help our French comrades against the invasion of a common enemy. You have to perform a task which will need your courage, your energy, your patience. Remember that the Honour of the British Army depends on your individual conduct. It will be your duty not only to set an example of discipline and perfect steadiness under fire but also to maintain the most friendly relations with those whom you are helping in this struggle. The operation in which you are engaged will, for the most part, take place in a friendly country, and you can do your own country no better service than in showing yourself in France and Belgium in the true character of a British soldier.

Be invariably courteous, considerate and kind. Never do anything likely to injure or destroy property and always look upon looting as a disgraceful act. You are sure to meet with a welcome and be trusted; your conduct must justify that welcome and that trust. Your duty cannot be done unless your health is sound. So keep constantly on your guard against any excesses. In this new experience you may find temptations both in wine and women. You must entirely resist both temptations, and, while treating all women with perfect courtesy, you should avoid any intimacy.

> DO YOUR DUTY BRAVELY,
> FEAR GOD,
> HONOUR THE KING.

Kitchener,
Field Marshal.

The soldiers of the British Expeditionary Force did not, in general, suffer from an excess of prudishness. Many had spent years in the Army, roughing it in barrack rooms from Aldershot to Dehra Dun, and they were far from being the bunch of effete innocents which the contents of this document seemed to imply.

It reduced the officers of the French General Staff to tears of laughter. That evening Lieutenant Spears was the butt of heavy witticism. 'Is it an army your Lord Kitchener is sending us, or is it a girls' school?' Attired in the khaki service dress, in which his Parisian landlady had unfavourably compared him to a dusty canary, feeling distinctly ill at ease in the company of the gorgeously uniformed French, Lieutenant Spears did not enjoy a comfortable dinner. But he contented himself by retaliating with the suggestion that, in order to avoid mishaps, the French would be well advised to teach their troops the difference between the uniforms of friend and foe. He himself had twice narrowly escaped being shot out of hand by zealous Frenchmen who were unfamiliar with khaki service dress and had inconveniently mistaken him for a German.

By the time the first contingents of the British Expeditionary Force arrived, attired in khaki as drab as his own, Lieutenant Spears was almost inclined to regard them as his personal reinforcements.

Chapter 6

They sailed to Boulogne, to Rouen, to Le Havre, and mostly they sailed by night. On 18 August the newspapers carried the official report that over the preceding week the British Expeditionary Force had been safely landed in France and that the operation had been carried out without a single casualty.

It was true that, so far as the troops were concerned, no one had succumbed to the effects of enemy action, to seasickness or to the occasionally over-hearty welcome of their rapturous allies. But some unboxed horses had died of heart attacks. They were overcome by vertigo and terror as cranes grappled the slings around their bellies, hoisted them up from deep holds, swung them high above the deck and lowered them, screaming and quivering, to the cobbled quayside. One of their grooms had also been struck off the strength as a casualty. His name was Allan and he was a groom in the 1st Battalion of the Ox and Bucks.

Allan did not approve of wartime conditions. He did not approve of the horses – his peacetime pride and joy – being stowed into cramped and fetid accommodation deep below the waterline and, no matter how long the voyage, he was determined to stay with them to see that they came to no harm. Nothing could persuade him to leave the airless hold lit by dim lanterns, where the tight-tethered horses neighed and stamped and sweated and scrabbled miserably to keep their footing as the ship yawed and rolled. Allan kept them company, dozing from time to time on a bale of straw, cheering them with a familiar clap on the rump and murmured words of encouragement, refilling water-buckets, and doing what he could to reassure them. The horses weathered the journey reasonably well, but when the Ox and Bucks arrived at Boulogne in the afternoon of 14 August Allan himself was found to be much the worse for wear. He managed to struggle up on deck to line up with his company, he managed to totter down the gangway, but it was beyond him to go further or do more.

The Ox and Bucks had been more than sixteen hours on board the SS *Lake Michigan*, waiting half the night in Southampton Water for the order to sail, waiting half the morning outside the port of Boulogne for a berth in its congested harbour. Despite the tedium the Battalion had, on the whole, had a good voyage and unkind spirits, loudly jeering, suggested that twenty-four hours of enforced teetotalism was responsible for Allan's dramatic collapse. The officers affected not to hear and wondered what the devil to do with him. There were numerous field ambulances and plenty of medical personnel in the Expeditionary Force, but battle casualties were their concern and they were hardly likely to be found, set up and ready for business, among the throng of rapturous citizens on the flag-decked quayside at Boulogne. The Battalion Medical Officer was equally at a loss. He had made a swift diagnosis. *Heat. Exhaustion. Lack of oxygen. Needs treatment.* Where the treatment was to be found was another matter. It was the adjutant, Lieutenant Crosse, who solved the immediate problem. He spotted two nuns, conspicuous among the crowd in long black habits, benign and smiling beneath white starched wimples. Trusting to Christian charity, he thrust Allan into their arms, begged them in limping French to look after '*ce pauvre soldat malade*' and before they could recover from their astonishment, dived back to his place at the side of the Commanding Officer as the leading company marched off. It was a crafty move.

The Transport Officer stayed behind with a detachment of men to see the horses safely ashore, but they could not begin to unload them until all the men had left the ship. The Worcesters and the Highland Light Infantry had not even begun to disembark and were still hanging over the rails exchanging waves and banter with the crowd on the quay. Some of the older sweats (apparently under the impression that any foreign language could be understood by any foreigner) were treating the French to salutations in Hindustani. It was perfectly obvious that it would be hours yet before the officers' horses could be landed and that even Colonel Davies would have to lead his battalion on foot.

They were all thankful to stretch their legs but it was a hot afternoon, the camp was four miles away on the heights above the town, and the march was mostly uphill through narrow, stifling streets. It was a steep hill at that, and it was the Tommies' first experience of marching with full kit on French cobblestones through such a crush of people that it seemed as if the whole town had turned out to watch them go by. They hung out of windows, they swarmed like flies on the pavements and gangs of shrieking children ran alongside the Battalion waving tricolour flags with such enthusiasm that some men on the flanks were in serious danger of being poked in the eye. Girls bombarded the soldiers with sweets, with flowers, with tricolour rosettes and begged for souvenirs in exchange. They snatched at buttons and cap badges and made off with so many that by the time the Battalion had covered the first half mile it was beginning to present a decidedly dishevelled appearance. One platoon officer was struck by the recollection that his pocket contained a pack of playing cards, greasy with use, that had helped to while away the monotonous voyage to France. Since they bore the Regimental Crest they made acceptable keepsakes and by doling them out one at a time to the most insistent souvenir-hunters, he ensured that his platoon kept its uniforms if not its dignity more or less intact.

The Ox and Bucks found it hard to credit that this was the fourth day of disembarkation, that some thousands of troops had got there before them and that the enthusiasm of Boulogne had still not abated. As the hill grew steeper, leg muscles began to ache, faces glistened with sweat, and the novelty wore off. At the summit, where the road turned and opened out in front of the old walled citadel, an ancient taxi cab trundled past. The Ox and Bucks had a clear view of its passengers. Allan was sitting at ease in the back between the two solicitous sisters. Beaming broadly, and looking much recovered, he was good enough to give his comrades a wave as he went by. This courtesy was not much appreciated.

There was another long hill to climb before they reached the camp, where they would join the vanguard of the BEF waiting for their comrades, their transport and their supplies to catch up with them. The arrival of the 2nd Worcesters an hour later completed the assembly of the 5th Infantry Brigade. They were almost the last arrivals.

The camp was one vast caravanserai of tents and men and animals on a square mile of heathland; in the middle of it all, Napoleon, from the top of the Colonne de la Grande Armée, gazed out to sea where the last of the troop-carriers still rode on the tide waiting their turn to make landfall in France.

There was a Field Post Office where letters scribbled on the boat could be handed in. There was a beer tent for each battalion, but the beer had to be paid for and in local currency and soon long queues of thirsty soldiers were waiting at the Paymaster's tent to change money into francs. The going rate of twenty-five francs to the pound was all very well for the officers but it was not much use to most Tommies who had not been paid for a fortnight. The Army's supply of French currency did not extend to unlimited quantities of *sous* and *centimes* and faced with demands to change threepenny bits and even pennies and halfpennies into francs the exasperated NCOs had made it emphatically known that no transaction lower than eightpence would be entertained. A soldier who could just scrape up the twopence for a pint had to find and join forces with three comrades in a similar state of penury before he could get one. But the thirst of the Army was legendary and, despite financial difficulties, a dump of empty casks mounted steadily behind the beer tents.

There was some grumbling over the food, for rations were 'carried on the man'. Yesterday they had included cooked meat, prepared in army kitchens before the men left their Home Barracks. Today they were down to iron rations of biscuits and bully beef. But the Ox and Bucks, at least, were cheered by an issue of cheese and the news that, without fail, there would be rations of bread and fresh meat tomorrow. This was stated in evening orders which added the welcome news that the rule against smoking cigarettes while under arms or on fatigues (strictly enforced in the Home Commands) was 'in the present circumstances' rescinded. The Tommies who, in the present circumstances, were theoretically 'under arms' for twenty-four hours of the day, were only too glad to hear it.

It was a fine warm evening and after the bustle had subsided in streets and harbour, civilians straggled up the hill to the camp to continue the entertainment. Most were young girls, not all of them respectable, and insistent cries of '*Tommee. . . Souvenir Tommee*' continued far into the night. Sentries had considerable difficulty in preventing the visitors from invading the camp itself and when darkness fell, the downs came alive with furtive shadows, with muffled shrieks and giggles and sudden bursts of laughter. Determined Tommies had easily slipped past the picquets and were now amicably engaged in promoting the *Entente Cordiale* at a more personal level.

Some way to the south in the port of Rouen the *Entente Cordiale* had suffered a knock and it was all the fault of the Royal Sussex. Rouen's welcome had exceeded even the clamorous receptions that thrilled the troops at Boulogne and Le Havre, for the ships bound for Rouen had sailed right up the Seine and the last stretch of the journey was a triumphal progress. People lined the river banks, covered every hillside, clung to precarious vantage points on cliffs and promontories. Flotillas of rowing boats struggled to keep pace with the troopships and bombarded the Tommies on their decks with friendly fusillades of fruit and flowers. When the troops finally disembarked at Rouen they were mobbed.

Buttons and cap badges were, as always, in demand and it was this that indirectly caused the trouble. The Sussex were proud of their cap badge. They were proud of the history of their regiment and they were well aware that the Roussillon plume on their insignia was a symbol of victory. It dated from Quebec where, as the old 35th Foot, the Regiment had soundly beaten the French. The Roussillon Regiment had faced them in the line and, elated with success, the victors had snatched the furled plumes from enemy hats and worn them gloatingly in their own. There was not a man in the 2nd Battalion who did not know the story and, in the very act of handing over their cap badges in the cause of Franco-British friendship, many soldiers managed to communicate a graphic version to the French, curious to know why this familiar Gallic device should adorn the badges of their Anglo-Saxon allies. Despite the language difficulty, the message came across loud and clear and the French did not take it well. There was almost a riot.

Next morning, Colonel Montresor, considerably put out, paraded the Battalion a company at a time to read them a lecture and to point out the necessity of tact. He suggested that in the circumstances it would be better to say, if asked, that the French had freely given the plume in recognition of the Regiment's bravery at the Battle of Quebec. There was no further trouble but, nevertheless, when orders arrived to move off, the Colonel and his officers were distinctly relieved.

The original plan was that the British Expeditionary Force should assemble in a pear-shaped tract of country around Maubeuge and Le Cateau before taking up a position close to the Belgian border on the left of the French army. It had been worked out years before in the course of the 'Military Conversations' and it had been worked out on the basis of the French conviction that the Germans would strike into France through the common Franco-German border where the bulk of the French army would be prepared to meet them. This plan, so far as the British had been concerned, was little more than a gesture. It was obvious that the six divisions agreed on were only a token force and in the remote eventuality of a British Expeditionary Force being sent to support the French, it would be called on to give little more than token support – to protect the French flank where it petered out near the neutral border while the French armies were engaging the enemy further east.

But with the declaration of war, the British Cabinet looked again at the theory, pondered the French plan in the light of the invasion of Belgium – and got cold feet.

The French made it clear that they considered the Belgian adventure to be a mere feint intended to lure their strength away from the main theatre of events. The British were not so sure. If the Germans were to sweep down in large numbers on this weakest part of the Front they might easily overwhelm General Lanrezac's Fifth Army. If the British were standing on General Lanrezac's left it was perfectly obvious that the Germans would only have to widen their sweep by a very little to encircle the Expeditionary Force, to scoop it up and to open the high road to Calais and Boulogne. The Cabinet conferred with the Army commanders and argued among themselves. Would it not be best to hold back the BEF, to concentrate around Amiens, to hold open the vital lines of communication which linked them to Britain and to be ready and in a far better position to support the French if they were pushed back by the first onslaught?

They were still arguing when the first troopships put to sea. By then it was too late to change their destination. It was also too late to avert the destiny that would plunge them in a few days into the Battle of Mons.

It was the first time that the Army had proceeded to battle by train – which was not to say that they travelled in comfort. Long before the war, the French had studied the problem of moving large numbers of troops and supplies over long distances and had come up with a practical solution. If the component parts of hundreds of trains had to be constantly changed to suit the requirements of different units, it would cause long delays in marshalling yards and need whole armies of couplers and shunters and drivers whose services, in time of war, could be made better use of elsewhere. But if men or animals or supplies could all be carried in the same sort of rolling stock – *voilà*! Forty box-cars would carry eighty horses and more than a thousand men and so, with the addition of a few carriages for officers and flat trucks for wagons, a single train could accommodate a whole infantry battalion and its transport. If required to transport a brigade of guns, without the slightest modification and in the fastest possible time the same forty cars would as easily carry two hundred horses, six hundred gunners, their guns and their ammunition. They could also serve as supply trains. What could be simpler! Only the Tommies, travelling in what they reasonably assumed to be cattle trucks, were less than thrilled with this versatile arrangement.

They took it in fairly good part, although the citizens of Le Havre, cheering the troop trains as they crossed the town tracks at the start of their journey, were startled when the Tommies responded with choruses of 'moo-o-o' and 'baa-a-a' in imitation of cows and sheep.

Travelling north with the 4th Royal Fusiliers, Bill Holbrook counted himself lucky to be there at all. He was well aware that, had he not happened to be the Colonel's servant he would still be kicking his heels at home with the Reserve Battalion.

Cpl. W. Holbrook, No. 13599, 4th Bttn., Royal Fusiliers, 9th Brigade, 3rd Division, B.E.F.

When I went with the rest for the medical examination the doctor marked me unfit. DATH – disorderly action of the heart. Well! When I told the Colonel, he couldn't believe it. He put his arm round my shoulders. 'Do you want to go?' he said. I said, 'I should say I do, Sir!' He said, 'Right you are, then. I'll see to it.' So off I went with the Battalion. We went to Cowes first and I always remember waiting on the quayside to go across to embark at Southampton, there was a big advertisement on the side of a house for a publication called *John Bull*. It covered the whole gable-end of this house and it said, 'The Dawn of Britain's Greatest Glory' – all down the side of this house. I remember sitting there and saying to myself, 'I wonder!'

Holbrook was a seasoned soldier. Although his Army age was twenty-three, he had lied his way into the service six years before at the age of fifteen. Nothing could have stopped him. The gardener in the household where young Holbrook was employed in the humble capacity of odd-job boy was an old campaigner and he fired young Bill's imagination with tales of soldiering and adventure round the world. Holbrook was undeterred by the fact that old Tedder stumped around on a cork leg (having lost the original in some distant outpost of the Empire) and Tedder himself dismissed this inconvenience as a small penalty to have paid for a large slice of life's good fortune. 'It's a man's life, that's what it is, lad,' he was fond of saying, 'and the world's your oyster.' Bill needed little encouragement. He joined the Army on 6 September 1908 and, being five foot seven inches tall and well set up for his age, had little difficulty in passing for seventeen. Although he had recently fallen on easy times with his appointment as the Colonel's servant, the early days had been rough enough to make the present circumstances seem like a picnic. Old Tedder had said nothing about *that*.

Cpl. W. Holbrook, No. 13599, 4th Bttn., Royal Fusiliers, 9th Brigade, 3rd Division, B.E.F.

I went home and told my mother and, oh, there was a hell of a row then. But I'd made up my mind, so the next morning away I went. I had nothing, not a toothbrush, nothing whatever except the jacket and trousers I stood up in. But my elder brother gave me a shilling and old Tedder shed a few tears and *he* gave me a shilling – so I had two shillings to go with.

I slept the first night at Stratford on some old straw bags. They gave me a warrant next morning to go to Hounslow and I went with another man. He was a deserter from the Navy, but I didn't know that until afterwards. It was a special reserve you went to, to prepare for the Regular Army, and most of them were fellows trying to get away from the police – convicted burglars, all sorts. These fellows were all right – but drink! By golly, they used to drink. They got fighting drunk. Frightened the life out of me that did. But they were ever so good to me and they treated me well, they did. I was the youngest there by years and I could hardly carry my rifle and bayonet, but I got on all right.

I only got a shilling a week, boys' pay. On Fridays we used to line up for our money. The officer sat at a table with a blanket on it and all the fellows would line up for their pay – they got six shillings most of them, and when they called my name out – 'Holbrook. One shilling!' – they all used to burst out laughing. The officer, Captain Birchall, once patted me on the shoulder and said, 'Never mind, Holbrook, you'll grow up!'

I liked it all right, but the food was terrible there! When 'Cookhouse' sounded, the fellows wouldn't stop to go out the doors to get to the mess hut, they'd jump out the window! There was about twenty in each hut and there was a window between every two beds and they was always open. Clean out the blooming windows they'd jump! Of course the first day I was a long way behind. When I got there there was a queue of thirty or forty men in front of me, pressing against the door and then somebody shouted 'GO!' and the door opened up and they went rushing in. On each side there was bare tables and there was forms each side with four men on a form, and there was a loaf cut in four and a piece of margarine slapped on top of it. That was your lot! You had nothing else, a piece of bread and some margarine. Of course they were hungry. What they used to do was this. Three men got at a table so there was a vacant place at the end with a bit of bread on it and they'd get a knife, spear it through the bread and stick it to the underside of the table. Then when the old sergeant came round he'd say, 'Where's yon bread gone to?' And they'd say, 'Oh, some other fellows got here first. They've taken it.' He'd look a bit suspicious like, but when he'd gone they'd get the bread, cut it into three and share it out. Of course someone would have to go without, because there was no more. You could eat your bayonet for all they cared!

The tea was in a big pudding basin, one between two and of course if you was sitting with a man older than you, as I *always* was, you didn't have much of a chance, you know. He'd grab it and have a drink and if you wanted one you had to pull it out his hand if you could. Then you'd find he'd have had a good drink and left you the tealeaves. You was done all ways! There wasn't no more.

We had stew for dinner – it was always greasy old stew with great lumps of fat in it, ladled out of a big dixie. And they'd take this fat out and they'd throw it on the bare table, the fellows would. And when they'd finish, the table was covered with fat and gristle and gravy. Terrible it was! Swimming! And when they'd gone, the chaps who had to stay behind to clean up the mess hall, they wouldn't clean it properly, they'd jump up on the tables with sweeping brushes and sweep it all into a big pile. Then it was sent off as swill for the pigs. It was only fit for pigs anyway!

Now, with only iron rations to sustain them yet again on a long journey, even a dish of greasy stew would have been welcome.

From Le Havre, the furthest point of departure, it was not much more than 150 miles as the crow flies to the area of concentration, but the locomotives did not have wings and every day 144 trains were travelling in both directions across the double track of the *chemin de fer du nord*. There were unconscionable delays and interminable halts for no reasons that were clear to the weary, thirsty passengers but were all too obvious to the legion of officials who were despatching the trains at ten-minute intervals and monitoring their progress to one small corner of France.

Even when the trains were on the move the journey was painfully slow for their cumbersome length and weight obliged them to travel at a maximum speed of twenty miles an hour. Not many reached even half that speed and, as the Tommies remarked derisively, a soldier who felt inclined could jump down, spend twenty minutes picking flowers or chasing butterflies and easily catch up with the train further up the track. Few indulged in such bucolic pastimes, though orchards of pear trees, heavy with unripe fruit, tempted some foraging parties and it was perfectly possible for a man who was no more than moderately athletic to sprint to the front of the train, fill a dixie with hot water from the engine and more or less at his leisure rejoin the wagon where his comrades were waiting to brew up.

Despite the cushioned comfort of first-class carriages, the officers too had to manage as best they could, for the coaches of ancient vintage did not boast the convenience of corridors. The train that carried the 15th Brigade of the Royal Field Artillery northwards to the war struck a clear stretch of line about midday and perversely puffed along for some miles at a faster pace than it had achieved all day. Lieutenant Cully Buckle and the other subalterns of the 80th Battery were obliged to clamber along the running-board to reach the compartment which contained their senior officers. It was a matter of some urgency, since it also contained the luncheon basket. The fare was spartan compared to the cold chickens, the game pies, the succulent Irish ham, which the basket normally provided for the officers' luncheon on shoots and field days; but the cutlery was silver and the napkins linen, there was fresh bread to go with sardines and bully beef, a couple of dozen hard-boiled eggs, a morsel of cheese, and – best of all – a bottle of port and one of brandy. At the Major's suggestion they went easy on the eggs and the cheese. At this snail-like rate of progress they would be glad of them long before the end of the journey.

But spirits were high. The fine weather, the atmosphere of anticipation, the strange foreign landscape and villages slowly unrolling as they travelled, all combined to give the journey the air of a holiday outing. No one had more than a vague idea of where they were bound for and no one was particularly worried.

Travelling rather faster (and it was just as well) was the convoy of large touring motor cars that carried the British Commander-in-Chief and his Staff on a break-neck round of courtesy calls and consultations with the French. He went first to Paris to meet the President and visit the Ministry of War, on to Vitry-le-François to meet General Joffre, and from there to Rethel, to the headquarters of General Lanrezac in command of the Fifth Army. This meeting, with the man with whom the British were to work most closely, was a disaster.

The keynote was secrecy. The French were obsessed with spies. Even interpreters, in General Lanrezac's view, were strangers and not to be trusted. To the astonishment of Lieutenant Spears, he ushered Sir John French into his private sanctum and firmly closed the door. Neither French nor Lanrezac had more than the most rudimentary understanding of the other's language. When they emerged some ten minutes later for a more general discussion with the French and British Staff Officers who had been left waiting in an anteroom, the expressions on their faces clearly showed that each man thought the other a fool. Had their deliberations concerned the whereabouts of the pens of their aunts or of the ball which baby had dropped in the garden, it might just have been possible for the two men to come to some constructive conclusion. They did not however. They were concerned with the whereabouts of the German army and with their plans to defeat it.

It was an inauspicious beginning and it sowed the seeds of doubt and misunderstanding that were to dog the relations between the British Commander and his allies through seven grim battles and a gruelling year of war. It was 17 August. Sixteen months later, to the day, Sir John French would be relieved of his command. Meanwhile, as he drove north to the concentration area and his headquarters at Le Cateau, his thoughts were concerned with the more immediate future. Lanrezac had been visibly irritated by Sir John French's assertion that the British Army could not be in position and ready to attack alongside the French before the following Monday, 24 August, but as the Commander-in-Chief drove through villages and hamlets, he had the satisfaction of seeing for himself that the concentration was well under way.

There were soldiers everywhere. They were billeted in school-rooms, in village halls, in barns, in farmyards, in mills, in cottages. There were makeshift horse-lines in meadows and orchards, there were wagons and lorries parked in village streets, and, looking strangely out of place, delivery vans and carts requisitioned from British firms.

The weather was glorious. The fields were rich with ripe grain and, with the Army's blessing, the Tommies stripped off their khaki tunics and helped with the harvest. The women, left to cope alone since their menfolk had left for the war, were thankful for able-bodied help and treated the soldiers like heroes. The Tommies loved it. The sun was warm, the work was enjoyable and liberal supplies of acid home-brewed cider were brought to the fields by the pailful to slake their well-earned thirst. There was one bizarre hold-up. A top-heavy haywain lumbering homewards along a narrow road to the village of Iron forced a line of army transport to slow down to a crawl. It made a strange procession. The 'transport' consisted of a Waring and Gillow pantechnicon, a van which proclaimed HP Sauce to be 'The World's Appetiser', and a scarlet line of double-decker buses covered with posters advertising London's West End shows. In this remote country region, where buses of any kind were few and far between, they attracted considerable attention. From the neighbouring harvest fields the soldiers waved and shouted and whistled derision. It was all part of the entertainment, and the war that had provided it might have been a figment of the politicians' imagination.

The officers were also grateful for a breathing-space and took advantage of it to knock the sluggish Reservists into shape. But even the morning route marches and the evening musketry practice hardly detracted from a universal air of leisurely well-being. There were hot meals at the end of the day, fresh bread and lusty stews of fresh meat ladled out from field cookers, and later there were campfires under the stars, stories to swap and, as the beer and cider flowed, impromptu warbling of lugubrious ballads that suited the mildly inebriated mood.

> *Though your heart may ache awhile –*
> *Never Mind!*
> *Though your face may lose its smile –*
> *Never Mind!*
> *For there's sunshine after rain –*
> *And then gladness follows pain –*
> *You'll be happy once again –*
> *Never Mi-i-ind!*

Not many months from now, a more disillusioned army would rewrite the lyrics to suit their own peculiar circumstances but not many soldiers of the Expeditionary Force now assembling among the summer fields of

France would be left to sing them. *If you're stuck up on the wire, Never Mind . . .*

News was in short supply. A mess president cantering into the nearest town in search of delicacies for the officers' table scoured the place in vain for reliable newspapers. He was lucky if he could find a copy of *Le Petit Parisien* to take back to the mess, to be deciphered, analysed and discussed by the hour. There was not much to go on. War news was confined to stirring but vague reports of battles and victories in the east where (just as Count Schlieffen had intended) the right wing of the French army was in close combat with the enemy and had even snatched back some sacred miles of the lost territories of Alsace and Lorraine. Of the left flank, where the British were preparing to move up to the attack, not a word. Of the vast force of Germans now surging westwards through Belgium to confront them, not a syllable.

It was the Royal Flying Corps who discovered them on 20 August – a week after they had caused a sensation on the south coast by the spectacular manner of their departure. Sixty-three aeroplanes had roared off one after the other from Swingate Downs above Dover and disappeared into the clouds over the Channel. The crowds who craned their necks to watch them had never seen anything like it and it was not surprising. With the exception of a single flight, left behind for coastal patrol work, the entire strength of British military aviation had taken to the air. Now, the aircraft, their pilots and their personnel were up front with the Army, clustered round Maubeuge. They had been there for two days and already this infant branch of the Army was showing signs of petulance. Visibility was bad. The weather continued hot, but the heat brought sudden thunderstorms and banks of steely cloud rolling across the sky, leaving mist and heat haze when they cleared. Behind the bald official phrase 'unsuitable for reconnaissance' a hundred frustrated pilots were chafing at the bit.

But their unproductive efforts had not been lacking in excitement. Already one aircraft had been shot down – not by the invisible Germans, but by the French. The same Civil Guards whose trigger fingers had itched at the sight of Lieutenant Spears were proving all too eager to take a pot shot at any machine in the sky – be it French, friend or foe. The pilot was fortunately not injured.

On 20 August the mist cleared and the aircraft buzzed off on reconnaissance sorties to sweep the clear blue skies above Belgium. Their orders were to find the German army, to pinpoint its position and to estimate its strength. They brought back disturbing news. They had finally spotted an army on the march. It was heading through Louvain, but it was difficult to estimate its strength for the long grey columns of marching men stretched as far as the eye could reach.

The main echelon of the German army was on the move at last. The swift advance, the wide sweep which had been intended to encircle the French army almost before they knew it, had been delayed for eighteen crucial days. It had been held up by the Belgians. Ill-trained, badly equipped, outnumbered by almost a hundred to one, but fired by a desperate fury, they had fought until they could fight no more. That Thursday, 20 August, was a fateful day. The Belgians were forced to retire to Antwerp. The Germans marched as conquerors into Brussels. And General Joffre ordered a general advance on his left flank to stem their main force flowing down the highway to France.

The leading columns of the British troops had already set off and were marching north to move into position around the town of Mons, on the left of the French army. It was a long, hot tramp on a brilliant summer day. Bill Holbrook managed it well enough (though marching with a full pack over French cobblestones was not his idea of fun) but it was too much for large numbers of the recent arrivals hobbling in new boots they had not yet had a chance to break in. Their younger, fitter comrades, a fraction wearied by the old soldiers' boasting and the tales of daring exploits they had heard so often over the last fortnight, jeered unkindly as they passed them, slumped and sweating at the roadside and nursing their blistered feet.

Sir John French addressed himself to his troops in an Order of the Day that had the ring of a clarion call.

> Our cause is just. We are called upon to fight beside our gallant allies in France and Belgium in no war of arrogance, but to uphold our national honour, independence and freedom. We have violated no neutrality, nor have we been false to any treaties. We enter upon this conflict with the clearest consciousness that we are fighting for right and honour.
>
>   Having then this trust in the righteousness of our cause, pride in the glory of our military traditions, and belief in the efficiency of our army, we go forward together to do or die for
>   GOD – KING – AND COUNTRY.

It was read out to the 4th Royal Fusiliers at the end of the day, when their stragglers had caught up with them. That night they were to bivouac in open country and it was fortunately a fine evening since they had strict instructions to build no fires and to show no lights. They were unmoved by the information that they were within rifle-shot of the historic field of Malplaquet where another English commander had once led his army to victory. They listened impassively to the ringing words of their own commander and were not much inspired by the war-cry of Do-or-Die. They were professional soldiers. Whatever tomorrow might bring would be all in the day's work.

Part Two
Strangers in a Strange Land

Oh, weren't they the fine boys! You never saw the beat of them,
Singing all together with their throats bronze-bare;
Fighting-fit and mirth-mad, music in the feet of them,
Swinging on to glory and the wrath out there.
Laughing by and chaffing by, frolic in the smiles of them,
On the road, the white road, all the afternoon;
Strangers in a strange land, miles and miles and miles of them,
Battle-bound and heart-high, and singing this tune,

It's a long way to Tipperary . . .

Robert Service

Chapter 7

They started off early in the morning, and in a few hours the spearhead of the British Expeditionary Force was fanning out across the countryside round Mons and into the town itself. It was not the first time that these roads had drummed beneath the tread of British troops. When Marl-borough's men had fought there, even when Wellington had rolled his army across this corner of Flanders barely a century before, it had made a fine battlefield – an open rolling plain, scattered with hamlets and villages, with low hills for vantage points, woods and copses for concealment. But times had changed, and the men of the British Army, still schooled in the principles of classic warfare, looked at their surroundings in dismay. They were not accustomed to soldiering among lines of flapping washing, in the gardens of suburban dwellings, in the streets of mining villages where the friendly inhabitants went, unconcerned, about their daily business, in the yards of factories humming with production, around slag heaps and pitheads where black-faced miners waved cheerily as they jostled through the gates off the morning shift.

The textbook battlefield had all but disappeared under a sprawl of industrial development – a conglomerate mass of blast furnaces, of glass-works, of mines and chemical plants, of smoking chimneys, and straggling around them a tangle of grimy villages that housed the workers. The Belgians called it 'le Borinage'. The Black Country.

Their commanders were even more dismayed than the troops. There was no room to manoeuvre, no open space for skirmishing, no point of observation that was not overlooked by another. The field artillery in support of the troops could not fire through slag heaps, nor could they shoot round corners. With no visible targets, with no clear view ahead and with nothing remotely resembling a 'field of fire', the guns would be blind and the infantry would be lost.

For the moment, though, the matter was academic. The BEF was not intended to stand and fight at Mons. As soon as they were in position and had linked up with the French on their right, the whole line would surge forward together to teach the Germans a lesson, sweep them out of Belgium and send them scuttling for home. The forward line of troops had been ordered to set up an outpost position along the line of the canal. It started at the River Sambre to the east of Mons, looped round it in a semi-circle to the north and then ran arrow-straight for twenty miles to Condé, where the great black barges unloaded their cargoes. In the absence of any other natural feature, the canal was a useful map reference. As events were turning out, it was also a position of acute danger. The British were out on a limb.

It was precisely the position chosen by the 'Military Conversationalists' years before and, in those war-gaming peacetime days, it had looked wonderful on paper. The British would stand on the extreme left of the French to extend the French line and protect the left flank.

It had seemed almost as simple as joining up two platoons of soldiers drilling on a barrack square. If one extended to the right and the other stretched out to its left, on the principle of stretching and knotting together two lengths of elastic, they would gain touch, as the Army had it, to present an unbroken front. But soldiers on a barrack square, even two battalions ordered to 'gain touch' under Active Service conditions on peacetime manoeuvres, did not labour under the difficulty that one of them was already locked in battle with the enemy. The war, which had not yet begun for the British, was well under way for the French, and it was not going well.

The Cavalry Brigade in the vanguard of the British Expeditionary Force was charged with two vital tasks. Their patrols must probe the country to the north to gain touch with the outposts of the enemy. They must range to the south to join hands with their neighbours the French. And when all of the BEF had moved up and assembled in force, then they would close the gap.

But the gap was nine miles wide from north to south and, as the Germans battered hard at the French Fifth Army, as the French fell back, it was widening all the time. The British were not yet there. But they were on their way. Marching to stand alone nine miles to the north-west, and marching on a path that would bring them face to face with the right flank of the Kaiser's Army wheeling round to outflank the French and to march on to Paris.

The men of the 15th Howitzer Brigade were asleep on their feet, for they had had no rest to speak of since they had left the trains at Landrecies the evening before. The 80th Battery had had a particularly trying time. They had shared a train with the Brigade ammunition column and they were the last to arrive. The evening was overcast and by the time they had reached Landrecies at ten o'clock, it was pitch dark. Unloading was a nightmare. One by one the nervous horses had to be led down narrow ramps on to the rails and since there were only three such gangways provided for the whole train, that took a long time. It was far from easy to harness the horses in total darkness, to hook them up to the guns and wagons and to guide them blind across a network of rails to the road on the other side. It was a miracle that only one wagon had come to grief. It missed the crossing and plunged one of its wheels into a deep depression between the tracks. Unfortunately it had been the last wagon of all and the rest of the battery had started off oblivious of the fact that one hapless subaltern, Rory Macleod, and several unfortunate gunners had been left behind. It had taken a good deal of sweating and cursing and heaving before they got back on the road and could set off in pursuit of the battery. Macleod had sufficient self-possession to remember that he was in France and to place his men on the right of the road, but he was not at all sure that it was the right road.

Half a mile on, he heard the rumble of wheels, the chinking of harness, knew that the battery was ahead of them, and broke into a sweat of relief. They joined on to the end, keeping a discreet distance. In the Stygian darkness of the country road it was impossible to see even a yard in front of them. They marched on for three miles behind their lumbering wagon.

Lt. R. A. Macleod, 80 Battery, XV Brigade, R.F.A., 5th Division, B.E.F.

The darkness wasn't our only problem. It was a frightfully hot stuffy night, we all had a raging thirst and the horses were in an equally bad state. They hadn't been watered for hours! It was dinned into us as young officers 'First look after the horses, then look after your men and last of all yourselves.' So the first thing was to look for water for the horses – but how on earth this was to be done when we couldn't see our hands in front of our faces was a problem. The word was passed back to halt and the battery turned off the road into what appeared to be a field at the side of the road. In a minute there was absolute mayhem. It was an orchard! The horses could see no better than we could but they seemed to know by instinct when there were obstacles in the way, but the drivers didn't, and the vehicles were crashing into the trees and you could hear this sound of splintering wood and horses whinnying and shouts and yells. Absolute mayhem!

Eventually we did manage to get ourselves slightly sorted out. We unhooked the horses and a party of us set off leading them to try to find a pond or a stream. We wandered around in the dark for ages and I was beginning to despair when a Frenchman who had been roused by the noise turned up with a lantern. He showed us where there was a pond by the roadside and stayed while the horses were watered, shining his lantern so that we could superintend the job. When we eventually got back to the orchard we were thankful to find a fire going and a hot drink of cocoa waiting for us. Major Birley had decided that there was no point in going on until we had some light to see by, so we wrapped ourselves in our greatcoats and lay down to rest for half an hour. By that time it was dawn! We set off again, feeling even more dead beat if anything and not too happy about what Brigade would say about the damage to the wagons.

But when the 80th Battery eventually caught up with the Brigade on the straight Roman road by Le Cateau where most of the 5th Division was now assembled, the Brigade officers had other things to concern them. The night before there had been a sad and horrible accident and they were deeply upset. As they approached Le Cateau they had prudently sent a small party of mounted men ahead into the dark to report and reconnoitre. The Civil Guard, recruited from the unsophisticated local peasantry, had been posted to watch the approaches to the town. They were edgy and nervous. They were also trigger-happy and unfamiliar with foreign tongues. The men guarding the railway bridge, deeply suspicious of the strange horsemen trotting towards them out of the dark night, challenged, panicked at the sound of foreign tongues and opened fire.

Even in the daylight their aim would have been shaky and the ancient weapons in their inexperienced hands were not calculated to do much damage, but the advance guard did not stop to argue. They turned tail and galloped fast back the way they had come. It was a natural reaction, but it was the wrong one. The picquets of the 5th Division, equally startled, equally nervous but far better equipped to do damage, met them with a fusillade of rifle fire, laid accurately along the straight line of the road and the consequences had been appalling. One man had been killed. Another badly wounded. Just as Major Birley was reporting the arrival of the 80th Battery, news came that the second man had died. The first British casualties to die in France had been killed by their own comrades.

It was a depressing start. The gunners had been allowed to snatch a few hours' sleep in a field, but they were still exhausted and still depressed when they set off after midday on the trek north to Mons. To cap it all there was a thunderstorm.

It was a journey of just over forty kilometres from the start just north of Le Cateau to Dour on the left of Mons – and there was to be no stopping on the way. As the Brigade set off the skies opened, and before they had gone a hundred yards men and horses were soaked by torrential rain. A mile or so on, when the sun shone again, they were wreathed in wisps of steam as the horses' coats and the sodden clothing of the men began to dry out in the heat. Clouds of dust were flung up as they travelled, and settled in a film on their damp uniforms. Although they were far better off than the marching infantry they passed on the way, it seemed as if the journey would never come to an end. Rory Macleod covered double the distance for he had to be constantly riding up and down the column to see that all was well and to hustle on any who fell behind. It was fortunate that he had two horses and to spare them he rode them alternately, for some of them were making heavier weather of the journey than the men. Late in the afternoon two of the limber horses collapsed with heat and exhaustion. There was no alternative but to shoot them.

Even marching along the western edge of the forest of Mormal, tantalised by the inviting shade in the glades among its tall trees, there was no relief from the dust or from the glare of the sun blazing down from the south-west. The villagers at every hamlet, thrilled by the sight of the guns, poured out of their cottages to line the road and to shower the gunners with fruit, with flowers, with cigarettes, and even with bottles of wine. There was hardly a man who wouldn't gladly have traded them all for a drink of water. The mouthful that Major Birley had twice allowed them to drink from their water-bottles did little to quench their thirst. They wanted water by the jugful, by the bucketful. They parted with such badges and buttons as they could decently spare to the village girls who, as usual, were clam-ouring for them. A few of the most competitive had managed to secure the badges of every unit that passed and the progress of the Expeditionary Force towards Mons could easily be deduced from the expanse of hardware that gleamed on their generous bosoms.

When the Brigade left the forest, progress slowed down. They were checked at every crossroads by long processions of cavalry. The cavalry had been the first in the field; now they were changing position and crossing from the right to the left of the British line. The orders were that the cavalry was on no account to be held up. The rumour was that they had already been in touch with the enemy.

It was perfectly true.

The cavalry could move far and fast. For days now they had been scouring the countryside, searching and probing, sending out patrols in a dozen different directions to pick up information, to reconnoitre the whereabouts of the elusive Germans.

Not a German had they seen, but every village was full of fugitives and they all had tales to tell. They had come from the north, from the north-east, the north-west, from villages that were twenty miles, sixteen miles, and as little as twelve miles distant. The Germans were everywhere – rolling

westwards as if round the rim of a gigantic wheel and marching as if down
its spokes towards Mons at its hub.

Major Tom Bridges had gone with C Squadron of the 4th Dragoon
Guards to bivouac for the night in a field outside a hamlet on the Mons to
Brussels road. He was not happy. There were too many rumours flying
about. To his suspicious mind, sharpened by the information gathered in
a day's reconnoitring, the villagers hanging about their camp were too
curious by half. The youths he had noticed cycling out of the village in a
northerly direction might have nothing more sinister in view than a meeting
with a country sweetheart, but he was not prepared to risk it. When night
came and the lamps in the cottage windows were dimmed, Bridges passed
the word for the squadron to pack up and moved them off to a safer spot
in a wood that conveniently topped a hill overlooking the road.

It was not a simple matter to move a hundred and fifty men and horses
quietly across country on a moonless night, but it had been managed. They
were all picked men and experienced soldiers. There was Corporal Thomas,
just twenty-nine, but with fifteen years' service to his credit. There was
Shoeing-Smith Corporal Old, who could croon the most nervous of horses
to silence. And there was Harry Savory. It was an open secret that he was
at least forty-five years old and should have been pensioned off years ago,
but the Dragoons turned a blind eye to this awkward fact. Savory was a
giant of a man who tipped the scales at more than seventeen stone, the
despair of the quartermasters who had to clothe him and of riding masters
who had to produce a mount powerful enough to carry him. But Savory
had more experience and had earned more campaign medals than any man
in the Dragoon Guards including the Colonel himself. In thirty years of
soldiering he had served in every campaign worth mentioning and he
sported a blaze of ribbons on his mammoth chest to prove it. He was a born
frontiersman, a brilliant keen-eyed scout with an uncanny chameleon-like
talent for losing his huge bulk in the background. Savory was worth his
considerable weight in gold and he was Bridges' right-hand man. At first
light he sent him with a picquet to the edge of the wood that overlooked
the road to try to spot the enemy. If any eyes could see through the mist
to spot the merest flutter of a tell-tale sign those eyes would be Savory's.
If there was even a muffled suggestion of men moving in the distance, the
faintest echo of a distant bugle call, the slightest stifled cough from men
concealed in ambush, Savory would hear it.

There was nothing. The road was empty. The countryside was silent.

Bridges pondered. It was not his job to attack the German army single-
handed. His task was to get information and that meant capturing prisoners.
He could wait where he was, ambush the enemy's advance guard, capture
prisoners and get away before the main force arrived. But that might mean

waiting all day. Already the horses were restless and had to be watered. Above all, the suspense was killing. He passed the order that the Dragoons should prepare to move.

By the time they started, the village was stirring and women drawing water from a well behind the outlying cottages stopped to stare as they clopped past up the road towards Soignies. Bridges was at the head of a hundred and fifty mounted men. The high polish of the riding boots and saddles had dimmed after a night in the open and the morning's heavy dew, the shining harness, the buckles and buttons, the gleaming spurs, even the sword hilts had been blackened for War Service, but they were still a fine sight, and the rifle-butts that protruded from canvas buckets, slung on the harness conveniently to hand, showed that the troopers meant business.

At the next crossroads and well screened from the roadway they found a stream where the horses could be watered. Bridges sent half a dozen men to conceal themselves in the bushes by the side of the main road and ordered them to keep a sharp look-out. The stream lay in a slight hollow below the level of the long straight road as it climbed the hill to the village of Le Cateau. The first troop had hardly dismounted when there was a low call from the hedgerow.

'Enemy coming down the main road, Sir!'

The Germans were still half a mile away, and moving at a cautious pace, but there was no mistaking them, for they were on horseback, they were carrying long lances and they stood out against the skyline as they came over the crest of the hill. A minute passed, then another – but no other troops appeared behind them. They were quite alone. Bridges congratulated himself on the good fortune that had taken his troop off the road minutes before they appeared. Now they were making straight for his hiding place, and when they reached it the Dragoons would bag them as easily as they might pluck four chickens from a roost.

Delighted, he gave the order. '4th Troop, dismounted ready for action; 1st Troop, behind, draw swords ready to go!' On came the Germans. Now others had breasted the hill and spread out across the broad highroad behind the advance guard. They were so close that Trooper Thomas could see quite clearly that the officer in front was unconcernedly puffing on a cigar.

Then they stopped, and it was clear that they had smelt a rat.

Perhaps the echo of Bridges' command had carried further than he intended through the still morning air. Perhaps the Germans had caught sight of the unavoidable flurry of movement behind the screen of trees. Whatever aroused their suspicions, they reined in their horses, hesitated, then, on a signal from their officer, turned and began to trot back the way they had come. There was an audible groan of disappointment.

With half his squadron dismounted, Bridges stood tight-lipped with dismay. But there were two troops still in the saddle, on their mettle and ready to go. 'Let *us* go after them, Sir!' Captain Hornby begged the Major to give the word. The change in the situation had put Bridges in a quandary. He had no idea how many Germans might be following the vanguard and it was not his job to engage the German army single-handed. His task was to capture prisoners, to find out their units and to report back so that the Command might estimate the strength of the enemy. But there was no resisting Hornby's entreaties. At Bridges' nod of assent, the two troops raced on to the high road and started to give chase. There was no need for silence now. By the time that Tom Bridges had ordered the rest of the squadron back into the saddle and was following at a trot, they were far ahead, galloping flat out in pursuit of the Uhlans. He could see sparks ringing from the cobbles under the horses' hooves. He could see the men crouched in the saddle, their right arms extended and the steely glitter of sword tips held as straight and as true as if they were going for a line of straw dummies on a peacetime exercise. And he could hear Hornby's voice above the mêlée. He was shouting 'Ch-a-a-a-rge'. And then they disappeared over the crest of the hill.

It was like every battle set-piece that had ever hung in a regimental mess. It was like every lurid illustration that had ever appeared in a boy's adventure book. Swords flashing, hooves flying, horses neighing, men yelling and charging. It might have happened at Waterloo. It might have happened at Agincourt. It was the most thrilling event in Ted Thomas's life and as long as he lived, he never forgot it.

Trooper E. Thomas, 4th Dragoon Guards, B.E.F.

My troop was ordered to follow on in support and we galloped through the little village of Casteau. We could see the 1st Troop using their swords and scattering the Uhlans left and right. We caught them up. Captain Hornby gave the order, '4th Troop, dismounted action!' We found cover behind a château wall and, possibly because I was rather noted for my quick movements and athletic ability, I was first in action. I could see a German cavalry officer some four hundred yards away standing mounted in full view of me, gesticulating to the left and to the right as he disposed of his dismounted men and ordered them to take up their firing positions to engage us. Immediately I saw him I took aim, pulled the trigger and automatically, almost instantaneously, he fell to the ground.

The strange thing about the episode – and it seems as clear to me as if it happened last week – was that I had not the slightest feeling of being in battle. It seemed to me like an ordinary action taking place in peacetime manoeuvres, until the bullets started whizzing round. And my shot certainly brought down an enemy who was no 'dummy'. It was the first shot fired by a rifle in the war. At the time it seemed to me more like rifle practice on Salisbury Plain.

Within a second or two it was mighty different. From every direction, as it seemed, the air above us was thick with bullets, the whistling noise of them, and the little flurries of hay they sent up like smoke as they hit the haystacks where the men were taking cover. This was something rather different to our days of make-believe!

The Germans had rushed troops to the crest of a hill and bullets were raining down on the Dragoons. There was nothing to be gained by staying. Bridges gave the signal to withdraw. They had done their job and Hornby was triumphant. They had captured five prisoners in the first sabre charge. It had not been difficult for the Germans had been armed with long lances, and found them hard to handle in a real hand-to-hand fight. They collected the prisoners on the way back, waiting in a disconsolate group by the roadside held at sword-point by half a dozen grinning troopers left behind to guard them. Three were wounded and all were bemused but tying their hands for safety's sake, they mounted the prisoners on their own horses and took them back in triumph for interrogation.

Holding the naked blade of his sword upright in the Attention position Hornby rode back in a state of high elation. For four thrilling inches his weapon was wet with German blood and he had no intention of losing so much as a single drop by returning it to the scabbard. Trooper Thomas had earned the distinction of firing the first British bullet of the war, but Hornby's sabre troop had been in action earlier still – and Hornby knew for certain that he had run his man through. In his own mind he was perfectly satisfied that the first German to be killed by the British in the Great War had died like a gentleman – by the sword. Later, when the blood had dried and before he was obliged reluctantly to submit his sword to be cleaned and sharpened he showed it off gleefully to fellow officers who had not had the good fortune to be in the fight.

It was past eight in the evening before the weary gunners of Macleod's battery reached the unlovely village of Dour on the left of Mons.

Lt. R. A. Macleod, 80 Battery, XV Brigade, R.F.A., 5th Division, B.E.F.

No maps had been issued because we moved so far and so fast that we were off one after the other. They were still in their boxes in the first line transport. But we knew where we were by asking the inhabitants and from signposts. We had a hot dinner. Then a thunderstorm came on about 10 p.m. We dived into our 'bivvies' and were soon asleep. My little bivouac-tent came in handy as we had some heavy rain that night.

At ten o'clock, just as the men of the 80th Battery were turning in for the night, Sir John French was finishing a late dinner at his headquarters some thirty miles to the south in the small town of Le Cateau and Lieutenant Spears, urgently waiting to see him, was pacing the drawing room. It was his second visit of the day and he was almost numb with exhaustion. It seemed as if a month had passed since this morning when he had chanced to meet Sir John French on his way to General Lanrezac's headquarters. In Spears' view the meeting had been a stroke of bad luck. He had been forced to tell the Commander-in-Chief that he would not find Lanrezac at his HQ but some miles north at Mettet, where the French general was anxiously following the fortunes of his forward troops. The two commanders had not met since their disastrous encounter of the previous week and Spears urged French to make for Mettet as fast as he could. He was dismayed when the Commander-in-Chief refused. It was too far. Time was too short. He was delighted to have met Lieutenant Spears. It had saved him a fruitless journey. He ordered Spears to get into the car. They would return together to Le Cateau.

A junior officer, even one engaged on vital liaison duties, was not accustomed to arguing with his Commander-in-Chief. Spears instructed his own driver to follow, and meekly did as he was told.

Le Cateau was bright in the August sun, but if Spears' spirits were momentarily lifted by the businesslike bustle of troops in its streets an interview with the Chief of British Intelligence very soon cast them down. Colonel McDonagh was uneasy. He was more than uneasy, he was furious. It was his job to analyse intelligence reports, to collate them and to pass them on to the Staff, and he had just received a snub as insulting as it was high-handed. The information passed on by the far-ranging cavalry, the shrewd estimates of the number of Germans who were advancing on a collision course with the British Army, had been dismissed out of hand by the Operations section. *The information which you have acquired and conveyed to the Commander-in-Chief appears to be somewhat exaggerated. It is probable that only mounted troops supported by Jaegers are in your immediate neighbourhood.*★

McDonagh was convinced that the reports were accurate. They were horribly confirmed by reports from the French, by reports from Belgian

★ *Army Order No. (O (A) 47) sent from GHQ to the Cavalry Division. 22/8/14.*

agents, and they were confirmed beyond any doubt by pilots flying above the web of roads that brought endless columns of marching Germans nearer with every hour.

Within the last hour, McDonagh had had another severe shock. He had heard – and only by chance – that as soon as the British troops were in position around Mons, they were to move up to Soignies ready to advance. By all his calculations the Germans were probably at Soignies already.

Together Spears and McDonagh went to the Operations Room (housed in the village school) to study the large maps hanging on its walls. They found its staff in paroxysms of laughter and only too ready to share the joke. A message had just come in from a unit which was detailed to cover the retirement of the cavalry as it crossed from the right to the left flank of the Army. They had been told to take up positions in some farm buildings and to prepare them for defence. And that was the trouble. Did this mean they were entitled to pierce loopholes in the walls? Opinion had been sharply divided. Mindful of the awful consequences for any soldier caught 'inflicting wilful injury to private property' while on manoeuvres, they had come to the conclusion that it would be wise to refer the matter to Headquarters. Spears had not joined in the general hilarity. He had left wondering bitterly just how long it would take to convince the British that they were engaged on the business of war and reflecting ironically that respect for law and order would doubtless prompt them to appoint a coroner in order to hold formal inquests on the first German casualties.

Now he was back in Le Cateau and he was dead beat. The intervening hours had not been pleasant. Travelling through the country behind the French army, long before he had caught up with General Lanrezac at the advance report centre at Mettet, Spears had realised that things were going badly. The 'rear area' was in the rear no longer.

Lt. E. L. Spears, 11th Hussars. Attached French Fifth Army.

Louder and louder grew the sound of the guns, until it became obvious that a great battle was raging close at hand. Empty spaces with not a soul to be seen, under a sky of brass, shaking with the concussion of artillery, now a single heavy discharge, then a pulsation of the whole atmosphere, as if all the gods in heaven were beating on drums the size of lakes. A little further on one might come upon a man working in a field, apparently quite unperturbed; then two or three country folk dressed in their best black suits and white shirts grey with dust, carrying odd packages, would hurry by. Then convoys hopelessly blocking the road, not knowing where to go, awaiting orders.

Presently it became all too obvious that the French line must have fallen back since the morning, for we were now almost in the firing line, whereas, according to the morning's information, we should have been far behind it. We began to encounter long pathetic processions of wounded men hobbling along alone or helping each other, their clothing torn, their faces black with grime or grey with dust. We had got even closer to the fighting line than we intended, for a few minutes later a couple of battalions in retreat crossed us. These were an even more poignant sight than the wounded. Hardly any officers, the men in disorder, terrible worn expressions on their faces, exhaustion dragging at their heels and weighing down their tired feet so that they caught on every stone in the roadway, but something driving them on. Was it fear? I do not think so – just the desire to find a place to rest, away from those infernal shells. These men were not beaten. They were worn out.

Now, back at Le Cateau for the second time, Spears was himself worn out by the exertion and emotions of the day, and he brought bad news. The French centre had been driven in, the French were falling back, the tide of Germans was still advancing. The gap between the French and the British was widening with every hour. The British troops at Mons were no longer in danger. They were in peril.

There was a burst of laughter and a buzz of talk as the double doors of the dining room opened and the Commander-in-Chief appeared with his Chief of Staff. They listened gravely and in silence to Spears' report. Then McDonagh, whom Spears had taken along for moral support, seized the chance to repeat his own information to the Commander-in-Chief in person. He stressed particularly the report of the airman who had spotted 'a whole German corps' marching down on the left of the British line. Still the Commander-in-Chief said nothing. Then he turned back to Spears.

'Have you anything further to say?'

Spears had had difficulty in wringing any information from General Lanrezac's Intelligence Staff as to the General's intentions, but he had conjectured them for himself. Now, without authority, against convention, but all too conscious of the plight of the Expeditionary Force, he played his own card.

'Only, Sir, that I am convinced that General Lanrezac does not mean to attack even if he were in a position to do so. And he is not.'

Spears and McDonagh were told to wait in the dining room while the two generals conferred. Spears looked back on it later as one of the most painful experiences of his life.

Lt. E. L. Spears, 11th Hussars. Attached French Fifth Army.

We sat down on a sofa facing the door. Round the table, the empty coffee cups pushed out of the way to make room for maps, the Chiefs of Staff of the two corps and of the cavalry, with a few officers of Sir John French's personal staff, were in animated conversation. A sickly feeling came over me as I realised that they were discussing a plan, evidently already decided upon, for a general advance upon the following day. They paid no attention to the two individuals sitting on the sofa, whose mood was so strikingly different from theirs. Round the table, keenness, suppressed excitement, joy and confidence, sparkled through the ordinary technical conversation of these men who already saw themselves marching to victory tomorrow, whilst we in our corner knew that their hopes must be dashed, that the advance we had all dreamed of would not take place, that – perhaps before it could even strike a blow at the enemy – the Army, *our* Army, might be forced to retire. My depression was increased by a gnawing doubt of my own judgement.

After the briefest period of reflection, Sir John French cancelled the plan to advance. If he had any doubt in his own mind whether a junior Staff Officer was competent to predict the intentions of the Commander of the French Fifth Army, it was dispelled within the hour and dispelled by a message from General Lanrezac himself. Sir John French was dismayed. Spears had prepared the Commander-in-Chief for the news that Lanrezac was unable to attack. He was not prepared for Lanrezac's request that his own small force, alone and isolated, should attack on Lanrezac's left to hold back the advance of the mighty flood of Germans that threatened to encircle them. Of course it was impossible. If the French retired, the BEF would have no alternative but to fall back alongside and few would have blamed the British Commander-in-Chief if he had immediately ordered them to do just that. But he did not.

Lights burned late in Le Cateau – in the cottages where officers were billeted, in the school where the staff had their offices, in the villa where French and his chiefs had their quarters. A Staff car waited outside, its powerful engine ticking over. Presently two officers hurried out and set off with all speed for General Lanrezac's headquarters. They carried General French's reply – and they carried a promise. Although the French had fallen back, although the gap between their armies was rapidly widening, although the British were now isolated in a forward position in a dangerous salient, General French gave General Lanrezac his word that he would cover his retirement. He would keep the Germans at bay. He would hold his present positions on the Mons canal and he would hold them for twenty-four hours. In his own mind, and in the absence of concrete information, Sir John French could not bring himself wholly to believe in the reports that vast hordes of Germans were advancing. It simply did not tally with their carefully garnered intelligence, with their estimate of Germany's strength, with their knowledge of her regular army. There were reserves, of course, but common sense dictated that they would be held well back, working as back-up to the shock troops, holding themselves ready in due course to supply reinforcements and replace casualties. With large numbers of men already engaged along the line of the frontiers in close combat with the French, with large numbers of front-line troops besieging Namur, and occupying Brussels, how could the German army possibly be bearing down on the left flank in the numbers that were being estimated by the French, by fleeing civilians, by spies, even by the inexperienced Flying Corps. It simply did not make sense. The reports must be wildly exaggerated.

As the car carrying his message to Lanrezac roared down the main street of Le Cateau and took to the dark country roads, the clock in the town hall was striking midnight. It was 23 August and another message of importance was winging its way through the night. It came from French Intelligence and its content was disturbing. It told of captured prisoners and of the astonishment of those who had interrogated them. Far from being the highly skilled professionals of Germany's standing army, a disquieting number were little more than 'ploughboys in uniform'. It was the first hint of an awful truth that was slow to dawn in the minds of the men who were disposing the troops to hit back at the Germans.

The Germans were gambling on surprise, on swiftness of movement, on a speedy victory – and they were prepared to wager every man they had. The Reserve Corps were not in Germany. They were here. Even if all the men of the British Expeditionary Force had arrived in their positions, they would have been outnumbered by two to one.

Time and again, as the British emissaries drove north-east to Chimay, they were forced to a halt by shadowy cavalcades of French soldiers. They hoped against hope that they were reserves moving forward, but they felt it in their bones that they were soldiers in retreat.

Not far to the east on either side of the forest of Mormal, the night sounds of the dark countryside were lost in the sound of marching feet as the men of the BEF streamed up to swell the numbers of their comrades in the salient round Mons.

Chapter 8

When night fell it was eerie on the canal bank. It was also cold and none too comfortable for there had been no shelter from the thunderstorm that plumped down at ten o'clock and the soldiers were damp and shivery. Mist hung over the water and clung dankly around the trenches scraped across a scrub of suburban wasteland behind the towpath. The Royal Fusiliers had scratched them out hurriedly in the last of the daylight and they were barely two feet deep. This was a point of small importance. The trenches were not meant to be permanent and the Tommies did not for a moment imagine that they were intended to stop there. They expected a skirmish – no more – and then, when the rest of the Army caught up and the powers-that-be gave the word, they would be ready to go, kicking the Germans along the road in front of them.

But, nevertheless, they had to take standard precautions. Foraging parties had gone off in search of bonfire wood and any waste material that would burn, for the canal was lined with empty barges that could all too easily be strung together to serve the enemy as a makeshift bridge. Conventional bridges carried roads and railway tracks across the canal, but the Royal Engineers had been busy all evening, laying explosive charges which, if the worst came to the worst, would blow the bridges up and leave the Germans spectacularly stranded on the opposite bank. But the barges were large, the canal was too shallow to sink them and, with so many men close by, it would be a risky business to use dynamite. The answer had been to set them alight. Now the burnt-out hulks lay askew in the water and the fumes of smouldering wood and pitch still smarted the Tommies' eyes.

Only this morning – and it seemed a hundred years ago – they had marched into Mons and into the bustle of the Saturday market that filled the Grande Place and spilled over into the streets around. In appointing this rendezvous it had not occurred to the Army to enquire if the streets would be clear. But the Fusiliers were not complaining and nor, apparently, were the citizens of Mons. The Tommies piled arms, balancing rifles together in threes, sat down on the sun-warmed cobblestones round the edge of the square, and prepared to enjoy themselves. Soon their rations were dished out. There was fresh bread – a large loaf to four men – and a tin of food between two. They were mysterious tins, innocent of labels and so battered and rusted that some Tommies loudly speculated on the probability that they came from some long-forgotten store left over from the Crimean War. It was literally pot luck. Some got sliced bacon, others got pilchards or herring and a few were surprised to find that their dinners consisted entirely of apple-dumpling.

It was lucky that appetites had been sharpened by the march for there was more, much more, to come. The market crowds vied with each other to shower the Tommies with eatables that were a distinct improvement on the Army's fare. There were apples, pears, and greengages by the bushel. There were lumps of tasty sausage, great hunks of cheese, rounds of country bread thick with fresh butter. What the soldiers could not consume on the spot they stowed into their packs as welcome insurance against future hunger pangs.

It was a long halt. Young Bill Holbrook, the Colonel's servant, made a token appearance at the restaurant where the officers were lunching and then, knowing that if he were missed he would be assumed to be with the Colonel, he set off with his mate for a stroll around the town. They had a most enjoyable time. They were hauled into cafés and treated to beer. They were lavished with fruit, with flowers, with sweets, cigars, cigarettes. A barber rushed from his shop to intercept them and almost frog-marched them inside for free haircuts. They were kidnapped by a teacher at a school for young ladies who entertained them to tea and polite English conversation, with much round-eyed giggling from her pupils. And they returned not a moment too soon, for they were just in time to slip into their places as the Battalion formed up to march through Mons to Nimy and on to its place on the bank of the wide Mons-Condé canal. Somewhere on the other side of it, so they said, were the Germans.

Now they were waiting, watching, listening. But there was nothing to see but the vague bulk of a bridge against the inky black of the night and nothing to be heard but the occasional cry of a night bird, the whistle of a distant train, and now and again the murmur of an officer's voice as he made his rounds.

Some distance to the rear – and it was just as well, for the sound of his fury would have roused any Germans within a mile of him – another officer, also on his rounds, was giving a subordinate the sharp edge of his tongue in tones that were anything but gentle. This unfortunate Lieutenant had been ordered to set up four outposts to cover the approaches to their makeshift camp in case the enemy surprised them in the hours of darkness. Three were in position when the Major made his rounds. The fourth was not and he wished to know the reason why. The answer came glibly enough from a subaltern whose polite deference was tinged with the merest suggestion that it was plain for all to see.

'I'm sorry, Sir. I didn't think it necessary to post one. The enemy would hardly come from that direction. It's private property, Sir.'

At the end of a nasty five minutes, still smarting from the indignity of having been called a dunderhead and brusquely reminded that he was engaged in war and not in a game of hopscotch, the Lieutenant hurried off to make amends and soon a corporal and four men marched into the grounds of a large villa to keep watch through the night. The Major checked on them himself and warned them to keep a sharp look-out, to show no lights and to make no sound.

But for many miles behind, the night was astir with noise and movement, with the marching of feet, the jingle of harness and the rumble of wheels as the troops and the guns were pushed at a spanking pace towards Mons. The infantry stopped at dusk to bivouac where they could and snatch a

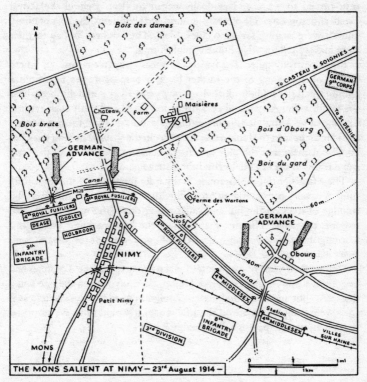

THE MONS SALIENT AT NIMY — 23rd August 1914 —

few hours' rest. The gunners kept going, for the guns were badly needed.

Riding just behind his Commanding Officer at the head of the 23rd Artillery Brigade, Jimmy Naylor was half-asleep in the saddle. The Colonel fell back and prodded him in the ribs. 'Wake up, Trumpeter. We're just crossing the border into Belgium.' He was too tired to pay much attention. They had moved so far and so fast that they had moved right off their maps. They still had a considerable distance to travel but when dawn broke, by consulting signposts and asking the way of a friendly farmer who was early up and about, they managed to find their destination and take up their position.

Mist hung over the canal as the sky lightened and a thin drizzle chilled the air. The men on the outpost line stretched their stiff limbs, gulped down mugs of tea, strong and sweet as only the Army could brew it, washed as best they could in the trickle of water that passed for a stream, slapped their arms, stamped their feet and tried to shake off the chill of the night. After a while the drizzle stopped and the sun broke hazily through, the mist turned to wisps and gradually began to clear. Behind the Royal Fusiliers, across a straggle of waste-ground and allotments, the bells of Nimy church were ringing for six o'clock Mass. The Fusiliers looked to their front and waited for what Sunday might bring.

It was perfectly quiet. The canal was still as glass. Just beyond it, where a few cottages clung to the further bank, a wisp of smoke rose from a chimney and the soldiers more than sixty yards away could distinctly hear the familiar domestic sound of a fire being raked and fresh coals rattling into the stove. It sounded disconcertingly like the rattle of musketry. Staring ahead into the mist the look-outs crouching in the shallow outpost trenches could just make out the blur of a fir-plantation on the crest of the long slope rising to the skyline beyond the cottage gardens.

Their first sight of the Germans was hardly more than a shifting of the mist. A cavalry patrol, edging forward with caution, moved out from the smudge of trees on the hill and came riding down the main Nimy road towards the canal. The first that most of the Fusiliers knew of it was a warning shout and then an urgent call of command. *At five hundred yards – five rounds rapid – FIRE!*

Despite their years of hard professional training few of the Tommies had ever fired a rifle in anger but, like Holbrook, every man in the line was a first-class shot and they fired now as coolly, as steadily, as accurately as if they were firing at targets on the rifle range. It would not have surprised them if an umpire had signalled the hits.

Cpl. W. Holbrook, No. 13599, 4th Bttn., Royal Fusiliers, 4th Brigade, 3rd Division, B.E.F.

Our Colonel McMahon, he was responsible for improving the fire-power of the British Army. Wonderful man he was. Before he came to us he was musketry mad! He started the fifteen rounds a minute. When I first joined the Army you fired at a bullseye, that was your target. He ended all that. You fired at moving figures – khaki, doubling – so from about five rounds a minute you went to about fifteen. You had to lie on the box, unloaded, with three rounds in clips of five in the pouches. When the whistle went you'd have to load your rifle and fire, tip the case out, *fire, fire, fire, fire* . . . and get it all into the minute.

His one craze was musketry. I was his servant, but you had to fire your course whatever job was on. You had to fire five hundred rounds a year. I got Best Shot in the Battalion, and I was as proud as Punch. I felt sure the Colonel would say something because I got the Battalion Orders from the Orderly Sergeant every night, and I used to take them in to him. This night my name was right at the top as marksman – Best Shot! He saw it all right. He sat at that table and he read it while I watched him. He never said a word! Just signed it and handed it, back and never said a word. I shed tears over that! I couldn't help it! I knew he'd seen it, I knew he'd thought a lot of it – but he wouldn't praise me for it.

That wasn't long before I went with him to France. I went as a marksman.

But, marksman or not, Holbrook was perhaps the only front-line soldier in his company who had *not* fired his rifle. He was also one of the few men who had not yet seen the Germans. There had been no time to look, for his job as the Colonel's orderly was to run from B Company Headquarters in the line to Battalion Headquarters in Nimy village, and to run like the wind to keep the Colonel abreast of the news. It was a third of a mile to Battalion Headquarters in a cottage in the main street of Nimy and the steady crackle of musketry had followed Holbrook all the way. By the time he returned to the canal it had stopped and the Germans had retired in some dismay.

At nine o'clock, the first shells began to fall and they went on pounding the canal for an hour. There were some casualties, but there was shelter behind, and they were not many. What hit the Tommies hardest was that not a single British gun replied. When the shellfire slackened they manned their shallow trench and stood indignantly to arms. When it stopped the German infantry started forward.

They came in a dense grey mass, swarming down towards the Royal Fusiliers on one bend of the canal and pressing hard against the 4th Middlesex on the other, as if squeezing a flimsy boomerang, to bend it and, by leaning the full weight of their numbers against it, to make it snap. Between them the two battalions were holding the tip of the salient round Mons. It was the weakest point in the line. They knew it – and so did the enemy.

Cpl. W. Holbrook, No. 13599, 4th Bttn., Royal Fusiliers, 9th Brigade, 3rd Division, B.E.F.

Bloody Hell! You couldn't see the earth for them there were that many. Time after time they gave the order '*Rapid Fire*'. Well, you didn't wait for the order, really! You'd see a lot of them coming in a mass on the other side of the canal and you just let them have it. They kept retreating, and then coming forward, and then retreating again. Of course, we were losing men and *lots* of the officers especially when the Germans started this shrapnel shelling and, of course, *they* had machine-guns – masses of them! But we kept flinging them back. You don't have time to think much. You don't even feel nervous – you've got other fellows with you, you see. I don't know how many times we saw them off. They didn't get anywhere near us with this rapid fire.

The Germans believed, and long after the war they went on believing, that the British had beaten them back with machine-guns. But there were only two, placed high above the canal on the buttresses of the vital Nimy railway bridge, and they made so conspicuous a target that they attracted the full force of the enemy fire. Team after team of gunners was knocked out. Time after time they were replaced, and on the canal bank the riflemen were firing as if every man was competing for his marksman's badge at Bisley. They were firing at a steady fifteen rounds a minute and they mowed down line after line of Germans.

A little way to the rear, from a pocket of open land to the left of Nimy village, a single section of field guns was valiantly attempting to give what help it could. But it was like spitting against the wind. The shrapnel fell on the Germans like a summer shower, and from a dozen or more of their own guns, well sited in the open country beyond the built-up area, they retorted with a hurricane of shells that all but swept away the fragile British line. By midday it was as clear to the soldiers who manned it as it was to the Germans who besieged it that it was only a matter of time before it would give way.

The trouble was that such British guns as there were were blinded by bricks and mortar – by the dwellings and churches, by the tall-chimneyed factories, by the pitheads, the slag heaps, the timber-yards, that stood between them and their targets. At the tip of the Mons salient where the Germans were concentrating their attack, there was simply no field of fire. And on either side of it where there was, the guns, as yet, had no targets to fire at.

For the moment it seemed hardly to matter. In the mining village of Dour the gunners of the 80th Battery were encamped in a ploughed field surrounded by houses and slag heaps. They woke to the sound of church bells and, falling automatically into the familiar routine of camp duties, they were finding it hard to adjust to the idea that they were on the brink of war. There was the usual cluster of noisy children hanging curiously round the camp. There were civilians going about their business. One good lady who had promised the night before to bring milk and eggs in the morning was as good as her word. She brought butter as well, and bread, newly baked and still warm from the oven. A modest amount of money changed hands and the officers (and the mess orderlies!) enjoyed an excellent breakfast.

There were the usual parades – Gun Inspection to ensure that all was in order and Stables to check on the grooming and welfare of the horses. It was then that they heard the faint but unmistakable sound of firing to the north-east. The church bells were ringing again and the local people, sober in Sunday black, were on their way to church, calling out and waving to the gunners as they passed. They seemed curiously unperturbed, as if they lived in an inviolate world of their own and the soldiers in another. It was as if bullets and shells were strictly the affair of the military and had nothing to do with them. But the Germans were already extending their attack and, by the time Mass was over, the fighting was closer to home.

Lt. R. A. Macleod, 80 Battery, XV Brigade, R.F.A., 5th Division, B.E.F.

About ten o'clock Major Birley and Mirrlees rode off to reconnoitre a battery position to support the infantry on the canal bank on the left flank of the 5th Division. They were the King's Own Scottish Borderers and they were having a very warm time of it. The Germans were shelling them and they had pushed up a field gun behind a hedge within five hundred yards of a house the KOSBs were holding. They were pounding it to bits. The Major went right through this shelling, looking for a suitable place for the guns. There wasn't one! The country was absolutely flat, cut up by ditches. No cover at all. The

party came back very despondent. Then the Colonel came up himself
and he and the Major set off once again on reconnaissance. By this
time it was about one o'clock and while they were away we had
luncheon. It was our last proper meal for days.

They got back about two o'clock and the Major gave orders for us
to move into the village of Dour. We harnessed up and moved off.
There was a field in the middle of the village close to Dour church
and we left all the vehicles there, dismounted the gunners and marched
through the village and turned into a turnip field with a railway
running at the bottom. Here we started preparing a battery position
along the only possible cover, behind a hedge bordering the railway.
It was on a forward slope and, somewhat to our surprise, it was facing
north-west.

As the sound of the fighting grew louder and fiercer, as more and more
German guns joined in and the shelling intensified, as they laboured to dig
emplacements for guns which in their view would face the wrong way,
the gunners' astonishment grew. No shell fired from this position would
be of the slightest use to the infantry in front. But although the gunners
could not know it, their guns could do nothing to save the day. Their task
now was to save the Army. And it would be touch and go.

Behind the battle, another German army was marching steadily towards
the open country to the west of Mons. Soon, perhaps in a matter of hours,
they would reach it. The guns were being placed to catch the Germans
when they appeared and if they failed to stop them, or, at the very least,
to make them waver and slow down, the Expeditionary Force would be
lost.

*Lt. R. A. Macleod, 80 Battery, XV Brigade, R.F.A., 5th Division,
B.E.F.*

At the top of the slope was a factory with a tall chimney we could
use as an observation post. We cut gaps in the hedge and dug the
gun-pits so that the top of the hedge would be level with the tops of
the gun-shields. And we made gaps in the hedge on the *other* side of
the railway line and filled in the ditches on each side with logs so
that the guns would be able to roll forward smoothly when the time
came to advance. We had no doubt that we *would* advance.

To the north of us there was another hedge, five hundred yards
away, and beyond it we could see the woods on the high ground
north of the canal. This was in the hands of the Germans, so we didn't
dare bring in the guns in daylight or we should have been shelled to

blazes as soon as they saw them. We knew the infantry were falling back from the canal bank because we could see them digging in along the hedge five hundred yards in front, and soon others came even further back and started digging in just in front of us along the hedge on the other side of the railway track. All the while the sound of the gunfire and the rifles and machine-guns on our right front to the north of us was getting heavier and heavier – and there wasn't a blessed thing we could do about it!

It was lucky that young Bill Holbrook was strong and fit. It was lucky that his feet had stood up well to the march, for time and again they had pounded up and down the road as the messages flew between Company HQ in the line and the house in Nimy where Colonel McMahon was anxiously following the fortunes of his hard-pressed battalion. The Colonel was also in touch with Brigade Headquarters and he knew that the 4th Middlesex on the eastern arm of the salient were faring no better. Holbrook did not know the contents of the messages he carried but, as the morning drew on, as the casualties mounted and the line thinned, he had no difficulty in guessing. The last time he sped back to the canal bank, pouring with sweat in the hot afternoon sun, he carried the order to retire.

Captain Byng was nowhere to be seen. He had rushed a platoon up to the bridge, where Lieutenant Dease, twice wounded, was still keeping the single machine-gun firing, as the Germans pressed ever closer. Holbrook handed the message to the only officer he could find. He read it grim-faced and scribbled a reply. Again Holbrook set off. It took him longer this time to reach Battalion HQ and by the time he got there, they were already packing up. The adjutant barely glanced at the message. He nodded to Holbrook. 'No answer. Cut along now and get back to your company.' It was easier said than done.

Cpl. W. Holbrook, No. 13599, 4th Bttn., Royal Fusiliers, 9th Brigade, 3rd Division, B.E.F.

Even in the little while I'd been away, the Germans had pulled a gun up on the other side of the road bridge over the canal, and they were firing right down the main street. People were running down the street, civilians, refugees, pushing little handcarts, or carrying what they could – or just running to get away as fast as they could, and they were all mixed up with troops coming back. They were trying to keep in some sort of order, but it was hopeless in all this crush. I couldn't see *anyone* of my own unit. Then a machine-gun started up and the bullets started streaming down the road, so I ducked through a gateway into a yard with a brick wall around it. There was another fellow sheltering in there leading a pack-mule loaded with ammunition that he was trying to take up to the front line. Poor chap! After a minute or so he put his head round the gatepost, cautious like, to see what was happening. He got a bullet straight through the head! He just spun round and collapsed at my feet.

That was enough for me. I was off! I went over the back wall. When I got to the house where the HQ was, *they'd* gone. So I just went back with the crowd. It wasn't confusion exactly, but you got mixed up, you were all over the place, because you had to get back the best way you could. I don't know who I was with. They were blokes from all different regiments, but I couldn't find any of our own chaps anywhere.

The Battalion diary (written up many days later) recorded laconically that the Royal Fusiliers had 'retired in good order'. That was one way of putting it. It was another thing to do it with nerves that twanged from hours of tension, with ears that rang from the sound of shelling, with muscles that ached from the exertion of the fight and brows that poured with sweat in the blistering sun. There was no question of waiting for a lull, for the enemy was almost upon them. The strip of land they must cross danced under exploding shells, the air zinged with the patter of flying shrapnel and a stream of bullets from hidden machine-guns spat and hissed at their heels. The soldiers had never been taught to retreat. But they were well schooled and disciplined in the art of 'strategic retirement' and they knew precisely what to do. It was discipline that got them away. It was discipline that kept them steady as they moved through the inferno to safety. It was discipline, standing fast with the rearguard, that held the Germans off while the rest got away. And it was something more than discipline that kept Private Godley firing the one remaining machine-gun until the last man had gone and the Germans rushed the bridge. Lieutenant Steele was the last man to leave the canal and a handful of the rearguard, sheltering by a wall, watched on tenterhooks as he worked unsteadily towards them, carrying Maurice Dease in his arms and staggering now and again under the dead weight of his unconscious body.★

On their right, the Germans had already managed to cross the canal at Obourg, and the Middlesex, the Gordons, the Royal Irish and the Royal

★ Private Godley remained a prisoner of war until November 1918. Lieutenant Dease died of his wounds minutes after Steele had carried him to safety and is buried in St Symphorien Military Cemetery near Mons. Both Dease and Godley were awarded the Victoria Cross.

Scots were falling steadily back. They were fighting as they went and they were fighting every yard of the way. The Germans were shaken, but still they came on. By five o'clock they were trickling into the streets of Mons and the British soldiers retiring in front of them were doing their best to get out of it. Now that the salient had cracked and the Germans were concentrating their attack on the long straight stretch of the canal to the west of the town, it was only a matter of time before that cracked too.

But, of course, it had never been intended to hold it and for that excellent reason the troops who had been moving into the area about Mons since early morning had not been sent forward to reinforce the outpost line. They had been deployed further back preparing a new line in a better position near the mining villages of Frameries and Paturages. It was to this position that the troops on the canal bank would retire. It was here that the BEF would stand and fight and, when the time was ripe, launch forward to attack the enemy.

The troops who were still holding on to the straight western edge of the canal bank had not taken a beating but they had taken a hard knock. There were many dead and the makeshift hospitals in the villages behind the line were full of wounded. Their ranks were horribly diminished, but they were still beating off the Germans and waiting for nightfall and the order to quit the line. They had clung to it, as the French had been promised they would, for twenty-four hours. But, even before dusk fell, the weary soldiers heard something that astonished them. It came distantly from the enemy's lines north of the canal and the Tommies listened in amazement. Just as they might have signalled the end of a day's manoeuvres the German buglers were sounding the Ceasefire.

Not long after, the soldiers of the Royal West Kents in the line at St Ghislain distinctly heard the Germans singing. They were soldiers of the 12th Brandenburg Grenadiers, they were singing '*Deutschland über Alles*', and they fully intended the British to hear them. Their audience obliged with catcalls of derision and shouts of 'Bloody sauce!' But, all the same, the Tommies quite admired the demonstration. They approved of pluck, and they knew very well that they had given the Kaiser's army a bloody nose.*

All along the line, even where the enemy had succeeded in breaking through, it was the same story. The Tommies, out-numbered by more

---

* The 12th Brandenburg Grenadiers had sustained more than five hundred casualties in the day's fighting. Those of the 1st Battalion, The Royal West Kent, were just over a hundred.

than three to one, had not merely thwarted the Germans – they had slaughtered them. In the course of the fighting, a bare dozen battalions at the sharp end of the puny BEF had lost sixteen hundred men, killed, wounded and 'missing', but they had delayed the advance of the enemy by one vital day.

The Germans had been hit even harder than the fighting soldiers realised, and they sorely needed a respite. They needed time to bury their dead, to tend their casualties, to bring up reserves and to gather their forces for the next onslaught. Both sides had fought like lions. Both sides were exhausted. Both sides were thankful to stop. Only the guns were fighting on.

Lt. R. A. Macleod, 80 Battery, XV Brigade, R.F.A., 5th Division, B.E.F.

As soon as it was dusk we went back to the Battery and brought it up nearer. Here we had a small supper of hard-boiled eggs and bread. When it was dark we brought the guns on to the position. Behind us a sixty-pounder battery in a wood yard on the crest of the hill was firing over our heads towards the north. We could see the shells bursting in a village which was on fire. In fact so many villages and farms were on fire that the flames lit up the whole horizon. Behind us, the arc lights of the factory and the lights in the town were on all night. It was almost as bright as day. We did some more digging, and then lay down for a couple of hours' sleep.

During the hours of darkness the troops on the outpost line retired 'in good order' into the main position that ran through the squalid villages behind Mons and slipped into line with the troops who had come up in the course of the day.

The distance was short but crossing it was a marathon of endurance, for it started to drizzle and the layer of coaldust that coated the surface of the cobbled roads – bad enough for army boots to grip at the best of times – turned in the wet to greasy slime. The troops hobbled and slipped and swore. They stumbled across endless slippery tramlines, crunched over cinder-heaps, blundered into ditches, tripped over fences in the half-light of the lurid night. Trees and chimney stacks, pitheads and spires stood black against the backdrop of the sky, flickering crimson above the villages burning at their backs.

Chapter 9

The Army had a vocabulary to fit the circumstances, and phrases like 'gradual withdrawal', 'readjustment of the line', 'conforming to the new position' had a comforting ring of assurance about them. They implied that someone somewhere knew what was happening – and it was just as well. To the soldiers on the spot – or on many spots, for all day they had been shuffled and shunted and moved about – the situation was confusing to say the least.

The Royal Sussex had reached the edge of the battle zone in an acute state of exhaustion. The Roussillon plume stood as proudly as ever on their badges and buttons but their owners were definitely wilting. They had had no rest but cat naps since they had left Rouen, packed into a train that travelled by day at little more than walking pace, stopping at nights at railway yards where the incessant shunting of trains and the penetrating sound of the guards' trumpets made sound sleep impossible. Three days' march had finally brought them to their destination a mile or so south of Mons on the eve of the battle. Crammed into the barns where they were to billet for the night the Battalion collapsed on the straw as one man and slept the sleep of the dead. On Sunday morning they were roused by the sound of church bells.

Sgt. F. M. Packham, No. 10134, 2nd Bttn., Royal Sussex Regt., 2nd Brigade, 1st Division, B.E.F.

After breakfast we were watching the local families going to church when we heard the sound of galloping horses coming towards us. As they approached we saw that it was a battery of sixty-pounders rushing up the hill. After about five minutes we heard the sound of the guns firing. Well! We all set off running up the hill. When we got to the top we were just in time to see our guns fire in anger for the first time. We could see the shells bursting far ahead and almost at once we heard in the distance the sound that we were to dread for the next four years – the sound of guns firing at us from behind the German lines. We could see their shells bursting just in front of our guns, and there was a rushing noise, like an express train tearing towards us. We soon learned that when you heard that sound the shell had already burst or that it had found its target and it was too late to duck, but we were green then! By this time our officers had arrived to round us up. They ordered us back to billets to 'stand to' at once and to be prepared to move at any time.

That day was 23 August, and it was a day of frustration and disappointment. We did nothing but march from one place to another and everywhere we went we could hear rifle and artillery fire from all directions, but we saw no signs of the enemy. Late in the afternoon we were ordered to dig a trench at the back of a row of houses and dig it deep! They told us we would be there all night and that we could expect the Germans to attack any time. We completed the trench, we posted sentries, and then – just as we'd been told to make ourselves comfortable – up came the Royal Munster Regiment to relieve us! So there was nothing for it but to scramble out and start marching back to the rear again. We went into billets for what was left of the night. We didn't know *what* was happening.

What was happening was that the new line was having to be given up. It was a matter of hours since Sir John French had given the instructions that had set the men digging for all they were worth. *I will stand the attack on the line now occupied by the troops. You will therefore strengthen your position by every possible means during the night.* Every possible means meant that battalions already weary with marching must rouse themselves and take to the road again to reinforce positions that were thinly held. Every possible means meant building barriers across roadways, stretching tripwires through copses, posting look-outs, doubling sentries. Every possible means meant that every man must remain awake and vigilant. Every possible means meant dig, dig, dig.

It was exactly ten days since the Worcesters and the Ox and Bucks had landed in France. Ten nights ago at this time they had been celebrating their arrival, queuing up at the beer tents in the camp above Boulogne, sneaking past the sentries to meet up with the local girls, revelling in the delightful novelties of the day. Tonight they were feeling considerably the worse for wear. They had been roused at half-past one that morning and set off two hours later, trudging northwards through Hargnies, to La Longueville, over the battlefield of Malplaquet, and across the Franco-Belgian frontier to Genly. It was a punishing march. It was swelteringly hot, there were perpetual checks and blocks on the road and they had had no breakfast. At nine o'clock, after more than five hours on the road, they were thankful when the officers called a halt and they turned into a field near Malplaquet for a meal of bread and stew and a badly needed rest. Fifteen miles to the north the Germans were battering at the canal bank and far-off roaring of their guns rippled and rolled across the horizon. Lieutenant Owen, making the rounds of No. 4 Platoon to see that his men were being fed, saw his younger soldiers look up enquiringly from their dixies of stew. He was well versed in the Regiment's history and he was struck by a sense of *déjà vu*. The regimental ancestors of the Ox and Bucks had camped on just the same spot ninety-nine years earlier as they tramped towards Waterloo and there they too had first heard the distant unfamiliar sound of the guns. On that occasion one old soldier had remarked, 'There they go, shaking their blankets again!' In that campaign 'they' had been the French. Now the enemy was the Germans and the sound was not the cannon of Quatre-Bras but the opening shots of the Battle of Mons.

The sound of the guns had, as Owen put it, 'a remarkable effect on our somewhat tired feet and jaded spirits' and the Battalion set off again with renewed vigour. But eight hours of moving from pillar to post had blunted their enthusiasm.

Lt. Crosse, 2nd Bttn., The Oxfordshire and Buckinghamshire Light Infantry, 5th Brigade, 2nd Division, B.E.F.

After the breakfast halt the march continued to the sound of the guns and the ringing of church bells, for it was Sunday. At three o'clock we arrived at Genly, settled into what seemed likely to be very comfortable billets and had dinner. This was hardly over when orders came to march eastward to Bougnies, there 'to entrench a back position, intended to cover a retirement'.

There was already a feeling, which nobody put into words, that all was not going well.

Lt. Crosse, 2nd Bttn., The Oxfordshire and Buckinghamshire Light Infantry, 5th Brigade, 2nd Division, B.E.F.

At five p.m. we marched out of Genly towards Bougnies where we found that other troops of the 2nd Division were already digging hard. We had just received our task and settled down to dig, when yet *another* order arrived. This time it was to close up and follow the Worcesters and the HLI north-westward to Frameries to fill a gap of some two miles almost entirely covered by houses. At nine p.m., therefore, we set off again, without transport or officers' horses, via Noirchain to Frameries.

The Brigade had then been on its feet and on the move for nineteen and a half hours and the men were exhausted. The Worcesters were the worst off for they had done the most digging and had all but finished their trenchline when they were told to hand it over and get going again as fast as they could. They were far from thrilled. It was already dark and it took some time to gather the men together, to collect the spades and implements, to form the Battalion up on the road and to check by companies and platoons that everyone was present and correct. At long last they marched off. It was little more than four miles to Frameries but it took them a good four hours to get there. Time and again they were caught up in the confusion of troops and transport and at every crossroads they collided with trails of refugees encumbered with salvaged belongings but hastening as best they could in any direction that would take them away from the guns and the fires that flickered against the sky behind them. The Battalion lost count of the times it had to give way and shuffle to a stop. There was not a man who was not bone-weary. Their muscles ached. Their feet throbbed. Eyes smarted. Heads ached. At every enforced halt on the interminable march the men fell asleep where they stood, woke with a start, and stumbled on again over the crippling cobbles of the rough road to Frameries.

To add to their difficulties, a brief shower of rain had made the road slippery, and (as the Colonel was uneasily aware) hazardous too, for every man marched with bayonet fixed and if one of them lost his footing it could lead to a nasty accident. But it was a risk they had to take; at any moment they might run into the Germans. The officers were carrying revolvers at the ready and as they neared Frameries the tension grew. It was perfectly possible that the Germans had got there before them.

The Germans had not advanced but the civilians left in Frameries were terrified that they would, and they were heartily thankful when the steady tread of approaching feet turned out to be British. It was an ugly mining village, a huddle of slag heaps, a straggle of streets and, late though it was, lamps were still burning in the windows of the low-roofed cottages. With the battle almost on their doorstep not many villagers had dared to go to bed. The Worcesters advanced slowly along the side streets, scattering to shelter close to the houses as a first salvo of shells screamed into the village and exploded in the main street. It was the nearest they had so far been to the unfriendly end of a gun and it was not agreeable. But their job was to advance to the slope beyond the cottages, to create a defensive line. To dig.

As they set to work again carving slit trenches across a stubble field it seemed to the Worcesters, now stiff with fatigue, that already in the past few hours they had dug up half of Belgium. They finished the job in the first grey light of the dawn. As the sky lightened and day crept in from the east the Germans renewed their attack.

In their billets, they knew not where, the Suffolks had been roused almost before they had properly gone to sleep. Once again they had set off without breakfast, bleary-eyed and moving at a shambling pace that bore little resemblance to marching as they normally understood it. They had not the faintest idea where they were bound. In the starless dark of the last hour of the night it was impossible to guess their direction and daylight, when it gradually enveloped them, revealed no landmarks. It was five o'clock before the sun began to rise and when it did they saw with bleary eyes that the pink glow of the eastern horizon was away to the left. They knew for certain now that they were marching due south and Sergeant Packham, for one, felt a sickening sense of failure. The Suffolks were retreating and they had not fired a single shot.

At midnight General French's fears had been horribly confirmed. General Lanrezac's army was being forced back. The news had reached him while his own troops were still taking up the new line that ran through Frameries and Pâturages, and before they had time to consolidate, the Commander-in-Chief had been forced to issue another order. It was the order for a general retreat. The bulk of the troops, and they had only just arrived, must be roused and sent back to the south. Their weary comrades now digging in to face a fresh onslaught on the new front line must stay put to cover their retirement.

With such a confusion of orders and counter-orders, it was hardly surprising that some units received no instructions at all, and the news that all was not well was conveyed to the 80th Battery of the Royal Field Artillery by the crack of rifle fire disconcertingly close at hand. It woke them at half-past three in the morning and their unease turned speedily to dismay. The trench in front of them was empty and the soldiers who had been holding it had gone. They were still trying to work out what was happening when a cavalry trooper pounded up at the gallop, stopped at the left section and shouted to Rory Macleod that the Germans were advancing and that they were just a few hundred yards away.

Lt. R. A. Macleod, 80 Battery, XV Brigade, R.F.A., 5th Division,
B.E.F.

The cavalry were apparently on our left, and they'd been astonished to find that we were there at all. The trooper pointed out a farmhouse about a hundred yards to our left front – no distance at all, and there were streams of bullets coming out of it – and told me that they would hold the position as long as they could to cover our withdrawal. I sent a runner off to pass the word to the Major and almost as soon as he got back with the order to withdraw I saw the gun teams coming up. In those few minutes I'd got the men together, gathered up what we could of our things so that as soon as the horses got to us we were ready to hook the guns to the limbers and get out. We retired at the trot, as fast as we could. It was obvious that there was no time to lose but we were very fed up at having to leave our position after all the hard work we'd done on it.

Our rendezvous was the church in Dour. As soon as all the battery arrived there, Major Birley called us officers together. He told us that a messenger had just brought the news that there had been a readjustment to the line. Reinforcements were needed further east and we had been put under the command of the 27th Brigade, RFA. The Major went on ahead to meet Colonel Onslow of the 27th and I brought on the battery. I was told to take it through the streets and down a steep hill to Petit Wasmes and to wait in a square with a fountain in it.

It was easier said than done. The shelling was now intense and it had been hard enough to get down the steep hill that led to Petit Wasmes, to keep the horses calm with the constant thud of explosions and the zing of bullets whipping above their heads and ricocheting off the rooftops. The brakesmen sweated and strained, the drivers pulled hard on the reins, the horses neighed and whinnied as the weight of the guns bore down on them and their hooves scrabbled to keep a foothold on the villainous curves of the close-set slippery cobbles.

Lt. R. A. Macleod, 80 Battery, XV Brigade, R.F.A., 5th Division,
B.E.F.

As we were advancing, an infantry officer warned me that the square was being heavily shelled but luckily the shelling stopped just as we entered it. A company of infantry was taking cover under the houses on the north side and the Mairie on the south side already had several shellholes in it. We just had room to form up in line, at half-intervals. There we waited. There was a furious fight going on not far to the north of us and, with the bullets still flying over our heads, the wait was most unpleasant. Eventually the Major returned with Colonel Onslow. They had gone to reconnoitre the new position and when they rode up a railway embankment only three hundred yards to the north of us they found that they were actually in our front line! Of course the Germans had started shooting at them wholesale. They were no distance away. In fact, they had already overrun the position *we* had been told to move into. So there was nothing for it but to struggle back up the hill again. The Major and Colonel Onslow went ahead to look for another position in the back gardens of some houses and I waited with the guns in the main street at the top of the hill.

It was a broad street, but there was hardly room to move. Now that daylight had come and the battle was pounding nearer and nearer the roadway was in turmoil with hurrying civilians intent on getting away before it was too late. Macleod's gun-section had squeezed in with difficulty behind the guns already there, waiting, like Macleod himself, for orders, and the narrow space of roadway that was not filled by their wagons and limbers, by the restive horses shifting uneasily in the shafts, by groups of dismounted gunners breakfasting as best they could on what the Army was pleased to call 'the unexpended portion' of yesterday's ration. In most cases this amounted to little more than dry and brick-like Army ration biscuits which some dissatisfied nibblers suspected had been left over from the Boer War a dozen years before. But hunger was a good sauce. Rory Macleod offered two of his own biscuits to an officer of the 27th Brigade who was eyeing them enviously and he consumed them with obvious relish.

Neither Lieutenant Chapman nor his men had seen so much as a crumb of food since Saturday evening, but they had seen plenty of action. Between munches he favoured Macleod with a lurid account. That morning they had been forced out of their position which by then, he assured Macleod, was 'literally in the front-line trench' but not before they had inflicted tremendous damage on the Germans.

'They came at us over a bank directly in front of us and as soon as they topped it we let them have it. The range was seventy yards, so we were firing at them point blank! I've never seen anything like it. Legs, arms, heads – they were flying all over the place! We absolutely smashed them! They simply *melted* away. Then the blighters got some machine-guns into action and, at that distance, we were like sitting ducks. So we had to get out of it and, by Jove, it was a close shave!' As proof of his story Lieutenant Chapman pointed out with some pride the hole made by a bullet which, miraculously, had passed harmlessly through the skirt of his service jacket. Macleod was suitably impressed. His own experience of getting the guns away in the face of the enemy seemed almost tame by comparison.

In his ears the sound of the gunfire seemed to be drawing ominously closer by the minute and there was still no sign of the Major and Colonel Onslow. The two officers had been gone less than ten minutes but, nevertheless, Macleod began to wonder uneasily if they had not already been killed or captured. It was galling to be hanging about with nothing to do but wait.

Those civilians, on the other hand, who had not already departed were determined to hang about no longer. They were pouring out of the houses now carrying babies, clutching small children by the hand, the older ones at their heels staggering under the weight of suitcases, heavy baskets, and even bedsheets and tablecloths hastily tied into unwieldy bundles knobbly with household possessions. A lucky few had handcarts. Others had resorted to wheelbarrows. And Macleod watched with mingled pity and amusement as one desperate householder stomped off with a bundle over his shoulder pushing a querulous grandmother before him in a barrow, deaf to her complaints.

Colonel Onslow now reappeared, shouting to Macleod as he dismounted, 'I am afraid the situation has changed. You must go into action at once. I will write fresh orders for the Major – I've left him in the back gardens of those houses over there – and I will also write a note to the commanding officer of the KOSBs to ask for a platoon to cover them, because I fear I must send you into an exposed position.'

The Colonel pulled a notebook from his pocket and, seeing a kitchen chair just inside the open doorway of a cottage, pulled it on to the road and sat down the better to write his messages, while Macleod ordered the section to prepare to move off. He returned to find the Colonel engaged in an undignified squabble. The occupants of the house were ready now to depart and the indignant owner, anxious to secure his property, stood angrily shaking the back of the chair in an effort to dislodge the Colonel, who was swatting him with the notepad as he might do a troublesome fly. Both men were red with rage and shouting at full pitch. A loud explosion, too close for comfort, resolved the argument. The householder reluctantly let go, locked his front door, picked up his bundle and made off with his tearful family as fast as their assorted baggage would allow. Macleod moved the battery off in the direction the Colonel had indicated and set off at a sprint to find the Major. In minutes the street was empty. The refugees had disappeared in the distance. All that remained was a solitary chair standing incongruously at the roadside and very shortly a well-placed shell reduced it to matchwood.

Lt. R. A. Macleod, 80 Battery, XV Brigade, R.F.A., 5th Division,
B.E.F.

On my return I found the battery in action and firing over open
sights. The target was a large body of Germans massing near a slag
heap nearly due east and moving south. The range was 2,400 yards.
We also had to keep under observation the park in the valley below
us in case the Germans tried to advance through it.

The situation was rather puzzling. We must now be on the right
flank of the 5th Division. What had happened to the 3rd Division?
Had it retired, or had the Germans driven a wedge between the 5th
and 3rd Divisions?

My section was on the right. The honour of firing the first round
in the battery would have been ours, but No. 1 gun could not clear
a tree close in front of it, so the centre section had been used
for ranging. Our field of view was a good deal blocked by numerous
slag heaps. The church on the left of the battery was an RAMC
dressing station, and a Union Jack and Red Cross flag hung from
the steeple.

We had not been long in action before the Germans replied. One
salvo fell short of the battery and shortly after another came over us,
nearly in our wagon-lines. They seemed to be ranging on us. But
after that shells were falling all over the place, some very near us.
Perhaps they were searching for us, or they may have thought the
church was an artillery observation post and were trying to shell that.
The houses round the main street were being heavily shelled, and a
cloud of brick dust and shell-smoke hung in the air. Our wagon-lines
escaped by a miracle.

I was now ordered to limber up my section and bring it into action
to support the retirement of the 2nd Battalion of the KOYLI. The
Captain went on to find a position taking with him my Sergeant
Prior. We withdrew at a trot by a gate in rear of the battery and along
the main street. This was under shellfire, and bricks were flying in all
directions. One salvo fell in the street just ahead of us. We passed over
the spot and turned to the right. Another shell pitched on the pavement
on the right, about thirty yards ahead, filling the street with dense
yellow smoke. My horse shied at this, but I got him through. One
shell pitched under one of Chapman's ammunition wagons in the
road, luckily without exploding the ammunition, and knocked off
and wounded the gunners on the wagon and hit all the horses, but
none was killed. We had passed them when Sergeant Prior galloped
up and said I had overshot the mark. Luckily the street was wide and

I was able to reverse without difficulty – just in time for immediately afterwards another shell pitched on the spot we had just left.

We went up a lane off the main street. The position was more or less in the open and exposed, so we unlimbered behind some houses and ran the guns up by hand to positions in rear of a low bank. The ammunition wagons were twenty yards away under cover of the houses and ammunition supply was by hand. I observed from the bank between the guns.

Young Jimmy Naylor had the most heady day of his life. It was as if the highlights of every adventure tale of derring-do he had ever read had been rolled into one stupendous adventure. All day he had stuck closer to the Colonel than his shadow, and he had seen it all. He had seen the dense grey masses of the enemy and watched them advancing, quite free from apprehension because as an avid reader and fervent follower of Mr G. A. Henty's adventure yarns, he knew that even when all seemed lost, the British always won. He had watched the shells exploding among them and with difficulty resisted a strong temptation to throw his cap in the air. He exulted in the noise, sniffed the pungent smell of cordite with an expression of bliss that might have put the Bisto Kids to shame and trotted about at the Colonel's behest like an enthusiastic terrier. He was as oblivious of the noise, the carnage, the danger as if he had been watching from the moon. If he had had a tail, he would have wagged it. He had even seen a cavalry charge. Admittedly it was in the distance and so far to the left that they had disappeared in a matter of moments, but the sight of the horses galloping, albeit in a cloud of dust, the long lances of the riders, the flying pennants, the glint of steel that even at that distance he imagined he could see thrilled him to the core. It was almost the crowning moment of his day.

But one matchless moment was still to come. It came when things were going badly, when it was time for the guns to go – and to go fast if they were to escape being captured by the enemy. But the guns could not move until the limbers and horse teams came up to trail them away. It was Jimmy who had taken the order to the transport, waiting with the ammunition wagons in the shelter of the village a quarter of a mile away. Now he was back, breathless and excited, waiting for them to appear. The infantry had been pushed back. They were close in front now firing on a mass of German soldiers whose ragged ranks faltered occasionally in their withering fire and then surged on like an incoming tide. Behind the racket of the firing Jimmy listened fascinated to the voice of their officer, steady and cool as any heroic character in one of his well-thumbed books.

Trumpeter J. Naylor, 3rd Division, R.F.A., B.E.F.

He was saying, *At four hundred . . .At three-fifty. . . At three hundred.*
The rifles blazed, but still the Germans came on. They were getting
nearer and nearer and for the first time I began to feel rather anxious
and frightened. They weren't an indeterminate mass any more – you
could actually pick out details, see them as individual men, coming
on, and coming on. And the officer, still as cool as anything, was
saying, *At two-fifty. . . At two hundred. . .* And then he said, *ten rounds
rapid!* And the chaps opened up – and the Germans just fell down like
logs. I've never seen anything like it, the discipline, the fire discipline
of those troops, I've never forgotten that, I was so impressed. As a
boy of sixteen I was simply astounded. I thought, '*What* a marvellous
army we are!' The attack was completely repulsed – probably not for
long, but it was long enough for us to get the guns away. It saved us.

But there was no time to gloat or to savour the immensity of relief for
the limbers had arrived, the guns were hooked up and the Colonel, turning
to Jimmy, gave him the order to sound the trot. It was the first time he
had sounded it in action. Putting the trumpet to his lips, taking a deep
breath to expand a chest already swelling with pride and elation, Jimmy
sounded the high, clear call that sent the guns galloping out of the battle
to safety.

The guns had to be saved, for in the face of the weight of German artillery
the Army could ill afford to lose them. A man was expendable. If he fell,
his rifle could be picked up and fired by another, but guns were less easily
replaced. For years, by long Army tradition, it had been dinned into
succeeding generations of gunners and infantry alike that it was a shameful
thing to allow the guns to fall into the hands of the enemy. There was no
trophy of war more highly prized than a captured artillery piece. The cry
of 'Save the guns' had rung down through the annals of war since the days
of Marlborough.

Infantry and gunners worked hand in hand throughout the long day's
fight. If the musketry of the infantry had saved the day on the 23rd, it was
the shooting of the gunners which saved the Army on the 24th. Later they
called it Shrapnel Monday. The Germans, advancing shoulder to shoulder
in wave after wave, dense-packed in close formation, presented such targets
as battery commanders, experienced in open-scale skirmishing, had dreamed
of only in their wildest dreams. Time after time, as small groups of infantry
fought desperate rearguard actions while their comrades slipped away, the
guns blasted the enemy to a standstill.

Lt. R. A. Macleod, 80 Battery, XV Brigade, R.F.A., 5th Division, B.E.F.

The KOYLIs were holding a slag heap about 2,000 yards to the north of us. We could tell our troops by their round flat-topped caps which appeared white in the sunlight. We could see the KOYLIs firing at something beyond them, and German shells were bursting among them with a greenish smoke. Nearer was another slag heap with a high conical mound on which was one of our machine-guns.

We could not see much beyond the KOYLIs but they were obviously in the front line and hotly engaged, so we opened fire beyond them at a range of 2,400 yards. One of our howitzer batteries was also assisting the KOYLI by dropping shells beyond the slag heap.

We had only been firing a few minutes when the Germans replied, but most of their shells fell twenty or thirty yards to our left in an open field.

Soon after this, the KOYLI began retiring by small detachments at a time, and they finally took up a position along a bank about 1,000 yards away. We kept up our shelling, but no Germans appeared to follow up the retirement.

A motor-cyclist now appeared but would not come up to the guns because he said he did not like the sound of the guns firing. I think he must have been a university man who had joined up at the beginning of the war. I went back to him, and he gave me a signal ordering me to retire. I quickly limbered up and trotted out by a lane which led round a copse in our rear as the main street was still being heavily shelled. We had to cross about fifty yards of open ground which we did at a trot, and, although in full view, not a shot was fired at us.

On rejoining the main road we found it blocked with marching infantry, but we fitted into a gap and retired south-westwards. At every halt I rode up and down looking for the remainder of the battery. I eventually found them ahead of me and managed to join up when the road became a little clearer. As the country became more open, the infantry took to the fields on each side, letting the guns and transport have the road.

As we retired we passed the other two batteries of our brigade in action to the west of the road, somewhere in the neighbourhood of Elouges. I could hear the range being called out, *2,400*. The Germans apparently were moving parallel to us to the west, but we on the road were concealed from them by a slight rise in the ground. The majors of both batteries were observing from seats on tipped-up limber poles.

The 119th Battery was also somewhere near here, and its Major Alexander got the VC for withdrawing his guns under heavy fire.

Elouges was far to the left, more than halfway along the road to Valenciennes, and Macleod was right. The Germans were creeping westwards, walking sideways like a crab and their plan was to hook out a crab-like claw, to reach round the left flank of the British force and, groping to its rear, to nip off its line of retreat. The fretting British commanders fully realised that so many men had been captured on Mons Sunday that, though every British soldier had fought like ten, the Germans had easily deduced that a mere handful of men stood between them and the road to Paris and that the small British force must be sadly depleted by losses the previous day. It was true that the Germans had lost far more men and their front-line soldiers were shaken and battle-weary, but they could be relieved and the gaps in their ranks easily filled by fresh troops surging down the highroads from the north. It was clear to the enemy that the British could have precious few reserves. They would be easy meat – and a fine prize for the Kaiser.

Around Elouges the main body of the 5th Division had already retired and the rearguard were preparing to follow them when Sir Charles Fergusson received a report that gave him considerable food for thought. It came from the Royal Flying Corps and it came in the nick of time. Captain Shephard's Avro had been airborne by half-past four that morning and hovering over the German right flank by first light. He was back with his report by breakfast-time but the Flying Corps was on the move, travelling south in a fleet of lorries to set up a new HQ at Le Cateau. It had taken Shephard a long time and a lot of hedge-hopping to find one convoy among many and but for a big red pantechnicon among the transport he might not have found them at all. It was well past ten o'clock before the vital information reached General Fergusson, Commander of the 5th Division, and when it did it shook him to the core.

Shephard and his observer, Lieutenant Bonham-Carter, had seen the Germans, and they had seen more of them than they could count to the nearest thousand. Some twenty miles to the north long columns of troops were passing through Grammont and Lessines and veering westwards. Beyond, and even further to the west, was another force, so large that it snaked over ten miles of road between Ath and Leuze. The head of the snake was already coiling south on a curve that would bring it behind the BEF and thus encircle it. They were still some hours' march away but on the way back, swooping recklessly low over the country north of Elouges and Quiévrain, the fliers saw signs of more immediate danger. A whole army corps was there. Split into four echelons like the prongs of a fork, the Germans were massing for an advance. Dodging lower still, for the smoke from the burnt-out villages still drifted a grey veil in the air, they were dismayed to see whole batteries of German guns had moved up to cover the attack. They could see them digging in along the Mons-Valenciennes railway, along the Mons-Valenciennes road, and on high ground to the north. When their artillery was ready, the Germans would be able to move forward and there would be nothing and no one to stop them.

General Fergusson's reserves were pitiful. He had one battalion of Cheshires, one battalion of Norfolks, and a single battery of guns in reserve. The heavy cavalry, rearguard of the whole division, had already withdrawn. Luckily, they had not gone far. Luckily, they could move fast. They rapidly took up position in the village of Audregnies and, by noon, the Norfolks and Cheshires had moved up and spread north across the mile that lay between the outskirts of Audregnies and the railway in front of Elouges. It was a long stretch for a small force to hold but it was high ground and

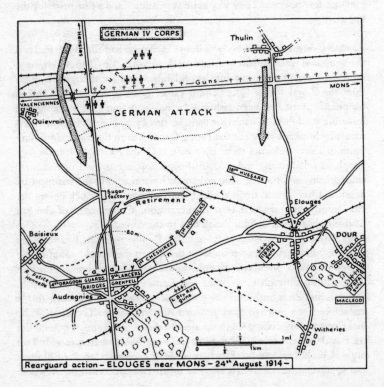

Rearguard action - ELOUGES near MONS - 24th August 1914 -

the land in front fell away in a natural glacis — just such a slope as might have been designed by the builders of some ancient fortress to expose an enemy intent on taking it to the vicious fire of bowmen intent on defending it. Now, in late August at the end of the harvest, it was covered with corn stooks and the air was sweet with the scent of fresh-cut grain.

It was the best that could be done. There was no time to think of digging trenches. The troops would have to make the best of it and take what natural cover they could find. The enemy came streaming from Quiévrain making straight for the infantry across the valley, with another wave coming out of a wood beyond them in close-packed formations that hinted at thousands more at their backs. If the Germans were to be stopped it was up to the cavalry to do it.

The cavalry charged.

The episode did not loom large in the bald official despatches but soon newspapers and periodicals, starved of instant victories, gratified their readers with colourful accounts in prose and in verse dripping with glory. There were no eyewitness accounts but there were artists to supply the omission with grandiloquent 'impressions' — rich in flashing sabres, rearing horses, cowering Germans, and so full of action that it was almost impossible to hear the shouts and yells above the thundering of hooves.

The reality was a little different. In Marlborough's day, even in Wellington's, the wide valley, bounded on the north by the great highway from Mons to Valenciennes, might have been ideal cavalry country where the troopers could have galloped hell-for-leather and wheeled and charged as easily as they had so often rehearsed these classic manoeuvres under the approving eye of General de Lisle on the wide reaches of Salisbury Plain. But now there were obstacles.

Roads and tracks cut across the valley. There was a main-line railway and a network of trolley tracks to serve the pithead and slag heap, and to carry the beet-crops for processing at the sugar factory across the fields. The fields were hedged and, worse, the valley was patchworked with small allotments each neatly fenced off from its neighbour. It was not the shells, exploding with deadly accuracy, that stopped the cavalry in its dash towards the enemy; it was not the German rifles that thwarted them, nor the merciless machine-guns that started up at once. They were not thrown into confusion by the stampede of riderless horses or the loss of troop-leaders hit at the head of their men. It was the tangle of wires and fences that brought them headlong to a halt. Horses tripped and fell on low-level signal wires running along the rail-track, or plunged into ballast-pits in a welter of flying hooves. They slipped and screamed and tumbled across railway lines, breaking their own limbs and more than one rider's neck. Galloping blind through clouds of cordite, heavy with coaldust, they ran full-tilt into fences and were caught, struggling, in the barbed wire.

It was gallant, it was reckless, it was glorious. And it was entirely fruitless.

Major Tom Bridges, whose squadron of the 4th Dragoon Guards had encountered the vanguard of the Germans at Soignies two days earlier, charged with the rest.

Major T. Bridges, 4th Dragoon Guards, The Cavalry Division, B.E.F.

Imagining that it was a matter of chasing away cavalry patrols, I debouched at the head of my squadron from the northern entrance of the village at a gallop, drawing swords as we went and dashing up a lane between wire fences on to a rise where there was a solitary cottage. But as we topped the rise we came under heavy rifle fire and my horse fell down on his nose with a broken leg, and most of the squadron and machine-gun section seemed to gallop over me, and I received a heavy blow in the face. I saw them swinging off to the right and then lost consciousness for a time.

I recovered to find myself inside the cottage which held one or two Red Cross orderlies and some wounded, whose rifles had been piled in a corner. There was also an old Frenchman and his wife who had put up the shutters, for bullets were pattering against the walls. Stiff and sore, I got a man to help me on to a chair where I could see through the fanlight over the door. I could scarcely believe my eyes! Marching through the corn in open order and perfect formation, with fixed bayonets glinting in the sun, were line upon line of grey-green German infantry. The nearest could not have been two hundred yards away.★

Later a legend grew up round Bridges' adventure. He had got as far as the sugar factory, they said, and there, finding himself surrounded by Germans, had taken a flying leap through a first-floor window straight on to the back of a charger, conveniently waiting below it to gallop him off. The reality was a little less heroic. It was true that he had gone through an open window at the back of the cottage (the back door being locked and barred) but his exit, as he later ruefully admitted, was more like a 'clown in pantomime' than with the dash and panache of a hero of old. He collapsed in a heap in the back garden and was picked out of a gooseberry bush by Shoeing-Corporal Old. But there *was* a horse. It was a chestnut, bleeding from a wound in the neck, but it was a horse nevertheless.

★ From the account in his book, *Alarms and Excursions.*

Major T. Bridges, 4th Dragoon Guards, The Cavalry Division, B.E.F.

I crawled on to his back and we ambled off in the direction of the village, sole target it seemed for a whole German army corps until we reached dead ground and the cover of the houses. Just outside the village at the side of the lane were a couple of guns in action, firing away at the advancing German hordes as steadily as if they had been on the rifle range at Okehampton.

The horse was making heavy weather of the journey. It was as much as he could do to drag himself along and, at the top of a hill on the south side of the village, his legs gave way altogether. The big chestnut lay at the side of the road breathing with difficulty, his eyes dulled with pain, his chestnut coat matted with clotted blood. Bridges drew his revolver, steeled himself, and shot him through the head. His own legs were none too steady, he was in acute pain and he strongly suspected that his jaw was broken. The village was quite deserted. The houses were shuttered, there was no sign of any troops and although he could see the cavalry rallying a mile away on a hill, Bridges had no idea what had happened and no idea what to do next. He sat down by the roadside to consider the matter. Presently there was a clatter of hooves and the 9th Lancers came trotting briskly through the deserted village. But although they were retiring and clearly in haste, the troopers did not seem in the least downcast, and Tom's friend Francis Grenfell riding in the lead was positively elated. He looked much the worse for wear. His clothes were full of bullet holes and his left hand, bleeding copiously, was wrapped in a handkerchief, the Germans were close on their heels but he was grinning all over his face. Under the very noses of the Germans, Grenfell and his troop had just saved some guns from being captured on the railway and they were still in a high state of excitement. They had no spare horse and no means of helping Bridges in his predicament but, as Grenfell assured him, some of his own men were coming up behind them.

Bridges' face was paralysed. He longed to ask Grenfell what was happening, what *had* happened, but he simply could not speak. By grunts and signs he managed to convey that he would wait where he was until help arrived. Grenfell nodded, waved and rode on leaving Bridges disconsolate by the roadside. The minutes passed. There was no sign of his men and after a fruitless attempt to hobble on, Bridges sank down again on the grass verge and resigned himself to the fact that the next soldiers he saw would be dressed in Kaiser's grey. It was then, as he looked anxiously down the road, that Bridges saw the most welcome sight of his life. It was a Rolls-Royce, a blue and silver sports model, and the cavalry signals officer was at the wheel.

He was scouring the country for stragglers. Bridges dragged himself painfully to his feet and, thanking his lucky stars, collapsed in the passenger seat.

He was incapable of answering Jackson's questions but his plight was self-evident. The car roared off along the line of retreat and presently, when they came to a large farm where a Red Cross flag hung lazily from a gable, Bridges was set down, patched up, given a hot drink, and put to bed by the farmer's wife on a heap of straw in the attic. Still in severe pain, but consoled by the doctor's diagnosis that he was suffering no more than a splintered cheek bone, bad bruising, and slight concussion, Bridges pulled the rough blanket around him and slept as if he lay on a feather bed. It was just before three in the afternoon.

At about the same time, at General Lanrezac's headquarters, Captain Spears was bearding the lion in the lion's den and he was shaking in his shoes. He knew he was in breach of etiquette, he might well be in breach of discipline, and the General was likely to erupt in such a fury that he would order him to be shot for his temerity. At least the General had, courteously enough, agreed to see him and now Spears stood in front of the great man in the small classroom he had requisitioned for his office. Lanrezac sat on a platform at the teacher's desk. Spears stood to attention in front of him and felt like a guilty schoolboy.

But his passionate concern for the plight of the British Army, the knowledge that General Lanrezac's Fifth Army was retiring rapidly and practically unharassed while the full brunt of the German push was falling on the British, gave him courage. He was also inspired by the encouraging attitude of some of the French officers. Naturally they sympathised with Lanrezac's desire to save his army to fight another day, but there was a matter of honour at stake and, since the French had virtually placed the British in a dangerous forward position, it would be dishonourable in the extreme to leave them there without some show of support. Mustering all his powers of tact and persuasion, Spears launched into his speech.

The gap between the two armies was rapidly widening and the French were already a day's march south from the isolated BEF, still fighting its way back from Mons. It was true that the Fourth French Army was also pulling back and that, since it joined General Lanrezac's right, his own army must fall back alongside. But, argued Spears, if the General were to use only part of his troops – particularly his Reserve Division which was closest to the British – to deliver an attack, then that would divert at least some of the Germans' attention and take the heat, even momentarily, off the BEF.

Spears' confidence mounted as he put his case. He tried as best he could to imply no criticism of the General's dispositions but, carried away by his eloquence, he finished up with an impassioned plea which astonished himself as much as it infuriated the General.

'*Mon Général*, if by your action the British Army is annihilated, England will never pardon France, and France will not be able to pardon you!'

The General erupted. He shouted, he ranted, he raved. He banged his fist on the table and he turned red with rage. Afterwards, in something approaching a state of shock, Spears could remember hardly a single word of his tirade. But he had given General Lanrezac food for thought and in minutes he had issued an order.

Capt. E. L. Spears, 11th Hussars.

An officer came out and said to me: 'Attack orders are about to be issued. They are to be taken by aeroplane to Le Cateau.' I felt like turning somersaults.

The whole Staff began to buzz with excitement. They did not take long to draw up the orders, but when I saw them I was bitterly disappointed, for they were not attack orders at all, but a preliminary order to the XVIII Corps not to retire beyond Solre-le-Château in view of a possible attack next day (25th) in co-operation with the British, in which the Reserve divisions were to participate.★ When I arrived at Le Cateau with a copy of this order, the first person I met was General Wilson. I told him my news. He shook his head. 'Too late,' he said.

In the circumstances, with the BEF punch-drunk with fatigue, painfully extricating itself from its perilous position and the Germans stretching out to grip it by the throat, the idea of a 'possible attack' with the French was a figment of General Lanrezac's imagination.

But Solre-le-Château was well south of Maubeuge and still a good day's march south of the BEF. But it was something that some of the French

---

★ The order read, QG, Chimay, August 24th, 1515.
General Order.
The XVII Corps will not fall back beyond Solre-le-Château. It is possible that it will be ordered to attack to-morrow in the direction of Thuin at the same time as the British Army, in the event of the latter's attacking towards Mons. It would in that case be linked up with the British Army by the Group of Reserve Divisions debouching from Maubeuge. The Group of Reserve Divisions will hold itself ready to debouch offensively, if it receives orders to do so, from the fortified camp of Maubeuge on the left bank of the Sambre so as to link up the attack of the XVIII Corps with the offensive of the British Army towards Mons.
Lanrezac.

at least would not be retiring further. With a bit of luck, the British might be able to catch them up, and luck, for the moment, seemed to be on their side. It would be going too far to say that they had fought the Germans to a standstill, but there were distinct signs that the enemy was beginning to slow down.

The rearguards, fighting desperate miniature battles, had saved the Army. Here and there tiny groups of men had been outnumbered by hundreds to one, but few had been overwhelmed. Time and again they had fought almost to the last round of ammunition, time and again they had retired in haste with the enemy on their heels, but they were not defeated. They had fought so fiercely and dealt out such punishment that, even when they had left their beleaguered positions, the Germans had hesitated to follow far in their footsteps. It was one thing for a vast army to beat a small one, standing fast to fight ignorant of the odds. It was an entirely different matter to conquer it while it backed off in an orderly retreat. The very size of their army made it hard for the Germans to follow.

As the men of the British Expeditionary Force had dug themselves into Mons so, leap-frogging backwards, they dug themselves out. They had not turned their backs on the enemy. They had retired in a series of carefully calculated moves, changing places methodically, turning to dig in on a new position to meet the enemy. Covered by their comrades, manoeuvring and sidestepping, retiring, stopping, fighting as they gradually moved back, the Army slipped away, until only small isolated groups were left to keep the Germans guessing.

The Germans might have chased an opponent who was palpably on the run. As it was, they were in no hurry to follow up. They had been hit hard and the BEF had made them pay a heavy price for the land they had won at Mons. They needed time to draw breath, to rest their soldiers, to see to their casualties, to deal with their prisoners, and to bring Reserve battalions to the line. Above all they needed time – time for the troops, now marching down through Belgium to complete their great wheel westwards. Anxious though the Germans were to set off down the road to Paris, it was no part of their plan to chase the British before them as they went, especially since they were showing such an awkward propensity to turn and fight. They had no desire to see the British in full retreat. The Germans wanted them to stay put until their great left wing, now almost upon them, could sweep round their backs and cut off their line of retreat. Then, attacked from all sides, they would be easily demolished.

There was another cogent reason why the Germans were not anxious to send the British fleeing southwards, and why they had not pursued them with determination. Not far behind the British line lay the fortress town of Maubeuge, protected, it was true, by mighty walls, by a widespread complex of defences and by powerful guns. But the Germans too had guns, great siege guns captured, ironically, from the fortress towns of Namur and Liège. They were the very guns on which the Belgians had depended to halt the invasion in its tracks. Namur and Liège had been captured. Maubeuge would be captured too. And if, instead of being put to a full-scale flight, the British could be pushed gradually back, if they could be manoeuvred into the shelter of the fortress, then their contemptibly small army (as the Kaiser had neatly described it) would be waiting, neatly packaged, ripe for capture, with no possible means of escape. The British, in fact, could be left to stew inside the fortress while the German army made its dispositions and dealt with them in its own good time. It would take only a little patience and a reasonably small number of men to force Maubeuge to surrender and the British, trapped inside it, to sue for peace. It would be merely a matter of time. Meanwhile, having left sufficient men to lay siege to Maubeuge and the fortifications round it, the bulk of the German army could sweep past and press on without delay to Paris.

The town of Maubeuge stood within ramparts designed some centuries earlier by the military architect, Vauban. It was surrounded by a series of outpost forts, strategically positioned to command important roads. They had been neglected in recent years but for the last month the French had been busy. The woods in front had been thinned and cleared. Buildings which might obstruct the guns were blown up or demolished and as the BEF had marched north to Mons they had been cheered by the sight of deep defensive trench systems, newly dug, protected by entanglements of heavy wire. The system stretched from fort to fort. It ran round twenty square miles. It looked impregnable. It was manned by thirty-five thousand troops of the French Reserve and it marked the point where the British and French had been intended to link up.

To Sir John French the temptation to retire into this haven was almost irresistible. All day it had gnawed in his mind like a dog worrying a bone. The Commander-in-Chief was not a happy man. The one bright spot of his day had been the sight of the 4th Division detraining at Le Cateau and nothing else he had seen or heard in the course of it had given him the least cause for satisfaction. Early in the afternoon, on the road from Le Cateau to Bavai, his driver had experienced considerable difficulty in making headway through streams of refugees flying from Mons.

Sir John French

They were lying about the fields in all directions, and blocking the roads with carts and vans in which they were trying to carry off as much of their worldly goods as possible. The whole country-side showed those concrete evidences of disturbance and alarm which brought home to all our minds what this retreat meant and all that it might come to mean.

After much delay from these causes I reached Bavai about 2.30 p.m. and it was with great difficulty that my motor could wind its way through the mass of carts, horses, fugitives and military baggage trains which literally covered almost every yard of space in the small town. The temporary advanced Headquarters were established in the market place, the appearance of which defies description. The babel of voices, the crying of women and children, mingled with the roar of the guns and the not far distant crack of rifles and machine-guns, made a deafening noise, amidst which it was most difficult to keep a clear eye and tight grip on the rapidly changing course of events.*

Although all the windows were open to the summer sun, it was stiflingly hot in the Mairie, and French's Chief of Staff, General Murray, was working in shirtsleeves. He had also ripped off his collar and tie and unbuttoned his shirt to the waist. The room was crowded with Staff Officers, collating information, issuing orders, awaiting instructions, poring over maps. Murray outlined the situation. The retirement was proceeding 'fairly well'. The left flank was a worry, but the action of the cavalry and the 19th Brigade on the left had greatly decreased the pressure on the 5th Division. This was a small comfort, but General French was well aware that the French were still falling back and that the Expeditionary Force was isolated. He knew from intelligence reports that his army was vastly outnumbered and that the Kaiser's was growing larger and stronger by the hour. He knew that he must make a decision, and that he must make it now.

Maubeuge beckoned to French like a beacon in the night. And yet he hesitated. He crossed to the open window and, turning his back to the noise in the room, looked down into the square. He thought. There was something, *something* niggling at the back of his mind, something he could not quite put his finger on. And then, in a flash of recollection, it came to him.

In years to come he often retold the story. He remembered his time at Staff College and his studies of the Franco-Prussian War. He remembered the example of the French Marshal Bazaine who, faced by the Prussian army in 1870, had retired into the fortress of Metz. He remembered, particularly, the damning judgement of Sir Edward Hamley, an historian for whom French had considerable respect. In writing of the episode,

* From French's book, *1914*

Hamley had described it as *the anxiety of the temporising mind which prefers postponement of a crisis to vigorous enterprise*. The Commander-in-Chief could see the words as plainly as if he had the book before him. *In clinging to Metz*, Hamley had continued, *he acted like one who, when the ship is foundering, lays hold of the anchor*.

The General's mind was made up. He turned back into the room and addressed his Chief of Staff. 'We will continue the retreat,' he said. And, beckoning Murray to follow him, he crossed to a map tacked to the wall, traced with his finger a line that ran from Le Cateau to Cambrai and ordered the British Expeditionary Force to retire to it.

When he left to return to his headquarters, it took the General's car some time to negotiate the streets of Bavai before it could turn into the crowded road to Le Cateau. The pathetic flow of refugees was thicker than ever, and their progress was slow, for now there were soldiers herding them into more orderly processions, strenuously trying to keep them from straggling, so that part of the road at least could be kept comparatively clear for the troops falling back on Bavai and passing beyond it to rest and bivouac in the fields on the other side.

As his car inched past, the General had leisure to observe his ragged battalions. They could hardly be said to have a spring in their step. Many were limping painfully. All were hollow-eyed and, to the last man, they looked dead beat.

Chapter 10

All roads led to Bavai. It was no more than a few miles as the crow flies from any point of the Front but it had taken the BEF many hours of methodical leap-frogging to get there, falling back, waiting – and frequently fighting – on a new line to cover the retirement of their comrades. And then it had to be done all over again until, at last, they were able to reassemble and plod towards Bavai.

It had taken the Worcesters fourteen hours to get there.

Capt. H. F. Stacke, 4th Bttn., The Worcestershire Regt., B.E.F.

The order to retire reached the Battalion about eight o'clock in the morning. Messages were sent forward to the trenches that the companies were to retire in succession through Frameries village and were to form up south of the houses. In accordance with the orders the companies left their trenches and fell back through Frameries.

The wretched inhabitants of the village poured out of their houses in a terror-stricken mob. In the streets all order was lost. Runaway horses and shrieking, sobbing women broke up the ranks of the platoons, while the houses around collapsed under the German shells. But the Worcestershire lads kept their heads. Orders were shouted to re-form on the road beyond the village and officers and men made their way as best they could through the stampede. On the road south of the village the companies were halted and reassembled. As if on peacetime training, the platoons closed up into column of fours and stood at ease. Rolls were called and every man was accounted for. The troops were cool and steady, in spite of the shells bursting among the houses close behind. When all was ready the Battalion sloped arms and marched off down the road, exactly as if they were marching back to barracks at Aldershot. 'I have always considered,' said an officer who saw much fighting afterwards, 'that this reassembly of the Battalion after the utter disorder in the streets of Frameries was the finest possible example of the discipline of the Old Army.'*

---

* From his account in the Regimental History.

Lt. R. A. Macleod, 80 Battery, XV Brigade, R.F.A., 5th Division, B.E.F.

We had a very slow march with frequent halts. We fed the horses whenever possible from corn-stooks gathered from the fields but there was no sign of any water for them.

We turned off south towards Bavai, and about six p.m. came into a position of readiness facing north in a field evidently to cover the retreat through the bottleneck of Bavai, but no Germans appeared and we did not open fire. We took the opportunity to have a snack of bully beef and biscuits from our luncheon basket. We waited here

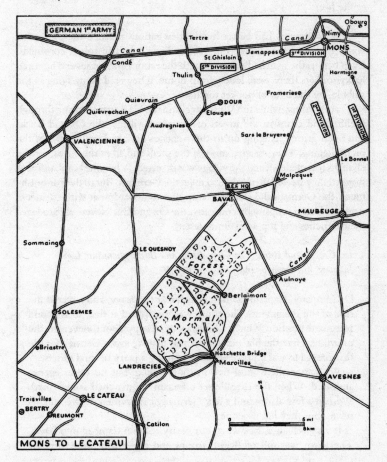

an hour, but nothing happened, so we continued our retreat to an area west of Bavai. It was pitch dark when we reached our bivouac in an orchard and we watered the horses as best we could from a small stream at the bottom. It was the first water they'd had, poor things, for twenty-four hours.

The Quartermaster-Sergeant went to look for rations and forage, but there were none that night. So we gave the horses a handful of oats apiece — that was all that remained of their feeds — and then we made ourselves a small fire. We raked up a tin of bully between five of us and for pudding we baked some apples we picked off the trees. Then we rolled ourselves up in our coats, and went to sleep round the fire.

The Worcesters had better luck. Their rations reached them — and it was a hot meal too, dished out as they bivouacked in rough cornfields. Even better, the mail had come up with the rations and for several hundred lucky soldiers there were letters from home. They read them, lying in the stubble, by the light of pocket torches.

That morning, while the Worcesters and the HLI were retiring through shellfire and chaos in the streets of Frameries village, the Ox and Bucks had been grimly hanging on to the trenches they had spent most of the night digging. They escaped most of the shells and all of the chaos, for the civilians had made off and the village was deserted. When the bombardment stopped they steeled themselves to meet the Germans. But to their astonishment, the Germans did not follow up their bombardment with an attack. An hour later, company by company, the Ox and Bucks were able to leave their trenches and slip away unmolested.

Lt. Crosse, 2nd Bttn., The Oxfordshire and Buckinghamshire Light Infantry, 5th Brigade, 2nd Division, B.E.F.

D Company, Captain Harden, was the last to leave, and covered the rear of the Regiment. The route was southward at first, to a second rearguard position which we began to occupy about eleven in the morning. Here the big excitement was that we saw a German for the first time. He was a prisoner brought in by a party of the Dorsets.

We stayed there until five in the evening, but no other enemy appeared! When the Brigade set off again we marched as rearguard. We had a few alarms and a few Germany cavalrymen showed themselves, but they left us alone.

It was well after dark when our weary column tramped into Bavai. The town was full of British troops and the streets were virtually blocked. After a long wait for orders (which involved the men standing drawn up in fours without any opportunity to fall out) the Brigade was directed to a stubble field beyond the town.

Extract from the diary of Lt.-Col. Davies, 2nd Bttn., The Oxfordshire and Buckinghamshire Light Infantry, B.E.F.

... and there at 10 p.m., dead tired, we bivouacked. We had been on our legs pretty continuously since yesterday morning. During the day our horses and transport rejoined us. The block on the road at times was very troublesome. Besides our troops there were great numbers of Belgians, fleeing from the Germans – men, women and children in crowds, some in wagons, some walking ...

The sight of those refugees was the most distressing aspect of the march. It was painful to reflect that only two days ago they had progressed through smiling villages on a wave of intoxicating welcome. But today, as the exhausted soldiers trudged away from the battle, the houses were shuttered, the villages seemed deserted, and the people fleeing with their pathetic bundles of belongings were scowling now. Some, more volatile than the rest, shook their fists and angry, tearful women shrieked *Perfides*. The Tommies were not accomplished linguists, but the meaning was clear enough, and they were shocked. They knew they had done well. They knew they had fought against huge odds and they were well aware that they had proved themselves more than a match for a foe who might have easily overwhelmed them. Few soldiers of the BEF were intimate with the sayings of Napoleon, but they would have agreed with his maxim that 'an orderly retreat is as good as a victory'. The Tommies did not feel that they had been defeated. And they were right.

Not all of them had got away. The better part of three thousand men had been left behind. But even before the casualties were totted up it was clear that there must be huge gaps in the ranks. A man knew which of his section were 'missing', and he did not need to refer to a casualty list to know which of his mates had been killed. As the soldiers inched back to safety they had seen churches, town halls, schools, farmsteads, where Red Cross flags hung from the gateposts, limp in the hot sun. Trudging past them, they had worried about the wounded they were leaving to the charity of the Germans.

Whole units were missing. Long after dark while exhausted battalions were still stumbling towards assembly points, brigadiers fumed and fretted and worried waiting for the reports that would tell them their brigades were complete. Some were a long time coming. Some never came at all.

During the pause while the German infantry caught its breath after the cavalry charge near Elouges the guns had been got away and most of the Norfolks had fallen back. They left a hundred wounded behind them and they also left behind the last platoon of all. The fact was that so many were felled by the shrapnel that sped them on their way no senior officer was left in a fit state to send the rearguard the order to get out. They held on fighting, alone and quite isolated in the path of what appeared to them to be the Kaiser's entire army.

The Cheshires also stayed where they were. Three separate messengers had been sent to tell them it was time to go. None had arrived. The Battalion was unaware that others had retreated although, as the afternoon went on, the lack of supporting gunfire became painfully obvious. And then, they lost the Colonel. The Germans were pressing in hard on both flanks. The machine-guns blazed, the Colonel was hit by three separate bullets and fell badly wounded. It did little to lift morale. It did a great deal to infuriate the men. They fell back to line the road that ran from Elouges to Audregnies, but the Germans had foreseen this move. Creeping out in front, they had cunningly placed two machine-guns in a dip two hundred yards away. Now they opened up, firing straight up the road. The Cheshires' own machine-guns, brought round at the double, blazed back, outshooting the German machine-gun teams, hammering them into silence. A sergeant shouted, 'Forward, boys!' and ten men rushed across the open, charging with bayonets at the ready, to finish the business and clear the Germans out. The Germans had actually run. Their wounded would run no more. And if the Cheshires had not behaved in strict accordance with the rules of the Geneva Convention, they were unrepentant. They felt a good deal better now. They only regretted that the Colonel had not been there to see their exploit.

They had gained the very briefest respite, but it was long enough for a few of the men to retire across the fields to the shelter of Audregnies Wood. Before the others could follow, the Germans attacked again. It took them three hours to overwhelm the Cheshires. At seven o'clock, when they had fired their last round of ammunition, when they were surrounded on all sides, when their number was reduced to a mere handful, they laid down their arms and, at last, they gave in.

Tom Bridges had a narrow escape. Despite the pain of his swollen face he had slept for many hours and it was after midnight when he awoke in his dark attic. He was stiff and cold and aching, and although all he could hear as he roused was the rustle of straw, he was sure that some other noise had disturbed him. Then it came again – the merest jingle of harness, a suggestion of movement and then the murmur of voices. Tom crawled cautiously to a tiny window in the eaves overlooking the farmyard. He could see with difficulty, but he could see enough to make out the spiked helmets of the horsemen below. A Uhlan patrol was circling the yard, staring at the darkened windows of the farm. Bridges held his breath. After a while the Germans rode off again and, since Bridges could think of nothing better to do, he lay down and went back to sleep. The Germans would clearly bag him in the morning. For the moment he was too tired to care.

But in the morning, to Bridges' delight and astonishment, there was no sign of the enemy. He was still in pain but his long sleep had restored his strength and he felt fit to walk. Borrowing a stick from his hostess, bidding her a hasty, grateful farewell, he hobbled off alone down the road as fast as he could propel his aching legs. He kept a sharp look-out for British troops, but it was a long time before he saw any.

To the relief of the British Army, the enemy had not taken advantage of the darkness, and after the violent activity of the day the night had been unexpectedly quiet. But the Germans had had their hands full. They had suffered huge casualties. Besides their own men there were large numbers of British wounded to be collected and carried back to hospitals behind their line. There were prisoners to be rounded up, marched off and interrogated. And there were the weary men of the assault troops whose crying need was for rest. It had taken the best part of the night to attend to all this business, to relieve exhausted regiments, to push fresh troops forward in their place, to weigh up reports from front-line battalions and try to guess the intentions of the British Commander-in-Chief and the number of men under his command. On balance, taking into account all the information they had gleaned, the Germans were convinced that the BEF would choose to stand on a line from Bavai to Valenciennes and that they would stand there and fight. German pilots had reported that a large contingent of troops was detraining near Le Cateau.* It would do no harm to give them time to reach the BEF and reinforce it. The whole army could then be outflanked and dealt with at one blow. All things considered, the British could safely be left to themselves for a short time, while the German's own right flank continued to march south-west to attack them from the rear.

The British Army and its commanders were unaware of the working of the German mind. They were merely thankful that the night had been quiet, that no enemy had appeared and that, in the morning, they were able to take to the road and make their departure undisturbed.

---

* This was the 4th Division.

Precisely what road they ought to take was a problem which had engaged the thoughts of the Staff for most of the night. Only the 5th Division was in the region of Bavai and the 3rd had fallen back to a position further east, resting on a ragged line between La Longueville and Maubeuge. The road behind the 3rd Division was clear. The route of the 5th Division was more of a problem. The forest of Mormal lay directly behind Bavai. It was a thick forest, almost seventeen kilometres long and, in places, more than ten kilometres across. Bavai was at the stalk of a rough pear-shape formed by the roads that ran south on either side of the forest, linked at its base by the road that wound from Landrecies to Le Cateau.

The forest was criss-crossed by narrow rides and a network of bridle-tracks, but they were felt to be unsuitable for the passage of the large numbers of troops the Army was anxious to keep together. There was no alternative but to send them down the roads. The eastern road would be safest, for the forest itself would lie between the troops and the great circling movement of the Germans to the west. If it continued at its present pace there was a real risk that troops travelling south-west on the other side might run straight into the Kaiser's clutches. But it was a risk they had to run and, if the troops got a move on, they might well get away with it. It took many hours to issue the marching orders, to determine the timetable, to appoint the rearguards, to make arrangements for stragglers and to send despatch riders carrying the vital instructions in search of the scattered battalions.

According to the timetable, the first contingent of troops should have left before dawn, but it was well past sunrise on what promised to be another scorching day before many units received their orders at all. It was not easy to rouse the Tommies, tired and weary as they were. They had been fighting, marching, digging continuously for forty-eight hours. Their few hours' rest had done little to restore them and, to the last man, they could have slept on without stirring for the rest of the day. Unrolling themselves reluctantly from greatcoats or blankets, rising stiff, sore and damp from the morning dew, struggling painfully to squeeze swollen feet into boots which some had been injudicious enough to remove, the Army gave vent to one great collective groan. It was a wonder that the Germans did not hear them.

But there was no sign of the Germans. Even their guns were silent. Shivering, breakfastless and unshaven (for most men had left their packs behind in the haste of yesterday's departure) the BEF prepared to slip away. Later in the day, when the right wing of the German advance sidestepped crabwise from the west and clawed round behind Bavai, its pincers closed on empty air.

★

It was a gruelling day for the men on the march. The sun shone relentlessly. The air was heavy and sultry with thunder. Dust swirled in clouds above the road, thrown up by shambling cavalcades of infantry, by the crush of desperate refugees and by some thousands of trundling wheels. There were six-horse farm wagons, dog-carts, handcarts, barrows, perambulators. There were gun-carriages, ammunition wagons, limbers, supply lorries. There were the spanking little Maltese carts. These were intended to carry the officers' kits, but before many miles had passed they were teetering under the weight of packs and greatcoats and anything else that would relieve the burden of the troops. There was no shade, no water, and no rest other than long waits on the road when the traffic came to a complete standstill. When that happened men slept where they stood. It happened often, and the progress of the BEF was excruciatingly slow.

There was hardly a Tommy or an officer who was not dazed and numb for lack of sleep, whose throat was not parched, whose eyes were not red and irritable, whose face was not streaked with rivulets of sweat, whose nerve-ends were not raw, and whose skin did not itch and stick, sweating, to his crumpled uniform. They were hot. They were dog-tired. But, although their morale was not what it had been on the way up to Mons, they were not completely dispirited.

Trumpeter J. Naylor, 3rd Division, R.F.A., B.E.F.

Whenever the column stopped, you fell off your horse and fell asleep. Then somebody started moving and we all got back on our horses and on we went again. But, under the circumstances, the morale was terrific. We were all quite sure that we were making a tactical move and that we were trying to lure the Germans into a trap. That's what we were told and it worked. We all believed it. Our morale was very high. We didn't think we were running *away* from the Germans. We thought we were luring them on, that the retreat was just a ruse and that when we'd got far enough back we would turn round and drive the Germans back again. And, of course, eventually that's what we did.

Lt. R. A. Macleod, 80 Battery, XV Brigade, R.F.A., 5th Division, B.E.F.

We were told that this was to be the last day of retreating, that we were to stand and fight in a position near Le Cateau with the First Corps on the right and the Second Corps on the left. We told our men that our retreat had been a well-designed trap to lead the Germans on to a position favourable to us so that the French could attack them in the flank. It was amusing seeing our soldiers trying to explain this by signs to the refugees.

We were moving along west of the forest of Mormal. The day was very hot and close, turning, as usual, to rain in the afternoon. The roads were choked with refugees and their carts, making our march very slow. There were frequent stops. Houses were being closed as we passed and more people kept coming on to the road. One pretty girl came out of a house and asked me where the French were. The only French I knew of were to our east, so I pointed in that general direction and they moved off into the forest. I hope they escaped the Germans! We'd had no breakfast. We tried to get some food for the men from houses we passed on the way, but most were shut up, and the others had no food to give us. I did get a raw egg at one place, and at another I got a couple of loaves of bread for my section. But that was all.

Whenever we could we watered our horses from wayside streams and wells, and we sent parties into the fields to collect stooks of corn and hay for them. And the men plucked apples and fruit from orchards and gave them to the infantry as we passed them, or they passed us. Some of them had had nothing since the previous Saturday, and they were very tired.

All the infantry officers I spoke to when we halted were full of praise for their men. Their rifle shooting was marvellous, and they had fairly slaughtered the Germans. They complained that they needed more machine-guns, as there were only two to a battalion.

This day, 25 August, our battery was detailed as rearguard battery, so we were with the infantry rearguard at the back of the whole Division. The Germans did not press forward – perhaps they had a respect for our gun and rifle fire – so we did not come into action, but all the way along our retirement the Major carried out reconnaissances in case we should have to.

In the course of the previous forty-eight hours the Germans had certainly developed a healthy respect for the 'gun and rifle fire' of the men of the force that their Kaiser had dismissed as a contemptibly small army, but whose skill and fighting spirit had thwarted them so frustratingly on the battlefields round Mons. But there was another reason why they did not immediately pursue the BEF as readily as they might have done. On the morning of the 25th, von Kluck had disposed his troops to attack the BEF at the point to which he knew they had retired the night before – and it was not so easy to change his plans now that the British had vanished into thin air. Were they retreating? Were they merely retiring a short distance to take up a position of greater advantage? It would be many hours before the situation became clear and before fresh orders could be sent out and acknowledged by the fifty different regiments scattered across the wide front from which the British had unaccountably disappeared. Von Kluck had not intended to drive them away. He had meant to play for time, to hold the enemy to the ground, to make him stand and fight to defend it. Now, what was to be done?

For most of the morning German aircraft followed the troops, swooping low over the slow-moving columns on the roads to the south. They terrified the civilians but they were a welcome diversion to the Tommies who snapped out of their lethargy, unslung their rifles and blasted fusillades of bullets into the sky. None of them scored a hit. High out of range, the pilots circled mockingly and flew back to report what they had seen. At von Kluck's headquarters the weight of information pointed to a wholesale retreat. But as the day wore on other reports began to filter back from advance guards and reconnoitring patrols on the ground, and they told a different tale. As they were probing cautiously forward, they had come up against some stiff opposition. The British were not on the run. Just as they had done as they retired from Mons, they were fighting as they went. All along the way they had been fortifying villages, manning them with rearguards, and there they were standing, ready to give any Germans who had the temerity to follow an exceedingly hot time and to make them think twice about giving the German commanders the green light to attack in force.

The Royal Engineers were a godsend to the weary troops of the rearguard. On Sunday, the 5th Field Company, Royal Engineers, had started off at dawn before the troops went into battle and reached Mons after many hours of march in time to dig the trenches that would get them out. In normal circumstances it would have been beneath the dignity of a full corporal like Alex Letyford to do anything other than supervise the work. As things were, the NCOs had buckled down with the rest. They had dug trenches for the Worcesters, they had dug them for the Ox and Bucks and now, on the long road back, they were digging trenches for anyone who needed them, preparing positions where the rearguards could stand and fight. They had been awake and on their feet since Saturday and they were sick with fatigue, but in snatched moments Letyford managed to scribble brief entries in his diary.

Cpl. A. Letyford, 5th Field Company, Royal Engineers, B.E.F.

24.8.14. The women in the small villages are all crying and we see a lot flying from their homes. Artillery firing all around us today and we have had to gradually retire from Mons digging trenches to cover the retirement. We are outnumbered by 6 to 1 so have to retire again to Lalongueville where we arrive at 7 p.m. having been on the go since 3 o'clock on Saturday (it's now Monday night). Hundreds of people are on the road with bundles leaving their homes in fear of the Germans. We are all very footsore and weary – also dirty! We bivouac in a field.

25.8.14. Off again at daybreak. The inhabitants are already on the move. It is a pitiful sight to see them leaving their homes, women and children crying and old and invalid people being helped along the roads. They know what it means if they stay behind, for on Sunday last the Germans, being unable to cross a bridge held by the Worcesters, drove the women and children from the village and drove them in front of them.★ In that way they got over the bridge. We march and put a lot of bridges in state of defence. We knock out the windows of houses nearby and make loopholes in them. All kinds of things lie alongside the roadway having been left in the hurry – soldiers' kits, bags of flour, loads of meat. We see a Belgian trying to give away a load of beef which he had killed and carried away before the Germans arrived.

In the afternoon we meet some of the French Army for the first time and we cheer each other. We march on, making for Landrecies, where we are told that we are to have a day's rest! The troops are getting very fatigued.

As it toiled south, plodding, halting, stumbling forward on feet that protested at every painful step, the Army was shepherded by the cavalry. Their horses were sorely in need of rest but the cavalry could still move fast. Travelling across open country away from the tortuous progress of the roads they could cover miles in minutes. They could search for the enemy and, when they found him, they could keep him busy and off the backs of the hard-pressed infantry. The men on the road had hardly set eyes on the cavalry all day, but they knew they were near, and without them, as Arthur Osborn put it, they would have been well and truly scuppered.

★ This rumour was one of the few which happened to be true. The episode took place at Nimy, where the Germans, knowing that the British troops would be unlikely to open fire on civilians, forced several hundred of the villagers to screen their advance. They were allowed to return to their homes the following day.

Capt. Arthur Osborn, 4th Dragoon Guards, The Cavalry Division,
B.E.F.

We seemed to spend the greater part of that day, 25 August, intercepting German cavalry and horse artillery coming apparently from Valenciennes. They kept pressing in towards the left flank of our retiring infantry at Beaudignies, where we lost our Colonel and Adjutant. We must delay the enemy's advance at all costs; we must prevent a frontal attack developing, lest our sun-wearied and footsore infantry, unable to continue their retreat, should be routed, perhaps entirely scuppered by German cavalry. At the same time we must prevent our guns and our lagging transport from being cut off. But, most important of all, thinned in numbers as we were, we must protect at all costs both flanks of the several divisions in retreat.

From flank to flank, from dawn almost to dawn, by mighty zigzags across an embattled front our cavalry rode throughout that retreat. From hour to hour we hung on till the last desperate minute, while the crawling infantry got clear, coming at any moment unexpectedly into action against German cavalry and horse artillery and then – most demoralising of all – bolting back to take up fresh and hurriedly chosen positions.

We opened fire on the advancing Germans from the ramparts of the walled town of Le Quesnoy because two regiments – one of them was the 2nd Battalion of the Irish Rifles – the men looking hot and evidently very weary and footsore, were being threatened from the west by German cavalry with their horse artillery. We bolted away from Le Quesnoy – only just in time – then, dashing through some fields, found that we were cut off by German cavalry on our right and by a gigantic hedge on our left. There was nothing for it but that several of us should seize the axes from the limbers and hack down the young trees that formed the hedge. We heaved away like demons, shrapnel, very badly aimed, coming over us. Then we were in action again near Vendegies. Near three hamlets, Maison Rouge, Maison Bleu and Maison Blanc, we were in action once more. An hour later, in a thunderstorm, we fell in with three of our other cavalry brigades and over a wide open plain of stubble dotted with dark wheat-stacks our brigades and regiments wheeled and galloped, formed and re-formed in column of squadrons, the German horse artillery making ineffectual attempts to drive us back. Over the brown masses of surging horsemen charging across that rather dreary plain beneath a lowering sky on that sultry afternoon came white feathery bursts of shrapnel. The threatening sky, the restless symmetrical movements, the whole scene reminded me in some strange way of Milton's description of the legions of dark angels practising for giant warfare with St Michael on the plains of hell. Anyway, the German Michael, for all his 'shining armour', did not like the look of things. By three o'clock his contemplated flank attack on our infantry had faded out.

Bill Holbrook was one of the stragglers. He had not succeeded in linking up with any of his battalion, which, on the night he had escaped, had bivouacked near the hospital on the eastern edge of Mons.

Cpl. W. Holbrook, No. 13599, 4th Bttn., Royal Fusiliers, 9th Brigade, 3rd Division, B.E.F.

It was days before I saw any of my lot again! I just kept following the crowd and there were so many stragglers they didn't notice *me*! It's a blank, really, most of it is, for that first few hours anyway. After a bit I came up with another bunch. There was an officer on the side of the road and he was rounding up stragglers and gathering them together, so I thought I might as well join up with them. They were *all* sorts. There was about fifty of us altogether, I suppose, and I don't believe there were two men from the same unit.

Well, we kept on going, and on and on, and the officer, he kept making enquiries, but he was as lost as any of us. So we just kept on making our way as best we could. I still had my rifle but not much else because being a runner, well, I couldn't run with my pack, could I? So *it* got left behind. We must have been well to the rear of the retreat because we kept on passing empty ration boxes by the side of the road. Any rations that were in them had long gone because the people who had got there first had taken them all. We were really hungry. Then, just getting dusk, there was a Uhlan patrol. It just seemed to come out of nowhere. Well, this officer, he got us organised along with some other troops – and we saw them off all right! There was no time to take up any sort of position, and no cover even if there had been. So we stood where we were and we let fire at them – rapid fire, standing. There were only a few of them and they got out of it pretty quick, I call tell you. Then we went on again. They were the only Germans we saw all day.

Thirty miles away, and well beyond the western edge of the forest, the Germans almost caught the Army at Solesmes. It was their biggest chance of the day – but they missed it.

The small town of Solesmes was a bottleneck. Three roads ran into it and converged on the one main road that ran out and, on the southern outskirts of Solesmes, that single road had been temporarily closed off to allow General Sordet's French cavalry to pass across to the extreme left flank of the ragged BEF. Solesmes, as a result, had come to a complete standstill. Even before the road out had been blocked, so many people had converged on it that, like a football crowd trying to pass through a single turnstile, they had to wrestle their way out. Now, by the sheer weight of the press of newcomers behind, the first arrivals were shuffled and squeezed into the narrow side streets, troops with their wagons and horses, refugees with their ramshackle carts, locked together – and locked, moreover, into the traffic jam of all time.

It was late afternoon. The Germans were in full pursuit now. They had lost valuable time, but they had made up for their belated start by sending a large contingent of infantry in a fleet of lorries down the same roads and a whisker behind the BEF. They were still just a whisker behind them. More were arriving every minute and they would soon be in a position to attack. Meanwhile their cavalry was in front of them and the German cavalrymen were on their way to Solesmes and north of Solesmes the British rearguard was waiting for them.★ They were not long in coming and, when they did, it was touch and go.

If the Germans had realised the situation, if they had guessed that Solesmes was filled with British troops, helpless to escape, they might have scored a pretty victory and a fine bag at the end of their day's hunting. But they did not know. The rearguard gave them a warm reception and, for all the Germans knew, the whole British Army might be lying in strength behind them. They stopped. They hesitated. They made up their minds to wait for their artillery to come up. Meanwhile they would conserve their strength and hold their infantry back.

But the sky was closing in. The heat was damp now and almost tangible, hanging thick as a blanket in the still, breezeless air. And then it erupted in a great rolling peal of thunder and the heavens opened.

Solesmes was at the centre of the storm. It was five o'clock in the evening and it raged for the best part of half an hour. Then the rain settled down to a steady torrent and when it did, the Germans gave up. Drenched and weary at the end of their long day they turned the streaming heads of their horses and, squelching in the saddles, set off to find billets for the night.

If anyone was thankful that the Germans had broken off their attack and that the bottleneck in Solesmes could begin to clear, that man was General

---

★ The rearguard comprised two battalions sent forward by the 4th Division (the 1st Wiltshires and the 2nd South Lancashires).

Snow in command of the 4th Division guarding the high ground behind the town. Their orders were to stay there, or at least to stay until the last of the Mons men had passed. Then, and only then, could they follow. They were then to place themselves on the left flank of the Army and, retreating with it, protect it as it went.

No one had dreamed that, even in abnormal conditions, it would take so long to cover the twelve miles or so from Bavai. No one had envisaged the full extent of the chaos on the roads, the long hold-ups, the miniature battles that the rearguards had fought on the way. And no one could have foreseen that the Germans would catch up at Solesmes nor that some units would be hopelessly stuck there for hours. As early as half-past four, as the sky began to darken with the gathering storm, and the troops were still coming on, General Snow was anxious. By six o'clock, as the light began to fail and the rain settled into a steady downpour, he began to be alarmed. He had received no reply to his message, sent to GHQ just before the attack. *The situation is becoming serious; it is getting dark. I cannot leave here until the 19th Brigade and the rearguard of the 3rd Division are in, and cannot therefore cover left flank yet.* The reply, when it came, was that he should prepare to withdraw and at six o'clock, in a lather of relief as the log-jam in Solesmes began to clear and the troops who had been held up began to trickle forward, he issued his instructions. As soon as all were through, the Division should be prepared to follow.

They had been there since half-past four in the morning. Or at least some of them had, for it was half-past five before the train bearing the last battalion of all had pulled into the station at Le Cateau. The 1st Battalion, The Rifle Brigade, had been two days on the journey from Le Havre and neither news nor rumours had reached them. They had no idea that a great battle had been fought at Mons and the first inkling they received that all was not well was when the train pulled in. Even at this unnaturally early hour the station was stiff with Staff Officers. A train, luxurious by comparison with the troop train, was drawn up on an opposite platform, guarded by watchful sentries. The doors of its baggage wagon were opened wide and a detachment of headquarters' troops was loading a mountain of valises and official boxes. They were heavy with maps and documents and they were clearly marked GHQ. Sir John French, his Staff, his entourage and his headquarters' personnel were moving down the line to St-Quentin. It was not a cheerful welcome.

Colonel Biddulph looked about him in dismay and he was not reassured by the agitated Staff Officer who hurried up to him with instructions. They were verbal instructions and, as the Colonel scribbled them hastily into his notebook, he gleaned a hazy view of the situation. But, taking his place at the head of the Battalion, now lined up and ready to march off, all he was sure of was that they were ordered to join the rest of the Brigade at Briastre, some miles to north-west of Le Cateau. How they were to find it was a mystery, for the harassed Staff Captain had merely gestured in the general direction. When the Battalion was clear of the station and had come to a quiet stretch of road the Colonel called a halt and ordered the map boxes to be opened. The contents unfortunately consisted entirely of maps of Belgium.

The only excitement that relieved the monotony of the march was the sight of a German reconnaissance plane sailing overhead. The Riflemen were tickled to death at being presented with such an early opportunity to give the enemy what-for, and they blazed away as if the outcome of the war depended on shooting it down. It was no more than a token gesture but it cheered the men up considerably and after an hour or two of hot and dusty marching, by dint of careful enquiries and a little luck, they joined up with the Division and started to dig themselves in. They had nothing but entrenching tools to dig with, for the transport – and therefore the tool-cart with their picks and shovels – had not yet arrived. As they worked they heard gunfire in the distance, saw the pathetic crowds of refugees on the roads, and watched in dismay as the troops – filthy, ragged and limping – plodded past them. The Riflemen were aghast. Their officers looked concerned and the snatches of information they were able to gather from shouted exchanges with the men on the retreat were not encouraging. Rumours flew.

Riding on the water cart in a line of spick-and-span transport wagons drawn by well-groomed horses, frisky after their long confinement in the train, Ted Gale felt almost out of place as they passed the dusty cavalcades and ramshackle vehicles that stretched all the way to the line. The transport was an hour or so behind the Battalion but they made good time and had almost reached the end of their journey when they met the 4th Middlesex – or what was left of them after their fight at Mons.

Rfn. E. Gale, No. 3774, 1st Bttn., The Rifle Brigade, B.E.F.

They didn't look anything like a battalion! There wasn't any more than a couple of hundred of them. The only officers were their Colonel and one subaltern, and *he* looked half-dazed. Lieutenant Barclay told me to stop the cart and he shouted across to the Colonel. We didn't know *what* was going on. And the Colonel shouted back, 'Do you see this party? Well, that's all that's left of my battalion.' I'll never forget the sight of those men. We didn't know *what* to think! No more did the fellows I spoke to when I dished out the water. But it didn't look good.

Tom Bridges was still some miles to the north, hobbling along in a mish-mash of stragglers and making slow progress. But the 4th Dragoon Guards had managed to collect a number of its missing men during the day, for those of them who, unlike Bridges, had not been parted from their horses had been able to detour through the forest and bypass the blockages on the roads. There had been no roll-call, no time for anything but the roughest of head-counts but, despite their losses in yesterday's charge at Audregnies, by the time they reached the outskirts of Le Cateau, the Dragoons reckoned that they were almost up to half-strength. By comparison with the sparse, bedraggled bodies of men they overtook on the road, they considered themselves lucky.

It had taken them more than three hours to cover the last few miles, and they still had six to go, but any rosy visions of billets, of food and rest, of warmth, that encouraged them over the last lap, quickly disappeared when they reached Le Cateau. The town was in a state of confusion that rivalled the scene at Solesmes. In some ways it was worse. The civilian inhabitants, who had been lulled into a false sense of security by the arrival of the 4th Division and the presence of British Headquarters Staff, were panicking now. The sound of the guns would have been enough in itself but when labourers returning early from the farms spoke of trenches dug across their fields and told of the Army retreating along the country roads, the civilians concluded that it was high time to get out.

If they could have seen the debris of abandoned belongings scattered along every road on the long trail from Mons, they might have decided to cut their losses and travel light. But, like the people who had fled from Belgium and the towns and villages to the north, the townsfolk of Le Cateau were determined to save as much of their personal property as they could. They had waited for the storm to pass and now they were pouring out of the houses, into the drizzly evening and into a press of troops and transport trying to pass in both directions through the streets. As it was they were making heavy weather of it. They could have done without a rush of civilians to add to their difficulties, and civilians, moreover who were driving their livestock before them. Cows, pigs, sheep, even geese and hens, lowing, bleating, grunting, screeching, scattered into the soldiers' ranks, pushing, flapping, squealing in terror as they kicked and swore and lashed out at them with the butts of their rifles. Feathers flew. Sheep, clubbed to the ground, were trampled underfoot. Soldiers tripped, fell, and narrowly escaped the same fate. Units disintegrated in a hopeless mix-up and still the refugees struggled and pressed, hysterical now in their determination to get away. Rickety vehicles packed with the contents of whole houses collided with army wagons. A grandfather clock teetered and crashed jangling to the ground. Children screamed, women, pressed against the walls and still clutching the skirts of aprons heavy with ornaments and cutlery, wept and fainted.

One battalion of French reservists trying to move north battled through the mob only to find that the way out of the town was barred by an inextricable jumble of abandoned farm carts whose drivers had made off to take their chance on foot. They had lost their officers in the mêlée, their ranks were hopelessly broken up and, even if they could have pushed past the carts, the men had only the vaguest of ideas where they were meant to be making for. Besides, they were tired of pushing and shoving. When the Dragoons, in their turn, had pushed and shoved down the hill to Le Cateau, the French *poilus* had given up the struggle. They were squatting on the ground beneath the high-slung wagons, sheltering from the rain and taking the opportunity to have a quiet smoke. Arthur Osborn was staggered.

Capt. Arthur Osborn, 4th Dragoon Guards, The Cavalry Division, B.E.F.

It all seems incredible now (I don't suppose the main street of Le Cateau can be anything like a mile in length; the town itself must be smaller than Oxford) but the 4th Dragoon Guards who had entered it perhaps two hundred and fifty strong, took two and a half hours to reach the top of the town – and then there were only about ninety of us left. In that wild scrimmage we had lost our Colonel and nearly all the officers who had not already been 'missing' since Shrapnel Monday. Although the day had been so thundery and sultry and one way and another we had covered a good forty miles, our struggle through the welter of Le Cateau had actually tired us out more than the whole of that day's march. Our first-line transport was lost, everything again was in confusion, nothing could be found and there seemed to be no orders.

One single business was functioning normally in Le Cateau and the Dragoons found it, to their astonishment, when at last they reached the top of the hill on the far side of the town. It was a tiny inn. Its window was lighted and welcoming and it was still open for custom.

After the exhausted horses had been watered and given a handful or so of oats, after the no-less-weary troopers had spread out their capes and settled down in a field to eat what remained of their iron-rations, seven of their saddle-sore officers who had managed to link up made their way thankfully back to the inn. It was well past eleven o'clock but, having been warned that there was more trade to come, the innkeeper had not yet shut up shop. He agreed to give them shelter for the night. He produced brandy, he went down to his cellar for some decent bottles of wine, and his two young daughters hurried to the kitchen and concocted the most gigantic omelette that Osborn had ever seen. After the ravenous officers had made short work of it, the girls cracked a few dozen more eggs and made them another. When the last delectable mouthful had been eaten, Osborn and five others wrapped themselves in their capes and went dreamlessly to sleep on the floor. The interpreter, Harrison, upholding his double reputation as a linguist and an enthusiast for feminine society, preferred to stroll into the kitchen where the girls were clearing away, and chat them up.

Not many men of the Second Corps were so lucky. There were precious few who enjoyed a hot meal that evening and fewer still who spent the night under the shelter of a roof.

Chapter 11

A good way to the north-east, on the other side of the forest of Mormal, separated now from Smith-Dorrien's force by miles of open country, the Guards Division had reached Landrecies and there they had been told to stay to act as rearguard to the First Army Corps when it passed through the area on its way south. The Guards had been in the vanguard of the First Corps and the rear battalions were still ten miles to the north with the enemy lagging a safe distance behind them. Safe in this knowledge, and knowing also that the great bulk of the Mormal forest itself protected his position to the west, the Corps Commander, Sir Douglas Haig, had set up his headquarters at Landrecies in perfect confidence that there were no Germans within miles.

The Guards were looking forward to a peaceful night, to decent billets, to a hot supper, and the troops roaming the small town in search of its limited attractions had been told that they need not report back to their billets for roll-call until 9 p.m. They were glad of a breathing space. There were still civilians in Landrecies. There were cafés where a soldier could buy a drink. There were water-pumps and, best of all in the heavy dog-days of August, there was the River Sambre where he could splash off the dust of the long day's tramp and soak his aching feet. There was nothing, it seemed, to prevent the Guards from enjoying a pleasant evening and the relief of a good night's rest.

Landrecies was too large to be, strictly speaking, a village and too small to be accurately described as a town. There were a few side streets, there was a main road that straggled into a market square and meandered beyond it to bridge the river and run past the railway station a little way ahead. The station and its level crossing marked the end of the town and, north of it, where the road ran up a hill, the cottages gave way to a scattering of villas and farmhouses.

Here, at the top of the rise, the country met the town. It was here that the main road forked and a minor road branched off towards the forest. It was not much more than a farm track. Its cobbles seldom carried any traffic faster than a country cart but the Guardsmen on the outpost picquet could distinctly hear a busy clatter of wheels and a disconcerting chorus of singing and whistling. It was barely nine o'clock but it had fallen dark early. It was late for refugees to be on the road and, even if they were, the voices sounded altogether too cheerful to belong to fleeing civilians.

By an irony of war, the Germans also had expected to spend the night at Landrecies, and they were so sure of finding billets, so certain that the village would be empty, that they did not trouble to send a patrol forward to reconnoitre. Instead they sent their transport on ahead, rumbling down the road in front of the infantry, to requisition billets and to unload the rations so that the cooks could start preparing a meal for the men. It had been a long day and they were all tired, but the Germans had made good time. As late as midday, according to the Royal Flying Corps, they had been just nearing Bavai, which the BEF had quitted hours before. But the Germans' own reconnaissance had not been entirely reliable – or rather, orders had been based on reports that had come in so early as to be useless later in the day when the position had changed. These had indicated – and perhaps it was wishful thinking – that east of the forest the British were in retreat towards Maubeuge and that, west of it, the roads from Le Quesnoy to the south were clear. And so they had been – at nine o'clock that morning. It was late in the day now and realising that their assessment of the situation had been wrong, German Intelligence reported in words that sounded more than a touch aggrieved that the British were 'now marching in a totally different direction to that which we supposed earlier'.

But no word of this revision of judgement had reached the forward column of the 27th German Regiment. Since the troops in front of them had dealt with the British rearguards, they had marched briskly to Le Quesnoy (by then in German hands) and there branched off to the left, travelling south-east along the southern edge of the forest to Landrecies. They were moving directly across the wide gap that split the Expeditionary Force and it was therefore not surprising that they saw no evidence of any British soldiers on the way. But their own troops were everywhere. The roads through the forest which the British had written off as being 'unsuitable for the passage of troops' had provided fine going for the German guns and cavalry and even for considerable bodies of infantry as well. The forest was full of Germans now, and the whole of the 5th German Division had already stopped to bivouac there for the night.

The Germans in the vanguard of the 27th Regiment were in good humour. The march had been so easy that it was almost a triumphal progress. The Tommies were miles away, skulking no doubt in the fortress of Maubeuge, and with billets almost in view, the prospect of a rest ahead, and the achievement of drumming the British out of Mons to their credit, the Kaiser's soldiers had every reason to sing their way into Landrecies.

But their choice of song was unusual. They were singing the 'Marseillaise'. This was France, after all, and it would keep the locals guessing. They would hardly expect a foreign invader to march in to occupy their town to the strains of the French National Anthem.

As the head of the column came up to the main road, the Coldstreams' challenge came as a severe shock. The German officer had to think fast. '*Français*,' he shouted.

Lieutenant Bingham hesitated, peering into the dark, and he hesitated a moment too long. The 'Frenchmen' broke into a run, rushed the machine-gun post, clubbed Bingham into the ditch and went for the gun, sending the gunners sprawling and making off with the gun itself, sprinting back up the road as fast as its weight would allow.

It was fortunate that Captain Monck was with the main picquet some twenty yards behind, for Monck was an old hand. He had been seventeen years in the Army, he had seen service in South Africa, and he knew a ruse when he met one for the rough-riding Boers had been up to every trick. Five years policing Egypt with the Battalion had not made Monck any less suspicious and he had learned to shoot first and ask questions afterwards. He was shooting now as he ran, firing his revolver into the dark towards the sound of the scuffle, and the picquet, firing blind with only the line of the road to guide them, unleashed such a storm of rapid fire that none of the raiding party escaped. The Coldstreams dashed forward, recovered the gun and stood to arms to await developments.

A runner sped down the hill to Landrecies to fetch help and reinforcements but long before they could get there the Germans had deployed and attacked in force. There was no means of knowing how many there were. It might have been a company. It might have been a regiment. In Landrecies itself, Sir Douglas Haig, urgently discussing the report with his Staff Officers, was equally at a loss. It was perfectly possible that the encounter was no more than a skirmish, an isolated stab at the soft underbelly of the long retreating column; it might equally be the spearhead of the great army that was sweeping round to outflank it. It was just possible that the fight outside Landrecies was the first move of the encirclement. They could only wait and see. Meanwhile they began to burn the secret papers that must on no account fall into the hands of the Germans.

The troops were working flat out to fortify Landrecies. They knocked loopholes in walls and windows. They blocked off the side streets, building barricades with whatever came to hand. It was not much. They dragged transport wagons across the roads, they pulled up paving stones, they requisitioned the ration-cart, the mess-cart, and the cart that carried the officers' kit. They dragged furniture from the houses and piled it in heaps across the roadway, and when they had emptied the lower floors of chairs and tables and dressers they dashed upstairs for bedding, for mattresses, for anything that could be lifted, and threw the lot out of the windows.

Staff Officers, accustomed to a gentler way of life, rushed furiously about and the tetchy commands of one unfortunate officer (not the best liked in the Brigade) were abruptly extinguished when a vast feather bed came billowing from above and enveloped him in its voluminous folds. By the time he had wrestled his way out of them, red with rage, the Guardsman who had carelessly let it fall was judiciously busy elsewhere.

The Germans had been taken equally by surprise. They had one section of guns, but it was far back at the end of the column and it took a full hour to bring it forward and to manhandle the guns into position. But now they had begun to shell the town.

A mile away on the outskirts, the Guards were still beating them off. They were fighting hand to hand, they were firing up the road and from the cottage gardens, shooting blind across the dark fields to the darker shadow of a wood where the enemy might be lurking. It was a lucky shot from a German rifle grenade that set fire to a haystack. It was summer dry and it burned with a fearsome light. Now the Germans could see – and they could see quite clearly that only a scattering of men stood between them and Landrecies. They charged again, running at the double, their bayonets glinting red and lurid in the firelight. They were a hundred yards away. They were fifty yards away. And when they were little more than twenty-five yards distant and the Guards were firing point-blank, Lance-Corporal Wyatt dashed out of the firing line. He carried a pitchfork and he went straight at the blazing haystack, flailing at it, forking at it, tearing it to pieces. He beat at the flames until the fire went out and he looked like a demon stoking the fires of hell. For a long time the eye-smarting stench of smoke hung acrid in the air while the Guards went on shooting into the night beyond the farmyard where a scattering of straw-wisps smouldered and glowed in the dark.

The news of the attack at Landrecies caused dismay at Sir John French's headquarters at St-Quentin. Coming on top of the battle at Mons it was too much for General Murray. He collapsed, worn out with lack of sleep and anxiety. Like Sir Douglas Haig, the Staff at GHQ had no means of knowing the scale of the attack. It contradicted all their information, but the last reliable reports had come in many hours ago. By now, anything might have happened and with half the First Corps still well to the north of Landrecies, the situation looked grim. Haig's message had read 'Attack heavy from north-west. Can you help?' GHQ could not – but Sir Horace Smith-Dorrien might. By the shortest route it was no more than three hours' march from Le Cateau to Landrecies. The Second Corps could easily go to the assistance of the First. A message to that effect was promptly despatched.

Sir Horace Smith-Dorrien's reply was couched in terms of restrained courtesy and it was a masterpiece of understatement. It gave little indication of his difficulties. It merely regretted, and, indeed, much regretted that his troops were '*quite unable to move tonight*'. Even the 19th Brigade, which GHQ had optimistically suggested might be spared if nothing else could, would be '*unable to reach Landrecies in a useful state*'. It was not that the fight had gone out of them. It was simply that they were worn out. Smith-Dorrien was well aware that, if the retreat was to be continued in the morning, they must have what little rest they could snatch. The troops were due to start along various routes at seven o'clock in the morning (the guns and transport earlier than that) and Smith-Dorrien had already issued the instructions, fervently hoping that they would reach his scattered divisions in time.

They reached General Allenby, in command of the Cavalry Corps, shortly after eleven in the evening, together with the order that the Cavalry Division was to cover the retreat, acting as rearguard and standing on the the high ground above Solesmes to protect the Army as it began to withdraw. The cavalrymen were tired too. The horses had covered more ground than any man on the retreat and they were exhausted. It would be difficult but, for the moment, it did not seem to be impossible. Then a second message arrived. It came from the 4th Division. It reported that the Division had completed its retirement from the ridge above Solesmes and it added the disconcerting news that the enemy was known to have advanced and was now in possession of the ground they had vacated. The Germans were occupying the very position which the cavalry had been ordered to hold to cover the next stage of the retreat.

Allenby called for his horse and rode to General Smith-Dorrien's head-quarters at Bertry. At midnight the lights in the villa were still blazing and Smith-Dorrien and his staff were still working, planning the move for tomorrow, waiting for news from outlying units, worrying about those which had not reported in. Allenby's news was a bombshell. The Germans were closer and the cavalry more scattered than anyone had realised and Allenby drew a gloomy picture. The cavalry could have held the ridge, or could at least have kept the Germans off it for a while, but with the Germans there already there were simply not enough of them to recapture it and boot the enemy off. If the Army was to make its escape it would have to fold its tent and creep off like Arabs in the night before daylight came and the Germans realised that it had gone. There were no options to be considered. There were no options available. It came down to one simple question. Could the troops move before daylight?

Even if they could, General Allenby added (with unaccustomed pessimism that impressed the Corps Commander more than all his urgent arguments), given the state of his men and his horses, it would be a miracle if the cavalry could protect the Army half as effectively tomorrow as they had succeeded in protecting it today. The only chance for the infantry and the gunners was to get a head start. There were three, perhaps four, hours of darkness ahead. Let them go *now*.

Smith-Dorrien had his doubts if they could. He had seen enough of the retreat to be appalled – and he was appalled not only by the conditions of the march, but by the condition of his men. Already they were dead beat. Already there were stragglers who had fallen, sometimes literally, at the wayside from sheer exhaustion. His mind was full of images of countless dust-streaked faces, of staring hollow eyes, of shoulders hunched with weariness, of feet attempting to march but which no amount of instilled discipline could prevent from limping. But he would put the matter to his divisional generals.

General Hamilton came in response to the Corps Commander's message to give his answer in person. So far as his 3rd Division was concerned, many of his troops had only just struggled in; many more had not. Even with luck on his side, he thought it most unlikely that he could retrieve his lost sheep, shepherd them into formation and have them ready to move off before nine o'clock in the morning. And *that*, he stressed, making no bones about the matter, would be at the earliest.

With infinite reluctance Sir Horace Smith-Dorrien made the only decision that was open to him. With Germans treading on their blistered heels it was clear that the men were incapable of marching for another day. If they attempted it the Germans would undoubtedly catch them up. The British soldiers were sorely in need of a respite. They must stand their ground, they must turn to face the enemy and they must fight for it.

Smith-Dorrien knew that it would be a gamble, he knew that everything would depend on timing, on fighting hard enough to check the enemy and on breaking off the battle at exactly the right moment to continue the retreat before the Germans were in a position to pursue. It would take a cool head to decide when that moment had come. It would take many stout hearts and a wealth of superhuman effort to reach it.

The 4th Division represented the one strong card in a desperately weak hand. It was true that they had been kept hard at it digging trenches and strengthening positions, but they were incomparably fresher and fitter than the ragged remnant of the men of Mons. The 4th Division, at least, was now safely resting on the left flank where they had been meant to stand as rearguard in the morning. By the time morning came they would surely be fighting fit. All that remained was to send the orders to all the commanders of all the units to stand fast. That task would take the rest of the night.

There was not a man of the 4th Division who would not have denied with the utmost indignation the implication that they had given up the high ground near Solesmes without waiting to be relieved by the cavalry. The order to retire as soon as the last of the retreating troops had cleared Solesmes had been sent out just after six o'clock and General Snow had confidently anticipated that they would leave within the hour. They had finally got away by eleven o'clock. They did not have far to go to take up their position on the left of the line round Fontaine-au-Pire, but it took hours to get there. The road was still crowded with transport and with stragglers, rain was still falling and the passage of many feet and countless horse-drawn wagons had churned the road into a mire. At every step their feet sank squelching into the mud.

The Brigade signallers had tried at first to cycle but the wheels soon clogged with mud, and the luckless cyclists had to plough ahead on foot like the rest of them, with the added burden of the useless bicycles slung across their shoulders. Wagons stuck so firmly that platoons of grumbling soldiers, on their own last legs, had to be brought up to dig them out and manhandle them forward.

Rfn. E. Gale, No. 3774, 1st Bttn., The Rifle Brigade, B.E.F.

We took up miles of road, our Brigade did. There was all the infantry for a start, four battalions, and the Brigade transport was in front of that. Our own Battalion transport was at the very back. There was two watercarts, there was three ammunition carriers, there was two limbers, there was a General Service Wagon – that's about twenty horses altogether. I had two horses, Charlie and a mare called Beth. We had to keep well on top of one another it was that dark. Just keep the horses right up close to the others. The Transport Officer, Lieutenant Barclay, he was up at the front leading the way, but we was at the back of the whole lot of them that night, with half the Battalion in front of us and the other half miles ahead with the Brigade Transport to give it a hand along.

When the 11th Brigade eventually reached Fontaine-au-Pire some hours later, the going was better, the paved surface of the village street came as a relief after the rough country road and, although they knew that there was little in the way of comfort awaiting them, Ted Gale for one was thankful to have reached the end of the journey. It was past two in the morning. The rain was still blowing in gusty squalls but it showed signs of lessening and even if they could hardly look forward to decent billets at least, with any luck, they would soon be able to take the weight off their feet. But it was not the end of their difficulties.

The twin villages of Beauvois and Fontaine-au-Pire straggled into each other sharing fully two kilometres of main road. The transport at the rear of the Brigade was just trundling into Beauvois when the head of the column was turning off at Fontaine to reach its rendezvous. The orders were clear. *Turn right at the far end of the village on the road to Cattenières.* Since there was only one turning it hardly seemed that they could go wrong. They turned right on to a good road surface at a perfectly respectable corner with houses well spaced on either side, but it did not lead to Cattenières. In twenty yards the paving gave way to mud. In twenty more the road had petered out into a narrow lane between two fields and the leading battalions, their ranks jostled almost into single file, discovered, cursing, that they were squeezed between two stout fences of barbed wire. They were also trapped there because several wagons of the transport column had trundled in behind them and were now stuck fast. The Brigadier, who had been riding near the head of the column, was trapped with the rest and the tail of the Brigade, spread along two kilometres of road, came gradually to a standstill.

It took a good half-hour of heaving and pushing to back up the wagons and horses and turn them about and by then the Brigadier had had enough. It was pointless to continue. He passed the word that the Brigade should rest where it was until daylight and find what shelter it could. Earlier in the evening, as nearby as Caudry a mile or so towards Le Cateau, some soldiers had been astonished to find the houses lit, the cafés open and the civilians comparatively unmoved by the stirring events on their doorstep. But Fontaine was deserted. Some sections of the infantry and even whole platoons were able to make themselves comfortable in empty houses. Some crowded in barns. The rest had to make the best of it in the fields and while the lucky ones made their beds on damp but springy corn stooks, others, in the malodorous meadows where cattle had been grazing, slid and tumbled swearing among the cow pats in the dark. The men who had wandered into the lane across the fields clambered through the barbed-wire fences and stretched out in the fields. In moments every man was asleep and dead to the world. Except, that is, for the Rifle Brigade which was pushed out in front of them to set up an outpost line.

The rain stopped. It was past three o'clock in the morning and they were by no means the last men home.

It was the twenty-sixth of August, and later people made much of the fact that this was the anniversary of the Battle of Crécy. At Crécy, and every schoolboy knew it, the honours of the field had been won by the English bowmen; at Le Cateau they would go hands down to the men who manned the guns.

The gunners – or, at least, their officers – were not regarded with undiluted admiration by other branches of the Army. Their colleagues of the infantry held the view that artillery officers thought themselves too élite by half, and there were not many gunners who regarded this opinion as an out-and-out insult. They *were* élite. They were proud of it, and in the hundred years of their history they had proved it in a hundred different fights. In peacetime it was a fine life. Lieutenant Roderick Macleod felt himself to be particularly fortunate. For the last two years he had been soldiering in Ireland, and they had been halcyon years. Like all artillery officers young Rory was mad about horses. The cavalry would have been the obvious choice, but for a young man who did not have a considerable private income there had been no question of a commission in the cavalry. The pay of an officer in that exclusive brotherhood was mere pin-money compared to the expenses of his aristocratic life-style. The artillery was the next best thing.

The Royal Regiment of Artillery prided itself on being singularly democratic. Its officers were selected on the grounds of brains and ability rather than wealth and influence, and a small number had even been commissioned from the ranks. But a subaltern with no other resources than his Army pay had a thin time. After four years' service Macleod's pay as a junior subaltern was £101 a year, and out of that he was obliged to pay for his own keep. His mess-bill, without so much in the way of 'extras' as a single glass of port, amounted to a basic £73, leaving a margin of £28 for all other expenses. He could never have managed if his parents had not been able to subsidise him to the tune of a comfortable, if not lavish, allowance of £200 a year. There was an odd four shillings and fourpence chipped in by the Army, but that did not help much towards the cost of dress and undress uniforms, of mess-kit, evening dress for social occasions, sports gear and civilian clothes, to say nothing of travel, subscriptions to games, to battery funds and, of course, the expenses of the hunt. Rory Macleod's pastime and his passion was hunting, and in the Royal Regiment of Artillery the officers were not only encouraged to hunt but were regarded as rank outsiders if they did not.

The efficiency of the Regiment was dependent on a large complement of well-schooled horses to pull the transport, to drag the guns and, when necessary, to gallop them into action. It went without saying that an officer should be an excellent horseman and the care and management of horses was an important part of his training. But hunting helped him to develop the science and the skills of his trade. It taught him the lie of the land and the art of moving speedily across country. It sharpened his reflexes, quickened his eye, trained him to spot cover where none seemed to exist and to detect the slightest fold or swelling of the earth, so that, when the need arose, he would be able almost instinctively to site his guns to the best advantage. Hunting kept a man and his horse hard and fit for active service.

It also provided a great deal of healthy fun and so long as an officer was professionally up to scratch and contrived to carry out his basic duties (and how he managed it was his own concern) his superiors were positively bounteous in the matter of time off.

Lt. R. A. Macleod, 80 Battery, XV Brigade, R.F.A., 5th Division, B.E.F.

If we had enough horses we could hunt six days a week, four days with the fox-hounds and two with the harriers. Even the subaltern doing section training could hunt occasionally. He would put on his hunting kit with a military greatcoat on top and a forage cap, and, on hunting days, took his section in the gunsheds by electric light on such things as gun drill at six a.m., and other drills, until it was time for him to leave and, on his return from hunting, his poor men were subjected to lectures in the barrack room to make up the time.

The country-house people were extraordinarily kind. We were often asked out to meals, or to tennis or dances, and sometimes we were invited to stay the night and hunt the next day. Once I drove to a place in the battery dog-cart, danced all night, hunted all next day (my hunter was ridden to the meet by my groom), then on to another house for dinner and more dancing. I got back to barracks in the early morning with only enough time to change my clothes and go straight on to parade.

Early in 1914 I decided to train my young mare, Be Early, for steeplechasing, with a view to the Grand Military at Punchestown. I wanted somewhere I could school her over jumps, and a friend advised me to apply to Major Honner, who had a large estate of 360 acres at Ardenode near Brannockstown.

He had a steeplechase course in his grounds and ran schools twice a week. So I used to ride over the thirteen miles before breakfast and the school took place between breakfast and luncheon. My little mare came on very well. She could jump like a stag and was very fast, so I had great hopes.

After luncheon I sometimes took Major Honner's daughter for a golf lesson in the fields near the house, and then rode Be Early back to barracks. It was a very pleasant existence.

The pleasant existence had come to an abrupt end just three weeks ago, but Macleod was not dissatisfied with his lot. In the hurly-burly of mobilisation and the preparations for departure the business of the battery had absorbed almost every waking moment of a subaltern's day but, pleading 'urgent business of a personal nature', Rory was given a few hours off and squeezed in one last visit to Ardenode. His business concerned the delightful Miss Honner, and it was of a highly personal nature. They had come to an understanding, both families had given their blessing and on his first leave Rory and Colleen would become officially engaged. He intended to buy her a handsome ring for, by a second stroke of luck, the Army had paid him £75 for the titular ownership of Be Early and the privilege of riding his own mare to the war. The money had nicely plumped out Rory's bank account which had been sadly depleted by the unfortunate affair of the Officers' Mess dining table. A Highland Fling vigorously performed by an officer wearing spurs had not improved its glossy surface and the £20 charged by the french polisher who restored it to its former glory had made an embarrassing hole in Macleod's allowance. Now, like the thick head of the following morning and a stiff wigging from the Colonel, all that was forgotten.

The 5th Division was spread across the heights to the west of the valley where Le Cateau clung to the banks of the River Selle and at three o'clock in the morning it was freezing cold. The gunners at least had had a few hours' sleep and in reasonable comfort. The baggage wagon had come up with the officers' sleeping-bags and even in the doubtful shelter of standing corn stooks they had been sound asleep near the wagon-lines outside the village of Reumont while most of the unfortunate infantry were still on the road. But they were the first to be roused because the guns and the transport were to lead the way on the next stage of the retreat. They harnessed up in the dark. There was no question of breakfast but the cooks had managed to make tea for the men and although, after three days without rations, the officers' luncheon basket had little to offer in the way of solid sustenance it still contained some cocoa. They were gulping it down now, fiery hot, gratefully warming their hands on the mugs as they waited to move off. It was a long wait and night was turning gradually to leaden dawn before orders came. The retreat was cancelled. The guns were to advance and fight, and they were to lose no time about it.

It was wide, rolling countryside of open swells and ridges, a high plateau that dropped sharply on the right to the Selle valley and rose steeply again on the other side. It was good shooting country and even a far less practised eye than the adjutant's would have had no difficulty in picking out positions for the guns, well placed to support the infantry, well concealed by the natural undulations of the ground. The manoeuvre had been practised so often, the men and the horses had been so relentlessly drilled, there had been such keen competition between batteries – and even between individual gun-sections – that it was mere routine for a six-gun battery to be ready for action within three minutes, well before an enemy could spot them and range his own guns on their position.

Just as they had done on a thousand exercises, the two Brigades of Artillery came dashing over the slopes on either side of Reumont, guns and horses swinging like pendulums from their jingling chains. There were thirty-six guns, thirty-six limbers, a dozen ammunition wagons and more than five hundred horses. It was a sight to behold. But there was no one to raise a cheer except for the sleepy infantry standing-to in a single line of sorry trenches that teetered along the edge of the hill a third of a mile ahead. And in seconds, it seemed, the guns had disappeared, tucked neatly into the landscape, and the grooms were trotting the horses and limbers back to the wagon-lines and out of harm's way. It was a textbook demonstration. No one had expected anything else.

The textbook had only lately been revised. As recently as a dozen years earlier, the guns had been placed well up-front with the infantry, ranging with the naked eye on targets they could clearly see, and using their formidable fire-power to inflict more damage than the muskets and even, later, the rifles of the infantry could inflict on an enemy on the advance. But the Boer War and the experience of fighting on the open veldts of Africa had made this long tradition obsolete. If guns deployed in the open could see the enemy it stood to reason that the enemy could see them too and would have no difficulty in knocking them out. Even a well-aimed rifle a thousand yards away could wreak havoc among the gun crew and put the gun out of action as effectively as a high-explosive shell aimed at the gun itself. Indirect fire was the modern way and it was far more satisfactory. With fine-precision range-finders, with the development of fast-travelling shells that could be fired accurately over long distances, the new method was simple. It needed only one observer placed well forward, to signal back to the battery in its place of concealment and simple mathematics took care of the rest. The gunners were scientists now and no amount of riding to hounds could equip a young officer with the expertise in signalling, the knowledge of science and the facility for mathematics he was required to demonstrate in promotion examinations. It took long hours of study and much sweating of the brow to master them.

Brigadier-General Headlam, in command of the 5th Division's artillery, was as familiar with the modern methods as any other officer of his rank. But, like many officers of similar vintage, he rather regretted the disappearance of the old traditions that went hand in hand with the old tactics. It was not that the modern method was inefficient – it had been proved in countless manoeuvres if not in battle – but it lacked gallantry. Some senior officers, mostly retired, went so far as to growl that it was downright ungentlemanly.

General Headlam was no fool, but with no time for written orders to reach him in the haste before the battle he had perhaps misunderstood the situation. He had certainly misinterpreted his Corps Commander's intention. There had been no time to spell out the niceties of Smith-Dorrien's strategy, of his desire that the battle should check the enemy just long enough to gain breathing space to continue the retreat. The two facts relayed to the Brigadier-General were, first, that the order to retreat had been cancelled and, second, that the First Corps was to stand and fight. In General Headlam's mind the two separate orders merged into one entirely erroneous understanding. They were to stand and fight and there was to be no retreat.

In the circumstances, envisaging a fight to the finish, General Headlam did not approve of the carefully chosen positions where the guns now waited for action. He wanted them moved forward. He wanted them out in the open. He wanted them placed as close as possible to the infantry in order to give the infantry the closest possible support. At 15th Brigade Headquarters, Colonel Stephens had no choice but obey and to send his Orderly Officer to the field to instruct his three battery commanders to quit their well-prepared positions. To move the guns up front.

This young officer did not relish his task. Even in normal circumstances he was accustomed to giving Major Birley a wide berth, particularly in the early hours of the morning when Birley's disposition was far from sunny. His wariness dated from the morning when, as a newly commissioned subaltern, he had found Birley at the mess breakfast table and greeted him with a polite 'Good Morning, Sir'. The Major had lowered the *Irish Times* far enough to fix him with a bloodshot glare. 'Good morning, good morning, good morning, good morning,' he snarled. 'Now let that last you for a week!' The snub had been a mere pleasantry compared to the stream of invective the Major spewed out now, and Majors Nutt and Henning of the 11th and 52nd Batteries were no more restrained. But there was no arguing with an order and no alternative but to comply. With deep misgivings, Colonel Stephens went forward himself to see the guns deployed. Etiquette, discipline and several hundred years of tradition debarred him from making any comment whatever. But his manner was sympathetic.

The message that Smith-Dorrien had sent to Sir John French outlining his intentions and the reasons behind them arrived at GHQ at five o'clock,

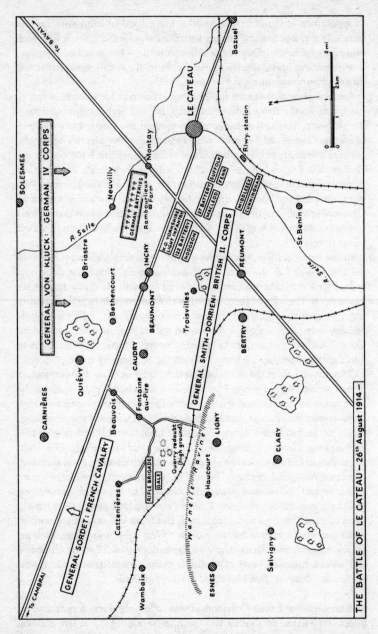

THE BATTLE OF LE CATEAU – 26th August 1914 –

for the Staff car which carried it had been held up on the way. This new development did nothing to lighten the anxieties of the Commander-in-Chief.

Relieved though he was to have extricated so many of his men from and under the Germans' very noses, the Commander-in-Chief, Sir John French, was now in a dilemma. He wanted to put a barrier between his men and the Germans. Some natural barrier, a sizeable river like the Somme or the Oise, would be a significant obstacle, easily defended by comparatively few men while the survivors of the retreat recuperated and waited for reinforcements. He badly wanted to continue the retreat.

And now this.

He was still unsure of the situation at Landrecies, and he still could not tell if the fight the previous evening was the prelude to a full-scale attack that would split his First Corps in two. But the fighting had died down and the Guards who had been standing to arms all night were, even now, preparing to retire and to put as much distance as possible between themselves and the Germans before daylight. Smith-Dorrien could expect no help from that quarter, so, if the Second Corps stood its ground it must be on the strict understanding that it would stand alone. The Commander-in-Chief understood Smith-Dorrien's dilemma, as any soldier would. He also understood the risks – and the risks were considerable. The maps were studied anew, the situation was reassessed, and a reply was drafted, but even the speediest method of sending it was slow and time was running out. Then someone had a happy thought. Sir Horace Smith-Dorrien's headquarters were at Bertry, at Bertry there was a railway station and the railway had a telephone line.

Daylight had broken before they got through and, by the time a messenger sped from the station and Sir Horace arrived to take the call, it was just after six o'clock. General Wilson was on the line. He gave Smith-Dorrien the gist of the message drafted by the Commander-in-Chief. He stressed his commander's reservations, passed on his reluctant acquiescence and emphasised his wish that Smith-Dorrien must nevertheless 'make every endeavour to carry out the retirement'. Drained through lack of sleep, keyed up with tension, Smith-Dorrien again spelt out the bleak unarguable facts.

There was a long pause before Wilson replied. 'If you stand to fight,' he said quietly, 'there will be another Sedan.'

As Wilson spoke, Smith-Dorrien heard a thud and then another.

'It's too late now,' he said. 'It's started.'

Not far to the north a battery of German guns was firing the opening shots of the Battle of Le Cateau.

Chapter 12

Ten miles of open country lay between the 5th Division on the ridge above Le Cateau and the village of Fontaine-au-Pire where the vanguard of the 11th Brigade had so unfortunately missed the way in the early hours of the morning. The main road from Le Cateau to Cambrai ran through rolling farmland, open slopes and valleys and wide fertile fields. The beetroot crops were well advanced, pastures scented the air with sweet clover, and sheaves of grain stood on the fresh-cut stubble between swathes of standing corn where the fields had been caught in mid-harvest by the war. Here and there, small groups of abandoned cattle, hobbled and tethered in the Flemish style, roused themselves at daybreak and began browsing in the meadows oblivious of the stir around them. Astride the road in the villages of Inchy, Caudry, and south of it in hamlets, fields and meadows, the Army waited for the day. No one had the faintest idea whether morning would bring an advance, a defensive action or retreat, and they were too tired to care. In barns and outbuildings, packed into farmyards, and, where there was no shelter to be found, out in the open in fields, in ditches, on the cobbles of village streets, the exhausted BEF had slumped down wherever there was space to rest its weary bones. In the minutes before dawn they stood to arms.

It was a long-established routine, instilled by rote and training into every prudent soldier since long before Caesar conquered Gaul. Dawn and dusk were the danger times. Then an army was at its most vulnerable and every nebulous bush, half-glimpsed in the half-light, might hide the darker outline of an enemy drawing near under the cloak of the shadows to take them by surprise.

It was on the left flank that they saw first spotted the Germans and it certainly came as a surprise to the 4th Division bivouacked round Fontaine-au-Pire at the far end of the tenuous line. They had received no orders of any kind and they had no information to go on – other than the shrewd suspicion that they were out on a limb on their own. To General Snow's displeasure, his Cavalry Squadron, the eyes of the Division, had been withdrawn to reinforce the Cavalry Division, without so much as a by-your-leave, and with no fast-moving horsemen to send in search of the

Germans, he had no means whatever of knowing where the enemy was. The General was not even entirely sure of the whereabouts of the three brigades of his own division for he had no communications. That was far more serious. The Signals Company was the vital link that connected the General at his headquarters with his battalions in the field and the Signals Company, with its miles of cable, its telephone equipment, its motorcyclists, its mounted messengers, its heliographs and signallers, had only just reached St-Quentin.

In their absence, General Snow sent three of his Staff Officers riding off at first light to find the Division and to pass on the Corps Commander's order to prepare for battle.

Captain Elles was the first to return and he reported with scant ceremony. 'They're already at it,' he said. 'They're at it, hammer and tongs!'

It was half-past five in the morning and the infantry had been 'at it' for more than an hour. It was already a full-scale battle and the 4th Division was indeed out on a limb. General Sordet with his French cavalry was somewhere on their left – but there was a long gap between them. And on their right another gap separated them from the 3rd Division at Caudry.

For the first hour it had been touch and go.

The Germans attacked the 4th Division with cavalry, with artillery, with machine-guns. They came at a hapless transport column, drawn up in the streets of Beauvois with nothing to defend it but the rifles of drivers and brakesmen. They spied the 1st King's Own on the march, all-unsuspecting on Haucourt hill, and opened up with a tornado of shells that set the transport stampeding and all but swept away the Battalion itself. They attacked with machine-guns, close-massed so that the bullets swarmed across like angry bees. They pushed forward wherever there was a gap. They filtered round the British flanks to try to take them in the rear. They came at them again – and again – and again. The line swayed. It cracked. But it held.

It held even before the artillery got into action, for General Milne had only begun to reconnoitre positions for the guns when the fight started. The musketry of the infantry kept the Germans off for a full hour before the guns were able to join in.

Of course they had to retire, but it was only a little way in the time-honoured tradition of 'adjusting the line', moving at a deliberate pace intended to demonstrate disdain to the German infantry, blundering knee-high through a beetroot field and making heavy weather of it as they came. When the Tommies stopped in their new positions and turned again to face them, the German soldiers hardly stood a chance.

Far to the right, during brief lulls in the fighting, they could hear faint bursts of fire from the skirmishing round Inchy and Caudry and, further off, the ceaseless hammer and thud of the guns at Le Cateau.

As the morning wore on it was clear that the Germans were pitting the bulk of their efforts against the flanks. They could afford to leave well alone. When both flanks had been pushed inwards, the situation in the centre would collapse of its own weight. By one o'clock a lull had fallen across the battlefront. The Germans were concentrating their attentions on Le Cateau and there the situation was worsening by the minute.

The 2nd Battalion, The Suffolk Regiment, had spent the night packed into the barns and outbuildings of a single farm.

Pte. A. W. Fenn, No. 8021, 2nd Bttn., The Suffolk Regt., B.E.F.

I can never imagine how we all crammed in, because there was near enough eight hundred of us, even after our losses at Mons. We tethered the horses in a field outside and by the time I'd seen to Major Wilson's horse you could hardly get through the gate. But I managed to squeeze into a corner beside my chums. There was four of us, Arthur Ashby, Spud Tatum and Joey Smith and me. We all joined up together and we stuck together whenever we could. We all came from Bury and we joined up on 28 April 1910, so we'd done four years peacetime soldiering by then. The old King, Edward, died that summer and we went up from the Isle of Wight to London and lined the streets for his funeral.

The nearest we got to active service before the war was the year after when there was the coal strike and we were sent to Chirk in North Wales on strike duty. It wasn't a job we looked forward to, but it was all right. In fact the miners were ever so friendly. They even arranged football matches with the Regiment. We played them quite a few times.

Just before the war broke out it was a bit more exciting. We were posted to Dublin. No trouble again, except for illegal gun-running by the Irish Nationalists. We didn't run into anything ourselves, but they pelted the King's Own Scottish Borderers in Dublin with bottles and stones. That was ugly. They gave them a lot of abuse. They used to call them 'King's Own Scottish Butchers'.

We came straight from there to France. We'd been up at Mons, but we only had two companies in action there on the canal, so for most of us Le Cateau was going to be our first taste of action. Well it was for Arthur and Spud and Joey and me, anyway. So there we were all jammed into this farmyard and Major Doughty came round and told us if any shells came over in the night we were to get out into the open and spread across the fields. I hate to think of the mess there would have been if they *had* shelled us, but everything was quiet, though we didn't get much sleep because there was no room to stretch out. We were all dead tired after the march from Mons but we were so cramped and shoved up together that when morning came we were quite glad to get ready to move again.

A couple of years before I'd been on a Mounted Infantry Course and learned all about horses, so I was Major Wilson's groom. I'd seen to the horse and got all the Major's kit strapped to the saddle and his overcoat rolled up neat behind it. The Battalion was all lined up on the road and I think we were actually mounted ready to move off when there seemed to be a hitch and the Major was called away. When he came back he said that we weren't going to retreat and we were going into the trenches ready for action. I suppose that would be just after six in the morning.

The Suffolks were not charmed with their trenches. They had been dug by French civilians. They were shallow and they were straight, with none of the curving bays so useful for deflecting the blast of exploding shells. They were also in the wrong place because the site had been picked as a rearguard position from which troops might have to make a quick getaway. There was 'dead ground' all around – invaluable cover for a rearguard to slip off unobserved when things got too hot, but all too convenient for an enemy intent on creeping up to outflank a battalion fighting to hold the ground; the trenches were on a forward slope, in full view of the enemy who could easily creep forward unobserved through a dozen tiny valleys and sunken roads that lay beneath their position, and to counter-attack over this terrain would be impossible. The troops would simply not be able to see where they were going, and because the land fell away in front of them twisting, bending, undulating as it went, the field of fire on their immediate front was, to say the least, limited. It was a rotten place to fight a battle.

RSM Bobby Burton looked over the position with the brand of furious disapproval he normally reserved for hapless new recruits. He was not an engaging man.

Pte. A. W. Fenn, No. 8021, 2nd Bttn., The Suffolk Regt., B.E.F.

We called him Old Bobby – and various other names when he couldn't hear us! Everybody knows the RSM is the regimental bully, but Bobby was damned insulting with it. If he had a recruit in line he would call his name out even if he wasn't on parade. 'Where do you live?' he'd say. And if the chap said Bury St Edmunds (because a lot of us *did* come from there) he'd say, 'Don't insult my native town. We wouldn't recognise scrap iron like you.' He had some repartee, did Old Bobby, and we got to know it all.

'Where do *you* live?'

'Essex, Sir.'

'Why the hell don't you go in the Essex Regiment? We don't want their bloody left-overs here.'

'What did you do in civilian life?'

'A shepherd, Sir.'

'Well wake up, bloody shepherd, you're not sitting on a gate eating a swede now!'

'What did *you* do in civilian life?'

'I was a musician, Sir.'

'I expect you knocked your old man down with a roll of music and ran away from home!'

'What's *your* name?'

'Swann, Sir.'

'Well wake up, Swann, and jump to it. You may have a neck like a swan but you've got ears like bloody rhubarb!'

Once he was inspecting a parade of recruits before Lieutenant Stubbs arrived, asking them all questions and passing his usual remarks. When the inspection started, Old Bobby toned it down a bit, but he kept on passing remarks about each recruit. When he got to the chap next to me he said to the officer, 'A most awkward recruit, Sir. I'll give you five bob to a pinch of snuff he's only a third-class shot. Aren't you, my lad?' Of course this chap said, 'Yes, Sir.' Of course Old Bobby knew this perfectly well, but he had the nerve to say to Lieutenant Stubbs, 'There you are, Sir, what did I tell you? I can pick them out just by looking at them!' He was a character, Old Bobby was.★

The RSM had served more than twenty-five years with the Suffolks. He was well over age for active service and strictly speaking he should have been left behind at the Regimental Depot when the Battalion sailed for France. But it was unthinkable to imagine the Battalion functioning without him and on the morning of the battle the sight of Bobby Burton's tight-lipped choleric face which had put the fear of God into recruits on the barrack square, was strangely reassuring to the younger Suffolks waiting with mixed feelings for their first taste of battle.

★ RSM 'Bobby' Burton was wounded at Ypres in December 1914 and invalided home where he died in Lincoln Hospital.

In the last remaining minutes before the morning exploded into battle, the RSM set the men digging. There was not much they could do to improve the trenches and they had nothing but entrenching tools to work with, but with many hands to help and some fruity encouragement from the RSM they scraped away at the despised ditches and made them deeper by the inch or so that would give at least a small degree of cover. Fortunately the soil was light, loamy and easy to dig in, so they managed to achieve a little. In the time available it was little enough, but as the morning wore on the Suffolks were glad even of that.

Fenn took no part in the digging. He was not even in the line. With the other officers' grooms his place was in a sunken road a hundred or so yards behind the trench and his job was to hold the Major's horse. It was almost worse to have to wait with nothing to do and he half wished he were out in front with Spud and Arthur and Joey, digging with the rest. They were within a few yards of 80 Battery busily preparing for action and Fenn knew full well that when the guns began firing it would be as much as they could do to keep the frightened horses under control.

Lt. R. A. Macleod, 80 Battery, XV Brigade, R.F.A., 5th Division, B.E.F.

We came into action in a turnip field in front of a field of standing corn and one hundred yards behind the crest of a low ridge. The ridge dipped in front of 37 Battery, and 11 Battery on our right was on slightly higher ground, so we seemed to be the best off for concealment. Captain Bartholemew, the Staff Captain, Royal Artillery, rode along the position and told us that there was going to be a big battle and there would be no retreat.

Captain Bartholemew had come from General Headlam's headquarters and his instructions were to go in person to every battery position to see that the General's orders had been understood. With time running short and with three brigades of guns already in position along the 5th Divisional front, it was a daunting task. Beyond the valley that divided the XVth Artillery Brigade from the XXVIII, 122 Battery was dug in almost alongside the Roman road and, because it had originally been designated as rearguard battery before the cancellation of the retreat, it was well dug-in and in a better position than 123 and 124 which had been moved up-front by General Headlam's order. Second Lieutenant Clarrie Hodgson, twenty years old and newly commissioned, was to be signals officer during the action, keeping the battery in touch with Artillery Brigade Headquarters from a position slightly in the rear, but he was up with the guns when

Captain Bartholemew rode over the hill and, after a word with Major Sanders, beckoned the men to gather round.

2nd Lt. C. F. Hodgson, 122 Battery, XXVIII Brigade, R.F.A., B.E.F.

He came, dismounted, and stood up on one of the limbers and looked out over all the chaps who'd gathered round and he told us what the situation was. He said that it was very, very serious and he was depending on us. He left us in no doubt as to what we were expected to do when we went into action. He said it was up to us, that we'd done well and he knew we'd do well again and wouldn't let him down.

I felt terribly elated. I was terribly young and quite inexperienced and I felt that this was something really exciting, that something was really going to happen in my life. I wasn't scared or apprehensive at all. Oddly enough I thought more about my brother – my twin brother, Victor. He was in 124 Battery, and I hadn't seen him at all though their battery position wasn't far away from us.

Lt. R. A. Macleod, 80 Battery, XV Brigade, R.F.A., 5th Division, B.E.F.

In front of us was Le Cateau. In the valley north-east of it ran a railway embankment on which we would put down our fire, and beyond the embankment the ground rose again to a ridge which was still hidden in mist.

We dug ourselves in as best we could, and the Major called us up to the crest in front where he had his Observation Post and explained the situation. The British Army was to stand and fight. The Second Corps was occupying a horseshoe-shaped position with the 5th Division on the right, the 3rd in the centre, and the 4th on the left. The Germans were known to be close to us in force.

A hundred yards ahead of us on top of the ridge the Suffolks were hastily digging themselves in with their entrenching tools. This was the front line! As the mist began to clear we could see the high ground beyond the River Selle on our right flank. I heard Major Birley ask the Colonel, 'Who is occupying it?' And the Colonel replied, 'First Corps.'

But the First Corps, a dozen miles away, had already taken to the road to continue their retreat. They were nowhere near. But for most of the day as they plodded south they could hear the relentless crash of the guns rolling across the sky above Le Cateau in the west. It was to be a gunner's battle, and it was not so much a battle as a duel.

In Le Cateau down in the valley, the 19th Brigade were having a lively time even before the first shots were fired. The 19th were nobody's children. The four battalions which comprised it had come to France to man the lines of communication and they had been hastily pressed into fighting service at Mons. Now, although they came nominally under the orders of the Second Corps, like many other units they had received no orders cancelling the retreat. No one had been able to find them. They had reached Le Cateau very late and bivouacked near the railway station. Captain Cunningham, in command of C Company, the 1st Middlesex, was fortunate in having Private McDonald as his batman and McDonald was a resourceful soldier. Nothing got him down and his cheerful demeanour had been a distinct comfort to his captain on the long road down from Mons. When the company had settled down in the station yard for the night, McDonald had taken it on himself to find a billet for the Captain. It was no palace, merely a railwaymen's shed between the points a little way along the tracks. It was impossible to stand upright and since the hut was a dumping ground for tools it was not too easy to lie down, but Cunningham had been grateful. McDonald had even managed to produce a mug of hottish tea when he poked his head in with the unwelcome news that it was time to get up. It was quarter to four in the grey dawn and already the sleepy Battalion was rousing reluctantly to move off before full daylight. The 1st Middlesex would be the last of the four battalions to move, for today they were to be rearguard to the Brigade and, as rearguard to the Battalion itself, the men of C Company were the last out of Le Cateau.

It gave them an unpleasant jolt when they were shot at as they left. How the Germans had worked round to the east of the town was a mystery but there they were and it was, as Captain Cunningham later jotted laconically in his diary, 'a lively exit'. This hardly summed up the heart-stopping excitement, the frantic dash to take up positions, to block the street with transport wagons. It only hinted at the smack of bullets ricocheting from walls and occasionally thudding into flesh, at the clattering hooves of the Uhlans as they wheeled and manoeuvred in pursuit, at the swift steady crack of the rifles, at the slow, yard-by-yard retirement. It said nothing of Captain Cunningham's relief when they were clear of trouble nor of his puzzlement over why they had been attacked at all. Where was the First Corps?

Their route lay along the valley floor and the guns now roaring above merely seemed to indicate that the artillery was fighting a rearguard action to cover the retreat. In accordance with their own instructions they struck off up the hill to Reumont to join the main road to St-Quentin. And here, as they hurried through the village, anxious to put as much distance as possible between themselves and the shelling, they were spotted and stopped by an astonished Staff Officer. It was the first the Middlesex knew of the battle. It was a quarter to ten in the morning and they had been fighting it for more than three hours.

Diary of Capt. J. S. Cunningham, C Company, 1st Bttn.,
The Middlesex Regt., B.E.F.

Told by Col. Cameron (Staff, 5th Division) that we were going to stand and fight – Told to take company behind a wood and join remainder of battalion – Did so – Argyll and Sutherland Highlanders and ourselves moved on to hill near Le Cateau – Took up position about 10 a.m. – Heavily shelled – Good many casualties – retired to second trench – Cavalry retired from our flank – Total of about 800 on our hill, Middlesex, Scots Fusiliers and Argylls – Masses of enemy appeared in front and both flanks – Must have been some thousands.

Lt. R. A. Macleod, 80 Battery, XV Brigade, R.F.A., 5th Division,
B.E.F.

We opened fire about 6 a.m. and registered a few targets including the railway embankment. When the mist lifted, we saw that the high ground on the opposite side of the valley beyond the embankment was crowded with Germans. We opened on them with battery fire 20 seconds at 4,000 yards gradually reducing the range as the Germans advanced, and for two hours we kept up 'battery fire 5 seconds' at a range of 2,400 yards on the line of the embankment they were trying to cross. They suffered severely.

The German artillery soon opened frontally on the trench in front of us. The fire became hotter and hotter and several 'overs' fell among our batteries. One of our first casualties was Lieutenant Coghlan of the 11th Battery on our right. He was killed, and I saw his body being taken to the rear on a stretcher along the back of our position to a sunken lane. We continued to fire at the German infantry. Some of them came within rifle fire of our infantry and were wiped out.

More and more German batteries came into action, a big concentration of them was Rambourlieux Farm which was now visible on our left flank (it had been concealed by the early-morning mist) and from there they could enfilade our position. A German aeroplane came overhead about 9 a.m. and started dropping stuff like streamers of silver paper over our trenches. Whenever he did this the German guns opened up on the spot he was flying over. He came over our brigade and did the same. A ranging round fell near the 11th Battery from a German battery enfilading from the left. Salvoes then began to fall on the 11th Battery, and their casualties started mounting up, we could hear them calling for stretchers, and many shells also fell on the 37th Battery on our left knocking out some guns and detachments. We, behind our low ridge, were more fortunate and only had comparatively few shells on the position. Wounded infantry and gunners began to trickle past us on their way back to the dressing station in Reumont.

Our infantry were splendid. They had only scratchings in the ground made with their entrenching tools, which didn't give much cover, but they stuck it out and returned a good rate of fire. The German infantry fired from the hip as they advanced, but the fire was very inaccurate.

The 'close support' that General Headlam had so strongly desired to give the infantry was doing the infantry no good at all. In the path of the shockwaves, hunched close to the trembling earth, ears ringing, teeth rattling, nerves screaming with every explosion, they could do nothing to retaliate and nothing to avert disaster when, all too often, a shell meant for the guns fell short and burst among the soldiers in the trench.

Fenn was still holding fast to the horses' bridles, moving as the terrified beasts pranced and whinnied, to stay between them in the shelter of their quivering bodies. The line was concealed by a rise in the ground and there was no telling what was happening. The wounded limping past were too shocked and dazed, too anxious to get out of it, to answer any questions but their expressions spoke volumes. He was all too close to the guns and he ducked and listened and looked and ducked again as the shells crashed among them. The Germans had fixed the gun positions to a nicety and with every bursting shell, it seemed, another gun was knocked out. Now, and Fenn could not understand it, there were bullets flying among the gun crews and, as one by one the gunners fell, they silenced the guns as effectively as a direct hit. Fenn wondered uneasily if the Germans had advanced, if the front line could be giving way and, as he strained to control the struggling horses, he wondered too how his comrades were faring in the fight.

But the Germans were biding their time and they could well afford to. When they had pounded the gun-line to atoms, their infantry would merely have to stroll across to capture the British trenches and what remained of the British Army. It would be as easy as taking a lollipop from a baby. In the meantime it was proving to be surprisingly difficult. It was true that the gunfire was slackening but, judging that their own guns must outnumber the British by some five to one, it amazed the Germans that the British fire continued at all.

They had already brought up fresh batteries and the shells were homing in on the 5th Division gun crews from everywhere at once – from the north, from the west and, what was worse, from the east from the high ground across the valley where the First Corps, as they thought, stood to guard their flank. It came as a rude shock. As if the shelling were not bad enough, machine-guns spitting from the Montay spur were whipping the trenches and the gun-line with a fury of flying bullets.

Through the clouds of smoke and dust there was a movement to the north-west. It was hardly more than a blur at first, but to observers in the line, training their binoculars on the heights around Rambourlieux Farm, it grew, sharpened, came into focus and they could see quite clearly a vast body of the enemy's infantry. They were massing for the attack, and they were massing so closely that they presented a target it was almost impossible to miss. It was a relief to the infantry that, at last, they had something to fire at. It was not so easy to signal back to the guns, for the telephone lines that linked the batteries to their forward observers had long ago been sliced to shreds, and signaller after signaller, trying conspicuously to semaphore back to the gun-line, had been promptly shot and knocked out of action. Major Birley gave up the attempt to relay orders and, seizing his chance in a brief lull, he rushed back to the battery to take charge on the spot.

Lt. R. A. Macleod, 80 Battery, XV Brigade, R.F.A., 5th Division, B.E.F.

German infantry were working round our right across the ground that we thought was held by the First Corps, and our artillery was given a switch to the right which meant some guns of my section (the left) being run up by hand to engage them. The 11th Battery also had to turn a section round to deal with hostile machine-guns in the valley actually behind them! Almost from that moment the Germans started to concentrate on them with the most intense fire. Two of their guns were completely knocked out, and there were so many casualties among the gunners that the battery very soon ceased firing.

Further to the left there had been intensive German artillery fire on other batteries of the Division and several of them fell silent too.

From his small funkhole just behind 122 Battery, the signals officer, Clarrie Hodgson, could see little of the action but, as breathless runners came and went, as Hodgson relayed their increasingly urgent messages, he knew precisely what was going on. And it was not good.

In this sheltered position the guns were better placed than those of the batteries fighting in the open. He knew that his brother Vic was there across the field – at least he hoped he was, for the casualties in 124 Battery must be devastating. For every shell they fired – and they were still miraculously firing – three rained back and they hardly knew from which direction, for the Germans were shooting from directly in front of them, from the left and also from the right – and when from the heights east of Le Cateau they started shooting at their backs, it was the last straw. It was the first time in the long history of the Royal Regiment of Artillery that gunners were forced to scamper for shelter in front of the gun-shields and under the muzzles of their own guns.

It was an ignominious situation and the gunners did not care for it in the least. But their fury gave them strength, and they needed every ounce of straining sinew and quivering muscle to drag the guns from their emplacements and manhandle them, pulling, straining, heaving them through a hundred degrees to face the enemy.

Even now they were not in a position which Major Kinsman would willingly have chosen. They were forced to fire directly over the guns of the battery in front. Already they had lost two guns, but with the four that remained they were at least able to reply.

2nd Lt. C. F. Hodgson, 122 Battery, XXVIII Brigade, R.F.A., B.E.F.

I noticed that our two flank batteries had swung back and were pointing at right angles to the original line of fire, so that the whole regiment formed an open square, just like the Napoleonic Wars! This indicated, even to a 'rookie' like myself, that things were not going too well – and subsequent events proved that this was putting it mildly!

By then we'd had about half a dozen guns knocked out and a *lot* of casualties in the gun crews. Then there was a lull (in fact the shelling almost ceased) but *still* we were getting casualties. We couldn't understand it. We were still firing, of course, but there wasn't much coming back and yet men suddenly dropped dead at the guns. *Then* we realised what was happening. We couldn't see into Le Cateau itself from where we were, but we *could* see the spire of the church through a slight dip between the high ground in front and the high ground on our right. It suddenly struck us that there was a machine-gunner in this church tower. Of course he could see us perfectly plainly and he was simply picking the chaps off and we hadn't even heard the bullets coming above the bally racket. So we ranged on the spire, put a few shells on it and put him out of action pretty quickly.

But it gave us a nasty turn, because it was only then that we realised that the Germans had occupied Le Cateau – and it was only a matter of a few hundred yards away!

Lt. R. A. Macleod, 80 Battery, XV Brigade, R.F.A., 5th Division, B.E.F.

About noon we saw the German infantry beginning to advance south between us and Rambourlieux Farm. Major Birley came down from the OP. He ordered 'Gun Control' to take them on. Hewson took charge of Nos. 1 and 2 guns, Mirrlees of No. 3 and I took No. 4. Because of casualties in the battery, the rest of the men of my section were distributed to the other four guns of the battery. All the men, in spite of the shelling and casualties, were as calm and as quiet and steady as if they were on a gun drill parade!

We swung the four guns round to the left to face the German infantry and began firing at 1,600 yards, each gun firing almost over the one on its left over open sights. The Germans went to ground behind a road embankment.

2nd Lt. C. F. Hodgson, 122 Battery, XXVIII Brigade, R.F.A., B.E.F.

The German infantry appeared almost in front of us. There were hordes of them! They were in very close formation and they were coming forward, coming forward, closer and closer, nearer and nearer the guns. The order was shouted, 'Gun fire!' That meant that all the guns had to fire at a speed of six rounds a minute. You can imagine the casualties they took. Men were falling down like ninepins, but *still* they came on. But their tactics were that they moved forward a few paces, dropped to the ground, then fired and then came on again. They were close enough to shoot at us with rifles, and we were firing back at point-blank range. Of course this created sheer pandemonium and devastation among the enemy. The poor devils never stood a chance! All the same, we knew it was only a matter of time.

Lt. R. A. Macleod, 80 Battery, XV Brigade, R.F.A., 5th Division,
B.E.F.

The German infantry began advancing again and we shortened our
range to 1,200 yards and increased our fire. We could see them
dropping down, taking shelter behind corn stooks.

We had to go easy now as our ammunition was beginning to run
out, so Captain Higgon ordered up three ammunition wagons, one
for each section. The first two for the right and centre sections came
up and the teams got away, but the team of the wagon for my section
got caught up in the Brigade telephone wire which ran through the
standing corn behind the battery. We ran to get them out, but the
horse were plunging and struggling. Some men ran to them, and tried
to unhook them, while I and some others ran to the wagon body to
start unloading the ammunition so that we could go on firing. The
Germans spotted us, and a salvo burst almost on top of us. All the
horses and men at the wagon were killed or wounded.

I was just pulling a shell out of the wagon body when I was hit by
shrapnel bullets in the head and arm and knocked to the ground.
Several of the rest of the battery came running to help us. Reay
Mirrlees put field dressings on my head and arm, and they helped us
back into the shallow pits we had dug behind the guns. I think I must
have passed out for a short time.

Besieged, bombarded, outnumbered by more men and guns than they
could count, Smith-Dorrien's Second Corps had held out for more than
six hours. They had gone far beyond the call of duty. They had almost
gone beyond the point of endurance. They had amply fulfilled their task
of checking the Germans, and still they were not defeated.

But they could not hold out much longer, and General Fergusson knew
it. Minute by minute he had kept abreast of the situation and at midday
he began to see unmistakable signs that the Front would soon crack. The
battlefield was a shambles. Men and horses, dead, wounded and dying,
littered the ground. The skeletons of guns lay askew on their wheels, their
barrels pointing uselessly at the sky. Limbers were overturned and splintered
to matchwood. Rifles still cracked and crackled, the guns still roared, and
men still laboured and fought on but, from the rear, small groups of soldiers,
daunted by the bombardment that met them as they tried to move forward,
had began to trickle away. It would be only a matter of time before the
trickle became a flood. Shortly after one o'clock, Sir Charles Fergusson
sent a message to the Corps Commander and told him it was time for his
Fifth Division to go.

They had held out for longer than Smith-Dorrien had dared to hope and he hardly liked to ask for more. But he asked it nevertheless. Could Fergusson hold on for just a little longer? He left it to his own discretion to withdraw as and when he saw fit. Above all, it must not be a rout. The Division must withdraw gradually, cautiously, in a calm and ordered manner. There must be no bottleneck, no congestion. Only thus could the Army hope to get away. Only thus could the roads be kept clear for the 3rd and 4th Divisions to follow. It was now twenty to two. Twenty minutes had passed since Fergusson had sent his message and the situation was now worse. The Germans were almost upon them.

In the shallow pit just behind what remained of 80 Battery, propped against the wheel of a shattered limber, Rory Macleod woke from his fainting fit and imagined that he was having a nightmare. He was unable to move. He seemed to be in the centre of a whirlwind of explosions and even as he tried to gather his wits a shell-splinter striking the wheel of the wagon a hair'sbreadth from his head almost put him back to sleep for good and all. As it was, it jarred him painfully and woke him to a full sense of the danger.

Lt. R. A. Macleod, 80 Battery, XV Brigade, R.F.A., 5th Division, B.E.F.

I had lost a good deal of blood and was feeling weak and dizzy but from where I was I could see Major Birley and Mirrlees, who had taken charge of No. 4 gun also, standing up behind their guns which were firing away rapidly at the German infantry. The German artillery now seemed to have our battery taped and concentrated on it. Salvo after salvo fell among the guns. No. 4 gun had a direct hit and my servant, Gunner Stewart, who was the layer, was killed. Mirrlees and the remainder of the detachment transferred to No. 3. Machine-guns started firing at the battery from the direction of the road, and you could hear their bullets rattling on the gun-shields. Our range came down to eight hundred yards.

Macleod still could not move. He could only wait, knowing that the Germans were now close in front and knowing too, as the firing grew louder at his back, that they were drawing close behind. There was no chance now of rescue. In minutes, and he resigned himself to the fact, he would be either killed or captured. With his good hand he drew his revolver from its holster and waited. If he had to go he would make quite sure that he took at least one of the enemy with him.

2nd Lt. C. F. Hodgson, 122 Battery, XXVIII Brigade, R.F.A., B.E.F.

The Germans kept moving forward, forward, until they were actually
shooting at us with their rifles. Then the order came down – *Save the
guns!* And the gun teams came dashing down, over the hill, right
through the middle of all this carnage. And then the Hun opened up
on them – artillery, machine-guns, rifles, everything! The horses were
silhouetted against the skyline and they made a perfect target. It was
absolute slaughter! Men and horses were just blown to pieces. One team
of four horses and a limber managed to reach one of the guns, limber
up and drag it over the high ground behind us. We were still in
position, doing what we could, although we were practically cut off
by the Hun and we realised our position was hopeless. Our Colonel,
the adjutant and two battery commanders had been killed, and many
of the men, and the place was a shambles. Then, to our intense relief
down came the order – *Every man for himself. Destroy the guns.*

I ran to one of the guns and I yelled to Gunner Major, an Irish chap
who was the limber gunner. The orthodox way to destroy the guns was
to put a round down the muzzle and one in the breech and then fire it
from a safe distance by using a lanyard. But there was no time for that.
All we could do was smash the sights and remove the breech which
would at least put it out of action. So that's what we did. Major took
the breech and we started to run up this hill behind us.

*Lt. R. A. Macleod, 80 Battery, XV Brigade, R.F.A., 5th Division,
B.E.F.*

When No. 3 gun was hit, Mirrlees moved to No. 2 and we now had
2 guns and 8 men left in action firing away as hard as they could go,
with salvoes bursting all round them. It was passed down that Hewson
had been hit in the shoulder by a shrapnel bullet, but Mirrlees standing
up behind No. 2 gun seemed to bear a charmed life. Suddenly someone
called out: 'The Major's hit.'

About 2.30 p.m. I saw all the brigade teams racing up at a gallop
from the wagon-lines led by Major Tailyour, the Brigade Major, and
ours by Captain Higgon. Shells were bursting all round them. It was
a magnificent sight! Now and again a man or horse or whole team
would go down. It was like Balaclava all over again!

Only two teams got to the guns and when they did they drove straight
into a salvo of shells. They erupted between the teams and the havoc was

sickening. Flying bodies, horses wounded, plunging, screaming, streaming with blood and struggling to get free of the shattered limbers, dragging the dead weight of others collapsed in the traces, and, beside themselves with terror, trampling on the bodies of the wounded and the dead. They reared and pranced so close to the pit where the wounded were sheltering that it seemed to Rory Macleod and his terrified companions that at any moment they might be crushed and trampled to death.

Before he knew it Macleod found himself on his feet, found that he was shouting, dragging at the reins, straining to hold the living horses while a gunner slashed at the traces to cut away the hopeless weight of the dead. Somehow it was managed. Somehow the ruined wagon, its wheels merci-fully intact, was hooked up to a gun. There were three horses left. The unknown gunner gave him a leg up and with almost the last of his strength Macleod heaved himself into the saddle and, spurring his mount as best he could, the gun bumping and thudding behind him, galloped No. 5 gun over the hill and out of the action. He held to the saddle with difficulty, for he still felt groggy and light-headed. But it was the most thrilling gallop of his life. It was a far cry from hallooing across the moors in Ireland. It felt *exactly* like Balaclava.

Fenn had long ago left the sunken road. He had taken to the fields and for some considerable time now he had been squatting behind the remains of flattened corn stooks. This shelter was purely psychological but at least he was far enough from the guns to escape the merciless shelling and to have some hope of controlling his horse and the Major's charger. It had been horrible to watch, and the last five minutes had been the worst of all. The guns were leaving, the infantry was streaming back, it was clear that the battle was over and still there was no sign of the Major. Fenn stood up and moved closer to the road, leading the reluctant horses, looking in vain for a familiar face among the troops going away from the line. He fervently wished he could go too but, in the absence of any new instructions, there was nothing for it but to stay where he was. He had watched Macleod dragging No. 5 gun from the ruins and tearing away over the hill. He had seen Tailyour help to hook up No. 6 and send its team galloping off to safety and he had watched him set off in the opposite direction, running against the tide of troops, running *towards* the line. He passed inches away, glared at Fenn in amazement and, hardly slackening his pace, yelled out, 'Do you want to get killed?' Fenn did not relish the prospect and said so. 'Well get the hell out of it then!' That was enough for Fenn. He jumped into the saddle and got the hell out of it, travelling across country and as fast as he could go.

Pte. A. W. Fenn, No. 8021, 2nd Bttn., The Suffolk Regt., B.E.F.

It was really rough going. There were wounded horses all over the place and they'd panicked, you see, and tearing around the way they were, panicking like, a lot of them had got tangled up in barbed-wire fences round the fields. Of course nobody could stop to help them or even to put a bullet through them to put them out of their misery. When I struck the road I was still leading Major Wilson's horse with all his kit on it and an officer of the Duke of Cornwall's Light Infantry came up to me and asked me whose horse it was. I told him, and he said, 'Well I've lost mine so I'll take Major Wilson's in the meantime.' And when I hesitated a bit, not knowing what to do (though I had to obey an officer), he said, 'It's all right. If Major Wilson turns up he can have it back right away.'

Of course the inevitable happened. Major Wilson *didn't* turn up – he was captured as I later found out – and he kept *me* as well as the horse until I caught up with what was left of the Battalion. That was days later. All that time I didn't see a single other man of the Regiment. Eventually we re-formed in a field, miles to the south it was, and then the roll was called. We had two officers left out of twenty-six, Lieutenant Oakes the Transport Officer and Captain Blackwall the Quartermaster. And there was only two hundred and fifty men out of more than eleven hundred.

2nd Lt. C. F. Hodgson, 122 Battery, XXVIII Brigade, R.F.A., B.E.F.

Everybody was running the same way – everyone who was left! We'd just got to the crest when Gunner Major tripped and fell forward flat on his face. At least I *thought* he'd tripped and I went back to help him up. Poor chap! There was blood coming out of his back. He'd been hit by a sniper's bullet and killed outright. There was nothing I could do but grab the breech and run on over the hilltop towards Reumont with the rest of them.

Just over the other side on the left of the road there was a farmhouse and of course it had the usual cess-pit in the courtyard. So I heaved the breech into the middle of this foul-smelling muck, jolly glad to get rid of it, and I remember thinking, 'Right! No ruddy Hun will ever find that one anyway.' The door was standing open, so in I went and looked round. There was nobody there, of course. The people had gone ages before. My chief concern was grub. We hadn't had a crumb of food all day and being more or less a growing lad still I was absolutely famished. But there wasn't anything that I could find. So I went on down the road to the rendezvous point, found my horse and waited for orders.

Not everyone had taken to the road. At two o'clock General Fergusson had issued the order for a general retirement. But it was one thing to send the order out. It was another matter to carry it to the soldiers in the trenches where they were fighting now almost hand-to-hand. The Germans were making a final all-out effort and the ground behind the trenches was swept by shellfire so intense that no messenger could hope to get through. They tried, and when the runners failed to return, they tried again. It was a full hour before some battalions got the signal to retire. Some never got it at all. So they fought on.

They fought with a remarkable tenacity. Now the Germans were only a hundred yards down the hill, inching closer still behind a barrage of machine-gun bullets that played back and forth, back and forth, along a ragged trench. It was held by a handful of Argylls and Suffolks. They would be massacred if they stayed there. They would be massacred if they moved back into the inferno of shellfire behind. They moved forward instead to a new position a good deal closer to the enemy, and there they went on fighting. It had not occurred to them to surrender.

A little to the right of them Captain Cunningham of the 1st Middlesex at last received the order to take C Company out.

Diary of Capt. J. S. Cunningham, C Company, 1st Bttn., The Middlesex Regt., B.E.F.

I personally was very pleased. I had had enough of Le Cateau! My company was the last of the battalion to retire – and it wasn't a moment too soon. I gave the orders a little less formally than the method laid down by regulations and started getting the men out. They wanted very little steadying and there was no panic. Two men, whose names I unfortunately forget, said to me, 'Why should we retire now, sir, when they're just coming on?'

The Germans certainly were 'just coming on'. They were massed in dense formations on three sides of the hill! We ought to have all been scuppered, but the men were A1 and we got away successfully. We were shelled all the way back and all the way through the village.

On the way back, during brief lulls in the shelling they could still hear the sound of rapid fire in the line and, behind it, the faint notes of a bugle.

In front of the Argylls and the Suffolks the Germans were sounding the British 'Ceasefire'. Some stood up, waving and gesticulating to encourage the British to surrender. The Highlanders took aim and coolly picked them off. Two of their officers, lying side by side, shouted out the hits, for all the world as if they were umpiring a shooting competition. They had knocked up quite a score when a detachment of Germans rushed them from behind. They had been fighting for nine hours but, at last, they were overwhelmed.★

★ The total losses of the three divisions engaged in the single day's fighting of the Battle of Le Cateau were 7,812 men and 38 guns.

Part Three
The Long Slog

Seven – six – eleven – five – nine an' twenty mile today –
Four – eleven – seventeen – thirty-two the day before –
(Boots – boots – boots – boots – movin' up and down again!)
    An' there's no discharge in the war!

Rudyard Kipling

Chapter 13

The Roman road that ran across the hills above Le Cateau and through the fields past Reumont to the south had never been intended to carry traffic such as this. But the line of the road was the one sure signpost that pointed away from the battle, and everyone was making for it. In their eagerness to be gone they looked to one astonished Staff Officer like crowds streaming away from a football match. Half dazed by their pounding, half deafened by the relentless thunder of the guns, half dead from their monumental efforts to hold the enemy at bay, and half asleep with exhaustion, the men milling on to the road were impelled by a single thought – to get down it as far as possible, to keep on their feet and keep going until darkness fell and concealed them from the enemy. There would be time enough then to think of rest.

The road could not possibly carry them all, for there were carts, wagons, ambulances, guns and limbers, and mounted men too, all entangled in the crush. In the hope of making at least some headway, most of the infantry took to the fields on either side and, carefully keeping the road in sight, stumbled on across the fields and farmland. Even if they had been fit and fresh it would have been rough going, and as the hours went on some dropped to the ground in spite of themselves and slept where they had fallen among the mangelwurzels and the beets. There was no one to rouse them. There were no orders. There was no one to give them. Not many detachments had managed to leave the field as a body and those which had had been split up and hopelessly confused among the throng. There was no question of proceeding in formation, no question of moving faster than a crawl and no means of skirting obstructions when crawling vehicles trying urgently to pass through brought the whole procession to a halt. There was no question of food, no question of rest and, with their enemy on their heels, no question of stopping. So the Army inched and shuffled and plodded on, half unconscious with weariness.

Apart from his rifle and ammunition hardly a man had any belongings other than the clothes he stood up in.

General Smith-Dorrien and his Headquarters Staff were only a little way ahead of the Second Corps as it shuffled painfully down the road. They had not left Bertry until the last possible moment and Smith-Dorrien had been reluctant to go at all. In an agony of apprehension, leaving the fate of his Command in the hands of his divisional generals, Smith-Dorrien rode south. As it was he was cutting it fine. The main road was beginning to be congested, so that by far the speediest and most practical means of making the journey was to strike out on horseback across country. Even so, by half-past four, the Staff had covered barely seven kilometres and they were still close enough to the battle to suffer the worst moment of a day which had provided more than sufficient bad moments as it was.

As they approached the village of Maretz, they heard a cannonade of gunfire coming from the west where, a scant ten miles away as the crow flies, the 4th Division had just been ordered to retire. Smith-Dorrien realised with a sinking of the heart that if the Germans were bombarding the unfortunate 4th Division such an intensity of fire would well and truly scupper their chances of getting away at all. He spurred his horse and galloped up a knoll that gave a view to the west. Even through powerful binoculars it was difficult to see much, but Smith-Dorrien was an experienced campaigner. He could see enough and – above all – he could hear enough to know that the bombardment could only come from the fast-firing French guns, the famous 'soixante-quinze'. And it was a powerful bombardment. He rode on reassured. Whatever was happening to the 4th Division, General Sordet and his cavalry were there too and, true to his word, were covering the British left flank. For the moment it seemed to be secure. And now that his right flank was retiring just as he had planned, although it was too soon to be absolutely certain that his gamble would pay off, it looked just possible that the balance of advantage had tilted by the merest fraction in his favour.

The French were doing more than covering the flank. They were hammering the Germans as they tried to push forward – and it was just as well.

Screened by the punishing fire of General Sordet's guns, the 4th Division far on the left flank was beginning to slip away.

The 1st R Bs were the rearguard and under the unremitting machine-gun fire it would have been suicide to attempt to march out as a body of men. The order had been 'every man for himself' and for a long time Captain Morgan Grenfell and Captain Sutton-Nelthorpe stood at the roadside in the lee of a railway embankment acting as 'whippers-in'. All they could offer was encouragement and for some men on the point of exhaustion a drink from their water-bottles. Morgan Grenfell was thankful that he was carrying an extra bottle and that he had taken the precaution of filling it with brandy. He reserved it for the walking wounded and it revived a few of them just enough to give them strength to limp on behind the long, retiring column. The officers had stayed until it was clear that there were no more to come.

Some troops had been left behind and there were enough of them to keep the Germans guessing. No orders had reached them and they waited on because no one had told them to go. At Caudry they stayed until long past nightfall, until long after the fighting had died down and, although they did not know it, until long after their comrades had left. As the hours wore on a rumour muttered its way through the ranks of the Gordon Highlanders and spread to the isolated companies of Royal Scots and Royal Irish on either side. The troops were saying that two Staff Officers had galloped along parallel to their line shouting the order to retire. What was more, a junior officer of the Gordon Highlanders had seen them too and Colonel Gordon, second-in-command of the Battalion, was convinced that the rumour was true. Lieutenant-Colonel Neish, the Commanding Officer himself, was not inclined to believe the report and despite all Gordon's urging refused to give the order to retire.

William Eagleson Gordon was an awkward man to have as a subordinate. He was a fire-eater renowned for the daring exploits that won him the Victoria Cross during the South African War and, less than a year before, the Army had raised him to the rank of Brevet Colonel. He was fully entitled to a command of his own but in the small peacetime Army, as an officer in a regiment composed of only two regular battalions plus a skeleton reserve, it might be years before a vacancy arose. It was an uneasy situation. In the eyes of the Regiment, Colonel Gordon was still a subordinate officer. By Army convention he was senior in rank to the mere Lieutenant-Colonel who was his own Commanding Officer. It was not the first time the two men had clashed but it was the first time it had mattered. The very idea of retiring was anathema to Colonel Neish. Until he received the order to do so at first hand the Battalion would stay put and the more Gordon argued the more determined Neish was to stay.

Hours passed. At half-past nine Neish agreed reluctantly to send three men to Troisvilles to find 3rd Division Headquarters and to ask for orders.

Troisvilles was no more than two miles away. Even in the dark and drizzle, even allowing for the unfamiliar country, two hours should have been more than long enough to make the journey there and back. There was ample time in their absence for an exchange of words between the two colonels. Neish was furious. Gordon was ruffled. Time dragged on. By half-past eleven when there was no sign of the messengers returning, Gordon at least concluded that Divisional Headquarters had long since packed up and gone, that the Germans were giving the orders in Troisvilles now, and that the particular order they had given their men was to raise their hands above their heads and surrender.

Already they had wasted valuable time in quarrel and argument, now it was time for action. There was no alternative, in Colonel Gordon's view, but to pull rank. Since the Battalion had scooped the isolated companies of other battalions under its wing, it was therefore a 'mixed force'. As such, and as the senior officer in army rank, it was Gordon's right to command it. He made it clear to Neish that it was a right he intended to exercise whether Neish liked it or not. There was a furious argument while precious minutes ticked by. The Army, in laying down the self-evident rule that a conglomerate of troops should be commanded by the highest ranking officer among them, had not envisaged a situation such as this. But the rule stood, convention won and the Commanding Officer of the Gordon Highlanders had no choice but to bow to the orders of his own subordinate. By the time Colonel Gordon had given the order to retire, by the time he had assembled his men from the outlying posts, it was long past midnight.

By half-past twelve they were marching south to Montigny – dark and silent, but for a single light in a cottage window. But two miles to the east, on the outskirts of Bertry, the Germans were waiting. There was little the Germans could do but fire into the dark and little the Gordons could do but spread out and fire back in the direction of the invisible enemy, gradually pull back, round up the stragglers and strike south-west towards Clary. But this village too was in German hands and, alerted by the noise of the fight at Bertry, the enemy had placed a field gun trained to fire straight down the approach road. In the years to come the men who formed the advance guard of the Gordon Highlanders that night took pride in the fact that they had rushed the gun before it was able to fire a shot. It was some small consolation for the unkind reputation that would dog them as long as that night was remembered. It was hardly their fault that they had not received the order to retire, and they hardly deserved to be nicknamed 'The Kaiser's Bodyguard'.

They had tried to fight their way through Clary. They had even overcome the guard and stormed a house where German officers were enjoying a well-earned rest. They had fought like demons to carve a way through the bastion of fire that met them at every turn and the men at the rear of the column had faced about to answer the shots that spurted from behind and gradually encircled them. They fought on for more than an hour. But they were trapped.

All across the country where the battle had been fought the crack of rifles stabbed through the thick dark of the night where isolated groups of men – a few hundred, a company, even a platoon – were trying to punch their way out of the trap.

Here and there a handful succeeded in dodging the Germans or fighting their way out. Days, weeks and even arduous months later they turned up.*

Long into the night and far to the south where the bone-weary men who had got away still dragged on down the road they could hear the distant popping of rifle fire. When the sky cleared after daybreak, anxious officers sought out vantage points to look for the enemy following in pursuit. There were none to be seen. But they could hear gunfire and from the high ground they saw with some astonishment and a touch of glee that German shells were exploding uselessly on positions they had quitted many hours before. It had been the longest night of their lives.

Rfn. E. Gale, No. 3774, 1st Bttn., The Rifle Brigade, 11th Brigade, 4th Division, B.E.F.

All night long, we never stopped all night. The Army Service Corps who had our rations, they couldn't stop. They just threw our rations on the side of the road and left us to pick them up. The drivers were retiring in front of us and they couldn't stop to deliver them to the regiments. They had to just drop them on the road and you had to pick them up if you had the chance, and that went on the whole ten days. And there were a lot of complaints, people saying, 'Why are we retiring? What are we retiring for? Why don't we turn round and have a scrap with them?' All the troops were saying that. They couldn't understand it.

---

* Major Shewan of the Dublin Fusiliers with a mixed bag of seventy-eight officers and men from almost every battalion of all three Divisions engaged at Le Cateau arrived 'after many sharp engagements' at Boulogne. A small group of the 1st Gordon Highlanders turned up after adventurous wanderings as far as north as Antwerp. At least two men, Trooper Hull and Corporal Fowler of the 11th Hussars, were hidden by villagers at Bertry. Hull was betrayed and executed as a spy. Fowler was hidden in a capacious kitchen cupboard under the noses of enemy soldiers who billeted in the same house and, despite hair-raising near-discoveries, survived the war. The two women who sheltered him, Madame Belmont-Gobert and her daughter Angèle, were awarded the OBE by King George V. But after the war they were found to be living in straitened circumstances. There was no official means of recompensing them but, since Corporal Fowler could technically be said to have been billeted on them, the Army had the happy thought of awarding them the standard additional messing allowance of two pence a day for the four years of his concealment. It amounted to two thousand and forty-four francs and fifty centimes – at that time approximately £1,700 – and a further subscription was raised as a token of gratitude by the officers and men of the 11th Hussars.

2nd. Lt. C. F. Hodgson, 122 Battery, XXVIII Brigade, R.F.A., B.E.F.

We were moving in feet. There was no proper movement. You moved a few yards and halted. Another few yards, halted. My big trouble was that I was so exhausted that I couldn't keep on my horse; I kept going to sleep so then I tied the stirrups under the horse's tummy and, of course, as I fell forward my feet didn't spread out so I kept on the saddle and this went on all night. It was lack of food that concerned me more than the fear of the Germans harassing us. The Army Service Corps people had dumped piles of biscuits and bully beef but we hadn't got time to open the boxes.

Capt. Herbert Stewart, 3rd Divisional Train, Army Service Corps, B.E.F.

I received an order to meet the Supply Column coming from Péronne and take it to my Division at Estrées, north of St Quentin. We were told not to take the road via Le Catelet because parties of Uhlans were reported to be on it, but I was to turn off to the right about six miles south of Le Catelet. The twenty-seven lorries of the column arrived at St Quentin about six in the evening and at dusk we started off taking the splendid broad tree-lined road north. We made good progress until 8.30 p.m., then through the darkness we suddenly saw the road ahead crowded with a mass of troops. I saw they were all infantrymen and guessed they must be our own people. They were in no military order, and without officers or senior NCOs. There must have been three or four hundred from a dozen different regiments from two or three Divisions. Some of them said that the enemy were close at their heels. If their story was true, I was in an unpleasant predicament. A tree laid across the road or a volley fired into the engine of the leading lorry would finish all chances of a dash through. However my orders were to get to my Division, so there was nothing to be done but get on.

All the headlights were lit in the hope that their glare would upset the enemy's marksmanship and would also show up any obstruction on the road. In addition, I took up about thirty men from the stragglers who were armed, and distributed them over the convoy. Then, telling the leading lorry driver to go at his best speed and the others to follow, I climbed into the first and away we thundered into the darkness. In time we reached the turning to our right which we had to follow, and leaving the broad high-road, we now found we were in a country lane. Suddenly round a corner came the head of a column of troops.

It was the British 5th Division retiring under cover of night. We pulled the heavy lorries as far to one side of the way as we could to let the tired men get past – infantry staggering along in utter weariness, horsemen lying asleep on their horses' necks, they went slowly by, an interminable stream of shadows. To add to the difficulty and discomfort it started to rain, making the foothold on the road slippery and treacherous.

Presently some Staff Officers rode up and in excited language demanded to know why I was blocking the road. They demanded that the lorries should be flung into the ditch so as not to impede the troops. Fortunately the argument was heard by a general officer who said that I must give up all idea of getting through to Estrées, as the roads leading up to that place were blocked with troops. He said that I should turn the lorries at the next cross-roads two hundred yards farther on and take them back to St Quentin. Slowly and with great difficulty this was accomplished, but our mission to the 3rd Division was not! However some good was done, for we distributed supplies to the men who were now struggling past, and they were greatly in need of them.*

Sgt. F. M. Packham, No. 10134, 2nd Bttn., Royal Sussex Regt., 2nd Brigade, 1st Division, B.E.F.

As we passed by, the drivers handed each man some items of food to carry. I was given a tin of Oxo cubes, a half-round of cheese and some tins of corned beef. The man next to me had a tin of army biscuits. These tins were about a cubic foot square, so it was difficult for him to carry with a rifle and his kit. But he was delighted. He thought he'd got the best of the bargain and he was reluctant to share or exchange with us. However, after marching carrying this tin for a few hours he decided to swap with us. This relieved our ration for a few days.

* From his account in *From Mons to Loos.* Major H. A. Stewart, DSO, Blackwood & Sons, 1917.

Rfn. E. Gale, No. 3774, 1st Bttn., The Rifle Brigade, 11th Brigade,
4th Division, B.E.F.

We were all half asleep, like, sitting in the saddle. Couldn't help it.
Just shut your eyes and hope you'll find your horse still on the road
in the morning. You couldn't stop. And it was pitch dark! We had
to keep well on top of one another, just to keep the horses right up
close to the others. I know I nearly went over a ditch into a field
because I couldn't see. There was other transport of other regiments
too and we was all mixed up. There was the East Lancashires, I
remember, and there was the Hampshire Regiment and there was
some Highlanders, they was all mixed up together on the retirement.
We had to take a nap when we could and it was really quite dangerous
if you came to a hill and you were asleep, because we never had brakes
on these wagons. All we had was things like stops made of steel, you
shove them under the wheels to hold the wagon back. And it rained.
You got soaked to the skin in the pouring rain and the clothes just
dried on you.

Down the road there was some attempt to sort them out. As they neared
Estrées, fifteen miles from Le Cateau, the bleary-eyed troops saw flashlights
glimmering through the dismal rain and the darkness. Staff officers were
posted at the crossroads shouting as the line of shifting shadows plodded
interminably by, '*Transport and mounted troops straight on. 3rd Division infantry
to the right. 5th Division infantry to the left.*' They shouted on and on incessantly
and when one voice faded to a croak another took up the cry. Somehow
the weary men were herded towards the makeshift rendezvous where other
officers calling into the night did their best to sort the mass into some
semblance of battalions, or at least into brigades. The officers themselves
were worn out with anxiety and exhaustion but they knew that the plight
of the men was worse. In the space of five days they had marched many
miles. They had fought two mighty battles. They had been taxed to the
limit. But it would be madness to let them rest now when it was all too
likely that the Germans were close behind and merely waiting for daylight
to catch up. Men who slumped to the ground because they could no longer
stand, and slept there because they could no longer keep awake, must be
roused – even kicked to their feet – and urged on down the road towards
St-Quentin. They had to keep going for the stark and simple reason that
it was their only chance.

But the Germans were not at their backs. They too had had some sorting
out to do and they were also not entirely sure what was happening. The

fact that the retreat was well under way before some fighting units got the order to follow on, the fact that those who had been left behind had fought on, the fact that now that they were on the move they were still fighting as they went, had placed General von Kluck in a dilemma. The scattered and excitable reports from his forward troops with news of a dozen different skirmishes across a dozen or more miles of battleground showed quite clearly that some of the British force had remained. What they did not show was how many. It might, for all the German commander knew, be half an army. The intervention of General Sordet's troops and guns late in the afternoon had come as an unpleasant surprise. They might even now be coming up in force.

Von Kluck had a whole reserve corps at his disposal. His cavalry had been resting all day during the battle. There was no doubt that the British were retiring, but this was unlike the retirement from Mons forty-eight hours before, when the enemy had duped him by creeping off under the cover of darkness. This time they had performed the feat of disengaging at the height of the battle and retiring in broad daylight and, as a soldier, von Kluck was to be the first to admit that it was a feat worthy of soldierly admiration. But it was past five before the main body had gone and, even if the road had been clear, even if the stragglers had not put up sufficient fight to keep the Kaiser's troops from storming forward, it was far too late in the day for the Kaiser's General to mass his troops to follow and to send his cavalry dashing through to rout them. It was too late even to send out reconnaissance patrols or aeroplanes to search for them before darkness fell.

It was past eight o'clock in the evening before the Germans had assessed the situation as they saw it, planned the next move and issued their order accordingly. Von Kluck's army was to 'continue to pursue the beaten enemy' and the order went on to lay down precisely the routes each unit should take. But they would lead them in the wrong direction. The German commanders, putting themselves in the position of their enemy, were convinced that the British would make for the coast, travelling westwards to the ports of Dunkirk, Calais, and Boulogne, just a short sea-passage from England. If they could cut them off before they got there the British could be easily annihilated. Two opportunities of enveloping the BEF, first at Mons and yesterday at Le Cateau, had now been missed. But, although the sweep they must make in order to encircle them must now of necessity be wider, it would clearly be third time lucky. Given the losses of the BEF, the number of prisoners who had fallen into their hands, the number of dead and wounded left on the battlefield with the mountains of supplies and equipment, given the exhaustion of the men, the BEF must be at cracking point. If the Germans did *not* succeed in catching them (and it seemed unlikely that they could fail to do so) they would chase them into the sea. They were to start before dawn, at four o'clock in the morning.

It did not occur to the Germans that the British would not make for home and retire on their lines of communication that led to Calais and Boulogne. It did not occur to them that the British lines of communication stretched much further south, as far as Le Havre in Normandy. Neither did it occur to the logical German mind that the British could do otherwise than follow the neat, convenient plan suggested by their own deduction. They did not consider the possibility that the British would not make for the coast, that they would retire alongside the French and that the line of retirement would be due south.

At four o'clock in the morning on 27 August, von Kluck's troops started on their way moving towards the south-west, marching, riding, rolling forward on a line that separated them from the British by an angle of forty-five degrees. Smith-Dorrien's men continued plodding south, and with every tortured mile the gap between them and the Germans widened.

But few of them were plodding now. They had begun to hobble. Blisters raised by the night's march had burst and raw flesh burned and chafed against matted shreds of wool and boots that gripped their bloated feet like vices. Yesterday evening one limping soldier, asked by his officer, 'How are your boots, McLagen?' had answered ruefully, 'Very full of feet, Sir.' Today, like most of his comrades in that bedraggled cavalcade, he would march until his boots were full of blood.

The rain stopped before dawn, the mist cleared early and the sun rose warm. By eight o'clock a steady stream of men were passing along the last stretch of the long road that led into St-Quentin. They looked less like an army than like a forlorn hope. Their unshaven chins bristled with days of stubble, their faces were drawn, their eyes red-rimmed and sunken, their tread heavy, their shoulders slumped. Their appearance did not excite the cheers of admiration that had greeted them just a week before, but it excited compassion. There were good samaritans at the roadside – white-aproned women armed with jugs of water, with bottles of wine, with baskets of apples and pears, even a crust or two of bread. At the top of a hill where a heavy kitchen table had been carried out and placed beneath a shady tree, two pigtailed schoolgirls poured endless cups of strong black coffee from outsize enamel jugs and behind them wisps of steam drifted through an open kitchen window as their mother boiled endless pans of water to replenish the jugs as fast as the Tommies could empty them. It could hardly be expected to put a spring in their steps but it gave them heart to struggle on over the last lap. In St-Quentin, so the soldiers had been told, there would be food, there would be a chance to rest and a chance to find their own units. Then (but not too soon they hoped!) they would set off to cover the last few miles that would take them to the new line behind the

River Somme where they could hold the enemy at bay while they recovered their strength. There they could wait for reinforcements to stiffen their ragged ranks. There, when they had retrieved their vigour, they would turn to meet the enemy. The next time they moved they would be doing the chasing.

Various rendezvous and collecting points had been hastily arranged in St-Quentin and Staff Officers posted at intervals along the route from the north were pointing the troops towards the town and directing them to collecting points where they would find food and drink and instructions. Frederic Coleman was not an officer. He was not even a soldier but as a private motorist he had volunteered his services at the outbreak of war and had come to France with the Army. At Mons he had had a close-up view of the fighting; now he had a grandstand view of the retreat. All morning he had been ferrying wounded men to the station to wait for the trains that would take them on to hospitals in Paris or Rouen or Le Mans, and now that the flow of wounded had dried up, a Staff Officer had stationed Coleman at the roadside to help usher the troops towards St Quentin. This officer wore a look of concern. He turned as he walked away, hesitated and then turned back with some parting advice.

'Cheer them up as you keep them on the move,' he said. 'They're very downhearted. Tell them anything, but cheer them up. They've got their tails down a bit, but they're really all right. No wonder they're tired! Worn out to begin with, then fighting all day and coming back all night – no rest, no food, no sleep, poor devils! Tell them where to go, and cheer them up, cheer them up.'

Coleman did his best and was amazed that his feeble attempts to joke prompted an occasional smile and even now and again a wisecrack in response. As a mere civilian he was unfamiliar with the regimental insignia of the grimy and disreputable soldiery and one ragamuffin group of Royal Fusiliers took him to task. 'You ought to know who *we* are, Sir. First in Mons and last out, *that's* who we are.' 'That's right,' chipped in another, 'in at three miles an hour and out at eighteen!' They actually laughed. It raised Coleman's own spirits quite considerably.

The rough attempt to sort the men into categories during the night on the long dark road from Le Cateau had hardly begun to disentangle the mix-up. Some men had been drawn into the fold of their own divisions, some had even found their own brigades. A few, like the handful of Royal Fusiliers who had joked with Coleman, had managed to stick with mates of their platoon. But there were so many lost sheep, so many individual men and even rumps of whole battalions who should not have been on that road at all, that for almost every man who found his rendezvous in St-Quentin there was another with nowhere to go.

By early afternoon, several hundred stragglers had drifted into the main square and were slumped exhausted on the cobbles. There was no food but there was plenty of wine and the shopkeepers and the locals had been generous. Many who had unwisely slaked their thirst on an empty stomach lay loudly snoring. They were waiting. No one had much idea what they were waiting for and they were too tired and worn out to care.

Down at the railway station, on the other hand, where the remnants of the Royal Warwicks and the Royal Dublin Fusiliers had piled arms and slumped down in the afternoon sun, they knew they were waiting to surrender to the Germans. Their commanding officers had told them so and they had seen for themselves the unedifying sight of Sir John French's Staff boarding a train and steaming off down the southbound track. They had booed the train as it puffed away, knowing that no train was likely to come for them.

After two days' footslogging on top of his adventures at Mons, Tom Bridges had linked up again with the cavalry, thankful to hoist his aching limbs on to a horse and be back in charge of a squadron. Since early morning they had been stationed to the north of St-Quentin, guarding the passage into the town, on the look-out for Germans, ready to protect the men on the road from further mishaps. Late in the afternoon, the great flow of troops had shrunk to a trickle of stragglers and now, but for an occasional lame duck arriving at long intervals, the road was clear. Bridges judged that they could safely leave their post and in accordance with instructions retire slowly through St-Quentin to their rendezvous south of the town. There had been no sign of the Germans, the First Corps was safely away, but nevertheless Bridges left a detachment of men to guard the bridge over the river before spurring his horse and making for St-Quentin at the head of his men.

He was shocked to find the town still swarming with stragglers. It was not precisely mutiny but it was extraordinarily close to it. In the Grande Place, the men were refusing to move and to underline the point many had thrown away their rifles. Hardly any had any equipment. The shop-keepers, so compassionate earlier in the day, were now irate and loudly complaining of soldiers who had elbowed their way into shops and dwellings, helped themselves to food and drink and had fallen asleep on beds, on sofas, on chairs, in doorways and even stretched out on shop floors. Bridges sent all his available subalterns, backed up by some muscular farriers, to clear the men out and propel them back to join the crowds of Tommies slumped sullenly in the town square. It would clearly be a long job. While they were getting on with it, Bridges himself circled the Grande Place urging the men to get up, to form up, to prepare to move on. A few struggled unwillingly to their feet. Some flatly refused. Most stared stolidly back in a dull stupor and stayed where they were. Others were dead to the world. No amount of kicks and exhortation could wake them and the officers who tried got snarls of resentment for their pains and it was perfectly obvious that even if they had the will to move, many were literally unable to walk. So, decided Bridges, if they could not walk they must be carried.

Accompanied by his interpreter he set off across the square to the Hôtel de Ville, and demanded to see the Mayor. Harrison, who had so recently employed his excellent French to flirt with the daughters of the café-owner at Le Cateau, now used it to impress on the Mayor of St-Quentin the urgency of requisitioning every motor car, every wagon, every cart, every wheeled vehicle in the town to carry away the exhausted men. The Mayor hardly seemed to be listening. He launched into an excitable diatribe of his own. Harrison interrupted him in mid-flow and turned to Bridges, startled and incredulous. 'He says they've surrendered!' he exclaimed.

At first they could make no sense of the story for they knew that the Germans were miles away. But the Mayor insisted that he knew better. Now his sole concern was for his town, the fine and beautiful town of St-Quentin. It was a known fact that the Germans were taking a terrible revenge, sacking, looting, burning the towns whose inhabitants harboured the British or impeded their own progress as they thundered towards Paris. Look what had happened in Belgium! The city of Louvain was reduced to ashes and ruins. What would happen if the Germans arrived – and they would surely be here at any moment – and found the town to all intents and purposes garrisoned by British troops? Even if the troops were capable of fighting (and anyone could see that they were not) the Mayor had no intention of St-Quentin being turned into a battlefield. His first duty was to protect its citizens. If the troops could not clear out they must surrender quietly. Everyone had agreed. The surrender document had already been prepared and signed and it was signed, moreover, by senior British officers. It was in the Mayor's possession (he waved it in proof) and he intended to hand it to the Germans in person. In order to demonstrate suitable respect for the conquerors he had donned his best black suit in anticipation of their arrival.

Bridges was strongly tempted to grab the Mayor by his Sunday collar and shake him until he squealed; instead he snatched at the document. It was properly drawn up. It listed the approximate number of troops in St-Quentin, gave sketchy details of their respective units and surrendered them unreservedly to the German army. It was signed by Lieutenant-Colonel Ellington of the 1st Battalion, The Royal Warwickshire Regiment, and by Lieutenant-Colonel Mainwaring in command of the Royal Dublin Fusiliers.

Bridges held on to the document, folded it and buttoned it for safe-keeping into his breast-pocket. Then, repeating his orders for the requisitioning of vehicles, deaf to the protestations of the Mayor that it was all too late, he made for the railway station to find the two officers who had signed the paper, to inform them that there were no Germans in the vicinity, that there was a cavalry rearguard behind them and that they would be well advised to think twice about surrendering. On the contrary, they had best collect their men and bring them to join the stragglers in the centre of the town. Bridges was not in a position to give a direct order to two officers of a higher rank than his own, but he made it very clear that this was an ultimatum and gave them a deadline of half an hour in which to comply. He also made it clear that the surrender document bearing their signatures was now in his possession. It was a damning piece of evidence.*

The men were another matter, for they were anything but docile. They had been badly cut up at Le Cateau, they had lost three quarters of their comrades, they were demoralised, they were dispirited and they were done up. They had no food, no orders, no ammunition. They had been told by their own officers that this was the end of the road, and they believed it. Standing some distance away, Arthur Osborn could not hear all that Bridges said, but he heard one of the men call out, 'Our Old Man has surrendered to the Germans and we'll stick to him. We don't want any bloody cavalry interfering!'

But their 'Old Man' was having second thoughts. When, eventually, the sullen procession trailed into the Grande Place, each colonel was at the head of his decimated battalion.

Two hours had passed, darkness was closing in, lights were burning in the shops and the shopkeepers and the few civilians who had chosen to stay and face the Germans rather than leave their property unprotected watched from the windows. There was still no sign of the enemy, but everyone was edgy. It was many hours since a patrol had encountered Uhlans at Gricourt and Gricourt was no more than eight kilometres away. If the Germans had not yet entered St-Quentin it was a distinct possibility that they had encircled the town and that the men inside were in a fair way to being trapped. Carts and wagons were rumbling into the square, flustered officers scribbled receipts for the drivers, the men were sorted out

---

* On 9 September, both officers were court-martialled and cashiered. Soon afterwards, Colonel Mainwaring went back to France, joined the French Foreign Legion under a pseudonym and fought on the French Front. He was quickly promoted to the rank of sergeant, and distinguished himself by his bravery and leadership. He was awarded the Croix de Guerre and, although badly wounded, survived the war. In the early thirties, in recognition of his outstanding war service, King George V reinstated Colonel Mainwaring and restored his former rank.

and the wounded, the lame and the most prostrate of the Tommies were bundled into the vehicles. Whips cracked, wheels creaked under the weight, and they rumbled across the cobbles towards the road to Ham and safety. It was an unconscionably long time before the last of them trundled away and Bridges could turn his attention to some five hundred men who were left and who would have to march out on their painful, blood-smeared feet. One of them was Bill Holbrook.

The men did not relish this prospect. It was past eleven o'clock now and they had been on the road for thirty hours. They were a miserable sight. Urged by Tom Bridges, a few weary subalterns did their best to rouse their men and he ordered his own officers and NCOs to quarter the square, shouting, cajoling, encouraging. Bridges himself had climbed to a vantage point on the fountain and urged them on in as cheerful a tone as he could muster. 'Come along, men, fall in now. I'm taking you back to your regiments.' He ordered his trumpeter to sound the Fall In. Nothing had any effect. 'If only I had a band,' he thought. And then he saw the toyshop. It was long past the normal closing time but it was still lit and the shopkeeper was standing at the open door.

A toy drum and a penny whistle were poor substitutes for a full military band. But the idea worked. Bridges was no musician, but the trumpeter was, and the high-pitched note of the whistle penetrated to every corner of the square. Bridges marched behind him, round and round the square, banging the drum for all he was worth, doing his best to match the beat to the music. He was playing 'The British Grenadiers' and he went on playing it until every man was on his feet. He played on while they formed up into some kind of order, paused, and then started up again as the column of weary men marched out of the square and on out of the town. Bridges' own men followed on horseback in the manner of solicitous sheepdogs but, with a sense of *élan* and leadership that even the French would have admired, Tom Bridges and his trumpeter marched at the head of the mob, banging and whistling as loud as they could to encourage the footsore men behind them. Long after they had cleared the town they were still banging and whistling the same tune, and here and there along the length of the column a Tommy pulled a mouth organ from his pocket and summoned up the breath to join in. The old tune had never sounded less appropriate. But it had done the trick. When they were well clear of the town the trumpeter tired of it and switched to a song that had been popular last summer. 'It's a long way to Tipperary', he whistled. The Tommies had no breath to spare to sing it, but they agreed with the sentiment. Wherever they were bound for it certainly seemed a long, long way.

A mile or so beyond St-Quentin, Bridges ordered his squadron to stop in its rearguard position and, keeping his orderly to lead his horse, marched on through the night with the lost sheep of the infantry. It was close to dawn before he found a collecting point and was able to hand them over. He also officially handed over the damning surrender document to the most senior officer he could find. Early in the morning he rode back to join his squadron and found to his relief that they had not been harassed in his absence. Later in the day Colonel Ellington and Colonel Mainwaring were relieved of their commands, charged with *shamefully delivering up a garrison to the enemy* and placed under arrest.

Later they would be court-martialled but for the moment there was no time to deal with military offences, no matter how serious. New orders had arrived from Noyon, where Sir John French had established his new GHQ. The troops were not to stay on the new assembly line south of the river. The French were withdrawing further than they had at first intended, in order to be in a better position to counter-attack the enemy, and since he was in theory prolonging their line, Sir John French had agreed to do likewise. The retreat was to continue. The men were to march on. Holbrook at least had the consolation of having caught up at last with his battalion.

It was the end of the first day of the retreat from Le Cateau and the fourth day of the retreat from Mons. No one from the Commander-in-Chief downwards would have believed that they would still be retreating and on the march for nine more days.

Chapter 14

The news that the Army had suffered two significant defeats in the space of three days did not reach the British public until 30 August – seven days after the Battle of Mons – and it came as a bitter blow. So far as the man in the street was concerned, when the British Expeditionary Force had marched away from the ports of disembarkation towards the hinterland of France they marched into deep silence broken only by the lofty official tones of Army Communiqués which told the public precisely what the War Office wished them to know. It was very little. If the War Office had had its way it would have been nothing at all and such scant information as it did disseminate gave news-hungry readers of the daily papers no reason to think that the BEF was not holding its own with the Germans and that any adjustment of the situation was not part of some Olympian military plan. *The BEF has been in touch with the enemy near the Belgian frontier.* (This was the battle of Mons.) *The BEF has reached its new position.* (This was the start of the retreat.) *British troops engaged on Wednesday against superior forces fought splendidly.* (This was the Battle of Le Cateau.)

Such misleading information gave the newspaper readers the feeling that it would be merely a matter of time before the BEF were trouncing the Germans.

There had been news from the men in France, but it mostly amounted to cheery messages of reassurance scribbled on the backs of picture postcards with pleasant views of French coastal resorts and happy holidaymakers disporting themselves on the sands, and they merely reinforced the cheerful holiday-like atmosphere at home. The humdrum concerns of daily life had been swamped by an unaccountable air of exhilaration, that sense of being on tiptoe on the fringe of momentous events that everyone was feeling in those hectic days of August. First, there had been the weddings. Young officers like Lieutenant Rory Macleod who were under orders to embark for France had made haste to pop the question, and jewellers were gratified by a brisk run on engagement rings. The smarter Army weddings tradition-ally took place in August during the long leaves due to officers after the busy months of summer training and manoeuvres; now brides-to-be in the throes of preparing for an elegant society wedding found themselves

summoned peremptorily to distant Army encampments and whisked off
to be married in a far less elaborate ceremony in some unfamiliar church
with only their mother and the bridegrooms' brother officers to witness it.
More fortunate girls whose fiancés were stationed in London or who served
under benevolent commanding officers, willing to grant a few hours' leave
even in the hurly-burly of mobilisation, were able to have their weddings
more or less as planned. Bleary-eyed dressmakers worked far into the night
to complete half-finished wedding gowns and fathers giving way to the
pleas of a cherished daughter and the insistent demand of some young
officer that he should bestow her hand on him without delay were mollified
by the reflection that Violet or Winifred or Dorothy had at least saved him
the price of a costly wedding reception. The August society columns were
almost entirely filled by notices of War Weddings. One of them reported
the marriage of Pat Fitzgerald of Tom Bridges' 4th Dragoon Guards.

CAPTAIN FITZGERALD AND
MISS CHARRINGTON

By special licence from the Bishop of Winchester the marriage took
place on Wednesday at South Tidworth Church of Captain Fitzgerald,
4th Dragoon Guards, only son of Lord and Lady Maurice Fitzgerald, of
Johnstown Castle, Wexford, Ireland, and Miss Dorothy Charrington,
second daughter of Mr and Mrs Spencer Charrington, of Winchfield,
Hampshire. Owing to the emergency of the wedding on account of
the Regiment being ordered on service in the war, only the Colonel,
officers and men of the Regiment and the parents of the bride were
present.

Everyone agreed that the Colonel had been extremely sporting. The
Dragoon Guards were under orders to proceed to France, so the Commanding Officer could hardly have given Pat leave for the occasion, but he *had*
paraded the Regiment and Dorothy and Pat had been greeted by three
rousing cheers as they left the church under an arch of glittering swords.
The groom beamed, the bride blushed, the officers agreed that she was a
jolly girl and that, given the circumstances, the whole affair was dashed
romantic. Three days later, on the very morning the announcement of the
wedding appeared in *The Times*, the Dragoon Guards sailed for France.

The flurry of hasty weddings was not confined to the upper crust. In
the humbler ranks of the Army and the Reserve there were large numbers
of Tommies and working men who also wished to be married before they
went to war and in certain cases it was a matter of some urgency. The
Archbishop of Canterbury had given special permission for ecclesiastical
offices to stay open round the clock to issue special licences and had also

given clergymen permission to perform marriages after the legal hour of twelve noon. But there was a snag. The price of a special licence was two guineas. This was a blow to one Hounslow man on the Army Reserve whose presence was instantly required at Hounslow Barracks by the 6th Battalion, The Royal Fusiliers. His immediate plans had not included exchanging civilian clothes for khaki but they had included marriage and, as his future father-in-law had made plain, the sooner the wedding took place the better. He had expressed himself forcibly on the subject and his daughter's errant sweetheart had been scrimping and saving for a month now to buy a guinea wedding ring on the instalment plan. When his mobilisation papers arrived he had paid off nine shillings and sixpence. Now, if he did not place the ring on the lady's finger right away, money would be even more of a problem. If she was respectably married the Army would endow her with a separation allowance and, in due course, an allowance for her child. Unmarried she would be not only disgraced but destitute.

The family had a whipround which raised enough cash to pay off the ring. The bridegroom was able to scrape up three shillings and sixpence for the marriage licence, the bride supplied the coppers for his tramfare to the West End and sent him smartly off to obtain it. It had not occurred to them that a special licence would cost many times the price of a conventional one. Two guineas was an impossible sum. It was two o'clock in the afternoon, the wedding was arranged for five and he was due to report for duty at eight the following morning. He paced the streets and racked his brains. Then, plucking up courage, he went back into the office and spoke to the Registrar man to man. The Registrar was sympathetic. He waived his own fee, stretched the rules, issued the special licence and paid the difference out of his own pocket. After all, as he later explained, the man was going off to fight for his country. It was the least he could do to help him out of his predicament and little short of a patriotic duty.

The streets were merry with military bands but by the third week in August the first enthusiastic rush of recruits had tailed off and the most desirable regiments were full up. The Commanding Officer of the Inns of Court Officers' Training Corps who had pleaded for gentlemen to join in the first week of the war was pleading again a few days later, this time begging the gentlemen to desist. Men of means, of birth or education, assuming a God-given right to be officers, bombarded the Army for commissions and blatantly used influence and pulled strings to get one. When the Army indicated that for the moment it had its hands full, they were undeterred and set about preparing themselves for the day when the Army would be ready to receive them. On the roof of their Oxford Street store the shooting range that Selfridge's thoughtfully provided for the benefit of sporting gentlemen was inundated by gentlemen anxious to get in some rifle practice with more belligerent sport in mind. Some were merely passing time while their wives raided the newly opened Red Cross Depot on Selfridge's ground floor which guaranteed to supply *Everything required by Ladies working for the British Red Cross Society or Nursing Associations*, gave hourly knitting demonstrations and supplied free patterns with every purchase. Men flocked to private gymnasia. Some who were particularly anxious to get a head start even engaged retired drill instructors at two shillings an hour to teach them the rudiments of Army drill and practised this new-found skill on their families. Neville Lytton was frustrated by the fact that his 'squad' of three (made up by his two young daughters and their governess) not surprisingly found it difficult to form fours, were incapable of telling right from left and were woefully unamenable to discipline. As a result of this early experience, he later confessed, when he eventually did have command of a company of soldiers he was nonplussed when they actually did as he said.

The stores were inundated by eager shoppers, by officers purchasing kit, by stranded travellers – mainly Americans newly arrived from Europe – replacing luggage and belongings left behind in the haste of departure, by servicemen patronising the photographic studios (*Three free copies to all sailors and soldiers photographed in uniform*). And outside on the pavements crowds thronged in front of shop-windows patriotically decked out in red, white and blue surrounding outsize maps of Europe on which flags were fixed to illustrate the progress of the war. Owing to lack of information they illustrated little more than the progress of the Kaiser's troops through Belgium towards a bulwark of French tricolours and British Union flags massed reassuringly in their path.

In the absence of any obvious cause for concern, the issues which had been occupying the attention of public-spirited British citizens for the last three weeks were issues of morality. There was no solid news to print and only a certain amount of a newspaper's space could be devoted to editorial diatribes against the wicked Kaiser and the beastly Huns who were laying waste to Belgium at his command, and though the atrocity stories gleaned from Belgian refugees were apparently limitless, there were nevertheless many column-inches to fill. The editors filled them with ream upon ream of helpful advice on *How to be Useful in Wartime* and readers enthusiastically taking up this notion rushed to contribute their own helpful suggestions. A nonconformist minister, seeing a golden opportunity to advance the cause of temperance, demanded that breweries and distilleries should be promptly closed down and the grain thus saved diverted to food production. Messrs Suttons, seed merchants, with motives which were perhaps not wholly disinterested, reminded the public of the *desirability of sowing and planting every spare piece of land with such food crops as there might still be time to sow before the autumn* and added a paragraph of useful tips on the cultivation of onions, cabbages and root vegetables. Mrs Osgood of Guilsborough Hall, Northampton, wished to make known to the military authorities that she was prepared to place her house and grounds at their disposal for the reception of wounded officers and men and hoped that this public undertaking would *encourage other patriotic owners of property to follow my example.* And there were other voices from the Shires. *Instruct your keeper immediately to cease feeding your pheasants with maize and corn. It will do them no harm and they may provide even better sport when the shooting season opens.*

Canon Foukes Jackson wrote from Jesus College, Cambridge, to appeal to *the propertied classes not to dismiss their servants and employees but to live themselves as poor men in order that no one in Britain may be in want of food.* Holidaymakers were sternly adjured to give up the unproductive pastimes of golf and tennis and *enquire in any rural village whether help is required with the harvest,* and Sabbatarians were outraged by the suggestion that harvesting should continue on Sundays. An octogenarian Frenchman, whose fighting days had included grappling with the Austrians in 1866 and with the Germans in 1870, offered his services and, with a flourish of Gallic compliments to his adopted country, publicly solicited the Secretary of State for War to give him authority to raise a Foreign Legion *enlisting as volunteers all foreigners resident in the United Kingdom, and he appeals to other foreigners to join him.* There were calls for theatres, music halls, picture palaces and all other places of entertainment to close their doors immediately. Time and money spent on such frivolities would be far better devoted to more earnest purposes. Other correspondents riposted with the argument that to throw out of work the artistes, musicians and others employed in the entertainment industry would merely cause hardship, place a burden on the State and do nothing to further the War Effort.

It was not enough to be patriotic. People had to be seen to be patriotic and women in particular were urged to set an example. The Mayoress of Wandsworth pulled off a double coup that met with universal approval. All through the fine warm days of August, seated on the pavement outside Wandsworth Town Hall, she encouraged passers-by to contribute to the War Hardship Fund. A large-brimmed white hat shaded her from the sun and from under its broad brim she smiled, nodded, encouraged, thanked those who dropped coins through the slot of a large black box more used to receiving votes in local elections, and all the time her knitting needles clicked. She collected a great deal of money, knitted up ball after ball of khaki wool and turned out two pairs of socks a day.

Everyone urged self-sacrifice and economy. No self-indulgence, no needless waste, no extravagance. These were the first duties of every citizen and the most stentorian voices railed against those who selfishly hoarded food. Before the war was two days old an irate correspondence had started in *The Times*.

5th August.

Sir,

When I went to the Army and Navy Stores yesterday I was disgusted to see hundreds of people whom one cannot dignify by calling men and women, laying in tons of provisions. It is a time of War, and we are fighting for our existence as a Nation. Surely the Government ought to confiscate these private stores and fine and imprison the selfish brutes who are hoarding them.

Your obedient servant,
J. C. Ker Fox, Brevet Major.

It was true that in the first days of the war, even on the Saturday before war was declared, many people had taken the precaution of laying in extra supplies. It was not that they were so pessimistic as to imagine that the war would bring Britain to the point of starvation, but there were bound to be scarcities, trade was ruled by the law of supply and demand, and thrifty people feared that prices would go up. Salaried people who ran monthly accounts at grocery shops and stores laid in the largest supplies, but even households of modest means took the precaution of laying in a sack of flour, a quantity of coal and potatoes, an extra pound or two of tea and sugar — if they had the ready cash.

The question of cash was a universal problem. By Bank Holiday Tuesday, when the banks should have reopened for business, rich and poor alike were in the soup. The banks had not reopened and by Government decree the Bank Holiday was extended for three more days. With the nation's economy firmly based on the gold standard, the Government was anxious to safeguard the nation's own reserves of gold. The war would place a huge financial burden on the Treasury and it would be nothing short of profligacy to eat into its resources by continuing to mint gold coins for general circulation. By Friday when the banks next opened for business there would be supplies of new pound notes and ten-shilling notes in place of sovereigns and half-sovereigns, and the Royal Mint was also making haste to increase the supply of silver. But they needed time. Meanwhile postal orders would be recognised as legal currency.

Ironically, the poor were better able to manage. They were accustomed to dealing in cash and for once some of them had cash in hand. On the eve of the Bank Holiday weekend, Holiday Club money was paid out to provident employees who had been saving throughout the year at the rate of sixpence or a shilling a week. It was a useful windfall and those who had not blown it over the holiday weekend had silver and even gold to see them through. The better off had not. A pound's worth of silver and copper was easily exhausted. Despite stern official reminders that it was unpatriotic to hoard gold no one wanted to risk parting with sovereigns and no one really trusted anything else. The only other currency in circulation was the five-pound banknote, printed on finest white paper, so large that it had to be folded twice to fit into a wallet and bearing no other embellishment than the flowing engraved lettering which conveyed the promise that the Bank of England would redeem it for five golden sovereigns on demand. Until now it had seemed as solid and reliable as the Bank of England itself. But now that the banks were shut the opulent crackle of a fiver had lost its charm and neither shopkeepers nor tradesmen, cabbies, restaurants, clubs, even railway booking offices were willing to change one. Only gold was acceptable and those who had it were reluctant to part with it. Everyone was in the same boat. Desperate parents were forced to resort to rifling the money-boxes of protesting children for a handful of coppers and threepenny bits. Well-dressed gentlemen struck by the thought that a score of five-shilling postal orders could be purchased with a five-pound note were politely snubbed by Post Office clerks who reminded them that the few coppers' stamp duty on each postal order meant that the transaction would not amount to a round sum. Having no small change available they were unable to oblige.

The situation was less acute in Scotland where pound notes issued by the Scottish banks were already in circulation among the canny Scots who preferred paper money to gold because, it was said, a sovereign was too easily mistaken for a shilling in the dark.

Most people managed to scrape by, but those who had more pressing expenses were in a real predicament. On the boat-train platform at Dover Harbour one man was seen accosting passengers for the Channel steamer, brandishing a five-pound note and offering to exchange it for three pounds, ten shillings in gold. Even at this bargain rate there were no takers. He was spotted by Julius Price, a journalist and artist who was travelling to France to report the war for the *Illustrated London News*. Apart from foreigners anxious to get home and French reservists hastening home to join their regiments, journalists were almost the only civilian passengers on board the *Viper* when she sailed for Calais on the day war was declared. For all the news they gathered in the first weeks of the war they might as well have stayed at home.

Every national newspaper had its own 'man in Paris', and these reporters had hurried to the French Ministry of War to be accredited as War Correspondents. But, like the British War Office, the French Ministry did not look kindly on journalists. They had attached an *Officier Informateur* to each of their divisions and such crumbs of information as they saw fit to impart must suffice to satisfy the public's appetite for news. The 'official accreditation' they now bestowed upon the journalists merely gave them the privilege of attending the Ministry at a stated hour each day where they were handed the Official Communiqué. Any suggestion that they should be allowed to travel on troop trains, enter the war zone, or even get within striking distance of the Army still in barracks, was treated with disdain and stamped on hard. The journalists stuck it for a few days and then, bored by inactivity, frustrated beyond belief, and sick to death of filing stories dripping with local colour about the touching scenes as the troop trains steamed out, the patriotic fervour of civilians left behind, they made their own arrangements and quietly slipped away in search of the war.

They were running a considerable risk. On the pretext of visiting his sister, conveniently married to a French officer, Julius Price had managed to obtain a pass to travel east to her home at Langres and from there by devious illegal means to Bruyères, where he was promptly arrested. Even the eminent Philip Gibbs of the *Daily Chronicle* was held under open arrest for two weeks as far from the front as Le Havre. Others who had managed to get closer to the seat of war and had picked up such shreds of information as they could from civilians, found that their despatches were at the mercy of War Office censors who were only inclined to approve stories of uplifting moral tone, colourful word pictures of gallant British troops travelling towards the Front, and tales of terrified refugees fleeing from the frightfulness of Hun atrocities.

As a sop to popular demand, the War Office had appointed Sir Ernest Swinton, who was also a colonel, to the Staff of the Commander-in-Chief. His brief was to write 'colour pieces' to supplement the official despatches. They were bland, anodyne and unfailingly optimistic, but even Colonel Swinton complained that much of his material was vetoed by the generals even before it left GHQ for London. They were published, ironically, under the pseudonym 'Eyewitness'. Two photographers had been sent with the Army to France but, like Colonel Swinton, they too were military men and their photographs were intended to form part of an historical record of the war. None of them found their way into the illustrated weeklies of the time. New periodicals like *War Illustrated*, which had sprung into being with much trumpeting as soon as the war started, were forced to fill their pages with photographs of French and German troops. For weeks after the war began, apart from pictures of newly joined recruits or of wounded arriving home, no photographs of any British soldiers appeared in any illustrated magazine and their editors had to resort to reproducing pre-war picture postcard views of Dinant, Soissons or Maubeuge, stirringly captioned *Where the Battle Now Rages*. The battles themselves were depicted in artists' impressions in which imagination run riot compensated for the paucity of information on the actual event.

Moore of *The Times* and Beach-Thomas of the *Daily Mail* were thrown into jail at Hazebrouck, but it was *The Times* and the *Daily Mail* which finally broke the story and they told a sorry tale. They told of defeat. They told of broken British regiments struggling down the roads in disarray. They told of terrible losses. The report was first published in a special Sunday edition of *The Times* and the same day an equally horrifying account appeared in the *Weekly Despatch*. It was Sunday 30 August. Astonishingly, the facts were published with the connivance of the head of the Press Bureau himself. He believed that it was in the national interest to publish the truth and he urged the editors to punch home the message that the need for reinforcements was desperate, and to urge men who had been hanging back to join the Army now.

Before the inevitable row, before the iron barrier of censorship clanged down again, the news had precisely the effect he foresaw.* Over the following two days thirty thousand men enlisted. In London the recruiting office at Scotland Yard could no longer cope with the number of men who were queueing to join up and a second office was opened near Trafalgar Square. It set up for business in the newly vacated office of the Hamburg-Amerika shipping line and this in itself was considered to be a cock-snooking blow at the enemy. Anti-German feeling intensified. German spa water, previously much in demand on fashionable tables, was replaced by English water from Buxton. Lipton, the grocers, placed large display advertisements in the press to protest that their firm was British through and through, and to announce their action for libel against their competitors, Messrs Lyons, who had tried to grab their custom by suggesting that they were not. By the end of the week Lord Kitchener had his second hundred thousand men, and public opinion was raging against the Germans.

Reports of German atrocities fanned the flame of moral indignation and oddly enough the Germans themselves were responsible for all but the most lurid. They had been quick to realise the advantages, as they saw it, of allowing foreign correspondents to put the German case in neutral countries – particularly in powerful, neutral America. Neutral

---

* Furious questions were asked in Parliament. The newspapers were accused of sensationalism. The head of the Press Bureau resigned shortly afterwards.

correspondents already based in Brussels or Berlin were welcome to follow the German army and given every assistance to report its triumphs and victories. But this hospitality to some extent backfired.

'Frightfulness' was the Germans' own word. With characteristic thoroughness it had been written into the Schlieffen Plan which had so successfully sent the German army bowling across Belgium and down the road towards Paris. If the Germans were to advance and advance quickly, the civil population of the occupied countries must be smartly brought to heel and harsh measures against *francs tireurs*, *saboteurs* and those who harboured enemy soldiers were calculated to spread terror and to implant in the civil population such a wary respect for German discipline that only a minimal number of troops would be needed to garrison a town and police its citizens. The rules were laid down efficiently and categorically. As soon as a district was occupied, hostages would be taken into custody as a matter of course. If a single German was molested or injured the hostages would be shot. If fighting broke out the place would be destroyed. If a German column was attacked on a road between two villages, reprisals would be taken on the nearest. If they happened at the time of the attack to be halfway between them, both villages would be destroyed. Impounded herds of cattle would be butchered to sustain the German troops and, since soldiers could hardly be expected to behave as plaster saints, in appropriate cases, looting would be permitted in order to drive home the lesson that the Kaiser's troops were not to be trifled with. No matter how much the Fatherland of Schiller, Goethe, Beethoven, might deplore such punitive acts, the Germany of Frederick the Great, of Bismarck and of Hindenburg, regarded them as nothing more than essential and sound military tactics. The Declaration of Brussels to which Germany herself had been a signatory laid down that *Any destruction or seizure of enemy property not imperatively called for by military necessities is forbidden*. This hardly affected the issue. In the view of the High Command, their policy of 'Frightfulness' *was* a military necessity, as all reasonable men must agree. The Germans had nothing to hide. Foreign journalists were free to report each and every detail of their victorious advance for the delectation of the world. They were genuinely pained when the world condemned them as barbarians after the sacking of Louvain.

A report from Copenhagen quoted the *Volkische Zeitung*'s attempt to justify the destruction of the historic city to the German public. *The art treasures of the old town exist no more. Lovers of art will grieve, but there was no other way of punishing this population whose devilish women poured boiling oil over the German troops*. This was not official, neither would it wash – other than with the most credulous sections of the German public who were equally willing to believe ghoulish accounts of vicious civilians gouging out the eyes of German soldiers. But the official explanation, intended for worldwide consumption, was hardly less damning.

> The distribution of arms and ammunition among the civil population of Belgium had been carried out on systematic lines, and the authorities enraged the public against Germany by assiduously circulating false reports. The only means of preventing surprise attacks from the civil population has been to interfere with unrelenting severity and to create examples which, by their 'frightfulness', would be a warning to the whole country. The increased war contribution levied on the province of Liège has also had an excellent effect. *

America demonstrated its neutrality by reserving judgement and endeavouring to be impartial, but it was not easy. The *Washington Evening Post* in a plaintive editorial wrote more in sorrow than in anger:

> One can but cling to a faint hope that there may be, as to the devastation itself, some exaggeration and, as to the provocation for it, some slight mitigation at least of what on the face of it is an appalling act of vandalism and ferocious cruelty. That the German government may find it possible to put itself in the position to throw off, either by an explanation of the deed or by the punishment of those who committed it, the fearful burden of guilt which otherwise will attach to that government and to the German nation we most sincerely hope.

The *Globe* demanded that the German Ambassador should produce the facts and lay them before the American public whose newspapers (in the absence of any first-hand accounts from the Allied side) had been regaling them with descriptions of German successes and praise for her wonderful

---

* Years after the war, when General Ludendorff wrote his memoirs he still clung to the propaganda myth that the Belgian authorities had encouraged the civilians to impede the progress of the German army (the civil authorities had in fact posted notices telling civilians to refrain from hostile acts for their own protection) and he was still blaming the civilians for bringing German reprisals on themselves by 'breaches of international law' in defending their property and in their reluctance to succumb to the invader without putting up a fight. He wrote: *The Belgian government took a grave responsibility upon itself. It had systematically organised civilian warfare. The Garde Civique, which in the days of peace had its own arms and special uniforms, were able to appear sometimes in one garb and sometimes in another. The Belgian soldiers must also have had a special civilian suit in their knapsacks at the commencement of the war. In the trenches near Fort Barchon, to the north-east of Liège, I myself saw uniforms which had been left behind by soldiers who had fought there. Such action was not in keeping with the usages of war; our troops cannot be blamed if they took the sternest measures to suppress it.*

army which had gone down well with the German–American communities in the big cities and in the farming towns of the Midwest. It added meaningfully, 'Germany's honour is no less on trial in this hour than is its great military machine.'

In the United Kingdom, Germany's honour had already been tried and found guilty. Germany's name was mud, and now that she had condemned herself out of her own mouth, no rumour of bestial outrage was too vile to be believed. They emanated mainly from the refugees who had fled half-terrified out of their wits from the towns and villages of Belgium. There were first-hand accounts from people who had escaped from the flames of Andenne, where two hundred hostages had been shot, from Tamines, where four hundred were gunned down and bayoneted, and from the inhabitants of Dinant who had aroused the ire of the Germans by destroying a vital bridge. The Germans' revenge was to round up more than six hundred men, women and children and to shoot them in cold blood. The youngest, aged three weeks, died in his mother's arms. These stories were true and the Germans made no attempt to keep them secret. They were, after all, intended to warn. Inevitably as they travelled they spawned fictions in their wake – of rape, of macabre killings, of mutilation, of breasts and hands sliced off by sabres, of crucifixions, of babies dipped into boiling water or swung for sport against brick walls. There were even whispers of cannibalism. Grains of truth swelled and grew into a crop of rumours of unspeakable villainies unsurpassed since the hordes of Genghis Khan had rampaged and pillaged across Asia. In France and in Britain the newspapers were full of them. Public opinion hardened. It was no longer merely a Just War, it was positively righteous – and people were out for blood.

'Mummy,' demanded the small girl in a *Punch* cartoon, pointing to her German governess in the background, 'Mummy, will we have to kill poor Fräulein?'

In Yorkshire another young girl in a more modest station of life was having her first taste of the war. She was the daughter of the landlord of the King's Head Hotel in Halifax Road, Keighley.

Eva Leach (Mrs Churchman)

On 3 August my parents went for the day to Morecambe and brought back a late newspaper. It seemed inevitable that war would break out. The newspaper said there would be a moratorium on the banks. I wasn't sure what this meant, but my father was distressed. The paper also said, 'Pawnshops will be full,' which seemed to me (at fourteen) nothing very dreadful. We were preparing to go on our annual holiday and Father had rented a cottage near Haworth for the school holidays. With everything being so uncertain he couldn't get away himself, but Mother took us four younger ones anyway. That was on 10 August. We were leaving in a wagonette and Father and my elder brother Ronald were outside to wave us off but just as Mother was about to get in Ronald took her aside and whispered to her. She looked absolutely shaken, but she kissed him and whispered back and then off we went. After we started off she told me that he had enlisted.

The pubs had to close for a few days because of the money crisis and when they opened again there were new regulations and they had to close at nine p.m. – or if they didn't close the doors they could only sell non-intoxicating drinks. Hoyle's, the local soft-drinks people, made quite a killing with 'Hop Ale'. It looked like bitter beer – in colour only! – and there was another drink called 'After Nine Stout' which was a form of dandelion and burdock. There was also a horrible concoction called 'Vegale', a hot soupy drink which smelt to high heaven of peas. Nobody bought it. We were also allowed to sell Bovril and Oxo but they weren't very popular with the men in the bar.

One afternoon when we got back from our holiday, Dad took me to a matinée at the local picture house. We were laughing at Charlie Chaplin when suddenly a message in writing was flashed on the screen. It said *Namur Falls*. Just that! A few people got up and left, but the audience stayed quiet and the film continued. When Dad and I left the cinema a newsboy was calling out '*Heavy German Losses!*' I remember it vividly, because it was the first time I'd seen this particular 'newsboy'. He had whiskers down to his waist! The regular newsboy had joined up of course, so this old man took the job on and every single day for the next four years of the war he called out the same thing. '*Heavy German Losses*' – it was routine with him, no matter what the news happened to be, and it consoled nobody.

Because of the newspaper stories and gossip that went round, I'm afraid we disliked the Germans very much. There were dreadful stories of the atrocities in Belgium, babies being bayoneted and women treated unspeakably. There were several small pork butchers in Keighley. Some of them had been there for generations, but they all had German names – there was Stein and Schulz and Schneider and Hoffman – and all these shops were attacked and looted. It was a Saturday night and we children were playing in the upstairs sitting room while our parents were busy in the bar. Being the eldest I'd put the baby to bed and then the rest of us undressed ready to scamper off to bed in case either of our parents came up. Near the pub there was an Irish club. It was usually pretty noisy on Saturdays, so on the night of the riots we kids didn't take much notice of all the noise. Then my father came upstairs and he said, 'I want you children to see this. You'll never forget it!' We scurried into our clothes and went out with my father (my mother didn't approve so she stayed behind). Stein's shop was quite close to us and we could hear the sound of shouting and the crash of breaking windows. There was a great crowd there, mostly Irish from the Turkey Street district which was a poor quarter, and they were mostly drunk.

We went up a slight hill, well away from the crowd, and my father lifted Jessie up and the rest of us scrambled on a wall to see the fun. The police soon arrived and they started making baton charges into the crowd. Ruth Hugill, one of our cleaning staff, sheltered in a public toilet – it was a Gents! The embarrassment worried her more than the fear of being clobbered or trampled underfoot. We thought it was quite thrilling! The police didn't do much damage, the intention seemed to be to scare people and scatter the crowd. No one was arrested. I don't think any of the German families was actually hurt. The crowd seemed satisfied to have pinched the pork and bacon. They went from shop to shop. The Schulz family were a nice couple with a baby. They lived next door to friends of ours in Low Street and they were all very good neighbours. When the looters started attacking their shop, the Schulzes rushed next door and sheltered with the Mitchells until the trouble died down. Mrs Schulz was in an awful state, quite terrified. The next morning we went back to Stein's to see the damage and picked up pieces of plate glass for souvenirs. Of course we were sorry for them, but we children thought that it was quite natural. After all they were *Germans*! Not knowing anything of the war at close quarters we youngsters believed everything we heard, and we were fired with enthusiasm.

Then the first German prisoners were captured and they had GOTT MITT UNS inscribed on their belt buckles. We were really indignant when we heard that. What cheek! God was on *our* side.

'*Got mittens, have you*?' shouted a grinning Tommy in the caption to another popular cartoon, pointing his rifle at a quailing German soldier and adding as he pulled the trigger, '*Well, here's socks*!' It was thought to be a splendid joke and for a time the slang phrase *giving the Germans socks* had quite a vogue on the Home Front.

But, jokes apart, the idea of the Kaiser invoking God was too much to be borne with equanimity. On the first day of the Battle of Mons, the German Crown Prince, who commanded his father's Fifth Army, had enjoyed a local success and thwarted a French counter-attack in the area around Verdun. The Kaiser's fulsome telegram to his daughter-in-law had been published and was picked up by the world press. *I rejoice with you in Wilhelm's first victory. How magnificently God supported him!* Coming on top of the news of disasters and atrocities this blasphemy aroused furious indignation. Feeling that no prose could do it justice, the versesmith Barry Pain dashed off a poem to slap the Kaiser down.

> *Led by Wilhem, as you tell,*
> *God has done extremely well;*
> *You with patronising nod*
> *Show that you approve of God.*
> *Kaiser, face a question new –*
> *This – Does God approve of you?*
>
> *Villages burned down to dust,*
> *Torture, murder, bestial lust,*
> *Filth too foul for printers' ink,*
> *Crimes from which the apes would shrink.*
> *Strange the offerings that you press*
> *On the God of Righteousness!*
>
> *Impious braggart, you forget,*
> *God is not your conscript yet.*
> *You shall learn in dumb amaze*
> *That His ways are not your ways,*
> *That the mire through which you trod*
> *Is not the high white road of God –*
> *To Whom, whichever way the combat rolls,*
> *We – fighting to the end – commend our souls.*

And that was telling him!

Chapter 15

If stories of atrocity caused consternation in the United Kingdom, across the Channel where the Kaiser was carving a relentless swathe towards Paris they put the fear of God into the French directly in his path. Now that General von Kluck's army was swinging away at a tangent from the British and moving south-west through Cambrai to begin the great sweep that would cut off the British, as he believed, and give him the elbow room he needed to envelop the French, the town of Bapaume stood squarely on the line of his advance. It lay on the extreme southern edge of the great plain of Calais and on the verge of the smiling country, so soon to become a killing ground – the Department of the Somme.

Bapaume was a prosperous town at the junction of two roads running north-west to Arras and north-east to Cambrai. It was smaller and less important than either but it was a thriving commercial centre and the inhabitants of more than a dozen villages and hamlets depended on it. It was there that they went to market, transacted business with banks and lawyers, took their produce to be sold, their grain to be ground at the mill owned by the Mayor, Gaston Stenne, their tools and implements to be mended at the garage workshop owned by Monsieur Verdel. It was to Bapaume that they cycled or rode to fetch Dr Cauchy or Dr Poisson when there was illness in the family, or Monsieur Lemarcy the vet when an animal fell sick. Bapaume had almost three thousand inhabitants and no fewer than nineteen owned a motor car. Dr Poisson's was the grandest of them all, for while his fellow motorists had only canvas hoods to protect them in inclement weather, the doctor's car was coachbuilt and equipped with real glass windows. Inside it he rode like a king, royally ignoring the taunts of children who ran alongside shouting '*There goes the fish in his aquarium!*'

Even added to the dozen or so strange vehicles that might rattle through the streets of Bapaume on weekdays, nineteen motor cars were hardly enough to cause a traffic jam, but they were enough to demonstrate that Bapaume was no backwater. It had an ancient church, an Hôtel de Ville with graceful arcades at street level and a fine tower far above. It possessed an abbey, and attached to it was a renowned college founded in the Middle

Ages. Bapaume boasted a château and pleasant walks among landscaped vestiges of its old ramparts and towers. There were smart substantial villas on its leafy outskirts and in the town itself there was a wide square lined with plane trees and stone-built houses of pleasant design. In the centre was the statue of the French hero, Faidherbe, scholar and soldier, who had commanded the northern army when the Prussians had passed this way forty-five years earlier, and not far away the monument to those who had died in that struggle was a familiar landmark on the road to Arras. The older generation still had vivid recollections of that event and through oft-repeated stories their fear and hatred of the marauding Boche had filtered down to the young. Now the jackboots were on the march again along the road from Cambrai just twenty-four kilometres away, and for the second time in living memory they were bearing down on Bapaume.

A mere ten days earlier it had seemed impossible that the town could be reduced so soon to such a state of terror and anxiety. Just after midday on 16 August, the British had halted in Bapaume on their way north to Belgium and, despite the fact that Sunday lunch was sacred to all right-thinking Frenchmen, people had streamed out of the houses into the pouring rain to crowd round the long convoy of lorries that stopped in the rue d'Arras.

Madame Paul Deron

I remember one of their vehicles was parked outside the Savings Bank and the soldiers lifted me up on to it give me some titbit or other. It was a sort of wagon or trailer like a merchant's, open on both sides and fitted out with benches. The wheels had no tyres and it was towed by an engine like a steam roller. It was painted bright scarlet (there was no camouflage then) and it was a very old-fashioned vehicle, archaic even for those days.

At the same time on the following day there was another convoy of fifty or more British cars and lorries coming in from the Albert road and making for Cambrai. They were full of soldiers who waved to us as they passed and shouted greetings, laughing and singing. Everywhere they'd gone people had been throwing bouquets and the lorries were covered with flowers and decked out in the French and British colours. One of them even had a little Belgian flag. Other convoys came over the next two days, and seeing these friendly troops passing through really put heart into the town. They were so confident that it did a lot to raise our hopes.

While they waited for their midday rations to be dished out, the soldiers had been only too pleased to stretch their legs and join in the fun. Wine, cigarettes, cakes, chocolate and souvenirs changed hands. They sang and laughed and joked and their attempts at conversation caused much amusement. It was conducted mainly by signs and grimaces, but the Tommies had managed to get across the message that the Germans held no fears for them. After half an hour or so of this entertainment when the French recalled to mind the *rôti* in the oven, the *coq au vin* bubbling on the stove or even congealing on their abandoned plates, quite a number of Tommies accepted cordial invitations to join a French family at their interrupted lunch.

In many households the man of the house was absent, swept into the French army in the first days of mobilisation. At the age of eighteen every Frenchman did military service and until middle age released him from his obligation every Frenchman was on the Army Reserve. Many had already gone from Bapaume. Many more were awaiting the announcement of the mobilisation order for their age-group to go off in their turn. There were no exceptions and no professional occupation or business interests so pressing, no personal problem so acute that their requirements could be allowed to come before the interests of France. Only ill-health or age could release a man from his obligation to serve and neither Paul Deron's new-born daughter nor Henri Baclet's dying wife took precedence over the order to mobilise. It was more than a week since Paul Deron, editor-in-chief of the *Courrier du Nord*, had left his office in Arras and exchanged his sober business suit for horizon blue, leaving his wife Marie to return with their new-born infant to her parents in Bapaume. Already she was beginning to wonder if she might have done better to stay where she was. By the time Sunday lunchtime came round again the troops were battling at Mons and there was no laughter in the streets of Bapaume.

Far to the east in the long-lost territories of Alsace and Lorraine, the town of Mulhouse had been captured and was French again after more than forty years of German rule. But Alsace was a long way off. In Bapaume, standing on the edge of Picardy, other news was of more immediate concern. The Germans had crossed the Meuse between Liège and Namur, the Belgian army was retiring towards Antwerp, and the Germans were on the march south.

Monsieur Lechire was known as 'the carter' or occasionally, with jocular irony, 'the lorry driver'. He did not own a lorry, or even anything that approached a wagon. But he did have a low trailer, little more than a wheeled platform which could be hitched up to a single horse. Leading it by its halter he perambulated the town and the outlying hamlets to deliver the goods and packages that arrived by train. He was a familiar figure in

Bapaume and, although he was officially employed by the railway company, if someone was moving house or required his services for a special delivery, Monsieur Lechire was usually happy to oblige. On the day after the Battle of Mons he was transporting an unusual load. The trailer was piled high with mattresses and blankets and he was taking them from the college to the primary school where Madame Deron, with the help of other local ladies, was setting up an ambulance to care for wounded soldiers. The municipality had voted four thousand francs for its expenses and all the signs were pointing to the fact that it would very soon be needed. Tired as she was after a long day of bed-making, Madame Deron sat down to record these sinister portents in her journal.

Extract from the diary of Madame Deron

Since the morning of the 24th we have been wondering why such a large number of motor cars have been coming down the road from Cambrai and travelling towards Albert. They are full of travellers, mostly women and children. Trunks and suitcases are strapped on to the cars with travelling rugs on top and sometimes sheets and quilts and sacks of provisions. Why? Naturally everybody is curious when in the course of one day two hundred motors pass through. One of them was even being driven by the mother of a car-load of children. They say that they have come from Valenciennes, Condé, or Cambrai. They say that the Germans are about to arrive at their homes. They have heard talk of the atrocities committed in Belgium and they are fleeing as the danger comes closer.

There were more ominous signs at the railway station. Flora Dignoire, the stationmaster's daughter, had been brought up almost in the station itself. The family house stood close to the line and all their lives the children had slept through the roar of night trains as they streaked down from Belgium, through Lille, Douai and Bapaume on their way to reach Paris early in the morning. Now they woke in the night listening for the sound of trains that never came. Even the local trains were few and far between. Flora was nineteen, newly engaged to Jean Verdel. Now Jean had gone off to the war and Flora was left to worry and wonder as she helped her father at the station and, in her spare moments, scribbled a record of her doings in the exercise book she had bought when Jean went away to keep him up to date with events at home.

Extract from the journal of Mlle. Flora Dignoire

This morning the train between Bapaume and Marcoing was followed all the way by a German aeroplane. About 11 o'clock this morning we heard a low heavy growling coming from the north. I heard it two or three times. I think it was gunfire.

No one is working at the station. There are hardly any trains and there is no merchandise arriving. The railway employees who have nothing to do pass their time cleaning up the station yard. People getting off the trains yesterday say that the Germans are in Roubaix and Tourcoing – and we haven't yet seen a single French soldier! We are beginning to get worried. This evening an urgent message arrived. All the locomotives at Bapaume must be sent to Marcoing, they must be sent right away this evening without waiting for daylight. Immediately the four engines puffed off into the night, one after the other. All this is not reassuring.

Extract from the diary of Madame Deron

Tuesday 25 August. Soon after two in the morning, the procession of vehicles started up again, motors and also horse-drawn cars packed with people and luggage. Now pedestrians too have started passing through, men, women, children, carrying a single suitcase, a parcel, a change of shoes slung over a shoulder, baskets of provisions. They are covered with dust thrown up by the cars on the dirt roads. Some lead their dogs on a rope, others, not bothering to bring any essentials, have escaped just as they were. By eleven o'clock a great crowd of them had collected at the station, most of them not knowing where to go or what direction to go in.

The Bapaume people were all asking them questions. None of them had seen the Germans but the stories the Belgians had told them had incited them to fly. Now people are beginning to panic here. Those who have children are terrified at the idea of what might happen to them if there is an invasion.

The town council was worried too. That afternoon Monsieur Lechire plodded once more through the streets of Bapaume with his ancient cart piled high with the same load of linen he had so recently delivered to the primary school. The council had changed its mind about the clinic. What was the point of spending money on expensive stores and medical supplies when in all likelihood only the invader would benefit? In the present situation, they reasoned, four thousand francs could be put to better use. They had requested Madame Deron and her helpers to strip the newly made beds and instructed Lechire to take the linen back again to the college. If the situation changed and if there did happen to be any wounded soldiers to nurse, the ladies could nurse them there. But it seemed unlikely. It was 26 August and so far they had not seen a single French soldier. That was the most disquieting circumstance of all.

As she made her way home after closing up the school Madame Deron met the Mayor and his news was not reassuring. 'Cambrai is on fire,' he told her. 'The Germans will be in Bapaume tomorrow and at Peronne the day after!'

All day the light westerly wind had carried the distant drumming of the guns at Le Cateau. It was hardly more than an echo, faintly heard in the far distance, but it was enough to decide some people that it was time to go.

Gaston Degardin (aged 12)

My father had been injured in a serious hunting accident two years earlier and he was not liable for mobilisation. That morning he went into the town and Georges Vasseur said to him, 'If you intend to go you can take my car if you will take my children Lucien and Marie with you.' Our own car was only a two-seater so we left it in the garage and about one o'clock we set off in Georges Vasseur's motor to go to Berck on the coast. Our departure was very hurried and we took the absolute minimum of luggage. One thing I remember about the journey is that when we got to Achiet-le-Grand only a few kilometres away, a Civil Guard was barring the road at the railway bridge. All he had in the way of uniform was a military-style cap and an armlet and all he had in the way of a firearm was a rusty old rifle. He was a Bapaume man, Auguste Desvignes, and he recognised his boss's motor car (because he worked for George Vasseur in his grocery shop and at his oil-pressing mill). My father spoke to him for a few minutes and although it was no joking matter, he asked Auguste what on earth he would have done with his gun if we hadn't had a permit to travel. He had no ammunition at all. Not a single bullet!

Extract from the diary of Madame Deron

It was raining and quite cold for the time of year, and the sky was dark and grey. On the road out of town there was an interminable procession of people leaving the district – women, children, young people and old – going on through the rain without the least idea where they were going to lay their heads. Bapaume was emptying too, and they were saying now that the enemy was as near as Havrincourt. All over the town you could hear the banging of hammers. The shopkeepers were all barricading their premises and nailing planks of wood over the shop windows to act as shutters.

That evening the first convoy of wounded arrived at the Hospice and we also saw French soldiers, but they were soldiers who had fled leaving their rifles and equipment behind.

The Curé spoke to them. Two of them were Territorials and they said that they had been surprised by the Germans at Cambrai when they were in the middle of cooking up some food. They had tried to defend themselves. With a few others they had made a barrier across a street and tried to resist, but one of them had his hand smashed and the other was half-scalped by a bullet. When they were escaping towards Bapaume they had met an English lorry and got a lift.

For the Curé, Edouard Fournier, who was also Dean of the Diocese, there was no question of leaving. In peace or war there was still his parish to care for, children to be baptised, the dead to be buried. There was a funeral this very morning and as usual on such occasions the Curé had put on a white lace surplice over his long black cassock to read the Mass for the Dead. Now, Bible in hand, walking from the church in front of the horse-drawn hearse and the cortège of mourners following behind, Fournier spotted the soldiers.

M. le Doyen Edouard Fournier

Just before we arrived at the cemetery I saw French troops marching with rifles slung from the direction of Arras. I slowed down to have a better look and as I watched they turned off the road and started deploying in extended order across the fields facing Favreuil. This made me realise that the enemy could not be far away. While we were in the cemetery I heard gunfire. I learned later that these troops were under the orders of General d'Amade and that they had come from Beugny where they had been trying to hold back the invasion. They had been sent towards the right flank of von Kluck's army which was marching on Paris by the road from Cambrai.

Extract from the diary of Madame Deron

About nine in the morning we heard the guns. We thought at first that it was thunder, then we heard that they were fighting at Beugny. As the news got worse and worse I thought of starting up my ambulance again. The Abbé gave me the use of the college and we prepared twenty beds right away. At 11 o'clock the first wounded man arrived at the college. By the evening we had twenty-seven.

Extract from the journal of Mlle. Flora Dignoire

There was terrible anxiety in the town. Everyone wanted to run away. Suddenly five French Dragoons came galloping in from the Peronne road. From the distance we could only see their helmets covered with khaki cloth and their long lances. There was a shout. *The Uhlans!* And people started running away terrified – from our own soldiers! Fear is blind! A horse without a rider stopped exhausted at the station and it looked as if it had galloped a long way! About midday some infantry passed through going towards Péronne. They said that many more troops would be passing through the town in the afternoon. Here, at last, were our soldiers! It turned very dull and started to rain but everyone turned out to watch them go past, infantry, artillery, engineers. They halted in the town and everyone rushed to give water to the horses and food and drink to the men. The soldiers told us that their orders were not to attack the enemy.

A company of engineers went to the station to blow up the railway line to St Aubin. We heard the noise of the explosion and then another huge explosion, this time towards Arras. A train arrived from the south with provisions, bread, coffee, beans, etc. There is no more bread at our own bakers.

M. le Doyen Edouard Fournier

During the afternoon the troop of soldiers which had been spread out up the Arras road fell back to Bapaume. I was impressed with the optimism of these Territorials. They were delighted to have harassed the enemy when they came up against them near Beugny, they felt they had done a good job and were very pleased with themselves. But the commander of this battalion was extremely worried. He no longer had any idea where he was supposed to go. The soldiers spread across the rue d'Arras and the rue du Péronne and piled their arms. Like many other people I was going about giving the men wine and some food when a closed car arrived with a staff officer inside. The Commandant stopped it. He shouted, 'What must I do?' The officer replied, 'I have no orders for you.' They spoke in low voices but I had edged a little closer and I just caught their words. The Commandant said to him, 'Can you give me any idea of what's happening?' The officer spoke into his ear, 'General retreat to the Somme.'

When I heard these words my first thought was for our poor abandoned town.

Extract from the journal of Mlle. Flora Dignoire

By now it was almost nightfall. As I went back to the station I saw a huge fire that scared me out of my wits. The engineers had just set fire to the huge pile of sleepers that could have been used to repair the line. The flames rose into the dark night and the sparks were flying over the station. I could see all the soldiers going hither and thither in every direction. A little later the ration train left again, and all the soldiers and engineers went with it. So we closed up the station and went back into town. The atmosphere in the streets was really sinister! All the people who had stayed were still up and dressed, ready to go – no lights in the houses, everyone speaking in whispers, nobody asleep. Some soldiers came back from the direction of Cambrai and very soon afterwards they were followed by a lot of the soldiers we had seen in the afternoon going along in absolute disorder.

Extract from the diary of Madame Deron

When I was coming back from the Ambulance I saw soldiers every-where in full retreat. They were harassed and quite demoralised. They were throwing away rifles, ammunition, haversacks – everything. There were hundreds of cartridges lying around! A little further on there was an abandoned ammunition wagon and rifles thrown down just anywhere. I got hold of a soldier and said, 'What's all this! Why are you all retreating in the face of the enemy?' He said, 'Ah, Madame, we have no artillery, no machine-guns. They're mowing us down like corn.'

It took the single officer some time to round up the troops and get them on to the road to Arras and, when at last they set off, a small boy, André Betrancourt, was at the front of the contingent marching beside his father.

Peace. Knightsbridge Barracks, April 1914. The 1st Lifeguards parade in all their splendour for inspection.

War. Knightsbridge Barracks, August 1914. The 1st Lifeguards parade in khaki service dress before leaving for France.

(OPPOSITE, ABOVE) Wellington Barracks, August 1914. The Irish Guards filling ammunition pouches and preparing for departure.

(BELOW) Mobilised Reservists of the Grenadier Guards reporting at Wellington Barracks.

(ABOVE) A Squadron, 11th Hussars leaving Newcastle on the way to the front.

(RIGHT) A joke played by the 2nd Scots Guards on their Quartermaster who obligingly fell asleep on the Channel crossing. They added the wine bottles and propped him in a compromising position.

A Company, The 4th Royal Fusiliers, resting in the square at Mons on 22 August 1914. Minutes after this photograph was taken they were on the march and on the move up to the canal bank at Nimy.

The Lancers photographed on the retirement from Mons.

Trumpeter Jimmy Naylor. He blew the call that galloped the guns out of the action at the Battle of Mons.

1911. Lieutenant Roderick Macleod as a newly commissioned subaltern in the Royal Artillery.

A brief rest period in the early part of the Retreat from Mons.

A Uhlan horse captured, complete with German equipment, at Néry.

Bridging the Marne at La Ferté-sous-Jouarre.

La Creste. Miss Mildred Aldrich's house on the hill at Huiry and the garden which gave her a grandstand view of the Battle of the Marne.

11th Hussars, resting at their Battalion Headquarters on the Aisne. September 1914.

A refugee family smiled obligingly for a British officer's camera as they set off from Antwerp with children and belongings in their dogcart.

Men of the Royal Naval Brigade in the makeshift trenches at Antwerp.

Duckboards across the Belgian sector where the land was flooded to stem the German advance.

7th Division on the road from Bruges to Ostend.

Consultation at a crossroads in Ghent, with the Germans just a mile behind the 7th Division.

One of Commander Sampson's armoured cars on the Menin Road. Just behind it is the level crossing known as the Halte, later better known as Hellfire Corner.

The lush and leafy countryside provided useful cover, soon to vanish as the land was devastated.

After the first shells fell on Ypres. '. . . *There is a terror in the air about the town now . . . many, many houses have been completely destroyed . . . There is looting all over the place . . .*' Father Camille Delaere.

The Queen's Own Oxfordshire Hussars (the first Territorial Yeomanry to take part in the Great War) leaving St. Omer to go into action in the First Battle of Ypres.

(ABOVE) '. . . The crashing of the shells, of wood, of stone blocks blown in every direction with a terrible force had virtually broken the building apart – holed, broken, destroyed – everything reduced to nothing! . . . We spent a good part of the afternoon scrabbling through the rubble looking for the Blessed Host . . .' Father Camille Delaere.

(BELOW) Charles Worsley with his wife Alexandra seeing him off as he waits on the quayside to embark for France.

(BELOW RIGHT) The temporary cross that marked Worsley's grave at Zandvoorde.

The garden west wing of Hooge Chateau just after the explosion of the shell that wiped out the Staff at the crucial moment of the First Battle of Ypres on 31 October 1914.

Transport retiring down the Menin Road while the enemy shells Hooge. 31 October 1914.

Troops crawling out to 'reconnoitre in force' from Zandvoorde village towards Gheluvelt to test the weight of enemy opposition.

The Cloth Hall still smouldering two days after it was set alight. '. . . *black sky, intense heat, flames like red clouds thrown up by a storm – sublime among the horror* . . .' Father Delaere.

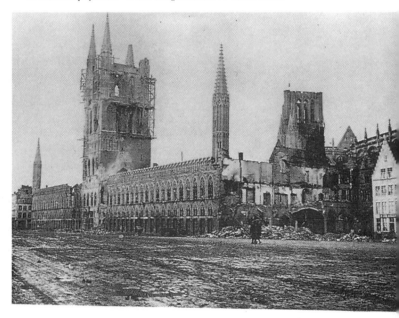

The 2nd Scots Guards, hastily entrenched at Zandvoorde.

Some remnants of the London Scottish after their blooding at Messines. They were the first Territorials to go into action in the war and suffered fifty per cent casualties.

(TOP) The French 75 mm gun – the famous '*Soixante Quinze*'. The French rushed them up to help the British troops at Messines.

(ABOVE) The troopship *Afric*. Her ship's newspaper scooped the world's press with news of the sinking of the *Emden*. The *Afric* herself was torpedoed and sunk on her next trip.

(LEFT) Ralph Langley, apprentice steward on the *Afric* 1914, photographed some months later as a newly enlisted soldier of the King's Royal Rifle Corps.

Eugène Betrancourt was not a soldier but he had a distinct feeling that this was his only chance of ever becoming one. For days now he had been on tenterhooks, agonising as the rumours mounted, fearing as the fighting drew closer that it would soon be too late and that the Germans would reach Bapaume before the arrival of his mobilisation papers. Standing on the doorstep as the troops were passing his house, struck by the thought that they might be the last French troops he would see, Eugène had suddenly made up his mind. He grabbed André by the hand and ran to catch up with the officer marching in front of the troop. The officer did not slacken his pace but he grunted permission. He had no objection to André coming along. Like everyone else he was quite convinced that the Germans were systematically cutting off the hands of all small boys so that they in their turn could never be soldiers of France. Even the Paris newspapers said so. In the circumstances there was nothing for it but to let the boy come too.

It was not easy for young legs to keep up, even with the pace set by such weary soldiers, but André trudged on without complaint and without speaking, for they had been warned to keep silent. He was terrified that they might meet the Germans but there was no sign of them. He was only aware of the tramping feet behind him, the grip of his father's hand on his shoulder, and the shadowy shapes of the poplars along the road flowing past against the dark of the night sky. And then, just as they breasted a rise, there was a light in the distance and the hum of a car approaching fast with headlamps blazing.

André Betrancourt (aged 12)

The soldiers shouted, 'It's a machine-gun car!' An officer halted the column and told us to go to the side of the road and hide behind the trees, and he stationed the soldiers there too. It was *not* a machine-gun carrier, but the officer, thinking the car belonged to spies, pulled out his sabre and rushed across the road waving it shouting, '*Halte-là!*' But the car didn't stop. The someone shouted, '*FIRE*' and the soldiers opened fire. The car was riddled with bullets and it skidded over to our side of the road banging into a tree. We had to scramble out of the way! Then the car recovered and went on. No one said a thing. They put us back at the head of the column and we set off again.

After this episode my father decided that we were going no further and that he would find another way of joining the army. My father's mother lived a little further on at Sapignies in a house on the main road and when we got there we left the ranks. My father told the officer what we were going to do but for some reason he was suspicious and he waited until my grandmother opened the door to make sure that my father hadn't spun him a yarn. We stayed the night there and went back the next morning to Bapaume. Then we heard the explanation for the drama of the motor car the night before.

The car had not contained spies. It contained Albert Lagnier who had been stopped by two French officers as he drove to Biefvillers with his friend Edouard Citerne. They had ordered Lagnier to drive them to the railway junction at Achiet and, having done so, the two men were racing back to Bapaume when they were challenged by the troops. Lagnier was convinced that they had been fired on by the Germans. Citerne, being dead, was unable to express an opinion.

In the barred and shuttered houses only the very old and the very young were asleep. The others kept watch, listening to the endless clatter of farm carts trundling over the cobbles, the flurries of bleating sheep, the lowing of cattle as farmers drove their livestock through the night. The entire village of Bancourt, two kilometres away, had taken to the road and in the morning many more people set out on the road from Bapaume.

The diary of an unknown evacuee

They come to fetch me at five o'clock in the morning. Everything is covered in thick mist and I walk without seeing a thing, feeling as if I were still asleep. On the outskirts of the town a few people stand on their doorsteps staring into the street at the scattered rifles and equipment the soldiers had thrown away the night before. The road is deserted, the morning breeze is cold on my face and wakes me up now. Apart from a sentry on the side of the road we don't see a soul outside the villages. At Biefvillers the people look anxiously at us as we pass and ask us if the Germans have reached Bapaume yet. We reassure them – a little!

At Bucquoy we find that word has just been passed advising people to go. On the square a lot of big wagons full of people are pulled up ready to go. They stop us to find out if the Germans are at Bapaume. Most of these people don't know where to go and they are very far from cheerful. As many as twenty people are squeezed into some of the two- or four-horse wagons, bareheaded with just a few blankets between them. Some have even taken the precaution of bringing their salt-beef barrels along with them! Others have nothing – they have even forgotten their money! Someone who must have killed his pig when the Germans were coming has abandoned it and the dead pig is lying in the middle of the square. A good-hearted woman has taken two lost children under her wing. A baker who was in the middle of making his bread has come just as he is, in his apron and slippers, bareheaded, without money and still covered with flour.

All the way from Bucquoy to Foncquevillers we travel in a long procession of carts and wagons. We pass through Sailly, where we are asked if it's true that the station at Bapaume has been burned down. At last we arrive at Souastre at dinner-time.

It was Friday, 28 August, and they had escaped just in time. That day there was a great battle on the plain and along the ridge where the road from Bapaume ran south-east to Péronne. And that day the Germans came.

They came to the farm of Hyacinthe Guerlet at St Aubin. Early in the morning a single Uhlan officer rode into the farmyard, dismounted and looked around him. To the farmer shushing his frightened children as he peered cautiously from a window, the German did not look particularly threatening. He made no attempt to enter the house, but merely poked around the yard, peered into the barn, and stayed leaning against the barn door as if to enjoy the morning sun. He appeared to be waiting, and Guerlet was in no doubt that his farm had been picked as a rendezvous and that the German was awaiting the arrival of his comrades. But it was the French who came, a troop of horsemen who promptly took the Uhlan prisoner and rode off in high delight with their unexpected catch. Unfortunately for the Guerlet family they omitted to capture their prisoner's horse, and when the Uhlans did arrive shortly afterwards and found the animal tied up riderless in the farmyard, they jumped to the worst possible conclusion.

Guerlet was not familiar with the German tongue, but even if he was unable to understand the drift of their irate questioning he fully understood the Germans' meaning when they thrust him against a wall and raised their rifles. Madame Guerlet screamed and wept. The children howled and Guerlet, still protesting, quailed and steeled himself to die. But something in the torrents of explanation had convinced the Uhlan officer that his colleague had not been foully murdered by the villainous French. He shouted an order, the troopers lowered their rifles, snatched sticks from the woodpile and ran to the house. They thrust the sticks into the kitchen stove to set them alight – and then they set fire to the barn.

The barn was full of dry hay and the fire quickly took hold. When it was well ablaze the Uhlans rode off. Hyacinthe Guerlet went too, hurrying down the road to Bapaume with his weeping family at his heels and his farm burning at his back. By ten o'clock everyone who still remained in the town knew the story. They also knew that it was now too late to escape.

There was fighting at Rocquigny, not five kilometres away, there was fighting at Le Transloy, at Sailly Saillisel, at Rancourt, and the drumming of guns echoed on and on through the deserted streets of Bapaume. People listening hoped against hope that some at least of the guns were French firing at the Germans, but they knew in their hearts that this was the sound of German field guns massed against the French. Shortly after midday the firing stopped.

Extract from the diary of Madame Deron

The town is deserted, all the shops are shut up and the people have sealed themselves into their houses, joining up with neighbours for company. Bapaume is almost empty and the men who are left have hidden themselves for fear of capture. Our butcher spends the whole day concealed in a tree! Others shut themselves in cupboards or even in grandfather clocks. Mothers of little boys are terrified and hide them too. We all expect the spearhead of the Germans to arrive at any moment. Towards midday a large number of wounded arrive, among them a lieutenant-colonel of the 338th Infantry Regiment. His battalion has been decimated, and while I am fixing a temporary dressing as we wait for a car to come to take them to the hospital at Arras I ask him, 'What is happening, Colonel?' He says, 'It's not going well. We have no guns. It's a rout!'

About half-past five in the evening, Abbé Ledoux tells us, seven Uhlans come through the town. Seeing them, three French soldiers rush into the house of Monsieur Delbecq who is not at home but whose door is half-open. Artemise, his maid, begs for mercy but the soldiers are taken prisoner and their rifles smashed. This first appearance of the Germans puts the whole population in despair and we spend an anxious night.

The French had been routed, the road was clear, and at four o'clock in the morning a long column of Germany infantry entered Bapaume *en route* for Péronne.

Extract from the diary of Madame Deron

At five o'clock we were rudely wakened by one of the night nurses shouting, 'Quick, quick, they're outside in the street, they're smashing all the windows and breaking down all the doors.'

On hearing the sound of glass being broken in the street, the Abbé had taken the wise precaution of opening the outer doors of the college and the door of the room where the wounded were was half-opened. At half-past five we saw three pointed helmets! One of the soldiers at the door made a sign with his hand as if to say, 'It's all right', and they went away. We thought we were rid of them, but at six o'clock four others came in, an officer with a drawn revolver followed by four soldiers with rifles, and bayonets fixed ready to run through the first one who moved. It was a terrible sight! I stayed calm, at least outwardly, but my heart was beating hard. The officer saluted me politely and said in French to the wounded, '*Bonjour Camarades.*' The four of them went round the room glancing at every wounded man, then they said, '*Bonne santé, Camarades*' and left.

By the time we finished the dressings for our poor wounded men the soldiers had moved on towards Péronne. I went into the town and what a sight the streets were! Shopfronts broken, doors smashed in! The shelves in the grocers' shops had been completely vandalised and hundreds and hundreds of bottled preserves and jars of jam were tossed down on the ground. But it was worse in the houses where the families had gone away. They had been ransacked and left in an indescribable mess with all their belongings tossed about pell-mell everywhere. It was dreadful!

After a day of brilliant sunshine it had been a night of bright moonlight and clear skies. All across the country north-east of Bapaume, beyond the long ridge where the Germans had trampled across the bodies of the French who had tried to bar their way, and for many miles behind where fresh German troops waited to continue the glorious march forward in the morning, bivouac fires glowed bright and bold across the fields. The Germans were not troubled by the thought that they might reveal their positions. There was little chance of a surprise attack. The French on their immediate front were broken, the British Army had been smashed to bits, and to crown their own successes the soldiers of von Kluck's army had heard news that night that the soldiers of von Bülow's had roundly thrashed the army of General Lanrezac not far to the east. Behind the shifting battlefront the jubilant official bulletin had been formally read to the troops and to assist the celebrations, some regimental bands unpacked their instruments and gave impromptu concerts in the fields. They played the Hymn of Praise. Lounging round glowing campfires, full of good German sausage and replete with excellent wine filched from a thousand French cellars, a thousand jubilant voices took up the refrain. In three days' time it would be the anniversary of the Battle of Sedan, the historic victory that had won the Franco-Prussian War for their Kaiser's grandfather. Singing happily in the mild moonlit evening the Kaiser's troops had not the slightest doubt that they would celebrate Sedan Day in sight of Paris.

They had every reason to believe that they had dealt the French a crushing blow. No one had yet had time to compute the losses of the day's fighting, but for the Germans, advancing behind massed machine-guns and a wall of supporting artillery, outnumbering their opponents by ten to one, the losses had been comparatively light. It was clear that the French had paid a high price. The heaped-up corpses testified to that, and all afternoon and evening the German troops going forward had seen with natural satisfaction long lines of prisoners passing to the rear. They had pulverised the French so soon, had broken through so quickly that they had captured several thousand troops waiting in reserve to go into action. They had taken a fine bag.

The Germans were right in their assumption that the French casualties had been chilling – 1,299 men in the 263rd Regiment of Infantry, 1,139 in the 338th – and most of them were dead. It was four weeks to the day since France had gone to war and for four blood-soaked years to come, no regiment, even in the cauldron of Verdun, would ever again suffer such losses in a single day. Already in the Battle of the Frontiers, 300,000 Frenchmen had been killed, wounded or captured. It was not surprising that the Germans were bursting with delight. Paris would be next. There seemed little doubt that all they would have to do would be to reach out and take hold of it as easily as they might pluck an over-ripe plum from a tree.

But the French had gained something. The Battle of Péronne is not much mentioned in the history books. It was only a small battle, a single morning's combat on a sunny summer day. It had been on a far smaller scale than the fight the British had fought at Le Cateau but, like Le Cateau, it had gained time. It had held up the Germans in their advance for one vital day, and as they fell back to Amiens, the remnants of the broken regiments pulled von Kluck's army on behind them as they went, drawing them further west, further away from Paris and further away from the British Expeditionary Force on its long trek south.

Dvr. J. Low, No. 47653, 117 Battery, R.F.A., B.E.F.

That retreat was the only part that shook me up in the whole war, and it was because we weren't getting any food and when there are no rations you have to put up with nowt. Oh, it was chronic! There was no rations. We had to live on the land, get what we could from the farms. When the people had gone they'd left the farms just as they was, you know. The coffee pot on the stove in the farmhouses, chickens running around the yard. They'd left the cattle and everything. Of course our chaps picked the chickens up, and the eggs and whatever we could get hold of to live off the land. We did that for three days, we did. Get hold of some chickens and when we got a chance to stop, kill them and boil them.

We were going along this road and we had to stop now and again, because it got jammed up with the military and it got jammed up with civilians with all their little belongings in handcarts. We'd pulled up for something and I dismounted, and I thought my luck was in. I saw a biscuit – one of those hard army biscuits – fallen in the mud at the side of the road and I picked it up, and when I looked at it, it was spread with marmalade. Well that brought me down, that did, because I really hated marmalade. But we were hungry! I managed to eat a bit of it, mud, marmalade and all.

It was starting to get cold at night (of course it rained quite a bit, and you got chilled. No shelter on the road.). So what I used to do was put my hand in the horse's mouth and just play with the horse's tongue at the back. I'd be afraid to do it now, but the horse knew me and it didn't mind, and of course its breath was warm and it warms up your hands.

Gnr. A. Crook, No. 69773, J. Battery, 5th Cavalry Brigade, B.E.F.

Rations were very scarce. It was almost impossible for rations to reach us. We had to resort to looting. Most shops and houses had been evacuated, and nearly every French family had a rabbit – so we had a choice of a rabbit in a hutch or a duck on the pond. Our trouble was being able to cook them. We had to form groups. Those that had done the looting had to share with those that had held the horses. We found our horses very useful. Grapes were very plentiful because quite often there were vines growing up the fronts of houses. Us gunners who rode single horses could ride up to the grapes and just pick a few bunches. Of course we had to share with the drivers on the guns and other vehicles. For some time we done very well. Then came the sad order *Looting must stop*. We had a very good officer commanding J Battery. Often if we were staying in a place for a few hours he would find the village baker and order him to bake bread for us. Bread was our difficulty.

Capt. E. J. Needham, 1st Bttn., Northamptonshire Regt., B.E.F.

All along these roads of France grew fruit trees, mostly apple, now in full fruit. Naturally all of us, officers and men, picked the fruit as we halted. It was nourishing and refreshing to our dust-parched throats and palates. What possible harm could this have done to anybody? The inhabitants had all left the countryside and everything edible left was food for the enemy. The same applied to food, bread, chocolate, etc. left behind in the shops when the owners had fled. Why should we not have been allowed to eke out our rations with them and why must they be left to feed the enemy? Yet, day after day I saw Staff Officers riding down the road giving orders for this and that man's name to be taken for 'stealing fruit in a friendly country'. What utter rot! The men felt this show of useless red tape very bitterly.

The same thing applies to the herds of cattle left grazing in the fields. In one case some regiment, I forget which, did drive a large herd before them for days and these were, I believe, eventually sent down by train to the base to be turned into beef for the troops. But I expect they got into trouble for it! If the cattle could not be driven by us, why could they not be shot, instead of being left behind to feed the Germans?

Drummer Slaytor, 3rd Bttn., The Coldstream Guards, B.E.F.

The marching was hard. The sun always seemed to be beating fiercely down – no doubt a very lovely summer on a sandy beach but most exhausting to the plodding infantrymen in retreat. I was sixteen years and ten months old, easily the youngest Coldstreamer on the retreat. I saw some wonderful pears in a walled garden and it wasn't long before I had my haversack full of juicy fruit. I had just got out of the garden when the sharp voice of the Regimental Sergeant-Major, Jack Carnell, brought me to a halt. 'What have you got there?' he enquired (as if he didn't know!). 'Pears,' I said. He said, 'If I see you going into other people's gardens again I'll put you in the Guardroom.' (This with the Germans just about to enter the place!) 'Get back to your company at once.' I was about to go, and thankful to get away, when he called me back. 'Come here, Drummer. I'll have a couple of those pears!' So I handed over three or four of my precious load and scuttled off to my platoon. I considered myself lucky to have got off so lightly!

Rfn. E. Gale, No. 3774, 1st Bttn., The Rifle Brigade, 11th Brigade,
4th Division, B.E.F.

I think we did about two hundred and sixteen miles in ten days and
no tea, no hot meals. All we had was army biscuits. You wanted a
sledgehammer to break them! We never stopped to camp anywhere
in those ten days. We'd stop on the road perhaps for ten or fifteen or
twenty minutes and we had to move on again. One night we was on
the road and the Staff Officer come along and said, 'What division?'
I said, 'Fourth.' 'What brigade?' I said, '11th Brigade Transport.' He
said, 'Go down the road. There's a field there, pull in there – you'll
see a wide gate on the left and you can pull in there and have a sleep
for the night.' He said to the old quartermaster, master cook, 'Get the
dixies up and get their field covers off and get some tea ready for the
troops coming in.' Well, they'd got the spuds going and they'd got
the tea and sugar all ready, and another Staff Officer come along and
he said, 'What the bloody hell are you doing here?' he said, 'Get out
of it, as quick as you can. Jerry's down the road about five hundred
yards away!' And they had to get out and left all the supplies just lying
there on the ground.

Gnr. A. Crook, No. 69773, J Battery, 5th Cavalry Brigade, B.E.F.

Our rest period during the retreat would be from about midnight till
three in the morning. In the daytime we would just get snatches of
sleep – if we were lucky! Sometimes we saw action. We might have
got some distance in advance of the Germans and the Major had
thought it was a good position to engage the enemy as they advanced,
perhaps a bridge or similar. We would then lay down in the sun
waiting for the Germans. But we always carried out the method 'They
who fight then runs away lives to fight another day.' I think we took
our toll of the Germans.

We had some good battles. On one occasion we fired every round
of ammunition we had. Our cavalry brought us back four prisoners
for interrogation. Usually when they made a charge they were ordered
to take *no* prisoners, but it was necessary sometimes to take a few for
interrogation. We had a good squadron of cavalry with us. They were
the 12th Lancers. On one occasion it was a weekend and very quiet.
Whether the Germans were going to take Sunday off I don't know,
but anyhow our Major went to a farm and got a calf. They cut it up
and started to cook it and it was just beginning to smell very nice

when the shells began to fall and we heard machine-guns firing further back, so we had to pack up and quickly. But our Major came to the rescue. He ordered the farmer to put our dixies containing the lovely stew on to one of his wagons and follow us. By the time it fell dusk we were in a town and we'd lit our fires in the square. Again our stew began to smell lovely! We had some French troops nearby. Excitable lot! Suddenly they began to shout and they started fixing their bayonets. What it was all about I *don't* know, but we had to make a hurried exit – and that was the end of our lovely stew!

Rfn. E. Gale, No. 3774, 1st Bttn., The Rifle Brigade, 11th Brigade, 4th Division, B.E.F.

I don't suppose we had more than an hour's sleep at a time that whole ten days. I tell you, us drivers going along the road with the transport got so sick and tired of riding in the saddle that we got off and walked at the head of our horses, your backside was so sore with riding all day. You were saddled up twenty-four hours a day. Of course, the infantry, they were in a worse condition than what we were. On transport we did have a chance to ride and they didn't. They had to hoof it all the way and, same as us, if they stopped anywhere they could only get a few minutes' sleep, that's all, and away they'd go again. I tell you, we never had our boots off for ten days! You daren't take your boots off because you might have a job to get them on, your feet was swollen so.

To the end of the retirement we never caught sight of our own battalion once. I still had the Battalion water cart but I don't know where *they* got their water from. They didn't get it off us! They never had a chance to catch up with us. No sooner had you stopped than you got a Staff Officer coming along and moving you out of it. On these water carts, you know, in the shafts you had two poles with, like, broomsticks on them. They were strapped to the shafts and if we got a chance to stop we'd unstrap them and let them down on the ground to take the weight off the horses' backs. We couldn't unharness the horses even. I remember one fellow got taken off the transport and sent back to the Battalion when we linked up with them. All during the retirement he hadn't bothered about the horses at all and when they finally pulled the saddle off they pulled half the horses' skin away from their backs. In those days your horse used to come before you. Of course, you could get a soldier for a shilling a day but a horse cost a hundred pounds.

Extract from the diary of Lt.-Col. Davies, 2nd Bttn., Oxfordshire and Buckinghamshire Light Infantry, B.E.F.

More than half the men were Reservists who, in spite of some route marches, had not got into proper condition for marching, and consequently there were a good many sore feet. A few of these were so bad that they had to be sent to hospital eventually, but the large majority of the sore-footed men stuck to it splendidly. We usually had no ambulances with us, so that even the men who fell down unconscious with sunstroke had to be got along on transport of some kind, even on artillery limbers. In spite of all this, the Regiment had only one man missing during the whole retreat. The officers all worked magnificently. They were tired to death themselves but they kept their companies together all through. Whenever there was a halt, men dropped down and slept on the road, and one had to allow extra time at each halt to wake them up before we could get on the move again. Sometimes a company commander going down his company to wake the men would find at the end that some of the men he had awakened first had dropped asleep again.

Cpl. W. Holbrook, No. 13599, 4th Bttn., The Royal Fusiliers, 9th Brigade, 3rd Division, B.E.F.

We did quite a bit of fighting on the way back from St-Quentin to the Marne. Of course they come up in lorries, the Germans. *We* had to walk back. So when the dawn broke in the mornings they were only a few miles away again, almost on our heels the Germans were.

But we never lost our morale. You see, the troops thought they were falling back and getting the Germans into a kind of a vee shape and then they would fall on them. We thought we were falling back on purpose. We didn't think we were being driven back. What they used to do, the people in the villages, the women and the elderly men (because all the young men had been called up), they dug trenches for us to fall back into – not deep ones, of course, little narrow things. Sometimes they were still doing it when we got there, the women and the elderly men. Then we'd get into that position so as to cover them and protect them while they got out themselves. Then we'd get out of it ourselves – but orderly, always orderly.

Food was the problem. The worst people to feed are people on the retreat. You see you've got to get transport up and you can't get it too near, can't take horses too near, because horses were as valuable as men in those days. So you had to get as near as you could and just dump it on the road. It was only biscuits and bully anyway, but of course the people who retreated first got it, and the poor devils who were last got nothing. So, as *we* were mostly last we lived on green apples and cabbage stalks and goodness knows what until we got to the Marne.

Sgt. F. M. Packham, No. 10134, 2nd Bttn., Royal Sussex Regt., 2nd Brigade, 1st Division, B.E.F.

By this time the continual marching was playing havoc with some of the men's feet. So it was decided to lessen the load we had to carry by leaving our greatcoats behind. We were told to roll our coats and then they were stacked in a barn and a party were left behind to guard them. These men were picked because of their sore feet and it was impossible for them to carry on any longer. They were taken prisoner the same day.

It was a long time since most of the Tommies had jettisoned every surplus ounce of weight to make the going easier. Some had done so by order – and in some cases with mixed feelings. One young officer of the 1st Battalion, The Rifle Brigade, reluctantly abandoning a gaudy angora blanket, was incensed to see it gleefully snatched up by a ragged Jock who promptly wrapped it round his waist in place of some hanging shreds of tartan that had once been a kilt. The Tommies tossed away packs, soap, razors. They dropped greatcoats, ground sheets, spare shirts, clean socks, mess-tins, mugs, knives and forks. They took off caps and jackets when they halted exhausted in the heat of the day and remembered, cursing, in the chill of night that they had left them behind when they moved on. They threw away whatever could be thrown except their rifles and ammunition.

A track of sleazy litter marked the trailing progress of the BEF down the roads to the south – a jumble of broken wagons, of abandoned equipment, of half-cooked food in overturned dixies, of ration boxes dumped by the roadside, occasionally even intact where some unfortunate stragglers had passed them by in the dark or had not been able to stop to cook or even to pick up and carry the cumbersome sides of beef and flitches of bacon that supply lorries, nosing forward as far as they dared, had dumped along the roads to sustain them on the march. To the Germans sniffing at their heels the trail of debris spoke for itself. It spoke of disaster. It spoke of disorder. It spoke of defeat. Believing this as they studied the reports, the German Command compounded their failure to appreciate the outcome of the battle at Le Cateau and were reinforced in their belief that the British had been so decisively trounced that they could be discounted as a fighting force.

It was lucky for General Smith-Dorrien's Second Corps, still marching in a confusion of entangled units, that von Kluck had swung away towards the west. They were troubled very little by the Germans. At every halt the wearisome business of sorting-out had been continued. There were still mixed bunches of stragglers but even they had been marshalled into some semblance of order with officers to guide them on their way, and by now most men were by now marching, if not with their own battalions, at least with their own brigades.

It was fortunate that the First Corps were in better shape. Marching south some ten miles to the east of the battle-torn ranks of the men who fought at Le Cateau, and on the left flank of General Lanrezac's Fifth Army, harried and hassled by von Bülow's cavalry, they were fighting as they went.

It was a matter of some concern to Sir John French that his two corps were far apart with a dangerous gap between them, but the retreat was going better than he had dared to expect and every day the gap was narrowing. Even so, he was a worried man.

To the east of the British Expeditionary Force as at last it approached the River Oise, General Lanrezac's Fifth Army was preparing to counter-attack von Bülow. He counter-attacked next day, on 29 August, and they called it the Battle of Guise. It gave the weary BEF a day of rest, a day to stretch out, to eat, to ease their aching feet and, above all, to sleep. It was the fifth day of the retreat from Mons and they sorely needed it.

Extract from the diary of Lt.-Col. Davies, 2nd Bttn., Oxfordshire and Buckinghamshire Light Infantry, B.E.F.

We had marched 59 miles in the last 64 hours, beginning the march in the middle of an entirely sleepless night, and getting no more than eight hours' sleep altogether during the other two nights. Many men could hardly put one leg before another, yet they all came into Servais singing. B and D Companies did not arrive until long after dark, but they also marched in singing. Captain Wood had hired a French wagon at one of the villages, and loaded it up with the packs of the men who were most tired. By doing this he was able to get them along well.

They slept all night. They slept for the best part of the day, and when they roused in the afternoon there was a hot meal for every man. They bathed in streams when there was water nearby and soaked their swollen feet. They soused their dirt-encrusted scalps and scraped the six-day bristle from their hollow cheeks. And then they slept again.

Late in the afternoon Colonel Montresor paraded the Royal Sussex on a village green, but his purpose was benevolent. He stood the men at ease and spoke a very few words, reminding them that B Company had won the Regimental Cricket Cup in the course of the summer. The Cup had naturally been left at home for safety, but the silver medallions had been mailed to the Battalion and had miraculously caught up with them. One by one each member of the cricket team was called out to receive his inscribed medallion and a handshake from the Colonel.

It was an investiture of a kind and it was not difficult to follow the train of thought of the soldier who remarked as they fell out, 'Any medal they give us for *this* lot ought to have a pair of boots on it!' Nobody disagreed.

Far to the north, in Bapaume, the townspeople had turned out en masse to attend another funeral. There were some twenty coffins to bury and each contained the body of a Frenchman who had died of wounds in the hospice. It also contained several rifles and a quantity of ammunition wedged neatly round the dead soldier's head and feet. The Germans had moved out of Bapaume, but there was little doubt that they would be back, and the citizens had seen enough of the enemy to make a shrewd guess at the penalty he would exact if any one of them was caught with firearms in his possession.

Chapter 16

On 29 August, General Joffre made time for an excellent luncheon in the middle of what was turning out to be a decidedly worrying day. All morning he had been contending with General Lanrezac. His task for the afternoon was to deal with Sir John French. Prickly and argumentative though he was, Lanrezac was by far the easier of the two to deal with, if only for the reason that he was Joffre's subordinate and was bound to carry out his orders. But Sir John French was the independent commander of an independent force with independent interests, and as an ally the British were proving to be a little less than staunch. Among the numerous misfortunes which had befallen France through the languorous days of that bloody August was the twist of fate which had placed the smallest and least dependable of the forces at Joffre's disposal at the most crucial point of the long battle-line that stretched to Alsace in the east. The British stood directly in the path of the German envelopment between, on the one hand, General Lanrezac's exhausted army on whom the brunt of the fighting and the retreat had fallen, and on the other the Sixth Army of General Maunoury.

It was an army in little more than name, for the bulk of the divisions Joffre had filched from his strong right wing to form it had still been on their way when von Kluck's great westward sweep had brushed against the embryo army at Amiens and rolled it back. But it had rolled back like a snowball, growing ever larger as it went, swelling and burgeoning as more and more divisions arrived from the east to join it. Joffre watched, calculated, and waited for the moment when the time would be ripe to strike back at the Germans. That moment, he judged, had almost arrived. He needed just a little more time. He badly needed the British Expeditionary Force to stand fast in order to supply it. For that reason General Joffre was exceedingly anxious to keep Sir John French happy. For that reason, and on that very morning, he had forced General Lanrezac into a battle that was not of his choosing, forcing him to swivel his army to face north-west and to attack the the left flank of von Bülow's army as it marched towards the vulnerable BEF.

The Battle of Guise had given the British soldiers their day of rest. Driving towards Sir John French's headquarters in the Palace of Compiègne,

Joffre fervently hoped that it would also put fresh heart into their Commander-in-Chief whose attitude was, to say the least, ambivalent. Papa Joffre was a formidable figure, tall, corpulent, taciturn, but with an air of benign charm that concealed a will of iron and a nerve of steel. Already today he had imposed that will on General Lanrezac, standing silent, watching, calculating, noting, and by his very presence at Lanrezac's headquarters spurring his general on as he orchestrated the Battle of Guise. Now, mounting the stone stairway that led to the long gallery where the British had set up their headquarters in the Palace of Compiègne, Joffre wished devoutly that he was in a position to bring similar pressure to bear on Sir John French. The Battle of Guise had reduced the danger to the British and that it had not been an unqualified success had been largely due to the failure of the British to co-operate. That failure could be laid squarely at the door of the British Commander-in-Chief.

Joffre of all people fully appreciated that Smith-Dorrien's Second Corps had been badly mauled at Le Cateau and might not yet be fit to fight. But the First Corps was a different matter. It had fought no major battle. Its losses had been far less severe. Through its long fighting retirement it had stayed intact. Its men had endured punishing marches, but most of them had seen little action. They were tired, but they were fit and they were standing alongside General Lanrezac's Fifth Army on the other side of the seven-mile gap that separated them from Smith-Dorrien's Second Corps on its straggling progress further to the west. The First Corps had not only been able to support General Lanrezac by joining in a battle that had an excellent chance of halting the German advance but, as Sir Douglas Haig had made clear, it had been ready and willing to do so. He had agreed to the plan with enthusiasm, *'subject, of course, to the approval of my Chief'*.

But Sir John French had refused.

He was suspicious of the French – above all he was suspicious of General Lanrezac, who only a week ago, in Sir John French's view, had left him in the lurch at Mons. He had no intention of being left for a second time isolated in a dangerous forward position if the French were to retreat again. There was still a gap of seven miles between his two corps as they marched south. He would not rest easy until the gap was closed and he did not mean to risk more casualties until he had made up his losses in men and supplies. He took a gloomy view of the situation. He intended to continue his retreat and no argument of General Joffre's would persuade him to the contrary.

The two men met in the Long Gallery. Despite the fact that several tennis courts might have been fitted into the area beneath the high windows it was almost impossible to hear themselves speak, for every section of Staff

Headquarters had set up for business in a different part of the Gallery. Desks, tables, chairs, had been brought in from the Napoleonic apartments under the brisk direction of orderlies. An army of signallers intent on connecting telephones was draping the wires between the august portraits of kings, queens, dukes, princes and gods that gazed down from their gilded frames on the walls, while another army of French workmen under orders from the Ministry of Beaux Arts did their best to remove the works of art for safe-keeping, oblivious to the requirements of the British Commander-in-Chief and his Staff. Since some gargantuan paintings weighed several hundredweight apiece, it was no easy task. Boots rang on the parquet floor, voices raised in argument rang back from the high, painted roof. There were ladders everywhere, and carpenters sawing and hammering oblivious of the military, and until they were persuaded to desist, the two commanders could not hear themselves speak. They retired with their entourages of officers and interpreters into a corner room.

In vain Joffre argued. In vain he urged Sir John French to stand fast. The British Army, he hinted, were comparatively safe between General Lanrezac's Fifth Army on their right and General Maunoury's Sixth rapidly forming on their left. Think of the danger, he urged, if the British retired and left a huge gap between Lanrezac and Manoury. Already they were a day's march south of the French. Think of the consequences if they fell back any further. If it was not yet time to advance, it was at least time to stand fast on the line they had reached. But Sir John French was adamant. He painted a lurid picture of the condition of his troops, of his losses, of his lack of equipment, of the weakness of the BEF. He had no choice but to continue his withdrawal. He proposed to retire behind Paris and there he would require at least ten days in which to rest his men, to reorganise, to reinforce and to re-equip. Only then would he be prepared to put the BEF back in the fighting line.

On the face of it, Joffre remained calm as he took his leave and later, in a formal despatch to London, French made a point of saying so. 'I strongly represented my position to the French Commander-in-Chief, who was most kind, cordial and sympathetic, as he has always been.' But on 29 August, Joffre was none of these things. He was in a towering rage. He would now have no choice but to abandon his plan to stem the German advance along the River Oise and to pull back his own troops to keep pace with the BEF. Driving away from Compiègne where a century earlier Napoleon had plotted his campaigns against the British, General Joffre might have been forgiven had he felt a certain fellow-feeling for the Emperor. He did succeed in wringing two concessions from his ally. Sir John French agreed to slow down his march to allow the French to catch up and, taking the point that to retire due west of Paris would take him across the line of General Maunoury's Sixth Army swinging back on his left, he also agreed to change direction and loop round Paris to the east. In a last-ditch attempt to maintain good relations with this awkward ally on whom the fate of the left wing depended, Joffre rewarded Sir John French with a message of effusive thanks. At the same time he felt obliged to inform the French government of his misgivings. They found it difficult to understand the attitude of the British Commander-in-Chief and said as much to the British Ambassador.

Sir John French had lost confidence in the French. It was also possible that he had lost his nerve. In his determination to remove his army to safety he intended to go a good deal further than he had indicated to Joffre. Clinging to the letter of his instructions from Kitchener, he intended to cut himself adrift from the French and, if necessary, to quit the battle entirely. In the light of these instructions he felt sincerely that his first and only duty was to save the BEF from being cut off and smashed by the German advance. There was little doubt in his mind that the first to agree would be Lord Kitchener who had written:

> It must be recognised from the outset that the numerical strength of the British Force and its contingent reinforcement is strictly limited, and with this consideration kept steadily in view it will be obvious that the greatest care must be exercised towards a minimum of losses and wastage.
>
> Therefore, while every effort must be made to coincide most sympathetically with the plans and wishes of our Ally, the gravest consideration will devolve upon you as to participation in forward movements where large bodies of French troops are not engaged and where your Force may be unduly exposed to attack. Should a contingency of this sort be contemplated, I look to you to inform me fully and give me time to communicate to you any decision to which His Majesty's Government may come in the matter. In this connection I wish you distinctly to understand that your command is an entirely independent one, and that you will in no case come in any sense under the orders of any Allied General.

The trouble was that Sir John French had not been informing Kitchener fully of his actions and decisions and, putting together such snippets of disquieting information as had trickled through to London, Kitchener at the War Office and the Cabinet in Downing Street were equally disturbed. Since von Kluck's army had marched across the roads that led to the ports of Calais and Boulogne (and if he were not stopped, would soon cut across the road to Le Havre) it had been prudently decided to move the British base south to St-Nazaire, on the coast of Brittany. From there, despite the inconvenience of a long sea-crossing, vital supplies and reinforcements could be transported by rail speedily and safely to the Army north of Paris. But what were they to make of Sir John French's latest request to London? He wanted maps, vast quantities of maps for an army on the march, maps that would lead him to the very heart of France, large-scale maps that showed in detail the two hundred miles that led south and west of Paris to the Atlantic coast. What were they to make of Sir John French's message to the Inspector General of Communications at Rouen that he *intended to make a definite and prolonged retreat due south passing Paris to the east or west*? What were they to make of the rumour that he had ordered the troops to abandon ammunition to speed up the retreat? His losses, by French's own estimate, were severe but not excessive and reinforcements had already been sent from home that were more than enough to replace them. What were they to make of the fact that they had not yet reached the Army since Sir John French had preferred to retain them at the base? Above all what were they to make of the murmurs that reached London through diplomatic channels that at this time of crisis the British commander proposed to retire from the line for ten vital days in order to re-equip?

It hardly made sense. At best it pointed to a deep breach of understanding between the British commander and the French at a time when good relations were of the first importance. For the next two days the wires and cables linking GHQ to London sizzled with an angry traffic of telegrams containing such a variety of conflicting views and information that they merely added to the confusion. Anxious though he was not to step on the toes of his Commander-in-Chief, Lord Kitchener decided that he must find out at first-hand how matters stood. Late in the evening of 31 August, with the approval of the Cabinet, he made up his mind to travel to France. He would reach Paris early the following afternoon and a last telegram to Sir John French made it clear that he was expected to be there too.

That very morning something had happened that was to change the entire course of the war.

The morning broke with a heavy ground mist that promised to usher in another day of shimmering heat. As soon as it had cleared, the engines of a dozen aircraft parked on the grassy oval on the racecourse of Senlis clattered into life. One by one they bumped and yawed across the grass, climbed into the air, circled to gain height and soared north through a sky of cloudless blue to search for the Germans. For the past week the Flying Corps, like the Army, had been moving gypsy-like round France sleeping wherever chance had led them, in barns, in châteaux, in lorries, under hedgerows, even occasionally in hotels. Every day they had spent many hours in the air searching for the enemy and half as long again searching to find their own base, for there was no guarantee that the makeshift airfield the patrols had left would still be in the same place when they returned. Standing orders were not much help – *Fly approximately twenty miles south and search for aircraft on the ground*. Some pilots had had hair-raising escapes and yesterday evening one mess had been buzzing with the exploits of two officers who had motored to Paris for spare parts and returned after dark to discover German officers dining in the billet they had left early that morning. This was nothing compared to the tale of the pilot who had landed his damaged machine under the noses of the Germans, set fire to it, given them the slip and escaped across country on foot. The story of such hairbreadth escapes had lost nothing in the telling.

Admittedly there had been casualties. The mere sight of a British aeroplane soaring far above the ground had been enough to attract fire, not merely from the Germans but from the French and even from the British troops. This annoyance had been partly overcome by the ground crews who had spent a sleepless night working by flashlight and the headlamps of parked lorries painting Union flags on the underside of the aircraft. But even this had not entirely put a stop to the nuisance, for British troops blinking up in the strong sunlight several hundred feet below could not easily distinguish the difference between the angular crosses of the Union Jack and the black cross of the Germans.* When in doubt they played safe by firing at it anyway and more than one aircraft came limping home riddled with holes made by British bullets. To the pilots swearing, dodging, swerving and climbing briskly out of harm's way it was all part of the game. A greater annoyance by far was their inability to deal with the Germans when they met an enemy aircraft on their wanderings. It was all very well for the observer to draw his revolver and shoot at the German pilot but it had little effect. And the strategy which their seniors had dreamed up for putting their adversaries out of action had turned out in practice to be nothing short of farce. They had fondly imagined that all a British pilot would have to do would be to fly above an enemy plane and keeping a parallel course at the same speed, drop a hand-grenade over the side to blow him neatly out of the sky. After a few attempts to put this theory into practice they decided that they could do quite as much harm to a marauding German pilot by shaking a fist at him.

But the fliers were not downhearted. On the contrary, they were rather inclined to be smug, for they were well aware that in a few short days they had proved their worth. Even senior officers who had previously regarded

---

* Such unfortunate occurrences very soon led to the adoption of the Roundel Identification Marking, still in use in the R A F.

them with starchy suspicion were beginning to show a certain grudging respect and to pay a little more attention to the observations of the Flying Corps than they had been inclined to do a week previously. They had spotted the unmistakable signs of the Germans' attempt to encircle the BEF at Mons. They had hedgehopped beyond the Army as it fell back and pinpointed the enemy formations in pursuit. Now they were about to glean the most vital information of all. Skimming across country north of Compiègne, flying up and down the roads from north to south and east to west, they spotted the first indications that von Kluck had changed direction.

Von Kluck's progress ever since Le Cateau had been to sweep towards the south-west. Now, skimming above the roads that led from Amiens, from Roye, from Montdidier towards the River Oise, the pilots plotting the course of the long caterpillars of German troops could see quite plainly that they had shifted in their course and were moving south-east towards Margny, towards Noyon, on a line that would bring them through the forest to Soissons on the Aisne. It was no haphazard movement. Half a dozen different patrols reported the progress of half a dozen different columns and this interesting information was flashed to the British Staff at their new HQ at Dammartin a little north of Paris. Plotting them on the big maps that recorded the progress of the German right wing on its great swing down from Belgium, the swerve to the east gave pensive Intelligence Staff considerable food for thought. Was it possible that von Kluck had abandoned his bid to envelop them? They would have given a good deal to be able to plumb the thoughts and intentions of the German High Command.

The fact was that over the previous forty-eight hours von Kluck had written off the British and by an unfortunate misjudgement had also written off General Maunoury's rapidly growing army on their left and was hastening south-east to support von Bülow in his drive against General Lanrezac's Fifth Army on their right. One sharp blow against its flank as it retired would, in von Bülow's opinion, demolish the French left wing. At Nancy some three hundred kilometres to the east a massive attack planned for the next day would take care of the right wing. The Kaiser himself had arrived at the Front with a retinue of *aides-de-camp*; his baggage contained the gorgeous ceremonial uniform in which he would ride in triumph through Rheims at the head of his victorious troops. The French could never withstand such a double blow. In days, even hours, they would be squeezed into submission. It hardly mattered that von Kluck was swerving away from Paris. Paris could safely be left to itself. No doubt the remnants of the French and British von Kluck had left behind would scuttle inside its defences. As surely as night followed day, if all went according to plan, the

Kaiser would very soon be riding at the head of his troops up the Champs Elysées. It would be 1870 all over again.

The French, and in particular the Parisians, were also remembering 1870 and the humiliation of occupation and defeat. Now Paris was again prepared for defence, troops were manning the gates and strongpoints of the city and in the outlying suburbs there were trenches in the streets. And there were stranger sights – peasants driving herds of sheep and cattle before them up the empty boulevards, leading them to graze in parks and formal gardens, or to browse along the elegant *allées* of the Bois de Boulogne. This time at least, if the worst came to the worst, there would be something in the larder to keep the city from starving. Paris was half-empty. Cafés, restaurants, theatres were closed and traffic in the once-bustling streets was sparse. Motor buses were few and far between, but peasants working many miles from the capital in the fields of the Marne and Champagne were startled to see whole convoys of Paris buses trundling past with soldiers bound for the Front, and still advertising their Paris destinations, *Mairie d'Ivry*, *Porte de la Villette*, *Concorde*, *Luxembourg*, *Bastille* – with an occasional extra embellishment where some optimistic *poilu* had chalked the word 'BERLIN'.

In the streets of Paris where the buses normally plied, would-be passengers waited for hours at bus stops and usually in vain. But there were not many passengers. Already a marauding German aeroplane had dropped three bombs on the city and although they had caused only a little damage it had been enough to make up the minds of many Parisians who had been hesitating whether to stay and take their chance or to leave while there was still time. At night above the silent, darkened streets, searchlights on the Eiffel Tower circled the Paris sky, machine-gunners perched shivering a thousand feet up on the highest platform kept a look-out for German planes, while below them in the wireless telegraphy station, army engineers, ears clamped to their crackling head-phones, strained to tune in to the distant bleep of signals transmitted by the enemy. One message was of special interest. The German cavalry were pleading for horseshoes and begging that several lorry-loads should be sent to them immediately to shoe their footsore horses. It indicated that despite their strength and their numbers, the Germans too were beginning to feel the strain of the long march south.

The Germans' horses were not alone in feeling the strain and the officers in command of the three battalions of the Brandenburg Grenadier Regiment were so anxious about their men that they joined forces and protested eloquently to their Regimental Commander. The Regiment had marched all the way through Belgium. They had lost most of their junior officers and almost half their men in the fighting at Mons. They had endured a week of punishing marches and now that von Kluck was hurrying east to join up with von Bülow the pace had been stepped up to twenty miles and more a day. The three officers were all of the same mind. The marching was excessive and their men were nearing the end of their tether. They put their case with some force, but their superior officer gave them a dusty answer. 'Sweat saves bloodshed,' he said.

The diary found in the pocket of a German officer, killed during a skirmish on the road, gave the first hint that von Kluck's army was running out of steam.

Our men are done up. For four days they have been marching twenty-four miles a day. The country is difficult, the roads are in bad condition and barred by trees felled across them, the fields are pitted with shell-holes. The men stagger forward, their faces coated with dust, their uniforms in rags, they look like living scarecrows. They march with their eyes closed, singing in chorus so that they shall not fall asleep on the march. The certainty of early victory and of the triumphal entry into Paris keeps them going and acts as a spur to their enthusiasm. Without this certainty of victory they would fall exhausted. They would go to sleep where they fell so as to get to sleep somehow or anyhow. It is the delirium of victory which sustains our men, and in order that their bodies may be as intoxicated as their souls, they drink to excess, but this drunkenness helps to keep them going. Today after an inspection the general was furious. He wanted to stop this general drunkenness. We managed to dissuade him from giving severe orders. If there were too much severity, the army would not march. Abnormal stimulants are necessary to make abnormal fatigue endurable. We will put all that right in Paris. There we will prohibit the sale of alcohol, and as soon as the men are able to rest on their laurels, order will reappear.

In contrast to the gloomy view of their own Commander-in-Chief, the British soldiers were also confident of victory. They were still weary and still dirty, still unshaven and unkempt, and they presented an appearance that was far from prepossessing – but they had got their second wind. Their day of rest, the blessed indulgence of uninterrupted sleep and a couple of square meals had worked wonders and restored them to a degree that some officers thought was little short of miraculous. Their feet had toughened up, their blisters had healed and that was all to the good, for their boots were worn away to shreds reinforced by makeshift cobbling with rough and ready insoles hacked from leather, wood or even layers of cardboard and paper where nothing better had come to hand. Their skins were tanned to bronze, their muscles had hardened, flabby reservists had shed superfluous pounds, the pace had slackened and as they took to the dusty roads again the Tommies were not in low spirits. Peacetime training and foreign service had bred a certain indifference to the whims of the higher command. The men obeyed orders, marched where they were told, fought as required – and usually won. Plans, dispositions and tactics were the officers' affair. Now in these admittedly unexpected circumstances they trudged on philosophically, sweating and sweltering in the relentless heat, but as confident as they had been on peacetime route-marches that someone somewhere knew where they were going and that it was all part of somebody's plan to beat the Germans. It was blisteringly hot, but most of them had endured far hotter marches in the tropics. There were no bands to encourage them over the miles but they were now in a mood to supply this deficiency for themselves.

The Tommies liked singing. Bill Holbrook had caught up at last with his battalion and the Fusiliers had adopted a ditty that rapidly became a favourite.

> *Hold your hand out, naughty boy!*
> *Hold your hand out, naughty boy!*
> *Last night in the pale moonlight*
> *I saw you, I SAW YOU! . . .*

It was a good brisk tune to cheer them over the miles. It was also their private joke. In response to a fervent rendition of the 'Marseillaise' during their wild reception at Le Havre, they had treated the French to a rousing chorus of 'Hold Your Hand Out, Naughty Boy'. This had the satisfactory result of making the crowd stand respectfully to attention apparently under the impression that this was their allies' National Anthem. Even now as the interminable slog went on, it was still good for a laugh and seldom failed to perk them up.

It was part of the mood to laugh at the Germans and in the course of encouraging pep talks by senior officers, the Tommies had not failed to notice that the name of the German general they were even now outwitting rhymed felicitously with their favourite swear-word and that the familiar tune of 'The Girl I Left Behind Me' – so easy to play on Jew's harp and tin whistle on the march – could be parodied with ease.

> *O-o-o-h we don't give a fuck*
> *For old von Kluck*
> *And all his German army . . .*

By a happy coincidence 'army' rhymed with 'barmy', though some preferred to substitute 'German Mausers' in the third line. This rhymed with 'trousers' and therefore gave more scope for describing the kicking they intended to apply to Fritz's posterior when at last the chance came to have a go at the Germans.

The men of the BEF knew that they had given a good account of themselves and they did not feel that they were on the run. In their view they had outwitted the enemy by giving him the slip and now they were leading him on, setting the pace while the Germans blundered on at their backs to a position of the British choosing. In *their* time, so their officers told them, they would turn about and give the Germans a bloody nose. The Tommies did not doubt it for a moment.

They were considerably heartened by an improvement in the rations which at last were catching up with them. In short, as one officer entered laconically in his diary, '*Since the 29th of August the retreat has become normal.*' But it had not been wanting in excitement.

The cavalry were having the best of it. Yesterday in a classic cavalry action at Cerisy, the 12th Lancers had fairly trounced the Germans and Bert Crook, who had had a grandstand view of the battle with the right section of J Battery, was not a little proud of having been one of the volunteers who dragged away the guns under the noses of the astonished enemy. The Germans had been far too wary to follow up.

The cavalry had their work cut out for them, for they were the only troops available to cover the open country that lay between Smith-Dorrien's Second Corps and Sir Douglas Haig's First Corps as they marched south, flirting and skirmishing as they went with General von Marwitz's Cavalry Corps who were doing much the same job in the gap between the German armies commanded by von Kluck and von Bülow. As the last hours of August ebbed away in a warm moonlight night, the 1st Cavalry Brigade of the British Army settled down to bivouac for the night in the village of Néry. If the morning of 1 September had not dawned in a thick fog they might never have met the Germans, for the cavalrymen had been roused early and ordered to be saddled up ready to move off at four in the morning. But it was pointless and dangerous too to set off into unfamiliar countryside while the fog persisted and visibility was reduced to a matter of yards. The order to stand down came as an extra bonus after a night of unusual ease. The officers had found billets in the houses. The troopers of the Queen's Bays and the 5th Dragoon Guards had bivouacked in the open on the outskirts of the village, wrapped in their warm cavalry cloaks, stretched round the dying embers of the bivouac fires, safe in the knowledge that there were no Germans within miles. The gunners of L Battery had also bivouacked in the open, although Major Sclater-Booth's trumpeter, young

Harry Gould, had enjoyed the luxury of a roof over his head for the first
time in the retreat. Harry was a friend of Jimmy Naylor, another of the
young hopefuls who had pleaded to be allowed to go to the war, and so
far the war had come up to all his expectations. He had hardly been able
to believe his luck when he was posted to the cavalry. He had had a fair
share of thrills at Mons. He had been in the fight at Audregnies and in
action at Le Cateau. He had acquitted himself well, and last night, well fed
and well satisfied, he had slumbered peacefully outside the Major's door,
ready for anything in the morning. Despite his youthful enthusiasm, he
was as pleased as the rest when the departure was postponed. There was
nothing much for Harry to do but mooch around within shouting distance
of the Major but the gunners and troopers were glad of the extra time.
There was time to give the horses a leisurely drink, taking them section
by section to the pond at the sugar factory above the valley, there was time
for a bit of extra grooming for the horses which had had short shrift over

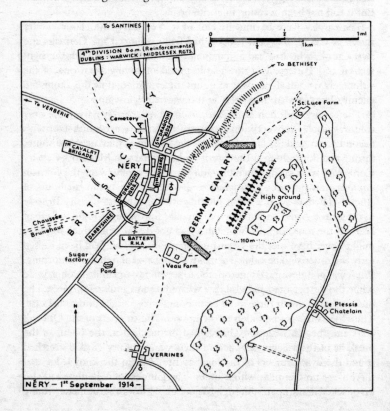

the previous days, and for the others time for a bit of extra breakfast, for a smoke and a chance to relax before the rigours of another long day in the saddle.

The German cavalry had not enjoyed the indulgence of a night of rest. They had been on the move, making their way fast through the forest, cutting across country to catch up with the left flank of the French to give them their first taste of what was in store. Some troops had lost their way and it was not until dawn that General von Garnier had gathered his cavalry division together and cleared the forest. By quarter past four they had made their way through the fog to the high ground east of Néry and settled down to rest. The village itself was just a stone's throw away, separated from the high ground by a stream that ran through a steep little ravine. Hidden from each other by a thick bank of fog neither side had the faintest idea that the other was there.

As a matter of course, Colonel Pitman of the 11th Hussars ordered a patrol to scour the vicinity for signs of the enemy. Pitman thought it exceedingly unlikely that there were any – so unlikely that he put George Tailby in charge of it. It would be useful experience. It was the first time that Tailby had been given command of a patrol but Corporal Parker was an old hand. He detailed two troopers to scout ahead and another man to guard the rear, and after they had scrambled with some difficulty down the steep rough slopes of the ravine, splashed through the stream and picked their way slipping and slithering up the opposite bank, they fanned out on the high ground beyond. The fog lay as thick on the plateau as in the valley below but on this higher ground there was the occasional eddy of breeze that rippled through the fog and trailed it upwards here and there as it rose. Tailby and his men must have passed within a few hundred yards of the Germans as they started their sweep to the north. They had almost finished it when they spotted them – so grey, so ghostly seen through the trails of the thinning mist that they could almost have believed that it was an illusion. But there was no mistaking the sharp-spiked helmets, the long, grey-green cloaks, and even at his first astonished glance Tailby could see that there were hundreds of men dismounted near their horses. At most they were half a mile away and God knows how many more of them were hidden in the fog beyond. Tailby might easily have turned his men discreetly back into the mist and on to Néry to raise the alarm that would give the Brigade time to slip away or time to prepare to meet the enemy. It was one of the scouts who gave the show away. Riding a little ahead of the patrol he had not seen the main body of Germans, but he did see a handful of horsemen not a hundred yards away. And he fired at them.

The crack of the rifle startled Tailby as much as it alarmed the Germans. They were shouting, running, leaping for their horses to give chase. Tailby knew that the game was up and, since there was no need for further discretion, he raised his sword, whirled his horse about and shouting at full pitch, '*Files about. GALLOP!*' he turned tail for Néry with his patrol at his heels. It was a little after five o'clock in the morning as they clattered at full pelt into the village through the lines of the astonished Dragoon Guards who were saddling up their horses on the village green.

At first Colonel Pitman refused to believe it. They must have been mistaken. The Germans were known to be miles away. Any cavalry they had seen could only have been French. But they had not been mistaken and when they had finally convinced him, Colonel Pitman himself rushed across the road to Brigade Headquarters to warn the General that the Germans were nearby and apparently in considerable force. An hour earlier, Major Anderson had waved off Tailby's patrol with 'a curious feeling that something was going to happen'. Now he began to organise defensive positions while Tailby, running to take his place in B Squadron, wondered uneasily why no German horsemen had followed in pursuit.

There was a very good reason why the German horsemen had not followed. They had been only too ready to give chase but they had hardly covered a mile when a bugle called them back. The Germans had also sent out a reconnaissance patrol and they had that moment returned with information that interested their general, von Garnier, a good deal more than the news that a handful of enemy horsemen had been sighted through the mist. The British were bivouacked at Néry all innocent and unprepared, and if, as he suspected, there were no other British troops within miles of them, it was a chance too good to miss. Fate had placed him in a position of natural advantage here on the high ground. His men were tired, they had covered four hundred miles since the start of the war, they had fought two major battles and last night they had had no sleep at all, but there were plenty of them. He had a whole division to pit against what he astutely guessed could be no more than a brigade and even allowing for losses – and his losses in Belgium had been considerable – he had four thousand men within call and, more to the point, he had twelve guns. He ordered the guns up now and began to range them in position along the ridge overlooking Néry in the valley below. He posted machine-guns between them and, just then, as if ringing up the curtain, the fog began to lift.

There was pandemonium in the village where the cavalry had been well and truly caught on the hop. Runners dashed from Brigade Headquarters to summon the senior officers and Harry Gould had gone along with Major Sclater-Booth, in command of L Battery, and waited outside while the CO hurried in to see the General. In less than a minute he was out again running back to the battery and shouting to Harry, 'Trumpeter, sound the Alarm!' Just as they reached the battery, and just as Harry was raising the bugle to his lips, the first shell exploded and it burst within yards of them. The Major was tossed into the air and fell unconscious. Harry was blown to the ground but he scrambled up, then, dazed and winded as he was, he blew the alarm.

Gnr. Darbyshire, I Battery, R.H.A., B.E.F.

Without the slightest warning a ranging shot dropped into the battery and we knew instantly that the German gunners were on to us and almost immediately the whole place was alive with shrapnel and machine-gun bullets. The battery was nearly surrounded by German artillery and infantry. It made havoc amongst the battery and the Bays alongside us and the losses amongst the horses were terrible. Crippling! Of course we were all over the place. The guns were ready for marching, not for fighting. Half the horses were away being watered and a lot of the horses and the men that *were* at the guns were killed or wounded. The gun crews were all anyhow, but Captain Bradbury shouted, 'Who'll volunteer to get the guns into action?' Every man who could still stand shouted 'Me!' and there was a rush for the guns to unhook them from the limbers and manhandle them into position. I was a limber gunner and it was part of my special duty to see to the ammunition in the limbers. But special duties at a time like that don't count for much! The chief thing is to keep the guns going.

Well, the first gun came to grief through the horses being terrified and bolting and overturning it on the steep bank of the road in front of us. The second gun had the spokes of a wheel blown out by one of the very first of the German shells. The third was knocked out by a direct hit from a shell that killed the whole detachment. The fourth was left standing, though the wheels got knocked about and all the horses were shot down. The fifth gun was brought into action but it soon fell silent because the crew were all killed. The sixth gun, which was ours, kept firing the whole time – though the side of the limber was blown away, the wheels were badly damaged, there were holes blown in the shield, and the buffer was simply peppered by shrapnel bullets.

As soon as we got No. 6 gun into action I jumped into the seat and began firing. These thirteen-pounder guns can be fired at the rate of fifteen rounds a minute, and though we were perhaps not doing that (because we were short-handed and the ammunition limbers were about thirty yards away) we were still doing splendid, and it was really telling on the Germans. As the mist melted away we could see them plainly – and they made a target we took care not to miss!

The concussion of our own explosions and the bursting German shells was so awful that I couldn't bear it for long. I kept firing for about twenty minutes, then my nose and ear were bleeding because of the concussion and I couldn't fire any more, so I left the gun-seat to get a change by fetching ammunition. Lieutenant Campbell took over, but he hadn't fired more than a couple of rounds when a shell burst right under the gun-shield. The explosion was awful and the poor young officer was hurled about six yards away from the very seat I'd been sitting in *seconds* earlier. He only lived a few minutes.

I began to help Driver Osborne to fetch ammunition from the wagons and I'd just managed to get back to the gun with an armful of ammunition when a shell exploded behind me, threw me to the ground and stunned me. When I came round I got up and found that I wasn't hurt but looking round I saw that Captain Bradbury had been knocked down by the same shell that floored me. Both his legs were blown off.

By this time our little camp was an utter wreck. There were horses and men lying everywhere, wagons and horses were turned upside down. Nearly all the officers and men were either dead or wounded. Not many minutes after the fight began in the mist only No. 6 gun was left in the battery, and there were only four of us left to serve it. Sergeant-Major Dorrell had taken command, and there was Sergeant Nelson, Driver Osborne and myself. We managed to silence several German guns, but very soon Sergeant Nelson was severely wounded by a bursting shell, and *that* left only three of us.

Lieutenant Arkwright of the 11th Hussars, affectionately known to his brother officers as 'Deafy', had not heard the first alarm. He had not heard the first shells. He had not heard the roar of the motorbikes as despatch riders roared off from Brigade Headquarters to find the 4th Division and beg for reinforcements. He had not heard the screams and clatter of hooves as the panicking horses of the Queen's Bays stampeded through the village. He had almost completed a leisurely toilet and was brushing his teeth when the gunfire intensified and sent him rushing outside to see what was happening. The men were frantically saddling up and getting the horses into shelter, penning them for safety into small yards behind the houses. It was a little while before all the troopers were ready to join the fight.

Lt. F.G.A. Arkwright, A Squadron, 11th (Prince Albert's Own) Hussars, 1st Cavalry Brigade, B.E.F.

I ran outside with my troop behind me and threw myself down in a gap on the bank by the side of the road. Looking about me, I saw the Brigade Major, Cawley, on one side of me with a ghastly wound in his head, obviously done for, poor chap. On the other side was a gunner corporal firing away with a rifle quite regardless of bullets all about, and cursing the Germans all the time, saying they had wiped out his battery and he prayed they might all be killed themselves. Just to my right front in a stubble field was the wreckage of L Battery, and a fearful sight it was too – guns lying all anyhow, a few men crawling about, and bunches of them behind two cornstacks in the fields. Lining the bank were my troop, about six of the Bays and their Maxim gun, which did great work. Opposite we could see five German guns eight hundred yards off, but L Battery had silenced three of them before they themselves were snuffed out, and the last gun plus the Maxim gradually silenced the others.

It was the ravine that saved them – the ravine and the cavalry, charging in the saddle, fighting dismounted, and beating off every attempt the Germans made to cross it. And when they had done that they crossed the ravine themselves and struck the Germans in their flank.

The despatch riders had found the 4th Cavalry Brigade waiting with I Battery for the fog to lift some four kilometres away at St Vaast and they had saddled up and set off at a gallop. At Verberie the Dublins and the Warwicks tumbled on to the road and marched off fast for Néry. The 1st Middlesex, alerted at Saintines, were the last to leave but with only two kilometres to travel they arrived on the cavalry's heels. But it was I Battery who did the trick. It was eight o'clock now. The fight had been on for more than two hours, the fog had long since thinned to a haze and now the sun began to pierce it, shining out of the eastern sky at the Germans' backs. The gunners of I Battery, still more than a mile away, saw it as they galloped over a rise, blazing down on the high ground beyond the misty valley and lighting up the German position like a stage set. They pulled off the road, unlimbered the guns, ranged on the tall chimney of the sugar factory and, as the three men on L Battery's last remaining gun slammed their last remaining shell into its breech, they fired their first shot. They kept on firing until the German guns fell silent, and the Germans began to retire, leaving a dreadful scatter of dead and wounded behind. Eight of their twelve guns were captured and Lieutenant Norrie was at the head of the troops that went for them. It was the thrill of his young life.

*Lt. Willoughby Norrie, C Squadron, 11th (Prince Albert's Own) Hussars,
B.E.F.*

We charged the German guns with a rousing cheer and drawn swords,
and captured eight guns and two machine-guns. This was a comparatively simple task as the machine-gun fire, particularly of the Bays,
and I Battery RHA, had practically silenced the gun battery. For
myself, it was a great thrill to lead a cavalry charge, even if the
enemy surrendered, shouting 'Kamerad, Kamerad!' My troop sergeant,
Sergeant Hailey, stuck one who was too slow in putting up his hands.
We then pushed on to another village, Le Plessis Chatelain, where
we captured another hundred prisoners until we were ordered back.
And what a terrible sight it was to see those gallant men of L Battery,
surrounded by so many dead horses.

Clearing up was a sad task. There were dead men and dead horses
everywhere and the sight was too awful to allow rejoicing. But the survivors
felt a certain grim satisfaction nevertheless. They had done a good job.
They had taken on an enemy force that outnumbered them five to one –
and they had beaten them.

They had won a greater victory than they realised, and the repercussions
of the fight were to stretch far further than the boundaries of one small
village in Valois. There was hardly a man in the Expeditionary Force who
had not learned in his schooldays to chant the moralistic verse intended to
demonstrate the virtues of care and perseverance to young minds.

> *For the want of a nail the shoe was lost.*
> *For the want of a shoe the horse was lost.*
> *For the want of a horse the rider was lost.*
> *For the want of a rider the battle was lost*
> *And all for the want of a horseshoe-nail.*

Néry was destined to be the 'horseshoe-nail' which in the course of a
very few days would puncture the balloon of von Kluck's plans and
aspirations and decide the final outcome of the Battle of the Marne.

Chapter 17

By late afternoon on 1 September, good relations had been restored between the British and the French and all was now sweetness and light. The only person who was not thoroughly satisfied with the results of Lord Kitchener's visit was Field Marshal Sir John French. Although Kitchener had called the Paris meetings in his civilian capacity as Secretary of State for War, he had turned up wearing the uniform of a senior Field Marshal of the British Army. He was perfectly entitled to do so and he had been wearing uniform as a matter of course since the start of the war, but Sir John French had taken deep umbrage. He was tired and he was worried. For the last ten days he had been under constant strain. The responsibility for the safety of the Expeditionary Force weighed heavily on his mind and he did not have Joffre's rare ability to sleep at regular hours, to eat regular meals, and even to make time for relaxation at times of crisis. His nerves were raw, his judgement clouded by misgivings, and with this new development it was hardly amazing that his dignity was offended.

Sir John French was far from pleased that Lord Kitchener had felt it necessary to come to France in person, and angered by the effect that his visit was likely to have on the French by giving them the impression that he himself could be overruled, that his authority was not absolute and that his plans and decisions could be reversed. But Lord Kitchener was all tact and the meetings had gone well. General Joffre had taken pains to explain the situation and he expounded his plans with care. He believed they were on the verge of great things. To the east his armies were doing well, they were holding the Germans to their ground and in places had even pushed them back, so now that von Kluck had clearly changed direction and was marching south-east, it would soon be time to strike him in the back.

Drawing his finger across the map, General Joffre traced the position of General Maunoury's new army massing to the north of Paris. Von Kluck, he stressed, was clearly unaware of its existence. He pointed to the strong defences of Paris and the fighting garrison that waited in the city. Sir John French, in his turn, pointed out the course of the Expeditionary Force marching now not many miles from Paris and conceded that von Kluck had clearly written it off. In his haste to make for General Lanrezac's Fifth

Army further east von Kluck was leaving both forces behind and, all unwittingly, putting himself in a position where they might deal a considerable blow at his exposed right flank as he went. They only had to draw him on. When he reached this point – and here Joffre's finger jabbed the map on the line of the River Marne – von Kluck would be well and truly trapped inside what could be described as an imaginary sack. At the bottom of the sack the British would be waiting, and when the Germans reached it, the French armies watching along both 'sides' could move in for the kill.

It was the chance they had all been waiting for, and although he was too diplomatic to put his thoughts into words, and too dependent on Sir John French's wholehearted co-operation to risk an altercation, Joffre was clearly of the opinion that the British Commander-in-Chief had been taking an unduly pessimistic view. Lord Kitchener was secretly of the same mind. After the departure of the French delegation, Kitchener and French retired to confer in private. No one knew what passed between them but when they emerged all had been decided. The British Expeditionary Force would retire to the Marne and there they would play their part in Joffre's plan. There would be no full-scale retreat. It was tacitly accepted that Sir John had perhaps been kept too much in the dark and, for his own part, Joffre had undertaken to keep the British more fully informed on the whole situation. He was determined at all costs to keep the British commander sweet and part of that cost was the sacrifice of his old friend Lanrezac. After all their misunderstandings, in view of the bitter loathing between them, it was clearly impossible to expect French and Lanrezac to work together.

It was unfortunate for General Lanrezac, who had so skilfully extricated his army from near-catastrophe in Belgium, who had kept it miraculously intact, who was now the direct target of both von Bülow and von Kluck and who was bearing the brunt of the fighting. Nevertheless, Joffre saw no alternative but to sack him. He meant to spare no pains to smooth Sir John French's ruffled feathers and to ensure that no disharmony, no misunderstanding, no grievances, no injured pride, would mar co-operation between his armies and their ally. If his plan were to succeed – and Joffre was determined that it should – they must fight as a united force. To tell the truth, he himself was beginning to find Lanrezac's constant cavilling and argument a little tedious. He would be not entirely sorry to see him go.

As the meetings in Paris broke up and the commanders separated to return to their troops, telegraphists keeping their round-the-clock watch on the airwaves picked up a wireless message which was to gladden all their hearts. From a position some ten kilometres south of Néry, General von Garnier was in contact with German headquarters, and he had bad news to report. *Have been attacked by the English at dawn and am unable to fulfil mission.* His orders had been to push south with his cavalry division towards the Marne and Paris, travelling on the extreme right of von Kluck's force, ranging far and wide, circling, probing, reconnoitring, protecting, and reporting back if danger threatened. But, for the moment, von Garnier's force was finished. His casualties had been enormous. He had lost two-thirds of his guns. In their haste to escape after the defeat at Néry there had been no time to rescue the transport and they had been forced to leave their ammunition wagons behind. The four remaining guns had been painfully manhandled from the battlefield, but with no horses to pull them, with no shells to shoot, they were useless. On the following day, to their great delight, the British Tommies found the guns abandoned in a wood and gleefully took possession. Von Garnier's force was withdrawn into reserve. Its mission unaccomplished, reduced now to a skeleton force, it would do no more scouting for weeks to come and there was no one else to patrol the sector where General Maunoury's Sixth Army was assembling. Unimpeded, undisturbed and unobserved, Maunoury gathered the last of his hundred thousand men around him, moved his army into position and stood ready to strike. Unaware that it was there, von Kluck, wobbling and wavering in his tracks, turned south and started marching into the trap exactly as Joffre had planned.

His motive in marching south was to settle with the British. For a defeated force – and von Kluck still believed that the Expeditionary Force was in disarray – the British were being exceedingly troublesome and were showing an irritating propensity to pop up all over the place instead of showing a clean pair of heels. Their victory at Néry had come as a distinct shock and a disquieting one, for General von Garnier had claimed in his report (understandably in view of the drubbing he had suffered) that he had come up against a force that vastly outnumbered his own. Time and again the Germans had blundered into remnants of its beaten enemy. Time and again the beaten enemy had shown an infuriating tendency to fight – and to fight with a dogged determination that ill became an army on the run. At the German Supreme Headquarters far off in Koblenz, even their supreme warlord, von Moltke, was beginning to feel the slightest bit uneasy as he studied gloating reports of successive German victories. If the French and the British had been as thoroughly thrashed as the communiqués suggested, where, he asked himself, were all the prisoners?

The ghost of Count von Schlieffen seemed to hover across the deliberations of the German High Command. The whole German strategy had been pinned on Schlieffen's grandiose plan. '*Only give me a strong right wing.*' He had been heard to say it a thousand times and this essential was the centrepiece and linch-pin of his strategy. '*A strong right wing.*' It was a well–publicised fact that he had murmured the words even as he lay dying less than a year before. But the 'strong right wing' was not so strong as it should have been. In the euphoria of von Kluck's rapid advance, deluded by the swiftness of success, falling into the trap of believing his own glowing communiqués, Schlieffen's successor had strayed too soon from the central tenet of Schlieffen's theory. He had already removed a considerable force from von Kluck's army and sent it east to deal with the French in Lorraine. By doing so, by going even further and withdrawing more divisions to send to the Russian front, by believing that the battle in the west was won, he had fatally weakened his own right wing. The massive sweep that had started so far to the north would not end now in the great envelopment of Schlieffen's grand design. The chance had been missed and it would not come again.

Returning to his headquarters at Dammartin, some ten miles north of Paris, Sir John French received a mixed bag of reports, several of which gave him some cause for satisfaction. To his great relief his scattered troops had at last linked up and the First and Second Corps were now in touch. The brilliant morning's work at Néry was most gratifying. There had been a sharp skirmish at Crépy with equally satisfactory results, and further east in the forest of Villers-Cotterêts the Guards Division had made a gallant stand against a thrusting spearhead of von Kluck's finest troops.

But another report was the reverse of reassuring. A patrol of Headquarters troops had spotted some Uhlan horsemen not far from Dammartin itself. It was merely a detachment of von Garnier's cavalry moving across country, dazed and unsupported after their hammering at Néry – but Headquarters Staff were not to know that. All they did know was that the enemy had been sighted behind the British front, between their headquarters and the nearest British troops, and that they had better get out fast. The secret maps and papers were packed up, the telegraph wires removed, the Staff cars summoned, and Sir John French and his Headquarters Staff left so hurriedly for the south that some unfortunate officers were left behind and had to cadge a lift.

Villers-Cotterêts was a small market town and, to the north of it, the forest spread thick and deep and dark across the slopes of a long low ridge. North of Villers-Cotterêts a valley of long rolling fields and mellow farmland rose to the horizon, and on the other side of it von Kluck's army was on the march.

A mile from the northern edge of the forest on the further slopes of the valley, young Eddie Slaytor had spent the night with the 3rd Battalion of the Coldstream Guards in the hamlet of Soucy and for once the Battalion had been in luck. After half a dozen nights of bivouacking in the open air they were actually in billets. Admittedly they were squashed up like sardines and more than twenty members of 13 Platoon were squeezed into a tiny cottage parlour, but somehow they had managed to fit in and even to stretch out on such floorspace as there was between the legs of the high-backed chairs, under the heavy oak table and beside the carved dresser whose many shelves were still laden with domestic bric-à-brac and china. Eddie had slept like a log. His feet were sore, his muscles were aching, but for the past week he had been thoroughly enjoying himself. Like the other fourteen boy soldiers in the 3rd Coldstream Guards he had been thrilled to go to France with the Battalion and the last month had seemed like one long glorious picnic with a spice of danger and excitement to add to its attractions.

Eddie was the pet of 13 Platoon. He was also the butt of their raillery and since coming to France he had acquired a new nickname. 'Poor Boy', they called him, and he didn't like it a bit. It had all been the fault of the old woman at Le Havre who had had the cheek to fling her arms round Eddie as he sat with his platoon on the cobbles waiting for orders, planted a kiss on his smooth and youthful cheek and in accents of maternal solicitude addressed him as '*mon pauvre garçon*'. Lieutenant Horlick grinned and kindly translated for the benefit of the platoon. They roared with laughter and

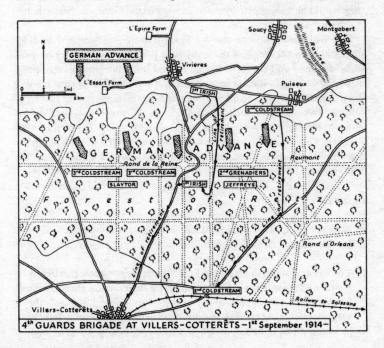

4th GUARDS BRIGADE AT VILLERS-COTTERÊTS — 1st September 1914

Eddie had been their 'Poor Boy' ever since. It still made him blush as furiously as two weeks earlier he had blushed with embarrassment. It was particularly galling for one who was six foot tall and considered himself to be a proper guardsman to be given away by his sixteen-year-old baby face. He longed for the day when the silky fluff which, with the aid of a magnifying glass, could just be detected on his upper lip would bristle into a respectable moustache and put an end to such insults. Although he was the youngest of the fourteen boy soldiers in the Battalion, Eddie was convinced, like all the rest of them, that without their services during the last fortnight the Battalion would have gone to pieces.

These services had, unfortunately, not included firing a rifle. Eddie did not even possess one, far less know how to fire it, although he had somehow or other contrived to get hold of a bayonet before embarking for France. He was forced to admit that, lacking a rifle to fix it to, the bayonet was useless, but it had made him feel good. Now, like his heavy pack and greatcoat, the bayonet had been abandoned during the long trek south and apart from haversack, water bottle and entrenching tool, the only weapons left in his possession were his bugle and his B-flat flute. He was the first to admit that, essential though such items were to his function as a drummer, they would be unlikely to do much damage to the Germans. Nevertheless his chance was about to come.

Day had hardly broken and 13 Platoon were still wrapped in deep slumber when the door of the congested parlour was thrust open with some difficulty and Sergeant Boden inched his way round it, trampling across the sleeping bodies wedged against the threshold. The platoon roused, disentangled itself with assorted groans and curses, struggled up and went outside. Lieutenant Horlick was waiting in the street. He sized up his platoon, frowzy, heavy-eyed, still stiff and still limping. It was plain that they were unrefreshed by their short night's rest and far from delighted at the prospect of another long day's march. He knew exactly how they felt. But Horlick also knew his men.

'Right,' he said, 'I'll give it to you straight. Would you rather march – or fight?'

Drummer E. L. Slaytor, 3rd Battalion, The Coldstream Guards,
4th Brigade, 2nd Division, B.E.F.

The whole platoon shouted out 'Fight!' Little did we know that before the day was out we would have fought a sharp action through the forest of Villers-Cotterêts and covered twenty-four miles into the bargain. Lieutenant Horlick also informed us that anyone who thought he was unfit to fight and march was to report sick. A lot of us were suffering from sore feet, but not a single man took advantage of his offer. He went on to give us instructions. I remember him telling us that if we were hit we were to take the ammunition out of our pouches and place it by our side for the others to pick up. Later I actually saw somebody do this.

We paraded with the Battalion and went off to dig some head-trenches in a stubble field and later we were ordered to retire on the forest. We did it under shellfire and my company – No. 4 Company – did it best of all. Later on, after the fight, we were complimented by our commanding officer, Colonel Feilding, on our orderly withdrawal. We were very proud of ourselves.

The Guards Brigade was standing as rearguard to the 2nd Division. No one had really expected that they would come up against the enemy in such force. No one had yet realised that von Kluck had yet again changed direction and was swinging south to 'settle with the debris of the Franco-British army'. They did not feel like 'debris' – and they were not. The 5th and 6th Brigades had passed through the Guards in the early hours of the morning and all the Guards were expected to do was to wait until both brigades had reached a safe distance and then retire in their own turn.

It was the morning of 1 September and, as usual, there was a thick mist. It began to lift shortly after six o'clock and just before half past six, to their surprise and consternation, the men manning the trenches across the stubble fields spotted German cavalry patrols in front. They saw them off with rifle fire at a thousand yards' range. Silence fell, and they waited on the *qui vive* but for a long time nothing happened. The Germans had galloped away, the sun began to rise and, just when it seemed that the Germans had been no more than an isolated patrol scouting on their own, just as the Guardsmen had received the order to withdraw into the forest, just as they began to leave their makeshift trenches to move back, the German guns had opened fire. It had not been easy to carry out the 'orderly withdrawal' which Colonel Feilding had been so quick to praise. Looking back as they went, the Guardsmen could see quite plainly that a mass of German infantry was crossing the ridge behind them and moving into position for action.

It was dark in the forest. The trees were tall and thick and the weak early-morning sun hardly penetrated through the leaves on the high branches above. The Guardsmen took up position along a wide dappled ride running across the top of the ridge and waited to confront the enemy. In front of them, spread in a thin line along the edge of the forest beyond, the Irish Guards and the 2nd Coldstreams would take the first brunt of the fighting and, if all went well, retire into the forest and through their ranks.

But it was a moot point if all would go well. Few military textbooks and still fewer planners of peacetime manoeuvres had dwelt on the difficulty of deploying a battalion for action in the middle of a wood, intersected in every direction by wide rides, where the field of fire ranged from a hundred yards where the trees were wide apart to nothing at all in places where they grew close together. The Coldstreams and the Grenadiers along the crest of the wooded ridge did the best they could, but it was little enough they could do. All that was possible was to post detachments to watch down the rides for the enemy to appear, to place men in force around the clearings and to spread the rest in a long thin line along the path that faced the trees on the downward slope. They stood with rifles at the ready, peering and squinting through the tree-trunks for the first sign of the enemy, listening to the rattle of rifle fire in front where the Irish Guards and the 2nd Coldstreams were having a hot time. By and by the fire diminished to a few scattered bursts and the Irish Guards fell back through the wood and passed through them. The tension heightened. Now they were facing the enemy alone.

There was a long silence. As they waited for the enemy to come on, the Grenadier Guards marvelled to see a herd of deer picking their way across their front, browsing beneath the trees, svelte and beautiful in the dappled sunlight and as unconcerned as if there were no war within a thousand miles of them. A sudden rifle shot sent them leaping off into the forest. Before the Guardsmen knew it, the Germans were upon them.

The enemy had crept up under cover of the trees and the first onslaught fell on the Coldstream Guards. They were just yards away when they opened fire and it was pandemonium.

Drummer E. L. Slaytor, 3rd Battalion, The Coldstream Guards, 4th Brigade, 2nd Division, B.E.F.

All you could hear was this heavy rifle fire, the blowing of bugles, beating of drums and the Germans shouting 'Hoch der Kaiser'. Of course we couldn't see them, we couldn't get at them, so our own fellows were calling out to them, 'Come out in the open and fight clean.' Captain Tritton was wounded, badly wounded in the hand and probably in the leg as well, because I remember seeing him on his horse, deathly pale, and the whole of his trouser leg saturated in blood. The Germans were treading on our heels! And they must have got round us because we could see them running across the ride on either side of us not many yards away, and there were bullets flying about in all directions, ricocheting off the trees – smack, smack, smack, smack – and flying about in all directions. It was terrible confusion.

On the right of the Coldstreams where the wood was less thick and the situation was clearer, the Grenadiers could see the Germans advancing in some kind of order, they could see them rushing up the long ride that led to the clearing they called Rond de la Reine, and they could hear the desperate confusion of the fight on their left where the Coldstreams were battling against the Germans among the trees. There were bullets flying everywhere. The enemy had dragged a machine-gun up the ride and bullets streamed into the clearing from straight ahead. Worse, they were streaming in from the Grenadiers' left and they knew without a doubt that the Germans had crept up under the cover of the wood, that they were now on a level with the Coldstreams and that they were in a fair way to surrounding them.

It was no place for a counter-attack, but only a counter-attack would save the situation. It was No. 4 Company of the Grenadier Guards who made it and, since rifles were useless in such surroundings, they attacked with the bayonet. George Cecil took them in, running with sword in hand in front of his company, slashing and slicing, shouting at the top of his voice as they plunged into the Germans. The enemy's machine-gun did desperate damage and Cecil fell almost at once. He was not the only casualty. When the remnants of the Company struggled back up the slope through the trees they left some scores of Guardsmen behind, wounded, bleeding, dying on the forest floor. George Cecil was among them. But they had thrown the enemy back.

Eddie Slaytor was fighting for the first time in his life. In normal circumstances he would not even have begun to learn to handle a rifle until he reached the age of eighteen and would not have expected to fire his initial musketry course until months had passed. But he fired it now in the forest at Villers-Cotterêts, snatching up a rifle lying beside the sprawled-out body of a dead Coldstream. He aimed it in the general direction of the Germans and, wincing from the recoil each time it kicked back into his skinny shoulder, he fervently hoped that some of his shots were hitting somebody who mattered.

Major G. D. Jeffreys, 1st Bttn., The Grenadier Guards, 4th Brigade, 2nd Division, B.E.F.

The first I heard of what was happening on my left was when Gerry Ruthven appeared leading a horse on which was the Brigadier badly wounded and obviously in great pain. He shouted to me that the enemy was held but that we should shortly have to withdraw, and disappeared to the rear in the forest. Then I saw Stephen Burton (3rd Coldstream) also badly wounded and staggering back. He said, 'For

God's sake help me get out of this or I shall be captured. I can't get much further.' By some lucky chance one of our ammunition pack-horses was coming along and I and the transport man hoisted Stephen on to him with some difficulty and he was got away. Shortly after this an orderly from Battalion Headquarters came to me with a verbal message that we were going to withdraw and as I knew from seeing the Brigadier taken away wounded that Noel Corry must be taking command of the Brigade, I concluded that I must be in command of the Battalion.

The Germans did not press us at all. They had evidently not only lost heavily but got very mixed up in the thick forest, and we could hear them shouting orders and blowing little horns apparently to rally their men.*

As we got back towards the railway bridge (I had some qualms as to whether I had read the map right with its maze of rides, but luckily I was all right), we began to meet parties of the 3rd Coldstream also making for it, and we let them cross first, as most of their battalion was already on ahead. I saw 'Cakes' Banbury on a horse, and rather rattled. He said, 'For God's sake get on out of this, or you'll be cut off!' I assured him we were not delaying and we rode on. Once over the bridge I assembled the Battalion and we then marched off down the road and through Villers-Cotterêts. We had no orders. The Brigade organisation had, I suppose, been upset by the Brigade Major escorting the wounded Brigadier out of action. Our CO had gone off with what remained of Brigade Headquarters, and so we just followed the rest of the Brigade. We passed through the town (the streets were quite empty) and emerged on to open ground south-west of the town. We could see what appeared to be enemy on the edge of some woods to the northward and I extended the Battalion, but we were not fired on, and passed through the 6th Brigade, who were lining the edge of the forest, and two batteries of artillery who were in action in the open just outside the edge of the forest. When we were clear of the 6th Brigade, I halted the Battalion and formed it up.

About half a mile further on General Monro himself rode up to me and ordered me to go back to Boursonne and take up a position there to cover the withdrawal of the troops in front. Accordingly, back we went to Boursonne, which is a straggling village with a number of gardens and enclosures surrounded by walls. We loopholed these and made such trenches as we could with our light entrenching

* The Germans had lost direction so badly that they were firing on each other and were forced to break off the action in order to reorganise.

tools and after two hours' work we had a reasonably strong position. At about 6 p.m. General Monro came back to us and told us that the guns had been in a tight place and that there had been difficulty in getting them back, but that the Germans were definitely held up. He stood (or rather sat on his horse) with us just on the northern outskirts of Boursonne where No. 3 Company was astride the road, when out of the forest about five or six hundred yards away to our left front some cavalry appeared riding quickly along and apparently going to pass our left flank. General Monro said, 'They've got their cavalry round! Quick! Get these men to change front and open fire!' I was almost certain they were British but I ordered the platoon to change front, but not to open fire, and got my glasses on to them and at once I saw the grey horses of the Scots Greys. I said, 'But it's the Scots Greys, Sir.' To which the General said, 'Thank God! Thank God!' I think he was tired and overwrought.

The time dragged on and gradually the 6th Brigade dribbled back through us, and last of all the 2nd Coldstream. I then collected the Battalion and followed the Coldstream. We had no orders and appeared to have been forgotten by our own Brigade Headquarters.

It was hardly surprising that General Monro was 'tired and overwrought'. Every man on the road was exhausted but there was nothing for it but to march on. By late afternoon Eddie Slaytor was faint with hunger. The 3rd Coldstreams had gone breakfastless into action and after the battle was broken off there were twelve miles to march before they reached their rendezvous. In 13 Platoon some pointed comments were aimed at Lieutenant Horlick who had given them the choice of fighting or marching. He had omitted to add that before the day ended they would be obliged to do both. It seemed a long, long way and with every step Eddie's empty stomach rumbled and protested. Marching beside him, Guardsman Mick Oban took pity on him and gave him his last remaining biscuit. It was better than nothing. Slaytor was suitably grateful and went so far as to assure Guardsman Oban, and with complete sincerity, that he had literally saved his life.

The lack of food presented Major Jeffreys with a dilemma. It was half-past ten in the evening before the Grenadier Guards reached Divisional Headquarters at Thury. The men had been on the go since three in the morning, digging trenches, fighting a battle and finally marching fourteen miles. They were drained, they were exhausted, they were famished, and Jeffreys, who was in precisely the same state himself, shrewdly suspected that they were near the end of their tether. They had done well and their major had every reason to be satisfied with their day's work. Now his first priority was to see that they got food and rest. He ordered the men to fall out by the roadside while he went to report at Divisional Headquarters. But he was in for a nasty jolt. The Brigade was at Betz four miles further along the road, and Jeffreys' orders were to join them there, ready to resume the march at three o'clock next morning. There were no supplies at Thury, no food and no accommodation either, since all the billets had long ago been occupied by the 6th Brigade and by Divisional Headquarters itself. A tired sergeant of the Army Service Corps informed the Major respectfully, but adamantly, that there was not the faintest hope of producing rations for a battalion – even one whose ranks were so diminished as those of the 2nd Grenadier Guards after their losses during the day.

Jeffreys was having none of that. He demanded to see the Assistant Quartermaster General and he refused to take no for an answer. This officer who had just settled down for the night was far from pleased at being roused. He was in no humour to co-operate and went so far as to give Jeffreys a piece of his mind. What did he mean by bothering him at this time of night? His battalion ought to be at Betz, and there was nothing he could do for them here. Holding his temper in check with some difficulty, Jeffreys squared up to this truculent colleague. His men could go no further, he declared, nor would he ask them to. He demanded to see the General himself. The Quartermaster grumbled and demurred. The General was tired, it was no good Jeffreys bothering him and he would do nothing for him anyway. But Jeffreys insisted and the Quartermaster, tired of argument, capitulated with ill grace.

The General, who had just sat down to dinner, was kindness itself. He perfectly understood the situation, poured Jeffreys a stiff whisky, pressed him to help himself to some cold chicken, and turned to the Quartermaster officer. 'Haven't you got a ration dump?' he demanded.

The Quartermaster replied that he had one a mile away.

'Well, Jeffreys,' said the General, 'will you wait while we send wagons for rations, or will you walk there?'

Jeffreys considered. It would take time to get the wagons out and send them down the road, leaving aside the matter of loading them up and fetching them back. As it was there was precious little left of the night, and if his weary men were to get any rest it would be better to take them to the rations than to wait for the rations to come to them. 'I think we can walk another mile, Sir,' he said.

'Very well,' said the General. General Monro was no fool and he had fairly sized up the situation. He nodded now to the Quartermaster and said, 'You go with them, Conway-Gordon, and see they get their rations.'

The look of disgust on Conway-Gordon's face gave Jeffreys considerable satisfaction.

Plodding through pitch darkness along the country road with his weary

THE LONG SLOG 267

men trudging stolidly behind him, Jeffreys walked in silence beside his brother officer, whose feelings towards him were all too clearly anything but fraternal. He did not speak until they reached the ration dump in a field by the side of the road.

'Here we are,' he said coldly. 'Take what you like.' And without another word he turned and strode off, breathing truculence, into the dark.

But discipline, even in such a situation, was better than a time-consuming scramble and Jeffreys had no intention of allowing a free-for-all. Calling up his platoon officers and NCOs, working by the inadequate beams of flashlights, he supervised the issue of a double ration of bully beef, biscuits and jam and, when they had eaten their fill, the Battalion lay down by the roadside to snatch what sleep they could. It was already well past midnight and they would have to be on their way at two o'clock in order to catch up with the Brigade before they took to the road at crack of dawn, but at least their stomachs were full.

A little later, stretching, grumbling, stiff, still weary and still bemused with sleep, the Grenadiers formed up and marched off down the road. As they left a party of the 12th Lancers began emptying cans of petrol over the piled-up ration boxes in the field and before the Battalion passed out of sight the dump was already blazing fiercely. Looking back over their shoulders the men watched with mixed feelings as the food went up in smoke. It was better that it should be destroyed than left to fill the bellies of the Germans. On the other hand, God knew when their own next meal was coming from.

But the rations they had consumed worked wonders and they had cheered up by the time they met up with the Brigade at Betz. The sun came up not long after they set off again and they marched on with a good heart. There were twenty-two miles to go and it was to be the hottest day of the retreat.

All along the roads that led to the pleasant country the French knew as the Ile de France, long lines of British soldiers threw up clouds of stifling dust as battalion on battalion dragged along them under the merciless blazing sun. Many fainted, many fell out, and there were few commanding officers so lacking in human feeling that they could bring themselves to blame them. They were a good deal more inclined to blame whoever had issued the orders that demanded the impossible.

Lt.-Col. Davies, 1st Bttn., The Oxfordshire and Buckinghamshire Light Infantry, B.E.F.

This was one of the worst marches we had. The Transport had to be sent off the night before, and as we were standing to arms in the trenches in the early morning, it was not possible to get any tea, so our breakfast was biscuits and water. The sun was very hot indeed, and after a few miles it began to tell on the men. Several fell down unconscious from heat-stroke, and others were quite unable to keep up. We had no ambulances and no transport, but some of the worst cases were taken up by the artillery who were with us.

Our orders were to hurry on as quickly as possible so as not to keep back the cavalry, as they seemed to expect that the Germans would press in on our rear. I went to the Brigadier and told him that too much hurrying would result in our leaving a number of men on the road. I pointed out that it was not a question of unwillingness on the men's part, but simply their inability to march fast with empty stomachs under a hot sun after all the previous hard marching – *and* on top of a night in the trenches with little if any sleep! The Brigadier quite agreed with me, but said that the orders were to push on as quickly as possible. However, he gave us one or two halts, which saved us a good deal and, fortunately, between Etrepilly and Chambry, we came up with our First Line Transport and found that Brett, the Transport Officer, had with great foresight made tea for the whole Regiment. This really saved us! We were allowed half an hour (which was extended to three quarters) and after some tea and something to eat the Regiment marched excellently for another three hours – well closed up in fours, and in good spirits. At the end of the march we bivouacked in a pleasant field.

Marching in the ranks of the 2nd Coldstream Guards, Eddie Slaytor had also found the going hard. The Quartermaster in charge of the ration dump at Betz had passed out as much food as possible to the troops before setting fire to what was left, and the bully beef, unfortunately, came in seven-pound tins. It was an unwieldy load to carry in the heat of the scorching sun and it seemed to grow heavier with every mile. The section took it in turns to carry their share and Eddie's turn came the last of all that morning. When they stopped for the midday break he dropped his burden with a howl of delight. But pleasure swiftly changed to consternation when the Corporal hacked open the tin. They had no need of jack-knives to divide the contents, for the bully beef had melted in the heat and turned into a pinkish, greasy porridge. They literally poured it into their mess tins and supped it up with spoons – a ghastly tepid mess, salted by a liberal hand. An hour later they marched on again under the relentless sun, tormented by raging thirst.

At nightfall they bivouacked close to a stream. When the order was given to fall out, men tore off their filthy, dust-encrusted clothing and leapt into it to swim and soak in the blessedly cool water. The thirstiest ran to the edge, knelt down and, scooping it up in cupped hands, lapped the water like dogs.

But they were in sight of the River Marne.

Chapter 18

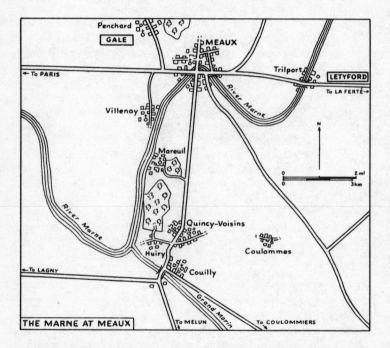

A third of the course of the long River Marne that rises near Langres, three hundred kilometres east of Paris, flows through a scant sixty kilometres of the countryside that lies between the capital and Le Ferté-sous-Jouarre, carving a long lazy course of loops and swirls, changing direction, circling back on itself to enclose hills and towns and villages, thrusting out canals and waterways to link up with the River Ourcq and with its own tributaries, the Grand Morin to the south, the Petit Morin to the north. The bridges were too numerous to count. A dozen alone crossed the waters that almost encircled the town of Meaux. There were not enough engineers, there was not enough explosive and, above all, not nearly enough time to spare to blow them all up as the Army went across.

Looking north across the valley from her garden on the crest of a hill above the sleepy villages of Quincy and Voisins, Mildred Aldrich could see the town of Meaux, just four miles away, and could count no fewer than five of the villages that clung to the slopes beyond it on the far side of the valley. It was a superb view and when she had been house-hunting that spring it was this prospect from the garden of the house on the hill that had finally clinched the sale. Mildred Aldrich was American. She was a newcomer to the hamlet of Huiry but she was no newcomer to France. For the past sixteen years Miss Aldrich had lived in Paris, augmenting her comfortable private income by writing and journalism. Now that she was approaching what the French gallantly called 'a certain age' and planned to take life more easily, although she wanted to leave the hurly-burly of Paris, she had felt no desire to return to the USA.

The last few months had passed pleasantly, settling into the house, planning her garden, arranging her books, admiring her view. Despite the urgings of friends at home and the persuasive arguments of American acquaintances in Paris who were on the point of leaving for home, Miss Aldrich was not inclined to uproot herself again, and had decided to take her chance. Even now, seated on a bench in her orchard, watching the tide of the war as it rolled across the valley, she did not regret her decision.

She had taken reasonable precautions. She had laid in a store of provisions, she had made a difficult trip to Paris on a local train packed with wounded soldiers, she had put her financial affairs in order and drawn a substantial sum of ready cash from the bank and hidden it safely against emergencies. She had packed a hatbox, the lightest piece of luggage she owned, with a change of shoes, stockings and underwear, and placed it at the foot of the stairs, ready to pick up at a moment's warning. She also shortened the skirt of her travelling suit and laid it over a chair in the salon downstairs with her hat and gloves on top and her strongest walking shoes on the floor beside them. Now, if Miss Aldrich were to be forced to leave, she could leave without loss of time. Meanwhile, she adorned her gateposts with a tricolour to demonstrate her patriotic feeling to the French and the Stars and Stripes to advertise her neutrality, if need be, to the Germans. After that she had nothing to do but wait for developments.

Far across the valley, where the church tower of the village of Penchard rose above the trees on its hill, puffs of smoke were erupting against the blue of the sky and, listening closely, she could hear the distant crack of rifle fire. They were fighting in the churchyard. The soldiers had known all day that the German cavalry were at their heels and there had just been time, before they caught up, to scrape the shallowest of trenches beyond the tombstones, along the verge of the road. Ted Gale was in the thick of it.

Rfn. E. Gale, No. 3774, 1st Bttn., The Rifle Brigade, 11th Brigade, 4th Division, B.E.F.

It was a beautiful summer's afternoon, really hot. The village was deserted – all the people had gone and the only civilian we saw was the old village priest. As we started to dig in, *he* was digging too. He was digging a hole where there was a patch of grass just outside the wall of the churchyard and he had the church silver piled around it. There was a big cross that must have stood on the altar, and goblets and plates, and he was obviously going to bury this stuff. He was still digging away when the Germans opened up, and he kept on digging and then wrapping all the stuff up in sacks and putting it down into the hole and covering it up. He was doing that all the time the fight was going on, as if there was nothing happening at all! All that time *we* were firing back. We were sheltered a bit by the tombstones and you could hear the bullets slapping into them, cracking bits off. We were only firing in the general direction of where we thought the enemy was. There were a few shells coming over and we could see the Germans – just a flash of them now and again, in among the trees. We went on firing for maybe half an hour, just to let the people behind us get further on. Then we gradually moved back to get away ourselves. But there couldn't have been many Germans, because they didn't follow us.

I've often wondered what happened to the priest, if he got his stuff back again. I couldn't get over the way he went on with the job, ignoring us, ignoring the firing and the shooting, just as if nothing was happening at all. We were taking cover, or as much cover as we could, but *he* wasn't! He was a brave man!

A mile or so to the right of them as they broke off the fight and retreated section by section down the road that would take them across the River Marne, they could hear a dull boom in the distance. The engineers had begun to blow up the bridges and the 5th Field Company of the Royal Engineers were given the task of blowing up the bridge at Le Trilport.

Cpl. A. Letyford, 5th Field Company, Royal Engineers, Extract from his diary.

3.9.14. We set off again before daylight and reached Meaux about 5 a.m. – a fine large town with a most beautiful cathedral. We thought until now we were on the road to Paris, but now we are on the main road to Metz. We reached the town of Trilport and prepared two of the Marne bridges for demolition. My section did the magnificent railway bridge. After about four hours hard work digging down round the arch, we found that the bridge had been built prepared for demolition, with a chamber in one of the piers below the water line. Apparently these two bridges were destroyed in 1870, and afterwards they were rebuilt. We blew the bridges up at 2 p.m. and it was very successful. We also sunk about fifty rowing boats here, some barges and houseboats. The towns we had been passing through are properly deserted and there is a lot of looting going on – especially in the poultry line! We march on to the village of Neufmontiers and have a good night's rest.

4.9.14. We move out of camp at 11 a.m. and do a hurried march, for we are surprised by the enemy. The whole Division entrenches and the Company dig trenches for the Coldstream Guards. We leave eventually about 4 p.m. and the Guards and Artillery get into action soon after. We march about nine miles and then bivouac. We have scarcely any food. For three days no rations have been drawn and the supply column is missing!

The first British soldiers to reach Miss Aldrich on her hilltop belonged to the 2nd Battalion of the King's Own Yorkshire Light Infantry. It was the best vantage point for miles around and it was not surprising that they chose to stop there, and that they posted a picquet on the road outside her gate. The Battalion marched on to bivouac on the other side of the hill and shortly afterwards Captain John Simpson joined Miss Aldrich in the garden. He was not the first of her visitors to admire the view.

Miss Mildred Aldrich

'Beautiful,' he said, as he took out his field-glasses. 'What town is that?' he asked, pointing to the foreground. I told him that it was Mareuil-on-the-Marne.

'How far off is it?' I told him that it was about two miles, and Meaux was about the same distance beyond it.

'What town is that?' he asked, pointing to the hill. I explained that the town on the horizon was Penchard – not really a town, only a village and that lower down, between Penchard and Meaux, were Neufmontier and Chauconin. All this time he was studying his map. 'Thank you. I have it,' he said. 'It is a lovely country, and this is a wonderful view of it, the best I have had.'

Miss Aldrich walked with him to the gate. She was anxious to know what was happening but she was too diffident to ask and merely enquired, as the Captain mounted his horse, if there was anything else she could do for him. There was nothing, unless – he looked down and gave her a winning smile – unless she could give the picquet a cup of tea. It would just about save their lives, he said, and Miss Aldrich was only too happy to oblige.

Miss Mildred Aldrich

I ran into the house, put on the kettle, ran up the road to call Amélie, and back to the arbour to set the table well as I could. The whole atmosphere was changed. I was going to be useful!

I had no idea how many men I was going to feed. I had only seen three. To this day I don't know how many I *did* feed. They came and came and came. It reminded me of hens running toward a place when another hen has found something good. It did not take me many minutes to discover that these men needed something more substantial than tea. Luckily I had brought back from Paris an emergency stock of things like biscuits, dry cakes, jam, etc., for even before our shops were closed there was mighty little in them. For an hour and a half I brewed pot after pot of tea, opened jar after jar of jam and jelly, and tin after tin of biscuits, and cakes, and although it was hardly hearty fodder for men, they put it down with a relish. I have seen hungry men, but never anything as hungry as these boys.

I knew little about military discipline – less about the rules of active service – so I had no idea that I was letting these hungry men break all the regulations of the Army. Their guns were lying about in any old place – their kits were on the ground – their belts were unbuckled. Suddenly the Captain rode up the road and looked over the hedge at the scene. The men were sitting on the benches, on the ground, anywhere, and were all smoking my best Egyptian cigarettes, and I was running round as happy as a queen, seeing them so contented and comfortable.

It was a rude awakening when the Captain rode up the street.

There was a sudden jumping up, a hurried buckling-up of belts, a grab for kits and guns, and an unceremonious dash for the gate. I heard a volley from the officer! I marked a serious effort on the part of the men to keep the smiles off their faces as they hurriedly got their kits on their backs and their guns on their shoulders and, rigidly saluting, dispersed up the hill, leaving two very straight men marching before the gate as if they never in their lives had thought of anything but picquet duty.

The Captain never glanced in her direction. He rode off behind his men, so stern and so forbidding that Miss Aldrich felt as guilty as if she herself were likely to be court-martialled. But when Captain Simpson returned a few minutes later, he was once again all smiles. 'Dear little lady,' he said, 'I wonder if there is any tea left for me?'

A small table was freshly set up in the arbour, and a fresh pot of tea brewed. As Miss Aldrich poured it out Captain Simpson gave her a gentle lecture on the requirements of military discipline and the exigencies of active service. He was unwilling to alarm her, but he felt obliged to point out the consequences if a detachment of Uhlans had rushed up the hill while the men were picnicking in her garden and holding teacups instead of rifles. He also informed her that a detachment of Uhlans were known to have crossed the Marne in front of them. As if to underline his point, there was a sudden loud explosion. Miss Aldrich leapt to her feet, but Simpson scarcely looked up. 'Another bridge gone,' he said quietly. 'Another division across the Marne.'

The three men guarding the road in the gritty heat of the afternoon were as anxious for a wash as they had been anxious to slake their thirst and refresh their dust-parched throats with Miss Aldrich's good strong tea. This time she knew better than to invite them in. Her handyman drew buckets of water from the pump in the yard, carried them to the gate and dragged out an old trestle table from the garden. The men took turns to strip off their shirts, to wash and shave, whistling and joking and splashing as happily as children in a paddling-pool, but all the time keeping a wary eye on the road below. They had barely finished when the order came to move on.

The Bedfords arrived in their place. Miss Aldrich found their presence distinctly comforting. As she shuttered her bedroom windows before going to bed, she could see the gleam of moonlight on the barrels of their rifles, and when she roused in the night heard the reassuring crunch of gravel beneath their feet as they paced the road and kept watch.

The pace of the retreat had slackened. There were soldiers bivouacking in every farm, in every village and in the grounds of all the country houses that lay across the lush and prosperous countryside of the Ile de France. Most of the villages had been evacuated and were deserted and the great houses were shut up with only an ancient retainer or two to keep guard. Now there was a little time to relax. The marches were shorter. Supplies had caught up. There was time to eat and there was time to wash. At Baron de Rothschild's estate a whole battalion plunged in relays into the swimming-pool and when the last man clambered out the water was completely black.

Men and officers alike took the opportunity to replace their lost possessions. There were cooking pots in abandoned kitchens, there were blankets on beds, there was clothing in cupboards, horses in stables and poultry in farmyards. They had no compunction about helping themselves but in order to preserve the good name of the British Army in the country of their ally the officers made a point of leaving requisition forms behind. It was stretching a point to call them requisition forms. In most cases they amounted to little more than scribbled sheets of paper torn from a field service notebook, but they were duly signed, the Army would eventually pay up and meanwhile honour was more or less satisfied. So the Army punctiliously salved its conscience and signed for everything from a half-used cake of soap found on a washstand to the string of bloodstock hunters they found in the Rothschild stable.

The horses, like the men, were almost on their last legs and badly needed reinforcements.

The fact that supplies had not kept up with the troops on the retreat had not been the fault of the Quartermaster-General. It was rather to Sir William Robertson's credit that any had reached them at all. Robertson was a soldier to the backbone. Although he was now a general he had risen to this dizzy eminence from the humble rank of private. He was held in much affection in the Army and known throughout its ranks as 'Wullie'. No one understood the mind of an ordinary soldier better than Wullie, no one cared more about his needs and his difficulties and no one had worked harder during the long days of the retreat to supply them. It had been a monumental headache.

The lines of retreat had been clearly laid down and after the first hectic days when the best he could do was to dump food haphazardly along the roads, Sir William had known in theory where the troops were supposed to be at a given date or time. Getting supplies through, even to the nearest railhead, was another matter. It was a long way from the coast to the forward area and the shifting of the supply bases from Le Havre and Boulogne to St-Nazaire far south of them had made his task no easier. Neither had the French. The railway system was dislocated by the weight of troop trains as soldiers were mobilised, as the troops were shunted from west to east, and back again according to the situation on the battlefronts. The supply trains from the British base were despatched by long and tortuous routes via Paris and when they failed to arrive at all it was because some frantic French official, whose priorities were not those of Sir William Robertson, had cleared the line by shunting the trains into yards and sidings. And there, all too often, they had stayed, overlooked in the general bustle. Wullie had sweated and worried, raged and fumed, and eventually sent his second-in-command, Colonel Percival, to board each train at a stop somewhere along the way and force the authorities to let it through by whatever means he chose. Sir William Robertson made it clear that, short of actual murder, he was not particular about the methods Percival adopted so long as the trains got through.

Now that most of the troops had reached the Paris region itself, things were easier. The ration trains had been brought up. There were fresh supplies of badly needed ammunition. Above all, there were men to replace at least some of the casualties and if they were not quite enough to bring the ragged ranks of the battalions up to strength, there were at least enough to stiffen and encourage them.

On 4 September, Lieutenant Turbutt of the Ox and Bucks Light Infantry arrived to join the 2nd Battalion at Champlet with a detachment of ninety-one men. Ninety belonged to the draft he had brought from Britain; he had picked up the extra man at Boulogne. It was Allan, the soldier who had been so overcome by the crossing nineteen days earlier that he had been left behind in the care of the nuns. Now he was back looking fitter than anyone else. In his absence the Battalion had been up to Mons. A dozen times or more they had grappled with the enemy, and in just ten days they had marched close on two hundred miles. As they took to the road that night to march the last twelve miles of the retreat, Allan's comrades regaled him with this information and described their experience in lurid and colourful detail. He didn't seem to mind that he had missed it and as the hours wore on he was injudicious enough to complain that his feet were killing him. He was lucky to arrive with a whole skin.

The last few miles were not without excitement, at least for No. 4 Platoon who had stayed behind to cover A Company when it moved off, and they had moved off just in time, for the Germans were at their backs.

Lt. J. Owen, No. 4 Pltn., A Company, 2nd Bttn., The Oxfordshire and Buckinghamshire Light Infantry, B.E.F.

Soon after the Company had moved off, I saw two mounted men coming along the road towards us. I got my glasses on to them, but

I couldn't make up my mind for certain whether they were Germans or our own troopers. I had my men across the road with bayonets fixed and rifles loaded. Meanwhile the two horsemen had come within a few hundred yards and there was no doubt that they were Germans of the Death's Head Hussars. They were quite by themselves, although I could see a few others about half a mile behind them. They continued to come along, quite unconcerned, until they got to within about forty yards of us. I called out to them and held up my arms to convey to them that they had better surrender. They threw their lances on to the road and we immediately doubled forward and bagged them! Two of my men took possession of the lances and were very pleased with themselves, and I took the better horse of the two and immediately got on to its back.

As this was our first capture there was tremendous excitement. The men were tickled to bits! A few more of the Germans were coming along, so I gave the order to open fire. We knocked out one fellow and killed his horse, and we wounded another of their horses. His rider picked himself up and scuttled like a hare into some trees alongside the road. By this time we were getting rather left behind, so we moved on and joined up with the Company. We felt quite happy!

They were more than happy. They grinned and crowed and gloated insufferably, as if the war was as good as won, passing the lances from hand to hand to be admired and taking it in turns to wear the German 'busbies' with their lurid insignia of skull and crossbones which had so recently adorned the heads of their discomfited prisoners.

But the best part was still to come. It was past one in the morning before the tail of the Battalion reached Le Fay Farm, and No. 4 Platoon was just settling down to bivouac for what remained of the night when Lieutenant Owen reappeared. He was grinning amiably and carrying the horse's saddlebags, whose contents he had now had time to investigate. They revealed quite a haul. There were several boxes of precious matches, two towels, a sponge, some tins of meat, some bread, some sausage, chocolate, a razor, clean socks and various odds and ends, and Owen generously presented these spoils to the Platoon. They shared out the eatables into tiny equal portions and tossed up for the rest.

The trouble was that no one knew quite where the Germans were. The Royal Flying Corps was working flat out and reporting back on the whereabouts and direction of von Kluck's main force, but not even the most daring of hedge-hoppers could hope to spot them all. With the meandering course of the River Marne, the impossibility of watching all its crossings, the hidden valleys, the lavish scatter of woods and spinneys across the land, it was all too easy for small groups of cavalry and mounted reconnaissance patrols to roam the countryside or to lie up in some secluded spot unseen and unsuspected.

One particular troop of German cavalry was lying up at the foot of Miss Aldrich's hill, not a thousand yards from her gate, and she knew very well that they were there for her maid Amélie had seen them crossing the road below and disappearing into the wood along the track that led to the canal. She told Captain Edwards of the Bedfords.*

Now that Captain Simpson had moved on, Edwin Edwards had taken Miss Aldrich under his wing. He had thought it ill-advised to attract attention by flying flags from her gateposts and they had been duly removed, but the picquet still stood guard outside the house and they had a cheering effect on her morale. She served them tea at the gate, listened to their banter, admired their snapshots, and enjoyed their company.

Miss Mildred Aldrich

Just after the boys had finished their tea Captain Edwards came down the road. He looked at the table by the gate. 'So the men have been having tea – lucky men! – and bottled water! What extravagance!' 'Come in and have some too,' I said.

While I was making the tea there was a tremendous explosion. He went to the door, looked out, and remarked as if it were the most natural thing in the world, 'Another division across. That should be the last.'

'Are all the bridges down?' I asked. 'All except the big railway bridge behind you. That won't go until the last minute.'

Miss Aldrich said nothing. She hardly liked to enquire what Captain Edwards meant by 'the last minute' and precisely how it would affect herself. Instead she told him about the Uhlans at the foot of the hill, that there was a cart road, rough and winding, running for over two miles, that it was screened by trees, had plenty of water and could provide shelter for a whole regiment of cavalry. Before he hastened off to report this useful information, she asked him to tell her outright just how much of a risk he considered she was running by staying put.

Edwards answered her frankly. 'None at all unless we are ordered to hold this hill. It's on the line of march from Meaux to Paris, you see, but we've had no orders to hold it yet. But *if* the Germans succeed in taking

---

* Lieutenant (Acting Captain) Edwin Edwards died of wounds on 31 December. Captain John Simpson was killed in action on 30 October.

Meaux and try to put their bridges across the Marne, our artillery on the top of the hill behind you will open fire on them over your head, and then the Germans will certainly reply by bombarding your hill.' He drained his teacup, rose, saluted politely and left Miss Aldrich to think it over.

Her thoughts were not entirely comfortable, but she had little time to dwell on them. Shortly after Edwards hurried off another officer came up the path and knocked on the front door. He was not looking for a cup of tea, as Miss Aldrich had at first assumed. He was looking for Germans, and he wished to know exactly where she thought they were hiding. She offered to take him down the road and show him.

Miss Mildred Aldrich

He stepped back into the garden, gave a quick look overhead – I don't know what for, unless for a German Taube! Then he said, 'Now, please come out into the road and keep close to the bank at the left, in the shadow. I shall walk at the extreme right. As soon as I get where I can see the roads ahead, at the foot of the hill, I shall ask you to stop, and please stop at once. I don't want you to be seen from the road below, in case anyone is there. Do you understand?'

I said I did. So we went into the road and walked silently down the hill. Just before we got to the turn, he motioned me to stop and stood with his map in hand while I explained that he was to cross the road that led into Voisins, take the cart track down the hill past the washhouse on his left, and turn into the wood along that side of the road. When I had explained, he simply said, 'Rough road?' I said it was, and wet in the dryest weather, that it was wooded all the way and, what was more, so winding that you could not see ten feet ahead anywhere. He said, 'Please wait just there for a moment.' He looked up the hill behind him, and made a gesture in the air with his hand above his head. I turned to look up the hill also. I saw the corporal at the gate repeat the gesture and then a big bicycle corps, four abreast, rifles on their backs, slid round the corner and came gliding down the hill. There was not a sound, not even the rattle of a chain or a pedal.

When I got back to my gate I found some of the men of the guard dragging a big long log down the road, and I watched them while they attached it to a tree at my gate and swung it across to the opposite side of the road, making a barrier about five feet high. The corporal took the trouble to explain that it was a barricade to prevent the Germans from making a dash up the hill!

It was just dusk when the bicycle corps returned up the hill. They had to dismount and wheel their machines under the barricade. I asked the Captain what had happened. 'Nothing,' he said. 'We couldn't go in far, the road's too rough and too dangerous. It's a cavalry job.'

All the same, Miss Aldrich knew that the Uhlans were there. That night she was careful to lock her doors. When she rose in the morning the road was deserted, the picquet had gone and Amélie, arriving a few minutes later, announced that not a single soldier remained in the whole commune. A little later the Germans rode boldly up the hill and stopped at the barrier. There were no more than a dozen of them and they were very polite. They merely asked – and in good French – exactly where they were and if all the bridges over the River Marne had been destroyed. Miss Aldrich told them the name of the hamlet in reply to the first question, and said that she did not know the answer to the second. They thanked her civilly and rode back the way they had come. She could not help noticing how smart they looked, in contrast to the hollow-eyed and travel-worn Tommies. It was not reassuring. Miss Aldrich had never felt so isolated in her life and, thinking back to her conversation with Captain Simpson, she wondered uneasily if 'the last minute' had arrived.

In one sense it had. The tide of battle had lapped to the foot of her hill – but it was at the flood, and it was about to turn.

General Joffre's moment had come at last. The Germans were now where he wanted them and he was ready to spring the trap. It was the morning of 5 September. That day the first skirmishes of the Battle of the Marne began in the valley below. But the British were on the march again, and they were marching away from it.

It was not precisely the fault of the British that they were marching in the opposite direction. Joffre had chosen his moment and made up his mind swiftly and the order that communicated his intention had only reached British GHQ at three o'clock on the morning of the 5th – the very day on which he intended to strike. Some sixty battalions of British troops were in bivouac spread over thirty miles or more and, partly in view of the continuing heat-wave, partly to allow them a few hours' rest at the end of the day, they had been ordered to march off early, some of them before sunrise. It was far too late to send out the order that would stop them and, although this day's march was intended to be a short one, the men were still too weary to be expected to turn about and come straight back again as soon as they reached their destinations. It was better to let them go, better to let them rest a little, and better by far to make sure that they would be fit to advance tomorrow.

Besides, they had been in the wrong place – too close to General Maunoury's army which was to advance east across the plain where the

Marne flowed round Meaux and too near Paris itself where General Galliéni was prepared to strike out, if necessary, to support him with the formidable armed garrison he called 'the Paris Army'. If that situation arose, and if the British had stayed where they were, he could find his troops advancing across the British front and there would be horrible confusion. So, if the British commander were to move his troops back a mere ten or twelve miles, if he were to swing them round as they moved so that they would be facing north-east rather than north, their allies on the left would have room to manoeuvre, and all three armies could advance in a single line in a bid to outflank the Germans and, if all went well, to victory.

Resignedly, the Tommies toiled on along the dusty lanes and highways. Most of them by now had lost all sense of time. With almost no rest and not much food to sustain them, they had been marching and fighting as they went for thirteen days and thirteen nights, but it felt to them as if they had been fighting and marching for a lifetime. It was the morning of 5 September, and the first day of the second month of the war.

General Maunoury's Sixth Army was already on the march, swinging east across the plain to attack towards Meaux. They had set out the evening before and already they had advanced six miles towards the unsuspecting flank of von Kluck's army, now well down into the trap that Joffre had set for it. But von Kluck was no longer unsuspecting. German pilots had been sending back disquieting reports of troop movements and of forces assembling, for the Sixth Army was now so large that it could not easily be concealed. The previous afternoon, as the first of Maunoury's troops moved into position for the advance, it dawned on the German Command at long last that the Allies had not been defeated, that they had not been routed, that they were not in disarray, but that they had *'withdrawn in good order and according to plan'*.★

The intelligence that the Allies were on the point of striking back came as more than a rude shock; it faced the Germans with a serious dilemma. Despite conflicting orders from the Supreme Command, von Kluck solved it in his own style. It was not his way to await developments. Like many soldier strategists before him, he believed that attack was the best means of defence. Accordingly he ordered his troops to halt, to turn about, to face towards Paris and to prepare to meet the enemy. He deployed his front-line troops across the valley in front of Meaux and placed his guns in the valley between the villages of Monthyon and Penchard on the hills on either side. Almost on the stroke of noon, as the French came into view, they fired. It was the first shot of the Battle of the Marne.

★ The words of Generaloberst von Moltke, spoken to Helfferich, then Foreign Secretary, and quoted in his book, *Der Weltkrieg*.

Miss Mildred Aldrich

Amélie rushed by me. I heard her say, '*Mon Dieu!*' I waited, but she did not come back. After a bit I pulled myself together, went out and followed down to the hedge where she was standing looking off to the plain.

The battle had advanced right over the crest of the hill. The sun was shining brilliantly on Mareuil and Chauconin, but Monthyon and Penchard were enveloped in smoke. From the east and west we could see the artillery fire, but owing to the smoke hanging over the crest of the hill on the horizon, it was impossible to get an idea of the positions of the armies. I tried to remember what the English soldiers had said – that the Germans were, if possible, to be pushed east, in which case the artillery to the west must be either the French or English. The hard thing to bear was that it was all guesswork. There was only noise, belching smoke, and long drifts of white clouds concealing the hill.

By the middle of the afternoon Monthyon came slowly out of the smoke. That seemed to mean that the heaviest firing was over the hill and not on it – or did it mean that the battle was receding? If it did, then the Allies were retreating. There was no way to discover the truth. And all this time the cannon thundered in the south-east.

A dozen times during the afternoon I went into the study and tried to read. Little groups of old men, women, and children were in the road, mounted on the barricade which the English had left. I could hear the murmur of their voices. I tried to stay indoors but in spite of myself, I kept going out on to the lawn, field-glasses in hand, to watch the smoke. In my imagination every shot meant awful slaughter. In the field below me the wheat was being cut. I remember vividly that a white horse was drawing the reaping machine and women and children were stacking and gleaning. Now and then the horse would stop, and a woman, with her red handkerchief on her head, would stand, shading her eyes for a moment, and look. Then the white horse would turn and go plodding on.

It was just about six o'clock when the first shell that we could really see came over the hill. The sun was setting. For two hours we saw them rise, descend, explode. Then a little smoke would rise from one hamlet, then from another; then a tiny flame – hardly more than a spark – and by dark the whole plain was on fire, lighting up Mareuil in the foreground. There were long lines of grain-stacks stretching along the plain. One by one they took fire, until, by ten o'clock, they stood like a procession of huge torches across my beloved panorama.

Late in the afternoon General Joffre drove to the headquarters of Sir John French. The British Commander-in-Chief had already agreed to co-operate, to take part in Joffre's grand plan, to turn his troops about and to send them into battle. But there had been some confusion and one liaison officer had reported his impression that the British were lukewarm. Joffre, on the other hand, was burning with zeal, and he could afford to take no chances. When courtesies had been exchanged, he launched into a long, impassioned appeal. He was prepared to throw everything – *everything* to his very last man – into the battle. It was literally do or die, for the chance would not come again. He begged Sir John French to support him to the limit. He begged him in the cause of the alliance. Then he paused, and delivered his punchline. '*Monsieur le Maréchal, c'est la France qui vous supplie!*' He was begging in the name of France herself.

There was no need for an interpreter. French had perfectly understood, but his own command of General Joffre's language failed him when he tried to say so. He struggled for a moment, uttered a few words, started again and then gave up. He turned to Major Clive. 'Damn it, I can't explain! Tell him that all that men *can* do our fellows *will* do.'

Sir John French had been deeply moved. Lieutenant Spears was touched and not a little astonished to see tears rolling down his cheeks.

The news that the British would not be able to advance before nine the following morning was something of an anticlimax, but General Joffre shrugged his shoulders. He had won his point, and it could not be helped.

Staff Officers hastened off to send out the orders, and that evening they were read out to the troops. They could hardly believe that the long retreat was over and that at long last the time had come to turn around and fight. It put new life into them and, despite their weariness, they could hardly wait to get going.

A little way to the north, Miss Aldrich was finding it difficult to get to sleep. Fires were still burning on the plain below and now and again a gun boomed faintly in the distance. In the silence that followed she tossed and turned, unable to wipe the battle from her thoughts, her mind awash with visions of the slaughter. She rose and opened the shutters. It was a beautiful night. The shadowy figures of the picquet were clearly visible on the road outside, but as Miss Aldrich stood and looked into the night she could only think of soldiers lying dead beneath the starlight.

Part Four
The Road To Flanders

Who's to fight for Flanders, who will set them free,
The war-worn lowlands by the English sea . . .

Charles Scott-Moncrieff

Chapter 19

On 9 September the weather broke, and at first the troops were glad of it. But refreshing showers turned into a steady downpour, scudding clouds banked into a sullen mass and the fresh breeze, so welcome after the near-tropical weather, blew up that night into a howling wind that chilled a man to the heart. The long-suffering Tommies, crouching uncomfortably in the open or at best in the flimsiest of shelters, grumbled and cursed the cold in much the same terms as they had reviled the heat. But they were not despondent. They were on the move at last. That day they had gone back across the River Marne driving the Germans before them and, although they could hardly know it yet, the Allies had between them won the Battle of the Marne.

But the Germans knew it. And they also knew that they had lost the mighty gamble on which they had staked their ambitions and failed to deliver the rapid knockout blow on which their hopes depended.

The French had launched their offensive all along the line, and all along the line they had done well. In the east they had baulked the Crown Prince of the victory he had so confidently expected and foiled his father of his triumphal march through Rheims. In the west von Kluck had failed to throw back General Maunoury's army and now it was the Kaiser's armies that were falling back. The Kaiser had returned disgruntled to Supreme Headquarters to review the situation and to brood on the disconcerting change in the fortunes of his armies.

But for twenty-four crucial hours it had been touch and go. When the French Sixth Army attacked, von Kluck had mustered every available man to meet them, even those who could ill be spared – even those in the British sector and they could not be spared at all. But he had taken a chance. Gambling on the likelihood that the BEF would continue their retreat, that a thin screen of cavalry could follow them up while he threw back General Maunoury, von Kluck rushed his First and Second Corps north-west and pitched them into the fight.

It was a desperate throw – and it very nearly worked. It was the dashing French who saved the situation and, in particular, it was the dash and imagination of General Galliéni. For Maunoury needed reinforcements;

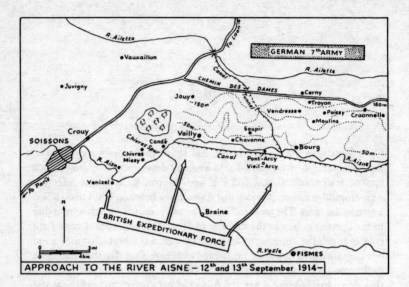

APPROACH TO THE RIVER AISNE — 12th and 13th September 1914 —

Labels in top map: R. Ailette, To Laon, GERMAN 7th ARMY, Vauxaillon, R. Ailette, Juvigny, CHEMIN DES DAMES, Cerny, Jouy, Troyon, 150m, Vendresse, Paissy, Craonnelle, Moulins, 150m, Crouy, Soupir, 50m, SOISSONS, Vailly, Chavonne, Chivres Spur, Condé, Bourg, To Paris, Chivres Missy, Canal, Pont-Arcy, Vieil-Arcy, 50m, R. Aisne, Vanizel, R. Aisne, N, Braine, BRITISH EXPEDITIONARY FORCE, R. Vesle, FISMES, 0 3 ml, 4 km

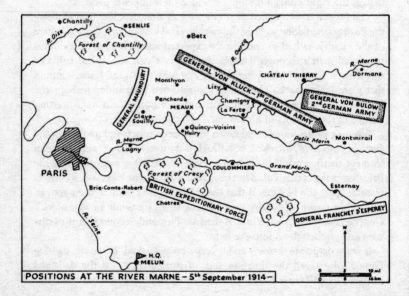

POSITIONS AT THE RIVER MARNE — 5th September 1914 —

Labels in bottom map: Chantilly, SENLIS, R. Oise, Forest of Chantilly, Betz, R. Ourcq, GENERAL VON KLUCK — 1st GERMAN ARMY, R. Marne, CHÂTEAU THIERRY, Dormans, Monthyon, Lizy, GENERAL VON BULOW 2nd GERMAN ARMY, GENERAL MAUNOURY, Penchard, Chamigny, MEAUX, La Ferté, Claye-Souilly, Quincy-Voisins, Montmirail, R. Marne, Huiry, Petit Morin, Lagny, PARIS, COULOMMIERS, Grand Morin, Forest of Crécy, Brie-Comte-Robert, Esternay, BRITISH EXPEDITIONARY FORCE, Chatres, GENERAL FRANCHET D'ESPEREY, R. Seine, H.Q. MELUN, N, 0 10 ml, 16 km he needed them fast; he needed them *now* – and it was Galliéni who provided them. Almost every vehicle in Paris, the buses, the vans, the motor lorries, had already been requisitioned to provide the troops with transport. Only the taxis were left. Galliéni commandeered them now, scouring the streets, the railway stations, the cab stands, whistling up every taxi plying for hire, packing them full of troops and pressing the astonished cab-drivers into the service of France. With the very fate of France at stake few of the drivers demurred and soon a procession of taxicabs, many miles long, was speeding out of Paris towards the Front.

They called it the 'Miracle of the Marne' and, after the heart-scorching sequence of defeats, after the anxious days of retreat, after the seemingly inexorable progress of the Germans across the north of France, it was little short of a miracle that the invader had been stopped at last. And not only stopped, but thrust back.

By pulling his army north-west to grapple with Maunoury, von Kluck had pulled away from von Bülow on his left. Turning northwards, the BEF moved into the gap. They moved slowly, they moved cautiously, and they moved just a little too late, for they had been a day's march away from the jump-off line when Joffre had given the word. But it was enough to force the Germans back to the line of the Marne, to chase them across it and, when they had reached the other side, to send them flooding back, counting the bitter cost, to take up a new position on the River Aisne. It was enough to tip the scales. Long years later, when the war was won, there were those who judged that the first seeds of the final victory had been sown, by some miracle, on the Marne.

It would be many moons before the Army won the war, but the Tommies knew that they had won a battle and it was the sense of winning that kept them going.

Cpl. W. Holbrook, No. 13599, 4th Bttn., The Royal Fusiliers,
9th Brigade, 3rd Division, B.E.F.

We gradually advanced a bit. Of course the Germans were trying to attack there too. One day I was sent with another fellow to a bit of high ground looking over the field where our Brigade was, because they expected the Germans to come along this road, or to send a patrol along it anyhow. And I and this other fellow were under cover on this road. We had to warn the troops further down if any advance was made and they'd got their eye on us looking for a signal. While we were there I saw a sight I'd never seen before and I don't imagine anyone ever saw it again. A German Uhlan regiment – the whole regiment – attacked the Lincolns (they were in our Brigade, they were on our left) and I saw these Germans from where I was. I looked down this little bit of a valley and I saw all these German cavalry attack the Lincolns. And the Lincolns held their fire until they were just two or three hundred yards away and then they let go. The Germans got nowhere near them, they got absolutely slaughtered. They slaughtered *hundreds*. I saw every bit of it as if I was watching a film. It lasted about half an hour.

I says to the other fellow, 'Just look at that!' And there were cavalry falling everywhere and wounded staggering about. An hour or two later I think every man in the Lincolns had a German helmet he'd picked up.

It did wonders for their morale. But the soldiers of the BEF were still ill-clad, still tired, still ill-equipped, and even after they had absorbed the first scanty reinforcements most battalions were still at skeleton strength.* They were lean and they were hungry. As the Front moved on, Sir William Robertson was labouring harder than ever to get supplies to the troops but so much transport had been lost that it was not always easy to send forward more than the bare minimum of rations. The Tommies were still short of food and, going back across invaded ravaged country, they could not live off the land as they had lived on the retreat, for the Germans had laid it waste and there were few pickings to be had.

In the battered villages where the shells had rained and the rearguards of the BEF had turned to fight, the flimsy country-built barns and cottages had crumbled and collapsed and the few walls left standing offered dubious shelter. Even hamlets that had escaped the battle had not escaped the ravages of war. Less than a week ago the troops had passed them, tranquil in the sunlight among fields of golden grain. Now as they came back, they could smell them a long way off. A stench hung over the villages – of slaughtered beasts and slow-decaying flesh, of filth from houses looted and defiled, of stale smoke that clung round burnt-out barns and rose from blackened stubble fields where the harvest grain had been set alight and reduced to ashes. It was hard luck on the Army's horses, weakening for want of forage.

In places where German soldiers had been billeted, people were eager to tell their tales of wanton damage and destruction.

* The 18th Brigade alone, after its losses at Mons and Le Cateau, numbered fewer than 2,000 compared to its normal strength of 4,400, and it was typical of many others.

Dr A. A. Martin, 15th Field Ambulance, 5th Division, B.E.F.

We came to a farmhouse that had been occupied by the Germans two days previously, and the old farmer brought me through the house to show what the Huns had done. His two wooden bedsteads had been smashed. All his wife's clothes had been taken out of a chest of drawers and torn up, and the chest had been battered badly with an axe. The windows were broken and two legs of the kitchen table had been chopped off.

An old family clock lay battered in a corner, and an ancient sporting gun was broken in two. The farmer showed me one of his wife's old bonnets which had been thrown into the fire by these lovely Germans and partially burned. Fancy burning an old woman's bonnet! Two German soldiers got into the fowlyard and struck all the birds down with their bayonets. A fine big dog lay dead at the garden gate, shot by a German NCO because the poor beast barked at him.

The old-fashioned furniture and ornaments of the house had been destroyed. All the pictures were broken except two – one of these was a framed picture of Pope Leo XIII, and the other was one representing the Crucifixion, so we guessed that the German troops must have been Bavarians, who are mostly Catholics.

It all seemed so stupid, so senseless, so paltry, and mean. Imagine burning an old lady's bonnet and smashing an old clock that had been in the family's possession for three generations! The old farmer was in tears and very miserable. He said that the German soldiers were very drunk and had brought a lot of bottles of champagne with them and spent a very hilarious night. One of the men had a very fine voice and sang German drinking songs, while the others hiccuped the choruses. There were certainly a lot of empty champagne bottles lying about. I don't think that the old farmer's drinking ever soared above vin rouge, so the bottles must have been German loot from elsewhere.

But their luck had changed so suddenly, their retreat had been so rapid that the Germans had not got clean away with all their spoils. All across the devastated country the Tommies were cheered to see the same signs of haste and disorder that had marked their own painful progress down the road from Mons – slow-moving wagons pulled to the side of the road, broken-down lorries half-toppled in a ditch, abandoned carts and even occasionally a gun. A few wagons even contained the supplies the BEF had been forced to dump as it went; many were piled high with goods looted from towns and villages *en route*. Among the furious populace the Ox and Bucks encountered one contented man – a farmer who had exacted reparation for his ruined crop by requisitioning the contents of a lorry full of grain conveniently abandoned by the Germans. He considered this booty to be no more than his due and was persuaded with some difficulty to sell the Quartermaster a bag or two to feed the hungry horses. Pleased though he was to see the Allies back again, he drove a hard bargain.

The soldiers too were happy to get their own back for the loss of their own supplies by helping themselves to the Germans' whenever they got the chance.

Cpl. W. Holbrook, No. 13599, 4th Bttn., The Royal Fusiliers, 9th Brigade, 3rd Division, B.E.F.

After we left the Marne we went to the Aisne and the Germans were retreating the whole time with a lot of fighting going on. I remember the stuff they'd pinched, cars, lorries, even stuff they'd pinched from the Belgians, they had to leave on the side of the road because they couldn't get them back fast enough. So I was marching along in fours between the Marne and the Aisne, and I saw some fellows in front of me diving out of the ranks and climbing up on this wagon and getting things out – bottles in straw covers it was – and then running to catch the troops up again. So I said to my mate, 'Here, hold my rifle. I'm going to have a go at this.' So when I got over there to this wagon I climbed up the wheels and got into it. It was all broken glass and straw in there, but I found two bottles in straw covers and ran and caught up my mate. He put one bottle in his pack, I put one in mine and we marched on. It must have been fifteen, even twenty blooming miles, but all the way we were looking forward to having a good drink at the end of the road – champagne as *we* thought! Well, we finally undone our packs and pulled the bottles out – and it was two bottles of Vichy water! That's all it was – and we'd carried them about twenty blooming miles! We didn't half swear!

The advance had not exactly been a walkover. Even after von Kluck rushed back two divisions to help, the Germans troops were few and they were thinly spread. But the country was rich in defensive positions. There was high ground that commanded the roads, there were woods where cavalry could skulk unobserved, there were valleys where guns could be concealed. Above all there were the formidable obstacles of three rivers and many smaller streams, too wide to swim, too deep to ford, too precarious to cross on the skeletons of demolished bridges. The Germans had fought with dogged fury to defend the bridges that were still intact and it had been no easy task to win them.

But it had been done. On the first day the BEF pushed forward almost eleven miles. On the second they crossed the Grand Morin and advanced another eight. On the third day they had moved ten miles and crossed the Petit Morin. On the fourth they had reached the wide waters of the Marne and fought their way across them to the other side. Now the tables had been turned and the Germans were in full flight. But they were fighting as they went.

Sgt. F. M. Packham, No. 10134, 2nd Bttn., Royal Sussex Regt., 2nd Brigade, 1st Division, B.E.F.

On the morning of 10 September we found ourselves right in the forefront of the army and my platoon was leading the advance. We stopped on the road in front of a village called Priez. We had an idea that something was afoot. The Colonel and the adjutant rode up and conversed with our company officer. Then our platoon was ordered to 'advance at the double'. With our platoon officer in the lead, we started to advance and we had to cross a small brook. Some of us were able to jump across but others jumped in and waded across. We kept on going, across a field and up a slight rise. When we reached the top we could see some Germans taking cover among some wheat stooks. We were ordered to lay down and open fire on them. We had a great time firing at them as they dodged from stook to stook, but very soon afterwards the German artillery opened fire on us.

They found our position with the first salvo. I saw the blinding flash as the shells burst in the air just in front of us and I could hear the shrapnel whistling past me. There were shouts and screams and I knew that some had been hit. I looked behind me and saw one of our corporals with his face covered with blood. We started again, firing at the enemy, then someone called behind us for us to get back. As I went to get up I was knocked down. I thought at first that someone had pushed me down, so I got to my feet again and started moving back. My shoulder strap was loose. I put my hand to the back of my shoulder to find out what was wrong with it and felt that it was wet. I was amazed to find that it was blood on my hand and that I'd been hit. I asked the man next to me to have a look at it and he said that I had quite a gash in my shoulder. So I went back to look for the First Aid squad, but it was a long time before I could locate one. I found one at last in the village, Priez. There were a lot of casualties waiting to be seen. The medical officer looked at my wound and the orderly put a dressing on it. That night some of us were taken by lorry to a rear field hospital. It was a very rough journey. One of the men had a stomach wound and had to lay on the hard floor of the lorry. He died just as we arrived at the hospital.

Many died that day. Their comrades buried them in the quiet hours of the night and in the morning pressed on to fight their way across the next few miles. The battle was not over, but it had moved so far ahead that the country of the first day's fighting, the place where the retreat had been halted, had almost returned to normal.

Miss Mildred Aldrich, 10 September 1914

Our communications which were cut on September 2nd were reopened in a sort of a way and we were told that postal communication with Paris was to be reopened with an automobile service from Couilly to Lagny on the other side of the Marne and from there trains were running to Paris. Of course we had no newspapers, and with our *mairie* and post office being closed there were no telegrams – besides, our telegraph wires are dangling from the poles just as the English engineers left them on September 2nd. It seemed a century ago!

We knew the Germans were still retreating because each morning the booming of the cannon and the columns of smoke were further off, and because the slopes and the hills which had been burning the first three days of the battle were lying silent in the wonderful sunshine, as if there were no living people in the world except us few on this side of the river. But the silence over there seems different today. Here and there still thin ribbons of smoke – now rising straight in the air, and now curling in the breeze – say that something is burning, not only in the bombarded towns, but in the woods and plains. But what? No one knows.

One or two of our older men crossed the Marne on a raft today. They brought back word that thousands from the battles of the 5th, 6th and 7th had laid for days unburied under the hot September sun, but that the fire department was already out there from Paris and that it would only be a few days until the worst marks of the terrible fight would be removed. But they brought back no news. The few people who had remained hidden in cellars or on isolated farms knew no more than we did, and it was impossible, naturally, to get near to the field ambulance at Neufmortier, which we can see from my lawn. However, the very day after the French advanced from here we got news in a very amusing way. I was working in the garden on the south side of the house (I had instinctively put the house between me and the smoke of battle) when Amélie came running down the hill in a high state of excitement, crying out that the French were coming back, that there had been a great victory and that I was to come and see.

Sure enough, there they were – *cuirassiers*, the sun glinting on their helmets, riding slowly towards Paris, as gaily as if they were returning from a fête, with all sorts of trophies hanging to their saddles. It was no army returning, only a small detachment. Still, I couldn't help feeling that if *any* of them were returning in that spirit while the cannon were still booming, all must be well.

It was. But there was still a long way to go. Next day it was miserable, wet and cold. It was 11 September and it happened also to be Eddie Slaytor's seventeenth birthday. Already he was a seasoned soldier. He had hung on to the rifle picked up in the forest at Villers-Cotterêts and since then had fired it in half a dozen fights and skirmishes. He did not go so far as to flatter himself that he was in the same class as the top marksmen in the Battalion, but he was becoming useful with his rifle. There was no denying it was a trial to carry it on the march and that it grew heavier with every mile, but Eddie would not for worlds have admitted it. His shoulder had ceased to protest at the fierce kick-back, his finger was at home on the trigger, his aim was steady if not always unerring, and although Lieutenant Horlick had not referred directly to his unofficial elevation from Drummer to Guardsman, Eddie was conscious of an occasional approving glance. For some days now no one had called him 'Poor Boy'. They had other things on their minds.

Drummer E. L. Slaytor, 3rd Bttn. The Coldstream Guards, 4th Brigade, 2nd Division, B.E.F.

I remember our platoon sergeant, who was always giving us good advice, telling us to prove our worth and to remember that better Coldstreamers had gone before us! I'd lost two very good friends at the Petit Morin, both killed – Mick Oban and Alec New – and the Coldstream had lost two fine soldiers. I felt sick at heart for they had both been good to me. After crossing the river our platoon commander got us into some sort of line, and told us we were going to charge (he always seemed to be wanting to do this!). We accordingly fixed bayonets, but I know for one I was relieved when it came to pass that the Germans whom we were about to charge had surrendered to our 2nd Battalion and the Irish Guards. Once again the 3rd Battalion had suffered many casualties.

On 12 September they reached the River Aisne and found that the Germans had stopped running and were dug in on the other side. They seemed to have every intention of staying there, they had blown up most of the bridges behind them and the British Army was stuck on the other side. That night, after a day of torrential rain and as if to emphasise the change in their fortune, the heavens opened, the wind screeched and the skies crashed and flashed. It was a tremendous storm, as if Wotan and a whole panoply of Teutonic gods were staging an almighty *Götterdämmerung* to show the British what was what.

It was bad enough for the Army trying to struggle across the Aisne. For the Royal Flying Corps the change in the weather was catastrophic. The rain had set in at the critical moment just as the battle started and ever since they had been in difficulties. It was bad weather for flying and with nothing to be seen on the ground through rain-spattered goggles and sweeping mist it was pointless to try. The Army, desperate to know where the Germans were digging in, did the best they could and waited and hoped for the weather to improve, for the fliers to take to the skies and for the all-important information to reach them. Now even that flimsy hope was gone, swept away by the storm as it had swept away most of the aeroplanes, so flimsy and so light that a twelve-year-old could have overturned them with a single hearty push. The storm picked them up, tossed them high in the air and hurled them back to earth in fragments.

The squadrons had newly arrived at their makeshift airfields at Sapenay, the storm was already raging and long before the machines could be secured more than half of them had been destroyed or badly knocked about. In No. 3 Squadron the damage was frightful and the pilots could do nothing but look on aghast. The Squadron diary painted a grim picture.

> Before anything could be done to make the machines more secure, the wind shifted, and about half the total number of machines were over on their backs. One Henri Farman went up about thirty feet in the air and crashed on top of another Henri Farman in a hopeless tangle. BEs of No. 2 squadron were blowing across the aerodrome, and when daylight arrived and the storm abated, the aerodrome presented a pitiful sight. The Royal Flying Corps in the field could not have had more than ten machines serviceable that morning.

All night long while the storm raged, the troops had been toiling and straining to cross the river. By the time it blew itself out in a wet and miserable dawn only a very few of them had made it to the other side.

The 4th Division had made it, for they had found a bridge. It could hardly be said to be intact. For one thing the girders had been cut through.

The charges had been laid for demolition, but they had failed to explode. In the rain and the dark it was impossible for the engineers to attempt the delicate and hazardous task of disconnecting the charges when at any moment a shaft of lightning might set them off. But the concrete roadway looked solid enough. General Sir Aylmer Hunter Weston inspected the bridge himself, weighed the danger of its exploding or collapsing against the advantage of stealing a march on the enemy by gaining a foothold on the other side, and decided that with infinite caution it might just be possible to cross it.

'Infinite caution' meant inching a brigade of some three thousand men across the bridge in silence, on tiptoe, and in single file. Infinite caution meant each man keeping his distance and adopting a light, almost mincing tread, placing his feet as carefully as if he were walking on glass. It meant unloading the ammunition wagons and passing the boxes from hand to hand, one at a time across a human chain. It was many hours before the last man was over and the job was complete, but the result was a resounding success. In the first grey light of the streaming dawn a soaked and sleepy German look-out on the heights beyond the river spotted the British massing for attack and raised the alarm. Within minutes the Germans had literally fled their trenches. They were only outpost trenches and they were thinly held, but the shouts and exclamations as the men were roused, the clearly heard sounds of astonishment and panic as they left, were music to the Tommies' ears. It lifted their bedraggled spirits and gave them heart to press on.

But the majority of the Expeditionary Force were still on the far side of the river and it was up to the engineers to get them across. Three hundred feet below a plateau the Aisne flowed deep and wide, carving a course in places through steep valleys and ravines between precipitous tree-clad banks reduced by the rain to glissades of slithering mud. The river was unfordable. There was no cover on the southern side and no suitable positions nearer than two miles distant on the southern heights from which the guns could cover the infantry as they crossed. All the advantages lay with the enemy, well entrenched in prepared positions on the high ground beyond the Aisne, and the enemy had made sure that the British would not easily be able to follow them. The roar of the German heavy guns ranged on the river and land beyond gave notice that their retreat had finally stopped, that they were well dug in, in a fortress-like position with the river as their moat. The few bridges that were still passable were defended by strong forces of infantry, but only the bridges could carry the Army across and there was nothing for it but to go for them.

Some of the troops were fortunate. In places where only a central span had gone the gap could be filled by a sturdy plank that men could cross with care. There were floating bridges too, barrels lashed beneath a makeshift deck of boards, ladders, trestles, linked by a half-sunken rowing boat or in one lucky instance by a barge. Engineers, working under a hail of shellfire, steeled themselves to the dangerous task of patching up bridges where they could or building pontoons where they could not. But they soon ran out of materials.

Cpl. A. Letyford, 5th Field Company, Royal Engineers, B.E.F.

12.9.14 Rise at 3.30 from our billet in railway carriages at the station. I go off to find an ambulance for sick men and find it 4 miles away. I lose the company and march along with the Guards. I find the No. 4 section just before dark taking down a large shed to provide timber for repairing a bridge. We march on a mile and billet at the bridge at Courcelle.

13.9.14. Awake in a rattle of artillery at 4 am. Off about 5, taking a cross country route and pass through Vieuil Arcy. On about a mile and make a pontoon bridge across the river. Shells burst amongst us all through the afternoon.

As they worked on steadily in the soaking rain, shaken by explosions, drenched by frequent shower-baths when a shell burst in the river, some troops of the 2nd Worcesters were already crossing, scrambling over the twisted girders of the broken bridge high above the engineers working at river level in the lee of its crumbling piers and presenting a fine target to the snipers high on the other side. All afternoon as they worked, Letyford and his section could hear the clang of bullets striking off the ironwork. It took until half-past four to finish the new bridge – and by a miracle there were no casualties. The Worcesters too had got safely across and were assembled on the other side and, as the day dulled and darkened into a false damp dusk and the engineers moved off, transport and guns were already clattering across their new-built bridge to support the troops who had reached the German side of the river and were pushing on to confront them on the heights above.

At the stretch of the river where Clarrie Hodgson was waiting impatiently to take across the last remaining gun of his section the bridge was not yet completed, but the 3rd Division infantry badly needed the gun and he decided to take a chance.

2nd Lt. C. F. Hodgson, 122 Battery, XXVIII Brigade, R.F.A., B.E.F.

They said we would be able to cross it any minute now, so I had a talk to the fellow doing it and he said, 'Yes, very well, if you'd like to risk it without side-rails.' So off we started trying to get across this river along the pontoon bridge. Well, just as the horses and the gun got halfway across a German shell pitched into the river. It frightened the horses so much that they slewed off the bridge dragging the gun with them. Of course with the weight of the gun they didn't have a chance. All the horses were drowned. The drivers managed to jump clear and they were struggling in the water. Luckily they could swim and they made it to the bank and we dragged them out and saved them – but the gun was at the bottom of the river. And it was deep! The gun was completely submerged.

Well, we were very fed up! We'd wanted to have a bash at the Germans after they'd pushed us back like this, but it was not to be. The question now was to try to get the gun. Sitting along the banks of the river were dozens if not hundreds of British troops waiting for something to happen. So one chap came forward and he said, 'Look, do you want us to save the gun?' 'Well,' I said, 'I certainly want it taken out of the river, if you can.' So he said, 'Well, as a matter of fact I used to be a diver.' So I said, 'Right, you're the chap! Come on.'

Well, he dived and dived and after a number of tries he managed to tie some rope round the gun and we got a dozen or so of these chaps heaving on the rope and eventually we succeeded in dragging it up on the bank. But it was no good! Water had got into the buffer, so that was that. We were finished. We hung about for a bit with the Brigade, but without a gun we were useless so as soon as things were established they sent us back to railhead to wait for another one. And that's where I found my brother.

Drummer E. L. Slaytor, 3rd Bttn., The Coldstream Guards, 4th Brigade, 2nd Division, B.E.F.

On Monday 14 September, we crossed the Aisne, and after ascending the heights on the right bank, which were quite steep in places – we had to pull ourselves up by branches of trees – we finally emerged at the top near Soupir Farm. We, No. 4 Company, were placed on the left of the 2nd Grenadiers, who appeared to be holding the farm itself. I believe our orders were to advance on the village of Ostel. This we attempted to do, advancing over stubble and across a beet field in extended order. We had gone just a few hundred yards when we came under heavy rifle, machine-gun fire *and* shellfire. How alone we felt! They could see that our thin straggling line couldn't advance any farther, so we were given the order to retire and to form a firing line by some haystacks to the left of Soupir Farm. We'd just started back when a shell fell between the next man and myself. We both fell to the ground, expecting to be blown to eternity – but it didn't burst! As I fell, the bugle I'd carried all the way through the retreat and advance slipped off my pack and fell under my chin. What a jolt it gave me! A real thump on the jaw. What with getting tangled up with the bugle cord, and the heat and excitement of the moment, I was in a fair old state. My comrade looked round and yelled, 'Chuck the bloody thing away.' That was a heinous crime of course, but I was past caring. Anyway I hadn't blown the wretched bugle since those far-off days in Chelsea Barracks (only a month before!). So I tore it off and slung it as hard as I could in the direction of the German line. I don't suppose it did the Germans much harm, but it certainly relieved my feelings.

We went on then and eventually we found ourselves near the haystacks. There we established a rough firing line – and there we stayed. We got no further, and after a couple of days a line on more or less the same spot was more or less stabilised. We bogged down. And that was that.

That would have been about 16 September 1914. In the three weeks since we were first in action at Landrecies, my battalion had lost twenty-two officers, of whom nine were killed, and nearly five hundred Guardsmen.

Even before the Army had reached the Aisne the first four days of the advance had cost many casualties, seventeen hundred alone in the four days that took them to the Marne. The crossing of the Aisne cost many more. With the BEF already weakened and depleted, the loss of even a single man was sorely felt.

The 4th Dragoon Guards had crossed the river at Bourg with their customary style. The road bridge had been demolished but two bridges over the canal were still intact, and the canal itself crossed to the other side of the Aisne on an aqueduct slung ten feet above the river. It was a wide aqueduct and on either side of the water-course there were high-walled towpaths, wide enough to carry the plodding horses that dragged the barges and wide enough, therefore, for the steeds of the cavalry to dash across, to capture the village and to open the way for the infantry to follow. But the village of Bourg stood on a high promontory which overlooked the river and the aqueduct. It also commanded the bridges that spanned the canal – those bridges that must be captured before the troopers could cross. A small force of Germans was dug in at the bridge; a large force was firmly ensconced up the hill in the village of Bourg. They were firing from machine-guns well sited on the heights, they were sniping from every vantage point, and the horsemen presented a fine target. While the Colonel conferred with his officers on the far bank of the canal, the Dragoons were forced to keep on the move, circling and manoeuvring to avoid the crossfire. Even so, with little cover to protect them, in the course of one uncomfortable quarter of an hour half a dozen men were hit.

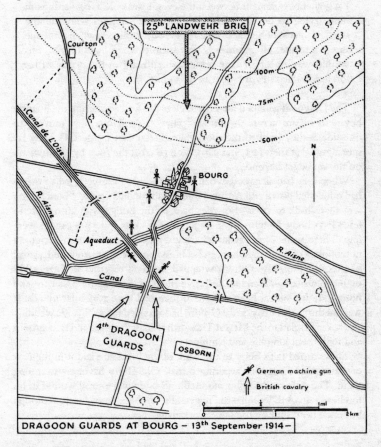

DRAGOON GUARDS AT BOURG – 13th September 1914 –

And then they formed up to attack.

The enemy, of course, were waiting for them. But it happened so quickly, they charged so fiercely that the German defence crumpled almost at once. The honours went to Lieutenant 'Sambo' Sewell, riding hard for the bridge at the head of his squadron through the lethal fire, slicing and cutting with drawn sabres, scattering the men on the outpost. And the credit went equally to Pat Fitzgerald rushing forward with his machine-gun team to finish the job. It was all over in less than five wild minutes. Pat was killed in the last moments of the fight.

Capt. A. Osborn, 4th Dragoon Guards, B.E.F.

Pat got a bullet straight between the eyes. I was only a few yards from him, trying to do something for Sergeant Langdon who had the subclavian vein of his neck ripped open with a splinter, when someone shouted to me. Fitzgerald was unconscious when I got to him. His wound was no bigger than a blue pencil mark in the centre of his forehead. Then in a moment he was gone.

The Dragoons galloped forward to clear the road ahead, and the infantry began to stream across the bridge. They stepped carefully, moving to one side as they reached the spot where Lieutenant Fitzgerald's body lay spreadeagled at their feet, and carried on to cross the river by the towpath on the aqueduct beyond.

When they had all passed, when Bourg had been captured, when things had quietened down and Arthur Osborn had patched up the wounded and sent them back to safety, he went back to the bridge with an orderly to fetch Pat's body. Osborn went through his pockets. Pat's possessions were few. There were a pocket-knife, a few French francs, four sovereigns, a notebook, a cigarette case and, in his breast pocket, two letters and a small snapshot of Dorothy. Osborn wrapped them all together in Fitzgerald's own green silk handkerchief and gave them to the Quartermaster to send home. He felt sick at heart. The two men had been particular friends. It was just thirty-three days since Osborn had attended Pat's romantic wedding and raised his glass in the Mess at Tidworth to toast the bride and bridegroom and wish them long life and happiness.

They carried Pat's body to the bank of the canal and laid it in the row of other dead Dragoons awaiting burial. Old Harry Savory was among them. The only mark on his mountainous body was a small wound in his forehead remarkably similar to Fitzgerald's. It looked suspiciously as though both had been shot by the same marksman.

Chapter 20

Bill Holbrook crossed the Aisne near Vailly during the dark and dripping night of 13 September with considerable difficulty since the whole of the 9th Brigade had to pass in single file over a precarious makeshift bridge, the best that the hard-pressed engineers had been able to contrive. In the wind and the rain and the pitch black of the night it was almost madness to attempt to cross at all. The sluggish river was flowing faster, swollen with rain, and foaming with a faint luminous light if a man was injudicious enough to look down as he teetered and swayed towards the pinprick light of a torch flashing encouragement from the far bank. Holbrook, who would rather have faced a dozen bombardments, was frankly terrified.

Cpl. W. Holbrook, No. 13599, 4th Bttn., The Royal Fusiliers, 9th Brigade, 3rd Division, B.E.F.

They'd blown up the bridge over the Aisne. There's a canal before you get to the Aisne, then the river, and they're only a few yards apart. And they'd left the canal bridge all right, but blown up the river one. So when you'd got over one bridge you couldn't get over the other. So the engineers had fixed up a temporary bridge, not a pontoon bridge, just a dump of boxes strung together. We had to cross that, one at a time over this Aisne. It was about sixteen feet below, you know, and we had to walk on this box thing – no rail! As you put your foot down the box came up to meet the other one. It was a hell of a job to get across. But *thousands* of us went across. I suppose it actually took about four hours to get even our own battalion over. It was dawn by then. We lost quite a few. Quite a few got drowned. Then we went up to where the German trenches were on some hills on the other side there.

It was exactly the type of bridge with which the sappers had been accustomed to traverse ravines in India, but crossing such a bridge with time to spare and in the bright Indian daylight was one thing; it was a different kind of feat and took a different kind of courage to attempt it in the slippery misery of a European autumn night. It was a long, long time before they were finally assembled on the far side and struggled up to the high ground above to extend the line of the 8th Brigade who had gone ahead of them. They were punch-drunk with weariness, but there was no time to rest for they were within slingshot of the Germans, and the Germans were waiting for them behind a heavy dripping mist. It was no help at all that their guns, still south of the river, had no means of seeing, no means of knowing where they were and that consequently they had no means of supporting them. After their steady advance of the last few days the events of the next few hours came as a nasty shock to the Fusiliers.

A cup-shaped spur of high land thrust up from Vailly at its base running north to Jouy and sweeping onwards, rising as it went, to a long road across the topmost ridge. They called it the Chemin des Dames. The 'ladies' of its romantic name were the ladies of the royal court and in the days when France had kings they had bowled along the Chemin des Dames in their cushioned coaches travelling east to Rheims. Now it was the Germans who were bowling along the road, hastening to support the regiments who held the trenches across the spur above the steep surrounding slopes where the Royal Fusiliers were toiling upwards to support their comrades on the open ground above. And they were making heavy weather of it. The slopes were thick with trees and undergrowth, dank with mist, slippy with mud, and swept by shrapnel. It was past seven o'clock before they managed to clear the woods and gain the upper slopes and almost as soon as they took up position the Germans attacked. Concealed by the fog the enemy had entrenched less than two hundred yards beyond the crest. The shelling and machine-gun fire were murderous. Lying in the open on either side of the farm they called Rouge Maison, the Lincolns and the Fusiliers held on, firing into the fog, holding the Germans back, aiming steadily when they could find a target and when they could not setting up such a barricade of fire in front of them that the Germans were discouraged from advancing and fell back to regroup. But it was only a matter of time before they would try again. Grimly conscious of the gaps in their ranks, knowing that their left flank was in the air, listening to the cries and groans of the wounded, peering ahead into the thick wall of mist, the Fusiliers waited for the next move. The next move was an order to counter-attack. It was some comfort that the Northumberland Fusiliers had arrived to support them. And none at all, had they known it, that although the 7th Brigade had received an urgent message to come up with all speed, they had been unable to cross the river by the pontoon bridge at Vailly which the engineers had worked so manfully to complete.

The shellfire was so intense and the shells were falling so accurately in the region of the bridge that it would have been suicide to take the men across. Instead they tramped upstream to the broken railway bridge to make the slow laborious crossing by its single plank. Just as the head of the Brigade reached it they met a stream of British soldiers filing back. The Lincolns, whom Bill Holbrook had watched so gleefully trouncing the Germans a few days earlier, had been forced this time to give way to their superior strength.

Holbrook was dismayed. He was still on the battlefield. The Fusiliers had been forced to fall back when the Lincolns withdrew, first to their original start line, then to a sunken road below the farm of Rouge Maison. Now that he was back in his old job as runner Bill had a fairer idea of the situation than most of his comrades, standing there stiff and tense, rifles poised as they stared into the mist awaiting the next attack. It was not good. The Royal Fusiliers were almost on their own. Even the reserves had been decimated, caught by machine-guns firing from either side as they trudged forward through a beetroot field. Beating their way between the waist-high leaves, tripping over the bulbous roots, stumbling across furrows and sinking deeper into the heavy earth with every dragging step, the Royal Scots Fusiliers had not stood an earthly chance. More than half of them were there still, lying among the tangled stalks, under the rain that still streamed down on the bloodstained furrows where they fell.

If the Germans had renewed their attack the Fusiliers would have been finished too. But they had not, so the Battalion hung on with what was left of their brigade, clinging to the precarious toehold on the slopes above the Aisne. The Germans held on too, and there the line would stay, give or take a yard or so, as the seasons changed and three more autumns and four more springs came to the valley of the Aisne.

The advance was over. In certain places along the extended front the troops had done better. On the left, where the 4th Division had crossed the river on its own initiative on the night of the 12th and pushed on to take the enemy by surprise. On the right at Bourg, where the attack that cost Pat Fitzgerald his life had opened the way for the guns to cross the aqueduct to support the infantry on the other side. There the troops had got far ahead – the 1st Division had got as far as the Chemin des Dames – but they could go no further, for between them there was no coherent line and between the hard-won lodgements beyond the Aisne there were wide gaps, bridged at best by some scattered outposts, at worst by nothing but air.

In its orders to the Army on 13 September, GHQ had repeated the injunction to 'continue the pursuit tomorrow at 6 am and act vigorously against the retreating enemy'. And if, in hindsight, the Staff at GHQ realised their error, if they were troubled by the thought that this now familiar formula contained no implication that time was of the essence, or were struck by the fact that they had given no guidance, no instructions, no specific plan to enable the troops to cross the river as a single fighting unit and no information on the opposition on the other side, they never gave the slightest hint that this was so. There had been no reconnaissance, no patrols sent ahead to send back information on the ruined bridges, to plot possible crossings, to slip across the river to reconnoitre the enemy positions and to estimate his strength. There had been little attempt to garner the vital intelligence on which GHQ might have worked out a concerted plan of action, and even the sketchy reports of the Royal Flying Corps, risking appalling weather in hastily patched-up planes, had been used to ill advantage. Commanders in the field, believing through lack of information to the contrary that the main force of the enemy was still on the run, were left to get their troops across the river as best they could and to blunder into battle when they reached the other side.

On 15 September, in the light of the dire results of the fighting of the previous day, GHQ issued a new instruction. It was terse and unequivocal. It intimated that the Commander-in-Chief desired the Army to entrench itself strongly where it stood and added that he intended to '*assume a general offensive at the first opportunity*'.

The results of the fighting had indeed been dire. The crossing of the Marne had cost the BEF seventeen hundred casualties between 6 and 10 September. In the fighting at the Aisne the First Corps alone had lost three and a half thousand men. Bill Holbrook in the 9th Brigade had lost almost seven hundred of his comrades, and there was hardly a battalion engaged in the fighting that could now muster more than a third of its mobilised strength.

But the Germans too had suffered heavy casualties. They were also suffering the pain of disillusionment. On the evening of 14 September, von Moltke was sacked and replaced by General von Falkenhayn. He was also put in a cruelly humiliating position for he was ordered not to leave Supreme Headquarters. The Germans believed that the news of his sacking would give comfort to their French and British enemies and might also demoralise their own troops on the French front, shaken as they were by the disconcerting reverse in their fortunes.

But, in the first of the strategic retirements which for the best part of four years would continue to irritate the Allies, the Germans had fallen back to some purpose. They had carefully chosen the position above the Aisne as a line of defence and it was well prepared. For more than a week now the BEF had been moving forward into enemy country, away from their own resources, drained and weakened by losses as they went. But the Germans were falling back on their own reserve, on their lines of communication, towards relief and reinforcements and to strong entrenched positions which others had been preparing even as they went. Even so, there was doubt in the mind of the German High Command, and von Falkenhayn's first act as Chief of the General Staff was to send a clear instruction to von Bülow. *If the First Army cannot hold the Aisne valley, it should retire in good time in the general direction of La Fère behind the river valley.*

But the depleted British Army, clinging to precarious footholds, with wide gaps between their positions, with no reserves, with shattered bridges at their backs and no chance of getting the guns across until they were repaired, could do nothing but hang on.

They hung on.

They had done so well, advanced so brilliantly, fought so purposefully, endured so stoically, that no one, from the Commander-in-Chief to the humblest boy soldier in the ranks, regarded the halt on the Aisne as anything more than a temporary setback. In typical British fashion they were half-inclined to blame it on the weather.

The weather had been to some extent to blame. For two vital days, badly needed reinforcements, the long-awaited 6th Division, had been riding out the storm on the Bay of Biscay unable to make landfall at St-Nazaire. But now they were on their way, still sick and groggy after their appalling voyage, packed into troop trains that, for once, took priority over all other traffic on the French railway system.

The shifting of the base to St-Nazaire had been responsible for the difficulties and delay in sending supplies and reinforcements to the Army. It had not been for want of effort, for the effort had been great. In just four days with the help of a fleet of ships and the muscle-power of every available man, more than 60,000 tons of stores, 800 tons of hay, 7,000 horses and 20,000 men had been shifted from the threatened ports in the north far south to St-Nazaire. It was an inconvenience that the Army could well have done without. But the hold-up in supplies was not merely due to the fact that St-Nazaire itself was inconveniently situated a long way from the Army grappling in the field, it was because nothing was ready. Bulk cargoes could hardly be transferred straight from the holds of the ships to the troops at the Front. They must first be unloaded, depots and dumps must be created, the supplies must be sorted into categories and broken down into manageable quantities, camps must be erected for the men who would do these jobs, there must be hospital camps for the wounded on their way back to England and transit camps for the men who arrived on their way to the Front. It was a daunting task. It had to be done at top speed. It required huge manpower and there was no alternative but to hold up some drafts of newly arrived reinforcements to do the job. One of them was

Victor Shawyer who had reached St-Nazaire in a draft destined for the 1st Battalion, The Rifle Brigade, whose losses had been so severe that the matter of his being under-age had been conveniently overlooked.

Bandsman H. V. Shawyer, No. 4142, 1st Bttn., The Rifle Brigade, B.E.F.

Words fail me to describe the chaos that reigned at St Nazaire in mid-September 1914. It was absolutely chronic!

If a whole platoon of quartermaster-generals tried to howl me down when I say that the whole business had panic written all over it, I would still howl back at them – *Panic! Chaos! Panic! Chaos!* No soldier of the rank and file, even in his wildest nightmares, ever dreamed up such a mess of concentrated confusion and misery as there was at that base while I was there. It was awful! The chief sufferer of course was a chap named Tommy Atkins. He always is! The BEF along the battlefront must have taken a hell of a licking to account for the terrible state of affairs at the base. It seemed to me that only one thing showed any sign of planned organisation, and that was that all the tents were going up in orderly lines.

Every day, more and more tents were going up all over the place, and where there were no tents, mountains of stores were growing bigger every day as ships down at the docks unloaded their cargoes.

We were on fatigues all day working on the dumps. Every evening, so much ration was issued to each tent and from that point it was up to us. A lump of raw beef, a smaller lump of bacon, biscuits, tea, sugar and jam was the usual issue, and we had to share it and cook it ourselves as best we could *in our own time*.

After working all day for long hours on heavy work we would return late in the evening to our tents and then have to prepare our own meal with the result that the food was often eaten half raw because there was no time to cook it and because we had no fuel to cook it with. Broken boxes on the ration dumps were almost as valuable as the tins of food the boxes had contained in the first place, and a man who got his hands on one when he was at work held on to it as though his life depended on it. At night there were hundreds of little campfires glowing all over the campsite and men squatting round on their heels cooking the evening meal, with other men hanging around hoping for a chance to use the hot embers after they'd finished.

Personal cleanliness was an almost overwhelming problem. Quite rightly we were forbidden to wash ourselves or our clothing in animal drinking troughs, which left us with only one alternative – the sea. Now ordinary soap won't lather in salt water, so you can image our predicament. As for our clothes, all our shirts and pants and socks ever got was a rinse in sea water and it left them anything but clean. I noticed soldiers who must have had foreign service doing as the dhobis of India did, beating the dirt out of their underwear by smacking it against a boulder. I tried my hand at that with fair results. But oh! the wear and tear. But what else could we do? *Then* we had to dry it!

Then came the crowning misery that turned our camp into crawling bedlam. The weather broke, the rain came down in sheets, day and night. We'd had rain on other occasions but there was always an end to it. *This* lot never stopped.

The mud became deeper and deeper as thousands of men, hundreds of horses and mules and big heavy wagons churned up the slush. Of course with no form of drainage we were floundering around in a sea of mud a foot deep and in some places it must have been nearer two feet deep. And still the rain came sweeping in from the Atlantic, lashing down on our tents perched up there on the high ground overlooking the ocean. At night, lying in our soaking tents, we could hear the sea pounding on the shore. Tent pegs just wouldn't hold firm in such soggy earth and all over camp the tents were collapsing on the poor blighters inside them. Then they had to set to in the pitch dark and the pouring rain to put them up again and try to sort out the chaos! Every night, before rolling ourselves in our blankets, we cleared as much of the mud as possible out of our tent, but by morning most of it had seeped back in again, and we woke up lying in mud.

The only fresh water supplies in the whole of that camp were in the horse-lines, and the further your tent was from horse- or mule-lines the further you had to walk for water. The Rifle Brigade detail were lucky for once. Our tent lines were only a hundred yards away from a remount depot, so we could fill our water-bottles quickly and often. Now those horses really did suffer! Almost every morning animals were being dragged out of the lines because they'd collapsed sick and dying at their picket ropes. And men were going down like flies too with all kinds of sickness.

One day towards the middle of the month we heard away across the other side of our camp boundary the old familiar sound of buglers on the march. Later we heard it was a unit marching to the railway station *en route* for the Front. There were many Light Infantry units in the army but we knew there was a chance that it was our own 3rd Battalion. How we wished we were going too!

It probably *was* their 3rd Battalion – or, if not, it was the Durhams or the Shropshires, for the whole of the 6th Division had at last arrived. On 16 September they reached the Army in the line as they were digging in on the further side of the River Aisne.

The Army could hardly believe it. The reinforcements looked like beings from another world. They were spick and span, their uniforms were neat and clean and bore a full complement of buttons, their haversacks were tidily filled with the regulation requirements and warm greatcoats tidily stowed above, their puttees were unfrayed and neatly rolled, and beneath them – miracle of miracles – were polished, stout-soled boots. The tattered, soaked, bedraggled Mons men gazed at their comrades in wonderment. They simply couldn't get over it. They themselves no longer looked like soldiers; with rags tied round their feet to hold in place the shreds that passed for boots, with several days' growth of beard, wearing a collection of miscellaneous garments to supplement lost kit and ragged uniforms, with sacks around their shoulders for extra warmth and thin protection from the rain, they looked less like an army than like a bunch of ragged tramps.

More than anything they wanted boots – and they ought to have had them. One perturbed Staff Officer at home, with inspired imagination, had ordered that each man of the 6th Division should be issued on departure with an extra pair of boots to be carried round his neck and handed over on arrival to a soldier in the field. Another, whose personality was more inclined towards desk-bound thinking than towards commonsense, had imposed his opinion that the badly needed boots should be dumped when the troops arrived at St–Nazaire. In due course, in due order, when due formalities had been complied with, the proper indents made and the proper forms filled up, they could properly be issued to the troops.

The ponderous bureaucratic mind, bound fast in red tape, nurtured through long well-ordered years of peacetime service, was driving Sir William Robertson to distraction.

There was hardly a man of the original Expeditionary Force who possessed more than the clothing he stood up in – and that was often woefully inadequate. During the long retreat, items which had not been lost or captured had been thrown away because, as 'Wullie' tersely answered when asked to provide an explanation for large numbers of missing caps, blankets, greatcoats, rifles, valises, shirts, shovels, machine-guns, tripods, entrenching tools, 'because they could not be carried'. In his view it was as simple as that. In the view of officialdom it was much more complicated. It was Wullie's immediate duty to see that they were replaced. And if officials did not precisely see it as their duty to thwart him, they were aghast at the very suggestion that they might circumvent long-established procedure by waiving the rules. Stores could only be issued against forms. Forms must be filled up (and in triplicate) with each item meticulously detailed, together with a full account (in the space provided) of the circumstances in which the required article had been lost. Moreover the forms must be completed and signed by no one of lesser authority than the Commanding Officer of each unit concerned. Such were Army Regulations and Army Regulations could not be flouted.

When the Commanding Officers of more than half the battalions in the field had been killed, or wounded or captured, when the troops on the retreat from Mons had not regarded it as a priority to burden themselves with Army forms and a battalion's stationery had been the first thing to be ditched, it was something of a problem to comply with the Army's requirements. Wullie did not even ask his troops to try. It was not in his nature to cajole. He thundered. He thundered in particular in the ear of Colonel Charles Mathew who had the misfortune to be Head of Ordnance Stores in France, and who was obliged, for his own part, to account to financial controllers in the War Office for every item of distribution and expenditure and to produce the paperwork and vouchers to back them up. Colonel Mathew was an understanding man, but the present circumstances defeated him.

Quartermaster-General Sir William Robertson, General Headquarters Staff, B.E.F.

He must often have thought me most irrational and unsympathetic, for I would listen to nothing about his regulations so long as officers and men were going about bareheaded for want of a cap, or had their backs exposed to drenching rain for lack of a coat. I insisted that the missing articles must be replaced at once, whatever the regulations might or might not be, and said that the entire responsibility would be mine if he got into trouble. In the end he played up well and the Army owed him much for the efforts he made to replenish it with the thousand and one things included in the term 'ordnance stores' of which it was short.★

The Army owed 'Wullie' a good deal more than it owed Colonel Mathew. But despite his relentless bullying and obduracy, it was October before some unfortunate units received as much as a pair of socks to ease their calloused feet – let alone a coat to keep out the cold. But even Wullie could do nothing for the officers. Officers provided their own kit, with

★ Quoted from Sir William Robertson's memoirs, *From Private to Field Marshal*, published by Constable & Co. Ltd. in 1921.

the aid of a cash grant from the Army, and no authority existed to provide them with free clothing or to compensate them for the loss of their own. 'They were expected to get it, I imagine,' remarked Sir William Robertson acidly, 'they were expected to get it as in peace, from Savile Row or other places inhabited by the military tailors of London!' Most young officers got it by writing pleading letters to their families at home.

The Army was short of more than clothing. It was difficult to carry out the instructions of the Commander-in-Chief to 'entrench strongly' when there were precious few tools and materials available to do the work, when the sappers were forced to dismantle huts for timber to repair bridges, when wire had to be removed from farmers' fences and laboriously coiled into protective entanglements, when brushwood had to be woven into revetments to support muddy trench walls, when there was little or nothing to dig with and plaintive messages were constantly passing along the line: '*Would A Company please lend C Company the spade?*'

They were entrenched at last but whether the Commander-in-Chief would consider that they were entrenched 'strongly' was a moot point. For want of any other protection, and rather in the manner of their bowmen forebears at Agincourt, they put tripwires in front of the trenches and built palisades of stakes, sharpened with clasp-knives, in the not-too-sanguine hope that enemy soldiers who attempted to approach in darkness would be impaled. Worst of all the Army was short of guns. Forty-two had been captured or destroyed in the three weeks' fighting from Mons to the Aisne. The first priority was to replace them, for until they did most of the hapless infantry must depend on their rifles to protect their positions.

In the third week of September, Clarrie Hodgson was sent with the few survivors of his section to the railhead south of Soissons, to pick up reinforcements and to collect new guns to replace the ones they had lost.

2nd Lt. C.F. Hodgson, 122 Battery, XXVIII Brigade, R.F.A., B.E.F.

There was a big Reinforcement Camp there where all the casualties were being replaced. We were put into decent accommodation, given fresh clothing and food. I was so hungry I could have eaten a . . . well, a scabby-headed child I think! There were some German prisoners there too, a little way off in a wire enclosure. We were kicking our heels, waiting for these guns to arrive and I was talking to three German officers who were boasting how they were going to win the war. They all spoke rather good English. So I was talking to them and I watched a stretcher go past and I could only see this chap's head. Somehow it looked familiar but it didn't dawn on me then. It was quite a while after the stretcher had gone that I suddenly realised that it was Nick, my brother, my twin. So I legged it to a place they were using as a Casualty Clearing Station – just a sort of barrack room, part of a farmhouse or something. As I went in the doctor was just coming out. He gave a terrific start when he saw me, and I said to him, 'Have you seen a chap who looks just like me, coming in on a stretcher just now?' He said, 'Good heavens, yes! I've just examined him. I thought it was *you* when I saw you standing there!' We were identical twins, of course, and this poor man got a terrific shock when he saw me because he'd just left Nick, and Nick was unconscious.

He took me inside to where he was. After a while Nick came round and he said, quite matter-of-fact, 'Well, Clarrie, I'm going to die. I want you to take all my things and see that they get home.' So I took these things – went through his pockets. There was nothing much of course, but there was some money and letters and photos and a few odd personal things. He wasn't wounded, so when I went out I said to the doctor, 'What's the matter with him?' He said, 'We don't actually know. He might possibly have been poisoned, because the Germans have poisoned all the wells round about here. But,' he said, 'we're not sure.' Well, when I got back there was word that the guns had arrived and I knew that meant we'd be going into action. I thought to myself, 'What the hell am I going to do with Nick's things? I'll probably be killed by tomorrow.' So I took them back to him and said, 'Look, it's no good me taking these things. We're going into action any minute.' So I handed them back to him.

I didn't see him again for about two years. But his ailment was a burst appendix. How he survived I don't know. Because it must have taken more than a day to get him back to England.

Nick was taken to St-Nazaire and got safely back to England. Clarrie returned to the Front to get on with the war. At least now they had weapons to fight with, to get a bit of their own back by harassing the Germans and at last they had the means of supporting the infantry when required.

But, for the moment, in the wake of some costly repulses, the Germans did not seem inclined to attack and now that they had received the long-awaited reserves and reinforcements, now that new bridges had been built across the river, now that rations were reaching them with dependable regularity, the infantry in the trenches settled down into something that strongly resembled a routine.

Cpl. W. Holbrook, No. 13599, 4th Bttn., The Royal Fusiliers,
9th Brigade, 3rd Division, B.E.F.

We were up there about a fortnight, if that. We lost quite a number of men up there. But what the Germans did, they'd got one of their big guns trained on this bridge – in the end of course the engineers had got a proper pontoon bridge across so we could get some artillery up. For a few days we couldn't get any artillery up there at all and all they had to rely on was infantry fire. What they used to do was this. The Germans would fire this big gun, fixed right on the bridge. Every quarter of an hour they fired this gun and we used to time ourselves by it in the trenches for sentry go. We'd say, 'Right, you go. That's four shells up now, you've done your hour!' Then we'd count another lot – one, two, three, four. 'Come on, your turn then!' It was as regular as that.

And I saw a funny thing happen there. I saw a horse hit on the new bridge and have his leg sliced off. I saw it cross the bridge on three legs! You can believe it or not. He got over the bridge on three legs, though it seems impossible. I saw another one hit that I thought was odd. He was hit in his side this horse was, lump of shell in its side, and I saw some fellow come along (I don't know if he was a vet or what he was) and stick his hand inside this horse, pull this lump of shell out – the horse is still standing on its feet, mind – and to stop the bleeding he got a lump of straw and plugged it over this hole, and the horse was on its way! Just stuffed the wound up with straw!

Horses and men were equally hard to replace, and the battle casualties had been huge. One of them was Colonel Adrian Duff Gordon, in command of the 1st Black Watch who, as Assistant Secretary of the Committee of Imperial Defence, had master-minded the War Book. Another was Jimmy Naylor's brother, but it was many weeks before Jimmy heard of it. By the time he did he was far from the Aisne, and the fire and excitement of the first weeks of the war had damped down to a dreary monotonous grind in the winter mud of Flanders. By then any diversion was welcome and even the long-outdated news in a crumpled sheet of newspaper packed into a corner of someone's parcel from home was passed eagerly from hand to hand and read to relieve the boredom. Near the foot of the page, in the small print of a long casualty list, Jimmy read the notice of his brother's death.

But that was some way in the future. Meanwhile, on the Aisne, the troops amused themselves by sniping by day and taking turns at night to patrol the darker reaches of the narrow strip of No Man's Land that lay between their trenches and the Germans.

At St-Nazaire some hundreds of miles away, the unfortunate men of the drafts held back to build the base camp were still wallowing in the mud and there was no sign of their being sent to the Front.

Bandsman H V Shawyer, No. 4142, 1st Bttn., The Rifle Brigade, B.E.F.

There were absolutely no amenities of any description. Every mother's son of us badly needed a haircut but, search where we would, we could never find a barber's tent in the whole of that sea of mud. Our hair became so untidy, and Bandsman Knight became so exasperated about it, that eventually he offered to cut my hair if I would return the compliment by cutting his, and damn the appearance of the completed job. At first I felt very dubious, but when I combed my hair and felt it hanging down behind to my tunic collar I realised something had to be done so I agreed. We selected the following Sunday morning to test our skill as hairdressers. That morning, for once, it wasn't raining.

Knight stripped to the waist, put a towel around his neck, sat himself on a couple of bales of new tents which were to be put up next day as an extension to our tent lines, and awaited my first attempt as a barber.

No need to be fussy about cutting hair neat and level. The damn lot was coming off somehow, anyhow. I surprised myself by making a reasonably good job of it. Certainly his hair looked tidy and neater, and after surveying himself in a piece of broken mirror, Knight was satisfied. Then we changed places. Knight put on his shirt and took over the scissors and I sat down on the tents and prepared for the worst.

About twenty minutes later, when I stood up, I was surprised to see a small queue of men lining up for a haircut – men of several units including a couple of kilted Scots. We tried to explain to them that we were not official barbers but they wouldn't listen.

'Sure! We can see you're not experts,' said a Jock, sarcastically, 'but it looks tidy, so do mine.'

'Righto,' said Knight, 'but it'll cost you a franc a time.'

The Jocks growled that it was bloody expensive, but they sat down just the same. We took it in turns to do the cutting, stripping the unkempt hair from their heads in handfuls. This went on till late in the afternoon and for once I was glad when the rain started again. My fingers were numb and it seemed to me that the scissors were losing their keen edge. By that time we'd amassed many francs, and for once we could afford the extortionate prices the French dealers were demanding for food and other things we hadn't been able to afford before.

It was Sunday 20 September, and their comrades at the Front had settled into a routine stable enough to make the idea of holding a church parade very close to the line unremarkable. The Germans held one too. They were only four hundred yards away, close enough for the sound of their brass band to be perfectly audible to the 1st RBs in front of them. The British Riflemen were not familiar with the hymn which the Germans had considered appropriate, *Heil Dir in Siegerkranz* (Hail to Thee in Victory) but the tune to which the Germans sang it was all too familiar. It was the tune of the British National Anthem. They took it as a deliberate taunt and a piece of infernal cheek and demonstrated their displeasure by throwing every available missile, stones, tin cans and, if nothing else came to hand, clods of earth in the direction of the German trenches. They would have dearly liked to treat them to a fusillade for their temerity, but no officer would give the order. So they made the best of it by belting out the English words to the Germans' involuntary accompaniment. *God Save Our Gracious King*, they roared. *Long Live Our Noble King*, they bellowed. *God Save the King*. They went on bawling it for some time after the Germans had stopped. *SEND HIM VICTORIOUS.* . . If victory had depended on decibels, the war would have been won there and then.

Across the Channel on that Sunday morning, the National Anthem was being sung no less fervently, if a touch less indignantly, at church services all over the country. In Gedling Street in the East End of London people arriving for the morning meeting at the Mission Hall were handed typewritten slips setting out the words of an extra verse, newly composed by the Mission Superintendent, Mr Alexander Brown.

> *God bless our splendid men,*
> *Send them safe home again,*
> *God save our men.*
> *Keep them victorious,*
> *Patient and chivalrous,*
> *They are so dear to us;*
> *God save our men.*

There was a school of thought which had felt and was still arguing that the Army should not have been sent to France at all. Britain's great traditional strength lay in her mighty Navy and some believed that the Army should have been held back until a suitable plan had been worked out for a combined operation on the European coast that would effectively punch the Germans out of Belgium and out of France in one knockout blow, rather than feinting and dabbing and ducking away from the enemy's blows as in some amateur boxing match.

Two situations now loomed up which fuelled these arguments and made it look as if their exponents might have been right. The first was the question of the Channel ports. The second was the situation at Antwerp. They were closely linked. Had it not been for the Belgians' refusal to give in (and who could have blamed them if they had?) the Germans would already have marched as boldly into Antwerp as they had marched into Brussels. But the Belgians had not given in, and a full two months after the Germans had forced their frontier and clubbed their way through Belgium to France, Antwerp was still holding out and usefully occupying the attention of two German army corps whose original role had been to push out 'Direction Calais' and which the Germans had been forced to leave behind. They were still there, sitting in front of the forts round Antwerp like cats in front of a mousehole.

Had these additional troops been available to von Bülow and von Kluck as they marched south, they might easily have reached out to the coast and seized the ports of Calais and Boulogne where there were no defences to speak of. In the opinion of certain people (and it made them break out in a mild sweat to think about it) the Expeditionary Force had been saved by the merest fluke. It was farcical, some argued, that all the iron strength of the Navy, its mighty battleships, the formidable fire-power of its mammoth guns, should be employed in nursemaiding the Army – patrolling the long sea-crossing to St-Nazaire, shepherding the ships that carried men and supplies to France, sweeping the Channel and the North Sea like a guard-dog at the gates.

If Antwerp fell, if the Germans reached out, as they easily might and grasped Dunkirk, Calais, Boulogne, Le Havre, much good would St-Nazaire be then, for with such ports at their disposal from which to operate their ships and submarines the Germans might then, without much trouble, reach out to Britain itself.

In the short term, there were practical considerations which made it desirable to winkle the Expeditionary Force out of its position on the Aisne. It was stuck between two French armies, General Maunoury's on its left and that of General Franchet d'Esperey on its right. Now that

General Maunoury had failed to outflank the Germans and to all appearances was stuck as well, there seemed no reason why the BEF should not be transferred to its old position on the left of the French line. There it would be within easier reach of England; it would be closer to its lines of communication and supply, it could be more easily reinforced and, in case of disaster, it could also be more easily evacuated. But in putting the British view to the French, it was not felt necessary to make much of that last point. What was clear to all was the overwhelming advantage of the British force taking up position between the open flank of the Germans and the unprotected ports beyond it on the coast, and to get there before the Germans turned towards the sea themselves. And it was only a matter of time before they did.

Now that the Schlieffen Plan had failed and the first grand project of a swift decisive war seemed doomed to fail also, the Kaiser's thoughts and those of his commanders were working along the same lines and considering the same possibilities that were causing such consternation in certain quarters of Whitehall.

Later, the history books would call it the Race to the Sea. But it began by stealth. Moving the troops slowly, carefully, unit by unit, giving the French time to move up. Marching them by night, hiding them by day so that no prying German aviator would spot that the BEF was on the move. Taking them by devious routes to railheads so that no increase in train traffic would give the show away, and dovetailing their complicated movements as they went to fit in with the French as they moved right across the French lines of communications. For most of them it meant marching fifty miles or more before there was a hope of trains or transport.

After the feat of endurance that had brought the earliest arrivals down from Mons and from Le Cateau, after the 'second wind' that had propelled the BEF across the Marne and back to the Aisne, the spell in the trenches had relaxed them. They had spent the bulk of their strength and drawn heavily on the balance of their fitness. The Tommies were done up and it half-killed them.

The cavalry were the first to leave. Travelling more comfortably on horseback, less exhausted than the infantry behind them, they were delighted to be back on the move. After the initial excitement, and unlike the infantry, they had had a quiet time on the Aisne and they were ready for some diversion. The 12th Lancers found it late on 1 October when they arrived in the Vallée de Nadon. It was a spot that appealed to the officers, for there was a trout hatchery in this pleasant place and, better still, several coverts of pheasants. They blessed the good fortune that had brought them to this auspicious spot on the very day on which the pheasant-shooting season opened, and those who had had the forethought to bring shotguns to

France in the expectation of some sport between the fighting spent the following morning happily potting away. Some of the troopers obligingly acted as beaters. Others indulged in a little fishing for trout. That night both officers and men ate better than they had eaten since they sailed for France. And if some purist, chewing his rubbery share of the spoils in the officers' mess tent, suggested that the birds should by rights have been hung for a fortnight or so to ripen, he was briskly reminded that there was a war on. Besides, who knew where they might be in a fortnight's time or what might have befallen them in the interval.

Where they would be in a fortnight's time was in Flanders and the fates had ordained that, for the British at least, Flanders was to be the cockpit and the crucible and the Calvary of the war.

Chapter 21

In Flanders, the presence of the BEF was awaited with some eagerness, for the Germans too were stretching out feelers and the only people at present who stood between them and the sea were the Queen's Own Oxfordshire Hussars and a certain Commander Sampson, and until the recent arrival of the Hussars, Sampson might fairly have been said to have been holding the entire sector single-handed. He had done so by bluffing the Germans and already his exploits were legendary.

Commander Sampson RN had arrived at Ostend on 27 August to carry out reconnaissance duties and to support a detachment of Royal Marines with a few aeroplanes of the Royal Naval Air Service, a couple of motor cars armoured Heath Robinson-style with 'home-made' steel plates and one machine-gun. It had been a useful diversion on the German flank and when news of the landing reached them, when they heard that the British were 'digging in at Ostend', it had made the German Command pause to reflect and consider caution. The Marines had indeed begun to dig trenches, but they were soon abandoned. The BEF, at that time still trekking inexorably to the south, was drawing further and further away, and in the circumstances more sanguine reflection concluded that three hundred Marines would do little to protect Ostend in the event of a determined attack by the Germans. Three days after they disembarked the Marines were withdrawn and sailed for home. Commander Sampson and his squadron stayed behind.

They stayed at the urgent request of General Bidon in command of the French garrison at Dunkirk, and beyond the obligation to carry out reconnaissance by such means as he could and to 'cooperate with the French', Sampson's brief was vague. He viewed it as *carte blanche* to take on the Germans.

His first chance came on 4 September at Cassel. The town of Cassel lay on the summit of a steep hill, a high volcanic outcrop that towered above the flat coastal plain of Flanders. The hill was a prominent landmark and an observer enjoying the famous view from its summit could as easily see Ypres some twenty miles to the east as Dunkirk fifteen miles away on the coast, and even Lille thirty miles off on the western horizon. Many travellers did stop to enjoy the view for they could hardly avoid Cassel. The main road to the coast climbed up to the summit and down again to the foot of the hill on the other side. The reason for this impractical piece of highway-planning in the middle of an otherwise flat plain lay far back in the mists of time in the days when Cassel was a fortress, and it was bizarre enough to have found a place in nursery lore. Cassel was known to every lisping tot, if not by name, at least as the place where the Grand Old Duke of York who had ten thousand men had 'marched them up to the top of the hill and marched them down again'. The Old Duke had had no choice but to march them down again since no other route was available. The German Staff car travelling from Bailleul had no choice either. Nor had Commander Sampson.

Sampson did not have ten thousand men. He had three. Two were driving the reconnaissance cars in which they were patrolling. The function of the third was to fire their solitary machine-gun in case they ran into trouble. They had attracted enthusiastic attention when they stopped in Cassel to scan the surrounding countryside for signs of marauding Germans and, having left their cars in the street in the care of the machine-gunner, they were on their way up a narrow lane that led to the highest vantage point when a breathless messenger caught up with them. There had been a telephone call from the post office at Bailleul and the Mayor had sent a clerk hot-foot to warn the British officers that a carload of German officers had just passed through the town square and had taken the road to Cassel. Bailleul was not twelve miles away. They would be here in minutes.

It would have been child's play to ambush a single motor car in the narrow twisting streets. Sampson was sorely tempted, but he was reluctant to put the townspeople at risk and a fight in Cassel itself, if it ended badly, might well bring down reprisals on civilian heads. He would meet the enemy in the open.

The two cars roared down the hill on the Bailleul road and halted at the bottom just as the Germans came into sight approaching fast on the long straight road. They set up the machine-gun, waited until the car was just five hundred yards away, and then they let them have it.

The German car was a large open tourer, it contained six officers, and even at a distance Sampson and his men could sense their panic as the stream of bullets smacked into the car. The Germans must have had revolvers but if they fired them the shots went far wide of their mark; Sampson's machine-gunner quite evidently found his. The car veered wildly, stopped and began reversing erratically down the road. The driver had some difficulty in turning it. It was a large car, the highway was not wide and it took several minutes of stopping, starting, reversing and

manoeuvring before the Germans were able to open up the throttle and
speed back towards Bailleul.

The British officers watched with glee and fired a few more rounds for
luck.

*Wing-Cmdr. C. E. Sampson, Eastchurch Sqdn., Royal Naval Air
Service.*

We had a tremendous reception from the inhabitants of Cassel, who
had enjoyed a splendid view of our little engagement from their
commanding position on the hilltop. I was pleased that they had seen
Germans running away, as it would remove from their minds that
1870 feeling which the Germans still produce in the minds of civilian
Frenchmen. This fight gave us a prestige in the villages far greater
than its result called for. Probably the six German officers reported
that they had run up against tremendous odds.★

It transpired that they had done exactly that. Not long after Sampson
returned another excited telephone call from the postmaster at Bailleul
reported that two officers had been wounded, that the car had halted briefly
in Bailleul before darting off towards Lille and that very soon afterwards
all the other Germans had gone too. Best of all, they had gone in such
haste that they had been forced to abandon a whole wagonload of wine
and champagne they had filched from shops and houses. Even as he spoke
the square was full of happy citizens who had reclaimed their property (or
in some regrettable cases helped themselves to the property of others) and
were happily drinking it in celebration.

The unsuspecting Germans had been distinctly shaken. Two days later,
at General Bidon's request, Wing-Commander Sampson made his way
towards Lille and, learning when they reached the suburbs that a large force
of Germans had just moved out, went boldly into the town centre.

*Wing-Cmdr. C. E. Sampson, Eastchurch Sqdn., Royal Naval Air
Service.*

We got through the crowd and took the cars into the courtyard of
the Préfecture, lining them up abreast facing the square. Practically
the whole of Lille appeared to be here. They were most enthusiastic,
cheering, singing, and shouting out, *Vive l'Angleterre!* I did everything I
could to impress the people with our discipline and military behaviour,

---

★ From Wing-Commander Sampson's account written after the war.

placing four of my men as sentries in a line behind the railings and one man standing by each machine-gun. Our sentries stood like Guardsmen, and even when beautiful French girls came on the scene and sponged their faces and brushed the dust off their clothes, they stood like lumps of granite.

I went inside to see the Préfet. He was pleased to see us and said that our arrival had reassured the town to a most extraordinary extent and demonstrated to the people that they were not entirely at the mercy of the enemy. He told me that the Germans had been quite worried over the fight at Cassel, and they had got the idea into their heads that there was a large force of English round about Cassel. He said there were about fifty French and a few English wounded in the town, left there by the Germans, and if I signed a proclamation to say that I had taken the town they could be evacuated to Dunkirk, otherwise the town would be held responsible.

This suggestion strongly appealed to Sampson's independent spirit. He had a shrewd suspicion that the Germans would shortly be back and he knew very well that he himself must return to Dunkirk within the hour, but he drew up the proclamation with a flourish.

To the Authorities of the City of Lille:
I have this day occupied Lille with an armed
English and French Force.

Signed: C. E. Sampson,
Commander, R. N.
Officer in Command of English
Force at Dunkirk.

He added this true but misleading description of his function with the deliberate intention of giving the Germans the impression that the British were there in force, and he was perfectly confident that the Germans soon knew all about it. He drove off to a wild ovation with the satisfaction of knowing that the Préfet had already ordered the notice to be printed and posted in prominent positions all across the city. Sampson and his men were pelted with souvenirs as they left and by the time they were three streets away the car was full of flowers, chocolate, even cigarettes. The only episode which struck a discordant note in an otherwise satisfactory afternoon was when one over-excited spectator, carried away by the general enthusiasm, threw a bottle of beer which dealt Commander Sampson a severe blow on the jaw. As he himself grew fond of remarking over the next few days, 'the man must have had German sympathies'. Sampson enjoyed a joke.

He was also enjoying his war and for two more weeks he ranged far and wide raiding, harassing and annoying the Germans at every opportunity and never missing a chance to lead them up the garden path. Sampson on his own had been worth a whole division and his admirers maintained that he alone had bluffed the Germans into keeping their distance. Now he was alone no longer. On 22 September a fresh detachment of Marines arrived and with them, as their Divisional Cavalry, came The Queen's Own Oxfordshire Hussars.

It was not mere chance that gave the Oxfordshires the distinction of being the first Territorial troops to embark for France. It was the influence of the First Lord of the Admiralty, Winston Churchill. The Marines were his baby. He had agreed to send them to Dunkirk at the request of Lord Kitchener, to hold the fort – quite literally – until the BEF moved north. But he did stipulate that a detachment of cavalry should go with them to provide a protective screen, to ride out on reconnaissance, to act as the eyes and ears of the Marines. Churchill was well aware that there was no cavalry to spare. But there *was* Yeomanry, and there was one particular regiment of Yeomanry in which Churchill took more than a passing interest – The Queen's Own Oxfordshire Hussars. The tradition and history of the Churchill family had been bound up with the Regiment for more than a hundred years, an ancestor had been one of its founders, most of the officers were Churchill's personal friends and his own brother, Major Jack Churchill, was in command of D Troop. It was only natural that when cavalry was required, the First Lord should request their services and that Lord Kitchener should be happy to let him have his way.

If there were those in their native Oxfordshire who referred to them derisively as 'The Agricultural Cavalry', the Hussars seldom rose to the bait. They had a high opinion of themselves and were quite sure that anyone who was not lucky enough to be a member of their brotherhood was a mere hobbledehoy and an object of pity. In 1908 they had been co-opted into the Territorial Force, but they considered themselves to be more than a cut above most Territorials who had not even existed five years ago. Their regiment had been raised in 1798 and everyone from the Colonel and his officers in their elaborate frogged uniforms to young Bill Huggins, the newest and rawest trooper, knew its history and was proud of it.

Lce/Cpl. Edward Organ, No. 1745, A Sqdn, 1st Troop, Queen's Own Oxfordshire Hussars, B.E.F.

I joined in September 1911. My first camp was a Brigade camp at Blenheim. On the Whit Monday we had a Sports Day. There was tent pegging, there was sprint races for troopers' horses, sprint races for officers, lemon slicing (that's galloping and slicing suspended lemons with a sword) and all kinds of sports. All our girl friends came for the Sports Day. Well, there was a break for lunch and we decided to go for a walk over High Lodge – that's a part of Blenheim beyond Monument Plain. There was a gate across the road where I was walking with my future wife and two gentlemen opened the gate for us and we went through. They raised their hats and of course I recognised who they were. It was Winston Churchill and King Emmanuel of Portugal. They smiled and said 'Good afternoon', very affable. Churchill was a jovial sort of man, but you couldn't call him a real soldier. As a matter of fact, without spilling any beans, you couldn't have called any of our officers real soldiers. They were more like country gentlemen, and most of us were countrymen ourselves, sons of tenant farmers and people of that sort.

It was true that the officers exercised their commands with a certain degree of informality which would not have been tolerated in the disciplined regular cavalry or, at the other end of the scale, in a battalion of the despised Territorials they called 'The Saturday Afternoon Soldiers'. Even after the war had begun General Peyton on a tour of inspection found it difficult to contain his wrath at their insouciance. 'Why is that man standing over there?' he demanded of one unfortunate officer after a particularly botched-up manoeuvre. This officer was the son of a lord. He was hot, harassed, flustered and far too irritated to recollect the courtesies due to his military betters. He replied through gritted teeth and with warm feeling, 'Because he is a *damned* fool!' The General was not amused. 'How dare you, sir! Do you call yourself a soldier?' He was not mollified by the reply. 'No, I don't! I'm a stockbroker.'

Most officers were landowners or the sons of landowners who had taken up some calling or profession. Besides Jack Churchill (who was the stockbroker) there were solicitors, bankers and merchants. The Colonel himself was a cloth manufacturer, Major Fiennes and Captain Fleming were Members of Parliament, Lieutenant Hutchinson was an Oxford don. Many owned estates in their own right or were heirs to substantial properties. Five of them had served in the South African War a dozen years before.

Tpr. Percy Batchelor, No. 1902, D Squadron, Queen's Own Oxfordshire Hussars, B.E.F.

Lieutenant Villiers' home was at Middleton Park and we used to do cavalry drilling there and I used to go on a Saturday afternoon and take my own horse. We were lined up in a long line and then we had to left turn, right turn, swing round in this long line and change into fours. It was a matter of this mounted infantry type of thing they used to do in the South African War. I'd only joined up in April 1914. It just took my fancy. I was going to market one Friday and I met Mr Fane in the bank and I asked him if I could go in. He was one of the officers and very keen and he had me sworn in by the local JP right away.

At the end of May we went to camp on Salisbury Plain – riding around nearly all day practising attacks on villages, all that kind of thing, for a whole fortnight. I thought it was a pretty good time! Of course, when the war broke out we were called up right away, although we were only Territorials. It was a quarter to seven in the morning when the postman brought the notice and it said that I'd got to appear at Woodstock at seven o'clock. Well, I didn't get there until nearly one o'clock, because I had to go to Bicester Fair to get some sheep. I did that, hurried back, collected my kit and went back to Bicester in the old pony and trap to get the train for Woodstock.

I didn't take my horse because the notice didn't say anything about taking your horse. Some fellows went back home later to fetch their own horses, but I couldn't because by then the Government had commandeered mine! I was handed out a big mount, a proper rough sort of horse and I'd never seen the like of him before! We were doing drill, galloping along across the park with the officers leading out in front and, like it or not, I found myself riding up alongside this officer! He shouted at me. 'What do you think you're doing here?' he said. I said, 'I can't hold him, Sir.' 'Can't *hold* him!' He couldn't understand a man that couldn't hold a horse. But I'd never ridden such a horse before – he had such a hard mouth. He didn't buck or kick or anything, but he made a noise in his throat. He wasn't sound really; he was a roarer. Whoever had him was lucky to sell him to the Army and get rid of him. I don't know what they got for him – but he wasn't worth much!

Tpr. G. H. Huggins, No. 2178, Queen's Own Oxfordshire Hussars, B.E.F.

I got a horse that was blind. We were there on the sands at Dunkirk having exercises and they gave the '*Form Squadron*' and then '*Charge*'. So we went along hell for leather, charging. And of course he could hear all the noise – you can imagine it, with the five hundred horses thundering along the sands – and away he went. Bolted. He was stone blind! So that was the end of him.

I could ride all right, being brought up on a farm, although at the time I was working as an office boy in a solicitor's office. I didn't get into the Hussars until after the war started. I was dying to get in! I went along the day after my seventeenth birthday – that was on 26 August – and on the advice of Sergeant Thomas, who was a friend of our family, I gave my age as nineteen.

I went through the riding school. That was all right. Then I had to go up to the rifle range for a test – five rounds at two hundred yards and five rounds at five hundred. Well, with the first five rounds I had three bulls and two inners. The instructor there says, 'Have you ever used a rifle before?' I said, 'No, but I've shot a few rabbits, and *they* didn't get much bloody chance!' So I was in. It was only a matter of days after that we had reveille in the *middle of the night* and we were ordered to saddle up in full marching order. And in not much more than an hour we were off.

Lce/Cpl. Edward Organ, No. 1745, A Sqdn., 1st Troop, Queen's Own Oxfordshire Hussars, B.E.F.

We finished up at Southampton boarding a ship. I can tell you it took all day to sling the horses up on the deck, but we eventually got aboard. All the horses were down in the hold, right down in the bottom of the ship.

Of course they were stifling hot down there in September and there was terrible ammonia fumes from these horses. We were about three days on the way and the horses were all sick. There was mucus coming out of their eyes and noses because of being confined in an atmosphere of nearly a hundred degrees and they were all overcome by fumes. Eventually we got into Dunkirk. It took a long time to unload at a jetty like a long pier. We connected the head ropes of the horses to the uprights of a canopy along this long pier. They stretched for nearly half a mile!

They had a royal welcome from the people of Dunkirk who were already revelling in the widely lauded exploits of Commander Sampson. Now with the arrival of the Oxfordshire Hussars, despite the nasty situation in Belgium a matter of miles away, they felt that the war was as good as over. The local paper reflected their enthusiasm.

There is but one destination for strollers in Dunkirk; that is the immense English camp on the Glacis de Rosendael. Approaching by the devastated square, or by the avenues denuded of their trees, people make their way to this little town of tents which, from the distance, reminds one of a big American touring circus. The inhabitants, wearing the little brass badges the soldiers have given them in buttonholes or pinned to bodices, keep going back to chat with them by their tents where the men express, by means of gestures, how they regret being away from their own beds and their own family circles.

  'I will come back,' say the soldiers to their hosts, and the moment they are free they take the opportunity of returning the visits, to enjoy the charms of family life again – now reserved exclusively for these horsemen of the Yeomanry.

But there was one entertainment the newspaper was too delicate to mention.

Lce/Cpl. Edward Organ, No. 1745, A Sqdn., 1st Troop, Queen's Own Oxfordshire Hussars, B.E.F.

We were camped on this long promenade place, and on the Sunday the people of Dunkirk all came up to see us. Very few of us could speak any word of French – I only knew copy-book French that I'd learned a bit of at school. Well, having a lot of men on this promenade, we had to have latrines. They were just rolls of hessian put round from pillar to pillar and behind them there were latrines – just poles and buckets. There was about fifteen hundred of us, so they were in use all day long. The Dunkirk people made a hell of a fuss of us, brought us bottles of wine and food, and I was with a chap called Bill Hayter, who was a farrier, and one Frenchwoman says to him, 'What's behind there?' pointing to the hessian. He said to me, 'What did she say?' I said, 'She wants to know what's behind the hessian?' He said, 'You tell her it's prisoners of war.' So I said, '*Prisonniers de guerre.*' Well, these women, of course, they *would* go and peep behind the hessian to see these prisoners, and of course what they saw was a row of bare bottoms! Well, they *did* have a laugh – you know what Frenchwomen are. And of course they went and told all their friends, and all afternoon there was *everybody* having a peep. Because they were all up there, it being a Sunday.

The Marines, subjected to an altogether tighter discipline, and encamped further off, did not join in these revels. Soon, they all moved inland, the Marines to kick their heels at Cassel, the Hussars to Hazebrouck, where they busied themselves patrolling, probing, diligently performing the duties of reconnaissance and, egged on by Commander Sampson, searching for the flanks of the Germans. They enjoyed some lively skirmishes. Thanks to the wide publicity the enemy had learned of their arrival and, drawing the logical but erroneous conclusion that cavalry was unlikely to be operating alone, German Intelligence believed (as it later transpired) that the Queen's Own Oxfordshire Hussars were merely the spearhead of a much larger British force. The fact was that after 3 October, when the Royal Marine Brigade was ordered north to Antwerp, the Oxfordshire Hussars enjoyed the doubtful privilege of being the only British troops between the Germans and the sea. The BEF was on its way from the Aisne, but it still had a long way to go.

In the four battalions of the Royal Marine Brigade, some seven hundred men were raw recruits and few of them had ever fired a rifle. The rest were tough, experienced men – but they were not in the first bloom of youth. Every man was an old campaigner with more than twenty-one years' service to his credit and one much-medalled platoon consisted entirely of pensioner sergeants and colour sergeants. Until their honourable retirement they had terrorised and disciplined several generations of recruits and none of them took kindly to the unaccustomed role of underdog. The air was often blue with acrimony and only their common enthusiasm at the prospect of fighting the Germans prevented outright insurrection in their bewhiskered ranks.

In ordering the Marines to Antwerp, no one was under any illusion that they would be able to provide much more than moral support, but even that was better than nothing, for the situation was coming to a head. The Germans had started bombarding the outer forts with massive siege guns brought up from Maubeuge and no one would have cared to wager on how long the garrison at Antwerp would be able to hang on. But hang on they must. Antwerp, for the Belgians, was the last resort. It was to serve as such that her two rings of fortresses dating from Napoleon's time had been reconstructed fifty years before and since the first day of the invasion, with 'the last resort' in mind, engineers had been working against time to improve them.

Now the Germans were holding Antwerp by the throat. Only the remnants of the Belgian army (some 65,000 men) and a garrison of elderly Civil Guards remained to defend the city with the government and the King within its walls. It was a despatch from Britain's Ambassador in Antwerp that caused the British Government to jump. It arrived on 2 October, the information it contained was passed on in good faith but it was quite untrue and when he heard of it, it infuriated King Albert of the Belgians. The King, it said, had decided to retire to Ostend the following day and he would take his army with him. This 'news' quite naturally caused consternation at the War Office who saw at one fell swoop the doom of Antwerp, the fall of Belgium and the loss of the Channel ports. Something must be done.

The Marines, who were already in northern France, could be sent post-haste as an emergency measure, and the 7th Division was almost ready to embark. But the BEF was still more than a hundred miles away and with the best will in the world their progress to the north could not be speeded up. What they needed was time.

It was Winston Churchill's idea to send the Royal Naval Division to Antwerp. There was no one else to send.

The men of the Royal Naval Division were delighted. It hardly worried them that since the arrival of their rifles a week ago, few of them had benefited from more than two days' instruction in the art of firing them, that they had little idea how to comport themselves as infantry, that they had neither transport nor equipment – no mess-tins, no water-bottles, no ammunition pouches, no entrenching tools – that only every other man possessed a greatcoat and that, for want of more conventional means of carrying them, those who had bayonets were obliged to stick them in their gaiters or, at a pinch, in their trouser pockets. The only qualification they could boast was a certain proficiency in seamanship which, in most cases, merely meant that they could row a boat or tie a knot. Nevertheless they regarded themselves as *bona fide* sailors and after they had disembarked at Dunkirk they were stung by the indignity of being forced to complete the journey to Antwerp by train. It was a circuitous, weary ride and it took a full thirty-six hours. Antwerp, argued the sailors, was a port. Why then must they be subjected to the humiliation of travelling overland like landlubbers when a flotilla of His Majesty's ships could have sailed them straight to Antwerp and in fine style. It made no sense.

Winston Churchill agreed with them. In addition to being First Lord of the Admiralty, Churchill was an incorrigible buccaneer and nothing would have pleased him more. The rub was that Antwerp lay far up the River Schelde. The mouth of the river and a large part of the coastline south of it belonged to neutral Holland, and Britain had gone to war to defend the principle that neutrality must not be violated. So the trains dragged north and the sailors grumbled, and as the slow hours passed the situation in Antwerp grew ever more precarious. The first train arrived early in the morning of 6 October. The men of the Royal Naval Brigade were stiff and cramped and weary, but they soon forgot that in the exhilaration of a wild welcome. The anxious citizens of Antwerp greeted them as saviours.

It was the second time in a matter of weeks that John Macdonald had enjoyed the unusual sensation of being the object of admiration but on the first occasion, in the streets of his native Glasgow on the day of mobilisation, he had been more irritated than thrilled by the experience. Thirty men of the RNVR had marched a mile to the docks from their drill hall in Scotland Street, and since the Navy had been mobilised on a Sunday, crowds of curious neighbours and passers-by had been on the streets to see them go. One enthusiastic patriot was not content to cheer them from the pavement. To the amusement of the onlookers and to Johnny's mortification, his ten-year-old brother chose to join the march, keeping in step with only an occasional hop, echoing the commands of the Petty Officer in a ringing treble, deaf to muttered threats and imprecations that grew more colourful with every stride. Hugh 'fell out' reluctantly as the contingent marched through the dock gates and they closed firmly in his face. 'Cheerio Johnny,' he shouted. 'See you don't get drowned!' His brother was scarlet with fury and embarrassment. 'Away home, you wee bugger, or I'll leather you!' It hardly qualified as a Soldier's Farewell.

Macdonald was not a soldier. He was not even a sailor. He was an electrician but like many young men who lived within sight and sound of the Clyde he had joined the Royal Naval Volunteer Reserve, changed from overalls to bell-bottoms on two evenings a week and enjoyed weekends of healthy exercise with the occasional bonus of a summer cruise in one of His Majesty's ships. The men of the RNVR looked on themselves as members of the Senior Service and the discovery that the Royal Navy could find no use for their services had not pleased them. It had been a severe come-down for the part-time sailors to find themselves involuntarily remustered as infantrymen in the newly formed Royal Naval Brigade, and they were not much mollified by the fact that they had been allowed to keep their uniforms and that their battalions had been given names, like Drake, Nelson, Hood, Anson, and so on, appropriate to naval tradition. Now, marching through Antwerp, the warmth of their reception, the sense of purpose and the sensation of being actually at the seat of war with the sound of the guns grumbling not far distant, more than compensated for the indignity. Breakfast was dished out in an open space in the middle of the town and before they fell in to march the six miles to the line of fortresses beyond it a few men took the opportunity to scribble a last few lines to their families at home. Macdonald pencilled his on a picture postcard of Canterbury Cathedral. He had purchased it during a few hours of liberty four days earlier, little thinking that it would be posted in Belgium.

Tuesday

Dear Mother,
This will perhaps be my last PC for a while. We are just going into the trenches. The Germans are only 7 miles away so we will be in the thick of it. The Belgian people gave us a great reception. They showered cigars, fruit and buns on us. My hands are just about shaken off. Love to everybody, Goodbye,

John.

The word 'Goodbye' was not likely to reassure his anxious mother when, some days later, the postcard reached 202 Weir Street on the south side of Glasgow. For the rest of the war she was tormented by two worries. One was for the safety of her eldest son, the second was of falling foul of the law. Like many provident housewives she had laid in a sack or two of flour in case of shortage and her younger children mercilessly teased her with reminders of the dire penalties that awaited unpatriotic hoarders. She was almost relieved when she shook the last few ounces from the bottom of the last sack to bake her last batch of all-white soda scones. That was in the autumn of 1916 and her sailor son was then still soldiering in the land-locked Battle of the Somme.

Despite the stiff resistance of the Belgian garrison and the stubborn efforts of the handful of Royal Marines, the battle for Antwerp was lost even before the two Royal Naval Brigades arrived. Already the defenders had been pushed back to the inner ring of fortresses only a few thousand yards from the outer edge of the city, and the city had spread since the forts were constructed. Fine houses and villas, pleasure gardens and coppices, cottages and orchards reached out towards the pleasant countryside, between the inner forts and stretching even beyond them in lush and prosperous profusion. The authorities might have paused to think that this provided useful camouflage, but they did not. Inspecting the defences, noting with consternation that many of the guns thrusting from the cupolas above the squat stone forts were trained towards barns and orchards and woods and that nowhere was there clear observation or a clear field of fire beyond, they had ordered the engineers to remove the obstructions. But the engineers had done more than clear the area: they had reduced it to a state of devastation. Now the guns stood fair and square, pointing towards the enemy from land as naked and as flat as a parade ground. The forts once hidden in the landscape could now be seen for miles. Had the Belgians set up a giant target they could hardly have done more to assist the German gunners to pinpoint their defences. To make things easier still, black smoke belching out each time a shot was fired hung in clouds round the barrels of the antique guns long after the shells had left them. It puffed backwards too. With no fans or ventilation to clear the fumes, the men inside the forts were half suffocated. Coughing, retching, choking, gasping for air, not many of them could stand it for long.

The trenches that ran between the forts were mere ditches, a foot or two at most in depth and the Royal Naval Division was not impressed with them. They gave no protection, there were no dugouts, no shelter but for an occasional stretch of muddy bank. The sailors set to work to build flimsy wooden barricades, to construct loopholed niches, to fill sandbags, to do the best they could to strengthen the positions. It wasn't much. Nor was there much they could do to save Antwerp. But they could try at least to save the Belgian army, to hang on long enough to allow it to withdraw, long enough to keep the escape route open, to keep the Germans at bay, above all to keep them from dispersing and striking out to cut off the narrow corridor strip of Belgian territory beyond the Schelde. That corridor was the one way out. It was the way home.

When the big German guns were at last dragged forward, when the shellfire lifted from the forts and began to bombard the city itself, when three key forts had fallen, when fires in Antwerp were blazing at their backs, it was time at last to go. It was the evening of 8 October. The Marines had been there for four days. The Royal Naval Division had held on for thirty-six hours. There was nothing to be gained by staying longer.

Chaplain H. Clapham Foster, 2nd Brigade, R.N. Division, B.E.F.

In order to cross the Schelde, we were forced to pass by the blazing petroleum tanks at Hoboken. The road was narrow, but it was the only road left. The fumes were overpowering and the intense heat proved too much for some of the men. The flames at times blew right across the road, and large German shells were falling in amongst the tanks at the rate of four a minute. Sometimes a shell would burst with a terrific report in the boiling oil, and flames shot up to the height of two hundred feet. As we approached the blazing tanks it was like entering the infernal regions. The burning oil had flooded a field on one side of the road and dead horses and cattle were frizzling in it.

'Now boys,' an officer shouted, 'keep your heads and run through it!' And we did – but I don't know how we did it!

Once we'd got past the oil tanks the road was sheltered for a hundred yards, but then for about a thousand yards again it was exposed to the enemy's fire. We were ordered to run at the double over this bit of road, and most of us were fortunate enough to reach the pontoon bridge over the river.

They marched all night and it was past dawn on 9 October before they found the trains that would carry them south-west down that narrow strip of land that passed so perilously close in places to the Germans.

The Governor of Antwerp had already asked for a ceasefire. On the 10th he formally surrendered the city to the Germans. They were astounded, and not a little annoyed, to find that the Belgian army had got clean away.

That day, what was left of the Royal Naval Division began to re-embark for home. They sailed from Ostend and they sailed into a furious row. Questions were asked in the House of Commons and the correspondence columns of daily newspapers erupted in a fury of letters to the editors. Most of them heaped calumny on the head of Winston Churchill, holding him responsible for the ill-fated expedition, reviling him for sending the untrained men of the Royal Naval Division like lambs to the slaughter and uselessly committing them to a lost cause.

Apart from its battle casualties it was a discomfiting fact that, although only 57 had been killed and 138 wounded, the infant Royal Naval Division had returned minus two and a half thousand men. Almost a thousand, a whole trainload, had fallen into the hands of the Germans. The rest had simply been left behind. The order to quit the trenches had not reached them. In the dark, the shelling, the confusion, it was several hours before they realised that everyone else had gone. By the time they had struggled into the burning city and out again through the press of frantic refugees, by the time they had crossed the river and marched aimlessly all night without orders and direction, the last of the trains had gone and with them their only chance of escape. They could not have struggled on much further.

Able Seaman J. S. Bentham, Benbow Bttn., 1st Brigade, R.N. Division, B.E.F.

We were on our own, my platoon. It was a ghastly march because everyone was very hungry and very tired and we didn't dare go to sleep when we stopped for a rest in case we might be left behind and find ourselves taken by the Germans. The atmosphere in Antwerp was absolutely chaotic, crowds of refugees taking up most of the road and spy mania everywhere. We guessed that because we even saw a few corpses hanging from lamp posts. Terrible. Eventually we got to the Schelde, but we'd missed the bridge and we'd no idea how to get across. After a long search someone found a boat and somehow or other we all crammed into it. It was a wonder we got to the other side! We had one little midshipman with us, he was only about fifteen, and this boy had a revolver. He was sitting there in the boat where we were all squeezed up and he was holding this revolver in his hand. We had a few old chaps with us, and I remember one elderly man of the Royal Fleet Reserve leaning across to him. He said, 'Give that to me, Sonny, before you shoot someone!'

When we got to the other side we started to march again. We Benbows really felt that we'd been let down, because we had received no information about any retirement whatsoever. As we drew away from the crowds we joined up with other small parties like ourselves and at long last we came to the Dutch frontier. We found our Commodore there and other officers and many, many other men all footsore and very, very weary like ourselves. After a long wait (while I presume the officers were parleying with the Dutch officials) we were ordered to hand in our rifles. We were told that the Dutch would let us through and give us twenty-four hours to get out of the country. It was all poppycock, of course, but we were very glad to take off our packs and relax on the straw in a large shed alongside the railway where they said we could rest for an hour or two. But some men wouldn't have it. They went off to try to find a way through Belgium themselves. We heard later that they were picked up by the Germans and made prisoners of war for the duration. The rest of us in the 1st Brigade – mostly of Hawke and Benbow and Collingwood Battalions – were interned.

The Dutch people were extremely kind to us while we were waiting, giving us food and drink which we very urgently wanted, and it was the same at all the railway stations when they eventually shipped us up to Gröningen in the north of Holland. But we were very fed up all the same.

At home in Britain, in a few days' time the men who had returned from Antwerp would start training in earnest. Next time they crossed the Channel they would be better equipped to fight the war. Meanwhile, oblivious to all but aching exhaustion, they slept. Some, like John Macdonald, managed to stay awake long enough to write brief letters and post them at the Field Post Office tent. Macdonald pencilled his on a leaf torn from his pocket diary. It read *Safe and well. Love, John.* It wasn't much, but it was all his anxious family wanted to know.

It took a little longer for reassuring postcards to arrive from Holland. The Red Cross had dished them out to some fifteen hundred sailors who languished in the barracks at Gröningen, hastily vacated to serve as an internment camp. They wrote them with mixed feelings. It was true that they were safe and out of danger, that they at least had not been captured by the enemy, but already the long inactive days were dragging. The Hawkes and the Collingwoods and the Benbows had the distinct impression that however long it lasted it would seem a long, long war.★

★ Bentham escaped in the spring of 1915 and succeeded in making his way back to the United Kingdom. He was commissioned and served for the rest of the war with the Hood Battalion. His experiences in 1916 are related in *Somme* (Michael Joseph, 1984) by the same author.

Chapter 22

The Marines and the sailors had not saved Antwerp – but they had bought time. Time for the Belgian army to get away. Time for the Expeditionary Force to reach further north. Time for the 7th Division to get into position, to start moving south to secure the left of the line and to reach out to the River Yser and to Ypres. There they would join hands on their right with the BEF as it took up its new line and link up on their left with the French and the Belgians who would extend it to the sea.

The 7th Division had started out from Lyndhurst Camp for Belgium on 4 October but it had taken them three full days to get there. In the frequently expressed opinion of gunners like Charlie Burrows, the infantry had it easy when the Army was on the move. All they had to do was pick up their kit, fall in and march off. For the gunners it meant a hundred back-breaking tasks, preparing the guns, the limbers, the ammunition, the transport wagons, the horses, manhandling them into the trains, heaving them off again at the docks and starting all over again to load them on board the ship. All this had been accomplished in the course of one long sleepless night. There had been a certain amount of swearing but the gunners were too full of excitement, too pleased to be on their way at last, to grumble very seriously. Charlie was not normally of a literary turn of mind but he had made up his mind to keep a diary to record his part in the adventure ahead and two days earlier he had purchased a suitable notebook in the post office at Lyndhurst. During the voyage, which was disconcertingly longer than anyone had expected, he had ample time to write the first entries on its smooth unsullied pages.

Gnr. C. B. Burrows, 104 Battery, 22nd Brigade, R.F.A., 7th Division, B.E.F.

Sunday, October 4th, 1914. Reveille 6.30 a.m. Stables, water and feed our horses, and are told to stand by, no one to leave camp. Infantry start marching at 8 a.m. They march all day long, battalion after battalion with drums and fifes and the Scots with their bagpipes. We are all tensed and anxious to move, ready with guns and horses to march to Southampton. As we leave Lyndhurst there are thousands of people cheering us as we move off about 1.45 a.m.

Monday 5th October. On reaching Southampton about 4 a.m. we are again met by thousands of people, the whole of Southampton is awake to receive us all the way to the docks. We think this is going to be a lovely war. After embarking on a Canadian Pacific liner we found that the ship is already crowded with the Scots Guards and Gordon Highlanders and we can only take half the Battery on board, 3 guns and 6 ammo wagons and 30 horses. We sail in complete darkness and are cheered by thousands of sailors on destroyers in Southampton Water. After trying to get some sleep on deck we find we are in Dover Harbour alongside of a destroyer, the *Cossack*. The sailors join us in a bit of fun. We hear we have put into Dover Harbour which is full of a convoy (about 15 ships) as a grain ship had been blown up by a mine previously, just in front of us.

Tuesday October 6th. Still in Dover Harbour and waiting!

Despite their impatience to be on their way and the mild tedium of the inexplicable delay, the day passed pleasantly enough for the 7th Division riding at anchor off Dover. There was plenty to see. There were so many ships that it looked, in the words of one Tommy, 'like a ruddy review of the Fleet', so many cutters plying importantly to and from the shore, carrying so many senior officers that they seemed likely to sink beneath the weight of gold-braid. There were so many jokes to be shouted from the Tommies lining the rails of troopships to the Tars on the warships, and so many rumours to be exchanged and passed round, that the troops were kept entertained for a long time. There was the view to be surveyed and enjoyed, with the grey walls of the Castle high above the town, and the cliffs and the promenades lined with sightseers, beetle-like in the distance, and the town itself. To the soldiers marooned offshore, the unattainable attractions of Dover, not least its well-known pubs, so near and yet so far, seemed more and more desirable as the hours passed. By and by a single plaintive voice began a chorus familiar to the Army and hundreds of like-minded Tommies took it up. It travelled from ship to ship in waves of thirsty longing.

> *There's a man selling beer over there,*
> *There's a man selling beer over there,*
> *There's a man selling beer,*
> *A man selling beer,*
> *A man selling beer over there.*

After a few repetitions some warblers drifted on to other verses that described in predictable detail the wares on offer by a girl selling love, but they failed to catch on. As the entertainment palled the men sought sheltered corners and settled down to the earnest business of card-playing or, keeping a wary look-out for sharp-eyed officers, huddled in discreet groups for a session of forbidden gambling. Today, with the Army in such close proximity to the Navy, the game of Crown and Anchor seemed particularly apposite. Most of them dozed off, woke up to find themselves still at anchor and went back to swapping rumours.

None of the thousand and one rumours that buzzed through the ranks came anywhere near pinpointing the real reason for the delay. The fact was that although the Army had embarked the 7th Division it was not quite sure where they should be sent. Almost the only man of the Division who was aware of this was their commander, Major-General Capper. Originally, it had been arranged for the Royal Navy to escort the 7th Division to Boulogne to join up with the Expeditionary Force as it dribbled up from the Aisne. In the light of the situation at Antwerp the plans had been hastily recast – but at such short notice it had not been so easy for the Navy to call up the extra ships required for a convoy of sufficient size to protect the troopships on the longer and more hazardous sea crossing to Zeebrugge in Belgium. Now they were rapidly converging on Dover and the word was that the convoy would soon set sail. They were, in theory, bound for Antwerp and General Capper's new instructions had been clear enough.

War Office,
Whitehall,
4th October, 1914

Instructions to General Capper
Commanding 7th Division.

1. You will proceed with your Division and disembark at Zeebrugge with a view to assisting and supporting the Belgian Army defending Antwerp, which place is being besieged by the Germans.

2. A French division, together with a French Fusilier Marine brigade, the latter 6,000 strong, and some cavalry will be associated with you in these operations as soon as they arrive.

3. The German forces besieging Antwerp are reported to be 4 or 4½ divisions not of first-line troops.

4. The Belgian Field Army who have been up to the present successfully holding them in check consists of about 60,000 men.

5. A vigorous offensive of the combined above force against the Germans should force them to retire and possibly place the heavy artillery with which they have been bombarding the forts of Antwerp in jeopardy.

6. As soon as these guns have been taken or silenced the future of Antwerp is safe and the object of the expedition of your force will have been obtained.

But early in the evening of 6 October, as the transports were standing by to cast off, the situation at Antwerp was changing for the worse. The Belgian army was withdrawing and the collapse of the city was merely a matter of time. Travelling in a fast destroyer, General Capper had arrived ahead of his division to assess the situation on the spot. In principle his orders still stood – but he had since received an amendment from Lord Kitchener himself. He was to run no undue risk. Above all, on no account was he to run the risk of being trapped in Antwerp. No one knew better than General Capper that his 7th Division was the last remaining reserve of Regular troops and by the morning of the 7th, when the first ships that carried them to Belgium were approaching Zeebrugge, despite the pleas of the Belgians that his men should entrain immediately for Antwerp, he had made his decision. The 'immediate' transporting of 12,000 men and all their transport and supplies could hardly be accomplished in less than a day. The bulk of the French troops who were expected to support him had not yet arrived. Antwerp was a lost cause. There was nothing to be gained by throwing his troops away in a vain attempt to save it. It would be better by far to link up with the French, to cover the retreat of the Belgian army and to live to fight another day.

When the 7th Division at last disembarked on Belgian soil on the morning of 7 October, they marched for Bruges. The anxious Belgians, seeing them as saviours, cheered them every inch of the way and Bruges went wild.

Gnr. C. B. Burrows, 104 Battery, 22nd Brigade, R.F.A., 7th Division, B.E.F.

Wednesday October 7th. We arrived at Zeebrugge, Belgium, at 5 a.m. By 9 a.m. when we disembarked the harbour was full of our ships. We marched with our guns and horses through Zeebrugge, which had a horrible smell from the canals (and there are many of them) and lots of bridges. The people gave us a great welcome with flowers, fruit, bread, chocolate and anything they could give us. Marched on to Bruges and had the same reception, everyone pleased to see us.

They showered us with gifts and were shouting out 'God Save the English'. We had a fine time. We thought this was a pretty good war up to now. The girls pinched our cap badges etc. for souvenirs. Marching on to a village named Oost, we billeted there and had some sport in the billet trying to speak the language.

Some of the troops attempted to overcome the language problem by speaking their native tongue suitably accented and enhanced by a certain foreign style in which the Regulars were accustomed to barter in certain eastern bazaars. It was the Padre who overheard one such conversation between a pair of baffled shopkeepers and two soldiers intent on buying postcards to send home. 'How moochee moonee?' demanded one Tommy in creditable imitation of an accent last heard east of Suez. The old couple replied with puzzled smiles. Brandishing his postcards under their noses he repeated his question, louder and more slowly. 'How moo-chee moo-nee?' Again they shrugged and smiled. The Tommies eventually gave up and departed postcardless. 'Stupid old buggers,' remarked the linguist, as the shop door slammed behind them. 'Don't understand their own bloody language!' The Padre tactfully pretended not to hear.

The Northumberland Hussars, who had come to Belgium in the vanguard of the 7th Division to act as its cavalry, were having similar fun in Bruges. Private Daglish of the Morpeth Troop adopted the simple method of responding to all salutations and acclamations in true Northumberland style, 'Vary canny, hoos yorsel?', which was as good an answer as any, while the chief entertainment of the junior officers was endeavouring to flummox the interpreters. They managed it eventually in a restaurant by demanding kippers all round. Harengs fumés hardly fitted the bill. In Europe, and well the Hussars knew it, there was no such animal. They settled for grilled sardines and the pique of the interpreters did nothing to spoil their enjoyment of a merry evening. The general verdict, like that of the gunners, was that it was 'a good war so far'.

News from Antwerp did very little to add to General Capper's enjoyment of his evening, but he was much relieved by receiving fresh orders from his new chief, Sir Henry Rawlinson. They instructed him to march the 7th Division to concentrate at Bruges. He was happy to be able to report that the Division was already there, and even happier to realise that he had made the right decision. New orders would shortly set the 7th Division on the move again. They would send them further west to Ghent and on to Ypres.

If Antwerp fell (and it was not so much 'if' as 'when'), the Germans too would be on the march and the two army corps which had been besieging the city would be released. There was little doubt then that they would pour through Belgium, to seize Ostend, Dunkirk, Calais itself. It was imperative to secure the line and on the evening of 7 October, as the walls of Antwerp cracked and crumbled beneath the German guns, the line was tenuous to say the least.

The French had trickled north to hold the line on the long German flank as far as Lens. From Lens, the British when they got there would extend it north to Menin and on their left the Belgian army, with a contingent of the French, would carry it on to the sea. When all were in position they would mount a joint offensive to turn the Germans' flank and drive them back. The trouble was that they were still a long way from the positions that French and Joffre had traced on the map when they agreed the plan.

The first men of the original BEF to leave the Aisne – the Second Corps – were just approaching Abbeville, and Abbeville was a hundred miles from Bruges. The Third Corps was only leaving Soissons. The First Corps was still standing on the Aisne. Until they got there, the future British sector was held by the cavalry. There were few enough of them, and along the fifty miles that lay between Ghent and the nearest British horseman there was no one at all, save for a small French garrison at Dunkirk and a few Territorials round Lille. The gateway to the sea was open and it must be slammed shut before the enemy moved.

The enemy, of course, was already on the move. The Germans needed a decisive victory, and they needed it in the west in order to be able to concentrate on the war on the Russian Front. Now that the situation on the French Front had turned to virtual stalemate, it was as obvious to the Germans as it was to the Allies that victory would only be won in the north. It was equally obvious that the Allies were planning a northern offensive to secure the safety of the seaports that Germany was equally anxious to grab. Already Germany was gathering her strength and preparing to get in first. Troops railed up from the Champagne Front were sideslipping northwards, keeping step with the French and the British, and fighting to push them westwards towards the sea. For the moment the Germans could do no more. They were biding their time. They were waiting for the troops, now tied up at Antwerp, to be released. There were 90,000 of them. And that was not all. A whole new army was on its way from Germany.

The realisation that the Belgian army had escaped from Antwerp came as an irritating jolt and even before the unfortunate city fathers had signed the official surrender the Germans sent off all but a few of their victorious troops on the heels of the retiring men.

With the 7th Division covering its retreat, the Belgian army had a head start, but they were retreating none the less. The British soldiers knew it, even if the civilians did not, and the cheering, the shouting, the rejoicing that greeted them at every village rang a little hollow in their ears. It was difficult not to feel guilty. They knew full well that it was the Germans who would be the next arrivals and that only the Northumberland Hussars were at their backs to stop them.

But, at best, the Northumberland Hussars, assisted by the gunners of the rearguard, searching and patrolling on the flanks and at the rear, could only delay the progress of the Germans. They were not intended to engage in a battle and their orders from General Capper had urged them to be cautious.

> If there is any molestation from the enemy he
> will be attacked silently with the bayonet.

This edict caused some wry amusement. It was clear that General Capper was innocent of the experience of a night ride with the cavalry on the noisy roads of Belgium paved with granite setts. The din raised by the hooves of even a single troop of horses was enough to broadcast their presence across several miles. In the light of this circumstance, the fact that they happened to possess no bayonets was unimportant. What mattered more was the confusion on the roads, the press of refugees as the news spread that Antwerp had fallen, the mixing up of troops as Belgians, French and British fell back from Ghent together clad in unfamiliar uniforms that made it hard to tell friend from foe. After several brushes with German patrols everyone was tense. Some, like Private Chrystal, were trigger-happy. He made no bones about his astonishment when Lieutenant Joyes ordered his men to the side of the road to make way for a troop of French Cuirassiers, gorgeous in plumed and shining helmets. 'Gox!' exclaimed Chrystal, when the matter was explained to him. 'Wey, I thought them buggers wor garman hoolans! I wor firin' at the likes o' them aal day yesterday!' It was fortunate that the thick accent of rural Northumbria concealed this revelation from all but his immediate companions. The French horsemen responded to the wave of laughter with friendly grins and comradely salutes as they rode on.

Nevertheless, Lieutenant Joyes, uncomfortably aware that Chrystal was one of his best shots, did not feel entirely happy until his allies were well out of sight down a side road.

On 14 October the advance guard of the 7th Division came to Ypres. Few of the soldiers had ever heard of it, fewer still could pronounce its curious name, but in the universal relief that they had arrived approximately at their destination, nobody much cared.

*

Ypres lay on the inland edge of the flat and marshy coastal plain of Flanders. Once it had been a town of princely magnificence. Its richly ornamented stone buildings, its cathedral, its churches, its towers, its spires, had been built in mediaeval times on the fat pickings of the wool trade for, like Ghent and Bruges, Ypres was one of the rich cloth towns of Flanders. Now it was a backwater. Swans sailed serenely on its moat. The great defensive ramparts designed by Vauban to keep out jealous foes had been breached and in parts demolished to allow the passage of the railway that had brought Ypres into the twentieth century and now brought a modest trickle of discerning travellers to the town to admire its architectural treasures and add their mite to the local economy. The highlight of an otherwise somnolent week was market-day when the farmers and smallholders came in from the surrounding countryside to buy and to sell, to barter and to gossip among the covered carts that served as market stalls. They lined up in the market square in the shadow of the Gothic Cloth Hall which, in times gone by, more prosperous merchants had erected to serve a richer trade. Nothing much happened in Ypres for years. And then the Germans came.

They had come on 7 October, a full week before the British. They had left again almost immediately and the town was still awash with relief. It had not been a pleasant experience. Camille Delaere, Curé of St James's Church, had good reason to remember it.

Father Camille Delaere, Curé of the Church of St Jacques. Extract from his diary

For some days people had seen Uhlans passing in small groups through neighbouring places. Towards eleven o'clock on the morning of 7 October, we heard several cannon shots nearby and then, about two o'clock, a dozen explosions at the entrance to the town. The whistle of shells, the explosions, the humming of bullets, the appalling sight of my poor people flying in terror. Fathers and mothers all weighed down with children and bundles, with pale faces and frightened eyes, running like madmen towards the Grande Place to hide from the enemy approaching so rapidly and to escape the bullets. The feeling of danger; the fight – or rather the flight – for existence.

Shrapnel balls made holes in the stained glass of my church and a great many were picked up nearby. One shell had exploded against the bell-tower; another went through an upstairs window of a house in my parish in the rue Grimminck, blowing holes in the staircase and the wall opposite.

After an anxious wait the German soldiers made their entrance into the town: cyclists, horsemen, infantry. People said there were 20,000 of them.★ Some of them only passed through, but a lot stayed to rest until the next day. Twenty or so cavalrymen with thirty horses took over my church hall. The next day I saw that they had written in French on the blackboard: *The Germans fear God, but apart from Him they fear nothing in the world. Germany for ever!*

There was ample evidence that the Germans had found nothing to fear or to respect in Ypres, and the Curé recorded an indignant catalogue of misdeeds that had shocked the population:

They showed their prowess in the town: the pillage of shops, jewellery shops above all for watches (at Madame Heursel's in the rue au Beurre, they stole 35,000 francs' worth), men's clothing, especially underwear, and of course food. They emptied the till at the post office – it was not much, 127 francs – and at the Hôtel de Ville they took the whole community fund – 65,000 francs. Early next day they left, making towards the French frontier, leaving only a few behind to patrol the outskirts of the town.

From the west, the towers and spires of Ypres were visible from a long way off across the flat Flanders fields. But north and north-east of the town the land began to rise in a succession of low ridges that ran round it in a rough semi-circle like the rim around a saucer. Ypres sat like a cup in the low ground below. On the highest of the gentle undulations and some six miles to the north-east was the village of Passchendaele. From the Passchendaele ridge there were fine views to the east where the land swept down again to join the plain that rolled off to the very heart of Belgium and swept down into France. The frontier post was at Menin, a mile or so away, and from there the road led on to Tourcoing, Roubaix, Lille, the great industrial agglomeration of northern France.

The roads that carried the troops from Ghent converged on the plain and they were bound to cross it. Roving troupes of German cavalry patrolled it. They were bound to clash.

The Germans were the first to come to Passchendaele. From her bedroom window above her father's grocery store at the corner of the Molenstraat Maria Van Assche, sixteen years old, was one of the first to see them.

★ There were approximately 8,000.

Maria Van Assche (Mrs W. Blackburn)

It was about seven o'clock in the morning. I heard the clatter of horses and I looked out and I saw seven Uhlans, Germans, in a lovely dress. They had helmets on and they had spears in their hands and on the other side they had their hands on their guns. They went up the road and just before the end of Molenstraat there is an alleyway and some Belgian soldiers was hidden in there as a trap. And they started shooting, the Germans, and I actually saw that. One German was shot and fell down, and another one was wounded. One German got off his horse, picked up the German that was wounded and they all rode as fast as they could back to the square. They got off their horses and told a man looking out of a door, 'Two wounded. See them to the hospital.' And they went off.

There was only seven of them that morning. But three days after we had about fourteen coming in. We were told not to look through the window. My father said, 'If you look through the window and move the curtains they will shoot you. They always have this gun ready, levelled at you, like that – and they will shoot you.'

Then one day we had about three hundred Germans coming, right through the village. They went into all the houses, they went in one estaminet – they call the cafés estaminets in Belgium – and they asked the woman where her husband was. And they called him by his name! She wondered why. She said, 'How do you know my husband's name?' and the German said, '*You* know me.' And she looked close and she *did* know him. He was a horse-dealer. Some of these Germans who came as Uhlans they were horse-dealers and they were spying before the war. Passchendaele was known for horse-dealing and they used to come and buy horses and now some of these people were officers in the Uhlan army. One fellow even knew my father! It didn't keep them from misbehaving.

They took every single man they could see, young men, old men, they put them all on the side. They'd come from Iseghem, not very far away, and they had two monks in a car behind them, two monks tied up as hostages in the back of this car. Then they made all the Belgians march in front of them and at the side of them so that nobody could shoot at them without shooting these civilians, and they went on again as far as Roosebeke and then they all turned back again. Roosebeke is the next village. They turned back again and let the men go. It was a terrible, frightening thing for them. We were all frightened. We always was hoping the English was coming, we were told the English was coming, but they didn't come.

The villagers of Passchendaele were not alone in anxiously awaiting the arrival of 'the English'. A French garrison of 4,000 Territorials had been holding on to Lille by the skin of their teeth, and were doing their best to carry on holding it until the BEF arrived in force. But the German reinforcements got there first, beat the Territorials back and occupied the city, this time for good. On a few street corners in the centre of the town copies of the notice so exuberantly drawn up by Commander Sampson more than a month before were still to be seen sticking to the walls. After some days of wind and rain they were a little the worse for wear but they were still legible. *I have this day occupied Lille with an armed English and French force*. The Germans scornfully tore them down. Where, they might have asked, was this Sampson and his force now!

They were at St-Omer. So was Sir John French and his Staff, for St-Omer was now British Headquarters. Ted Organ was there too, with the Oxfordshire Hussars. The Commander-in-Chief was there because the BEF had all but completed its move to the north. The Hussars were there because they had all but mutinied. By rights they should have been back in England, for now that the Royal Naval Division had gone back home there had been no obvious need for their services. After a week of tame activity at Dunkirk, spent mainly in training and shooting practice on the sands, they had been ordered to Boulogne to embark for home. They had found the pursuit of German cavalry much too enjoyable to take kindly to the idea. It went without saying that there was no arguing with orders, but on the road to Boulogne the officers debated and discussed what could be done and twenty miles south of Dunkirk they came to a unanimous decision. It was undoubtedly unmilitary, but they felt that it was decidedly yeomanlike. On their own initiative they broke off the march, commandeered billets in the village of Oye, and while the troops enjoyed their unexpected rest, despatched the adjutant with Lieutenant Fane (to back him up) to St-Omer to plead with the Commander-in-Chief himself to let them stay. They travelled in Lieutenant Fane's fast car, and it was not many hours before they returned with jubilant news.

Sir John French had liked their cheek. He also liked this evidence of keenness and he had been easily persuaded. He could not, he explained, absorb them as a fighting force, since they were not officially part of the BEF, but he was quick to see a use for them. They might come to St-Omer as Headquarters troops and thus release a fighting unit for the line. The Oxfordshire Hussars were delighted. By daybreak they were on the road to St-Omer.

Lce/Cpl. Edward Organ, No. 1745, A Sqdn., 1st Troop, Queen's Own Oxfordshire Hussars, B.E.F.

My troop was chosen to be General French's bodyguard and I was on guard outside in this street at two o'clock in the morning. We had our horses in the stable yard behind the Town Hall in St Omer. The General's horses were there too and all along the small streets were parked private cars, mostly belonging to British officers. A lot of officers had brought their own cars to France and their own chauffeurs. Consequently these chauffeurs were enrolled, but they didn't have any uniforms apart from their chauffeurs' uniforms of peaked hats and double-breasted coats. Anyway, I was in this little dark side street and there was a row of cars outside where I was standing with my rifle and bayonet, and I saw somebody come out in a dark double-breasted suit and peaked cap. He was peering round the cars, as if he was looking for a certain one, and he got up close to me and I said to him, 'Hello there, mate.' Well, he said 'Hello'! I said, 'Who do you drive for, Chummy?' Chatting to pass the time. He turned round and *then* I saw the braid on his cap! He said, not at all snooty, but he said, 'I'm the Commanding Officer of the Royal Naval Air Service at Dunkirk.' It was this Commander Sampson! Of course we'd heard all about him so I said, 'I beg your pardon, Sir!' And I gave him a very flash Present Arms – you know, like the Guards do! Well, twelve hours later, in the daytime, I'd just come on guard again and this officer and our own Colonel came along on the other side of the little street and I gave them another very flash Present Arms. As they went past I saw this officer whisper to the Colonel and they both burst out laughing. I felt a real idiot! I knew perfectly well he must be telling the Colonel about my taking him for a chauffeur and asking who he drove for!

At St-Omer, apart from ceremonials and guards, the duties of the Oxfordshire Hussars were not unduly onerous. There was time to spare for badly needed training, for the officers were anxious to earn their right to be there at all by bringing the troops to a peak of excellence that would justify the confidence of the Commander-in-Chief and convince him, when the time came, that their men were not just willing but well and truly able to hold their own in battle. They were perfectly sure that the time *would* come, and that it would come soon. Close as they were to GHQ, with their ears cocked to discreet hints dropped by Staff Officers of their acquaintance with whom they happened to drink a glass of port or smoke an after-dinner cigar, they knew that a joint offensive was brewing and that, as soon as the Front was secured, it would start. They dearly

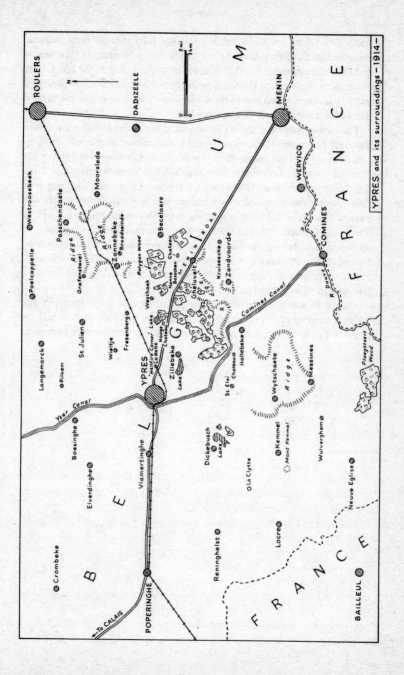

YPRES and its surroundings – 1914 –

wanted to be in on it. Meanwhile, as the BEF fought into position, contested by the Germans all the way, they took advantage of their leisure and their motor cars and took it in turn to go joy-riding to the Front. The nearer they could get to the fighting the better they liked it, and they vied with each other, when out of the Colonel's earshot, to regale the mess at dinner with tales of hair-raising adventure.

They were only very slightly exaggerated, for as the British moved into line, trickling north to face the Germans and, where they could, pushing east to try to turn the enemy flank, there were scraps enough to gratify the heart of the most avid seeker after thrills. They were fighting round the slag heaps at Béthune, Givenchy, La Bassée. They were fighting near Hazebrouck and north of it at Meteren and Bailleul. Beyond that, the cavalry had secured Messines and the long low ridge running north to Ypres. It was almost over. There was now a thin and tenuous line, so sparsely manned along the British Front that they depended on connecting files of cavalry to cover gaps of many miles. But it was a line nevertheless and it stretched uninterrupted from distant Belfort in Alsace to Flanders. But not quite to the North Sea.

On 14 October, at the end of the gruelling trek from Antwerp, the Belgian army stopped on the River Yser and the 7th Division entered the town of Ypres. The Race to the Sea was ended. The line was now complete.

Chapter 23

A spiteful fate, with a jaundiced eye cast on the distant future, felt it appropriate to decree that when the British came to Ypres it should be raining. It poured all morning in torrents and made it a matter of some urgency to get the horses under cover, to dry them off, as well as feed and rest them after a long trek that had started (at least for the advance guard) early in the morning. Charlie Burrows' 104 Battery had been told to cover them on the march from Roulers and at nine o'clock in the morning they entered Ypres, filing down the road from Zonnebeke, across the moat and through the breach in the ancient ramparts where once a city gate had barred the way. But it was many years since Ypres had been threatened by anything more lethal than a runaway horse or a fast motor car; the gate had been dismantled long ago and at the foot of the grassy slopes leading up to the ramparts a pair of stone lions, standing innocuous guard, gazed peacefully at travellers on the road.

As the advance guard passed them, marching towards the spires of Ypres, the clock in the tower of the old Cloth Hall was chiming nine o'clock. They halted in its shadow in the wide market square and were charmed with what they saw.

There were soaring spires, curious bronze domes, there were Gothic arches, high-pitched roofs adorned with intricate gables and pierced by rows of rooftop windows, there were elaborate façades, delicate with tracery, florid with statues and sculptures. Ypres was a feast to the artistic eye. Even the less aesthetically inclined were pleased by its quaintness and marked with approval that there were shops and estaminets by the dozen, and smiling faces everywhere. The Burgomeister with a deputation of leading citizens came hurrying across from the Town Hall to give the British an official welcome that amounted to the freedom of the town. Nothing was too good for them. Billets would be difficult, for there were French soldiers in the town, but somehow they would squeeze the Tommies in. The Burgomeister even proposed that the horses might be stabled in the Cloth Hall itself and personally saw to it that the doors of the old market hall opening on the square should be flung open to admit them.

But this splendid stable did not suit. The floor was of marble and the horses slipped and slithered on it, neighing fearfully as they struggled to keep their footing, and they had to be led out again and tethered in the open between the Cloth Hall and the cathedral. Luckily the rain tailed off and by noon when the whole of the 7th Division were assembled in the town the weather had cleared and field kitchens steaming busily in the square and in the wide street by St Martin's Cathedral were dishing out dixies of thick soup. There was bread to be had (the bakers of Ypres had worked an extra shift to make sure of it), and the population of Ypres was plying the troops with a largesse of fruit and smokes, beer and chocolate, as generous as any that had so far been showered on them in Belgium.

The Gordon Highlanders, kilted and sporraned in their Highland dress, came in for special attention and some of the troops, less gorgeous in dingy khaki, were of the opinion that they were getting a good deal more than their fair share of admiration. Ypres had never seen the like of them before and the Gordons were making the most of it. Some were positively strutting and showing off, warbling their favourite ditty to the girls. 'The Cock o' the North' was a melody favoured by most Scottish regiments, but the Gordons were treating the maidens of Ypres to the unauthorised version to which they were particularly attached.

> *Auntie Mary had a canary,*
> *It whistled the Cock o' the North,*
> *It whistled for 'oors*
> *And frightened the Boers,*
> *And won the Victoria Cross.*

The theme was somewhat dated, but since no one but the Gordons understood a word of it, it hardly mattered. Some respectably trousered members of the Border Regiment, communicating in such fractured French as they could summon up, endeavoured to puncture the conceit of the Gordons (and get a dig in at the Sassenachs at the same time) by spreading the calumny that these weirdly skirted warriors were not men at all, but the wives of English soldiers. They added that the sporrans were their handbags.

But the occasional crack of gunfire not far to the south was a crisp reminder that they would shortly be in action, and they were all anxious to get at it.

By three o'clock the next morning, the 7th Division was back again on the march. They were to fan out round Ypres, to take up a line and, when all were in position, when the French were standing firmly on their left, when the Belgian army they had rescued were stretched along the Yser to the sea, they were to attack. What was more they would attack across the whole north line from La Bassée in the south to Dixmude and the sea. The chance had come at last to outflank the Kaiser's force, to roll up his line and kick him smartly where it hurt, to liberate Belgium and to fling the Germans out of France. The northern offensive was designed to win the war. They would all be home by Christmas.

Charlie Burrows, with the 22nd Brigade, was on the extreme left of the British line where it joined the French.

Gnr. C. B. Burrows, 104 Battery, 22nd Brigade, R.F.A., 7th Division, B.E.F.

Thursday October 15th 3 a.m. March out of Ypres, north-east, wait in a field. Received our first mail at noon. Move again about 1 mile to another field. Thousands of French infantry with us. Would sooner be with our own boys. All quiet. Nothing doing. We billet in a factory which has been closed. No sleep for me, I'm on picket!

Friday October 16th. 2 a.m. March north about 2 miles. Stop in a lane for about 6 hours! We are getting fed up with all this waiting and all are anxious to get in action. Weather dull and cold. Heard that the enemy advance guard was falling back a few miles ahead and had set fire to a village. Billet in a small village.

A mile or so ahead, the cavalry was ranged around the saucer's rim of ridges. A horseman on the high top road riding from Roosebeke to Beclaere could see the towers of Ypres on the low ground to his right and, looking to his left, the miles of rolling plain, the distant chimneystacks of Roulers, the small town of Menin almost at his feet. It was a fine vantage point, but the cavalry were not given to travelling on main roads. They preferred open country where the horses could have their heads, where they could practise their skills of surprise and ambush and fight as hard as their officers had hunted across the shires at home. The 7th Cavalry Brigade was billeted at Passchendaele and, after the villagers' experience of the Uhlans, their arrival had caused some consternation.

Maria Van Assche (Mrs W. Blackmore)

It was about midday and two soldiers on horseback flew through our street to the square, and the Belgians there all put their hands up. They were in khaki and they must have thought they were Germans. I rushed out. I could hear them and they were calling out that they were English. That's all they could say. '*Anglais, Anglais*', they were saying.

There was a woman in the village who had been to America. I told the policeman, 'She's been to America. She must speak English.' So she came and they explained. There was just two of them, but then we had the whole cavalry coming and they commandeered all the rooms. My mother's bedroom was downstairs, through the shop. She'd just died in the summer and the room was still like it was when she died – we never used it. They took that room and across the road there was an empty shop and they made that their headquarters where all the big officers were.

I remember there was one there in the Headquarters, he was either a prince or a lord. He came into our shop with his butler and asked me to come with them to the butcher's shop. The butcher was a Flemish speaker and he couldn't understand French, so I had to go along with them and order two chickens, which of course the butcher had to kill.

It was perfectly possible that the officer was a lord, for there was no shortage of lords or of earls and viscounts, marquesses and baronets in the cavalry. There was even a duke or two. Mere honourables were commonplace and the roll of officers of the 7th Cavalry Brigade at Passchendaele read more like a roll-call of the blue-blooded families of England – for the 7th was the Household Brigade, the soldiers of the Sovereign himself. It comprised the illustrious Life Guards, and the Blues – the equally illustrious Royal Horse Guards. The Wyndhams, the Stanleys, the Grosvenors, Hoares, Thynnes, Pelhams, Astors, Cavendishes, Leveson-Gowers, Castlereaghs were among those represented. All were waiting on the Passchendaele line and they were raring to go.

On the march down from Zeebrugge, where the 7th Cavalry Brigade had landed the week before, they had guarded the railways, they had patrolled assiduously but they had seen little action. But some of their comrades had, for at the outbreak of the war a squadron had been withdrawn from each battalion and combined to form a separate force. They called it the Composite Household Battalion. It had travelled to France with the BEF, it had had many stirring adventures and the story of the part it played at Néry had fired the spirit and imagination of the officers and troopers left behind. They were frankly envious and waited with considerable impatience for the orders that would send them in their own turn to the war. The orders had been a long time coming, for the Brigade first had to be brought up to strength and the only people who did not chafe at the delay were certain troopers called up from the Reserves who had been co-opted of necessity to make up the numbers of the squadrons now in France. They belonged to slightly less exclusive regiments known by the Army as the Cavalry of the Line and none of them was loath to be transferred to the exalted ranks of the Household Cavalry. It meant an extra sevenpence a day, for the Household troopers were paid one princely shilling and ninepence against the daily one and twopence of other cavalrymen. Even that was better than the one and a penny paid to a private in the Guards and the humble shilling a day with which the Army rewarded the services of a private soldier in the infantry.

The Household Brigade magnanimously overlooked the fact that the new troopers did not quite reach up to the statuesque proportions they normally demanded of their rank and file. Despite their lack of inches, they were useful men: they had seen service in India, they were hard riders and sharp shooters. They would do. And now that the waiting was over, now that they were at full strength and ready to fight, now that they were actually at the war (and what was more were the advance guard of the 7th Division) there would soon be action and excitement enough to satisfy the most ardent young officer in the Brigade. But it was tedious to be marking time and young Lord Worsley, writing home from his billet in Passchendaele to his parents, the Earl and Countess of Yarborough, expressed the feelings of them all.

> . . . It all seems so strange; if it were not for the everlasting sound of guns, which seem quite close, but are probably several miles away, one would think one was on manoeuvres. One often catches oneself wondering which day manoeuvres are going to end – and one would give a good deal to know. The day before yesterday we were in the saddle for 17 hours – scarcely off one's horse all that time – then two hours' rest and off again for 16 hours. Needless to say men and horses absolutely stone cold, but we are having an easy time now, and very nice too. We do very well in the way of food, but we've been on the move ever since we landed . . . Did you send out the cigarettes and tobacco and pipe, or was it Alexandra? If you, thank you very much. They were very much appreciated, and as I had a pipe, I gave it to a Corporal who had broken his. Two of my drivers are just like music-hall turns and they keep us all in shrieks of laughter all the time we are halted on the road; they are priceless.

But the 'manoeuvres' were almost at an end. The First Corps had now started on its way from the Aisne and would arrive in a matter of days. Meanwhile the 7th Division was given what the Command considered to be a simple task. They were told to advance down the plain and to capture the town of Menin, sketchily held by a few isolated German outposts. At the same time the Cavalry Brigade was to join up with the French and occupy Roulers.

It was Sunday 18 October. The Division spent the day pivoting on its position to face south-east and the guns moved up to cover them. There was a certain sense of excitement as the infantry geared up for action, but for the gunners moving up to support them it was, on the whole, a boring day.

Gnr. C. B. Burrows, 104 Battery, 22nd Brigade, R.F.A., 7th Division, B.E.F.

October 18th. Stayed in a lane for 8 hours from 3.30 a.m. Got paid 10 francs near a small village named Frezenburg. Received mail. Very quiet. No sign of the enemy. Moved off at 4 p.m. Passed hundreds of refugees. All seem terrified. They blocked the roads and we cannot move until they get back towards Ypres. Heard plenty of rifle fire to our front. We expect to be busy soon. Our section officer tells us that a great battle will soon be fought here. Sleep in a field.

In the course of the day and according to plan the Germans had been driven out of Roulers. They had hardly put up a fight for they were only a token force and General de Mitry's French cavalry had easily turned them out, while the British cavalry protecting the French right flank had barely caught even a glimpse of the enemy. Only the Blues had seen any action, so tame that it was hardly worth mentioning. A patrol had been fired at from a row of isolated houses and Lieutenant Lord Worsley, galloping up with his machine-gun team, had blazed away and smartly put a stop to it. The others had had no fun at all. They returned to dine and sleep in Passchendaele and passed a quiet night. Most of them turned in early in anticipation of a more exciting day tomorrow.

During the course of the evening the ubiquitous Commander Sampson pressed well forward with his armoured cars to reconnoitre and, apart from dodging patrolling horsemen and spotting some isolated outpost trenches round Menin, he had seen nothing untoward. Reports from spies of the occupied zone told of large numbers of German troops detraining south of Brussels and other troops were noticed concentrating at Courtrai; but the general impression, as put forward by GHQ, was that the enemy had not arrived in force. The following morning the 7th Division would begin to move forward. Such opposition as they might encounter would be light and easily dealt with.

But the Staff at GHQ, like the troops they were sending forward, were misinformed. And the Germans had had a stroke of luck. Their patrols had captured a British officer and he was carrying in his pocket the orders for the offensive. They were detailed and specific and since they listed every unit, its position, its objective and its role in the attack, they all but amounted to an Order of Battle. The Germans now knew exactly who was there, who was where and what was what, down to the smallest detail of the plans for the attack. They were well prepared to forestall it.

The Germans themselves had intended to advance. They still intended it. Now, with full knowledge of where the British attack would fall, fully aware of the strength and purpose of the enemy, they had disposed themselves to meet it. They had set strong forces in the key positions, they had carefully disposed their guns; as soon as the troops began to move the shells began to fall among them and as they pressed forward the Germans advanced to meet them. They were astonished to meet any infantry at all, there were far, far more of them than anyone could have guessed – and there were more to come. At 10.30 in the morning, when the first startling reports of reverses and of unexpected opposition had begun to filter in to GHQ, a report of even graver news came back from pilots flying high above the battle and with a bird's-eye view of all the land beyond. They had flown as far as Courtrai and the news they sent was disconcerting to say the least. They had spotted the Germans on the move. They were moving in their thousands. As the pilots quartered the sky and scoured the horizon they could see, in several directions, long columns of troops and guns. The Germans were coming up fast on the roads across the plain. And they were making for the battle-line in front of Ypres.

Roulers was soon lost. Menin could not be captured. But the Royal Welch Fusiliers at the head of the 22nd Brigade had got within two miles of it before they were pushed back. The gunners behind them were ordered back and forth in their support. As the day went on they were merely ordered back.

Gnr. C. B. Burrows, 104 Battery, 22nd Brigade, R.F.A., 7th Division, B.E.F.

We move off at 5.30 a.m. Stay in a large field for two hours and heard sharp rifle fire to our front. Move on two miles ahead, passing the 106 Battery in action. We wait in a small village all deserted, move forward at 11.30 a.m., take up a position in a field, advance again. A shell burst about 550 yards from the battery. We go back to another field. Shells burst in the next field to us. We go further back and take up position in a turnip field. All the people are running for their lives. The village is burning just in front of us. Wagonloads of wounded pass us as we wait on the Menin road. We have to go back again so they are pushed into a field on our right to clear the road. As we move on the Germans start shelling again and we see the shells are falling all among them. Poor things! We go back to another village and billet there. It is completely deserted.

By nightfall they were back where they had started out that morning. It was a bleak, cold night. The infantry and gunners of the 7th Division bivouacked in what shelter they could find in the fields and villages on the rising land in front of Ypres. On the high ridge ahead of them, spread in a thin line that stretched from Roosebeke to Passchendaele, the cavalry waited and watched and patrolled and looked down on the fires burning in the plain. Down there the Germans were waiting too. Under the cover of darkness a whole new army was moving into position, stretching out, creeping ahead, ready to strike forward at daybreak.

It was 19 October and the end of the first day of the First Battle of Ypres.

Maria Van Assche (Mrs W. Blackmore)

Every so often the sentry came in, knocked on the door of this officer who was staying in our house and he answered. Then a cyclist came, one of the special cyclists that was with them, and the officer went out, and the cyclist told my father, 'The Germans are breaking through. If I was you I'd go away with those children.' (Because my father had us children and one was a baby.) He didn't take no notice of it at first, my father didn't. He was a master-builder and we also had the grocery shop, so we had property. He said, 'You should cling to your home. We don't want to lose everything.' But later when we looked out it was frightening.

The next town, Roulers, you could see it all on fire. And it frightened us, because on the train it would only take you half an hour to get to Roulers – it's near. That was *all* on fire, and you could see black clouds of shells bursting in the air. Then the refugees came. They all came from past Roulers driven away by the Germans. We took them all in. All our houses was full.

The refugees got frightened, they all run away again. Of course they heard all this noise. All the soldiers running that way and soldiers running this way. Anyway, you know, I was young, I was cruising in the street with my brother watching it all. They was rushing past outside, and all the French (because the French was there) and all went towards Roosebeke. We was quite happy seeing all that. It was exciting for young ones. We didn't feel the danger. We just thought, 'whatever's happening?' That was the night before, when the chap said, 'The Germans are coming. Go away.'

Next morning my father got up and he went and he looked in our kitchen (like, next the shop is a bedroom, then the kitchen) and they was all gone. But they left all bullets and things, on the floor, a whole heap of it. My father gets frightened when he sees all this ammunition left. He said, 'We're going to get shot if they find we've been having soldiers in here.' So we got the old dog-cart – a dog harnessed to a little cart – and we saddled the dog, put a few blankets on, a few bits of clothes, that's all we took, and we thought we'd go to Langemarck to my auntie's.

As we moved out, all the bullets came sizzling round – there's a lot of woods in Passchendaele all round – and they were already in that wood, the Germans were, as we came round. That's where they got through, you see. And you could hear the bullets going. But all the soldiers, the English and the French had all run away. They only left us civilians there. And the whistling of the bullets coming through! We run and we run. Everybody! Some had their cows with them. Farmers and everybody run away.

Gnr. C. B. Burrows, 104 Battery, 22nd Brigade, R.F.A., 7th Division, B.E.F.

Tuesday October 20th Move off at 4.30 a.m., go forward about a mile and go into action at 7 a.m. in a turnip field near a farm. The farm is deserted. In a lull a driver and I go to the farm and have a look round. The poor cows have not been milked. A dog chained to a kennel is raving mad. We can't get near it to help it – and there are puppies with it. A meal is still on the table. The people must have fled at a moment's notice. Get back to our guns. Heavy artillery fire to our right. The battery starts firing again at 9 a.m. and we fire at intervals for about 6 hours all told. Heard that the enemy's infantry were attacking very fiercely. About 10 a.m. a naval armoured train arrives just to our right. It had 2 six-inch and 1 four-inch naval guns, manned by sailors. They must be giving the enemy a hot time as they fire continuously as fast as they can. Our battery fires all day. The news is that we are slaughtering them, as they were attacking in mass formation. Heard we have captured 300 prisoners and disabled 44 guns. We keep firing until dark, then retire to a small village and billet there. All the houses are deserted. Move off again at 10 p.m. for a night attack and go into action in the same place. Second day of battle.

Even for a gunner shunting and shifting and fighting behind the immediate line, with nothing but rumour to go on, it was not difficult to deduce at the end of this second day of battle that they were fighting against huge odds and that the enemy had the advantage.

Now it was the Germans who were encircling the saucer's rim and the British troops were struggling not merely to maintain a foothold but to throw them back. But by the evening the village of Passchendaele was in German hands. And so it was destined to remain for the next three years.

The orders for the previous day had, inexplicably in view of the circumstances, ordered the continuation of the attack. That night a fresh order from GHQ placed the troops on the defensive. It read: *Action against enemy will be continued tomorrow on general line now held, which will be strongly entrenched.*

It omitted to say with what and by whom. There had been many casualties, and it was taking every ounce of effort for the remaining troops to hold off the enemy. Even when the 7th Division first landed they had been short of tools. They had no heavy spades and many of the lighter implements had now been lost in the fighting. Quartermasters, scouring the hardware and agricultural stores in Ypres, turned up twenty spades and no wire.

But the First Corps had at last arrived from the Aisne and they had arrived not a moment too soon. Even when the divisions were shoved pell-mell into the battle the men holding the line round Ypres were still hopelessly outnumbered. The first job of the 5th Field Company Royal Engineers was to dig trenches for the HLI and the Ox and Bucks.

It was cold in the north. Autumn had set in with chill winds and bleak drizzle and the sticky turnip fields and dripping woods round Ypres were a far cry from the mellow cornfields of the Marne. Forgetting the fatigue and privations of the retreat, remembering only the hot sun and the smiling countryside, the troops felt almost nostalgic. They had not, it was true, had an easy time on the Aisne, and the First Corps had held on there longer than most. The Royal Engineers had done two weeks of hard slog after the others had gone, digging trenches, strengthening positions, repairing the damaged bridges, right up to the last minute, and all for the benefit of the French who had relieved them. Now they almost envied them. Bad though their time on the Aisne had been, they had never experienced fighting and shelling such as this.

Day after day, as the battle raged on and the casualties mounted, Alex Letyford, in the thick of it with the infantry, took time in his meagre hours of rest to record the numbing details.

*Cpl. A. Letyford, 5th Field Company, Royal Engineers, 2nd Division,
B.E.F.*

22.10.14 We hear our brigade suffered very severely yesterday. The
battle is still raging. For an hour at nightfall we prepare barbed-wire
entanglements. At night we see four or five villages blazing. The firing
is too thick to enable us to go up with the barbed wire, so we dig
trenches in the rear for supports.

23.10.14. Back this morning at 2.30 a.m. A few killed in the section
last night. A little rest during the day. The artillery of both sides keep
at it continuously. We go out about 5.30 p.m. and dig more trenches
for the HLI Heavy rifle fire all round and heavy shelling.

It was not surprising that the German artillery fire was overwhelming.
They had more than 250 guns while the British had only fifty to spread
around their front. None of them were heavy enough to do much damage
to the enemy's batteries, but their shrapnel shells were lethal and the
Germans were suffering heavily. The 46th Battery had fired at short range
at the target of a lifetime – waves of enemy infantry advancing in massed
formation across the fields near Langemarck. In the moment before the
Tommies raised their rifles and the guns began to shoot, before they started
to mow them down and rip great rents in their ranks, before the long grey
lines of enemy soldiers came faltering to a stop, astonished observers in the
British firing line saw that they were advancing arm-in-arm, and through
the urgency of shouted orders they heard the sound of other voices singing.
Squinting through binoculars for a closer look they could see quite clearly
that the caps they wore with the field grey uniforms were not the regulation
headgear of German soldiers on the battlefield. They were the caps of
German students, and the Kaiser's young soldiers striding into battle were
wearing them now as they had worn them striding the streets of Heidelberg
– to show the world they were a band of brothers.★

The decision to send the new Reserve Corps to the line at Ypres had
caused much heart-searching among the officers of the German Command
and, in years to come, brought bitter condemnation on their heads, for
these young men were not part of the great military machine which (like
the French and the British) depended on trained reservists to augment its
numbers and bowl it into action in time of war. They were volunteers.

★ Many of the students who fell that day are buried in the impressive German cemetery
at Langemarck. At the entrance, a chapel panelled in wood from the forests of Germany
commemorates and bears the names of all the students from German universities who
died at Ypres.

Germany was not short of men, but the authorities knew that there were large segments of the youthful male population which had not yet reached the age of military service and therefore formed no part of the Reserve, and older men, whose liability to serve had now run out. On 16 August they announced their intention of forming new Volunteer Reserve Corps and recruits had queued up, some of them for days, to join.★ The students had been first in the queue. Three out of four of the new men were under military age. The cadre of experienced reservists who made up their numbers were all above it. Their junior officers were hastily commissioned cadets from military academies and the senior ranks were filled by officers from the Retired List or Reserve. Only one of them had ever seen active service as a captain, and he was very old. A huge majority of the rank and file had joined in groups from universities or high schools, and schoolmasters who volunteered were roped in as their NCOs.

None of them had more than six weeks' training. When Antwerp fell, when it was realised that the Allies were prolonging their line and engaged in troop movements which put them, for the moment, at a disadvantage; when it was clear that the road to the Channel ports was open, it was decided to make an army of four of the Reserve Corps and to send it to Flanders where it might just tip the scale. It was obvious that the Allies would attack soon in the north and equally obvious that it was far too late to forestall them by diverting their attention with a huge attack elsewhere. It was also too late to exchange the schoolboy soldiers for tried and tested troops and send them to learn their trade of fighting in a quiet part of the line. In Flanders there were ample guns to support them, five strong cavalry divisions to show them the way, the Sixth German Army standing at their elbow to the south. They had every reason to believe that opposition would be weak. Even so, it would be a gamble, but speed was of the essence and the prize was worth the risk. The prize was Belgium and the Channel ports, the envelopment of the British and the fall of France. It had seemed to be hanging, ripe and juicy, for the taking.

Now the Germans were having second thoughts. They had been right in assuming that opposition would be 'weak' in terms of manpower, but it was proving to be remarkably tough. The Duke of Württemberg, in command of the fledgling Fourth Army, was forced to the irritating conclusion that it would be impossible to break the British line round Ypres and punch through it to the sea with the forces now at his disposal.

★ They became the XXII, XXIII, XXIV, XXV, XXVI and XXVII Reserve Corps of the German army. The last-named was the Bavarian Reserve Division joined by large contingents of students from the University of Munich.

A whole new army of the best available troops must be formed to come to his assistance. When it arrived they would press on. Meanwhile they would keep pressing in on Ypres and gain what ground they could, hitting hard and hitting home and whittling away the British resistance before smashing it for good and all in one irresistible onslaught.

The German casualties had been fierce. In the single attack at Langemarck, according to British estimates, six hundred German soldiers had been captured and fifteen hundred had been killed. German reports ascribed their losses to the fact that they were contesting '. . . *a war-experienced and numerically superior opponent entrenched in strongly fortified positions*'. Every man in the BEF would have laughed himself silly if he could have read them, not least Alex Letyford and his comrades of the 5th Field Company, RE, who slogged all night under incessant shelling to carve out as best they could the short and shallow ditches that must serve the thin ranks of the infantry for trenches and, like the infantry, would be battered to bits next day.

Letyford was in Polygon Wood now. So were the HLI, the Worcesters and the Ox and Bucks. They were not displeased to have been relieved by the French after four days of hard fighting, though 'relief' had lost much of its meaning in recent weeks. The ranks were sparse, for they had lost 1,400 men, but as they marched in sequence across country in front of Ypres the battalions of the 5th Brigade had been reliably informed by their officers that they could look forward to three days' rest. They marched through Potizje and out to the Menin road and stopped at the place where the country road from Zillebeke crossed the wide main road to Ypres. Not many months ahead they would be calling it Hellfire Corner. Now it was shown on the maps as the Halte. Here the tram-cars stopped to pick up passengers from the farms and cottages to take them the two miles into Ypres or, travelling in the opposite direction, to Menin or to Courtrai, or to Roulers. With patience (and numerous changes) it was even possible to travel as far as Brussels on the network of trams that ran on the roads of Belgian Flanders and further, for the tramlines crossed the border into France linking Menin to Tourcoing, Tourcoing to Roubaix, Marcoing to Lille. Now the Germans were in all these places. Until three days ago a few trams had still been running cautiously up the Menin road at least as far as the Halte, but no passengers had any desire to travel further. Now that the crossroads was within sight and sound of the shellfire and the people from the farms and cottages had fled, there were no more passengers and it would be six years or more before the trams would run again.

★

Private John Cole of the Worcestershire Regiment was more than a little disgruntled. The Worcesters had been the last battalion of the 5th Brigade to leave the line near Langemarck, for the Germans had attacked again just as they were being relieved by the French and there had been no alternative but to stay and help to beat them off. They had been fighting shoulder-to-shoulder and it was dangerously close to dawn before the troops could be sorted out, the relief completed and the Worcesters were able to march away. They had been the last to arrive at the Halte. The rest of the 5th Brigade had long ago settled down. The officers had billeted in the villas along the road to Ypres; the troops had to shift for themselves in fields but they were old campaigners and after years in the Army they were well able to contrive tolerable bivouacs from sticks and groundsheets. The Worcesters fell out and began to follow suit. Two fields away towards Zillebeke, Alex Letyford and his fellow sappers, with their superior practical skills and the tool-cart at their disposal, had succeeded in making themselves reasonably comfortable. They had also breakfasted and, despite the grumbling of guns beyond the ridges on the skyline and the prospect of spending the morning digging latrine pits for the Brigade, they were not unhappy. Like everyone else they would have given a week's pay for the chance of a good wash, but even that was not out of the question. Some parties had gone off with buckets to explore deserted farms in search of water. Most of the others were asleep when the weary Worcesters plodded up to join them.

*Cpl. J. Cole, No. 12645, 2nd Bttn., The Worcestershire Regt.,
2nd Division, B.E.F.*

The Germans who attacked us the night before must have wondered what had hit them. We rained lead into them! But we lost Sergeant Billingsly, sniped through the head. We'd had three days' hard fighting holding the Germans back. Every man of the 2nd Worcesters was exhausted and unshaven and we were relieved to go back into reserve. But those days there was no such thing as rest! We'd only just arrived when the word came that we were urgently needed to stop another German attack, this time up the Ypres to Menin road. We were absolutely fed up to the teeth!

The line they had just handed over to the French had quietened and the Germans in front of it were digging in. The German commander had come to his decision. Now he was pitching all the weight of his numbers and all the power of his guns against the British on the ridges around Ypres – and they had broken their line at Polygon Wood.

*

Sleepy and hungry, the Worcesters set off marching fast up the Menin road with Major Hankey at the head of the Battalion. When the alarm was raised they had got as far as issuing rations to each platoon, but there had been no time to share them out, still less to eat them. One man in every seven was carrying a seven-pound tin of bully beef, and every man in the Battalion was marching forward to fight on an empty stomach. It did not make the march any easier. Jack Cole was also humping the tripod of the Vickers gun and it was no light weight.

They breasted the first rise, glimpsing the turrets and gables of Hooge Château through the trees, passed the long wood beyond it and hurried north-east across the fields to the shallow valley below Polygon Wood. They could hear rifles firing long before they got there. Thin wisps of vapour drifted above the tree-tops and wounded men were limping or crawling back from the wood in a steady stream.

The line had broken at the north-east corner and the Germans had poured through the gap and swarmed through the wood and almost out of it on the other side. A battalion of the Warwicks rushed up from reserve had prevented them from getting any further, and the Northumberland Hussars galloping up from the Menin road, plunging dismounted into the wood, had helped to finish the job. They had even managed to push them slightly back and they were still holding on – those that were left of them.

But the Germans were holding on too, clinging to the topmost corner of the wood, and the task of the Worcesters was to drive them out. It was not the easiest of tasks.

So many men were still fighting the Germans off from the points on the perimeter where the line had not given way, so many were fighting deep in the wood itself, grappling hand-to-hand with the enemy, dodging among the trees in groups of fifty, twenty, even a dozen men, and they were scattered in so many different directions that it was impossible to see what was happening through the thick screen of trees. There was no connected fighting. There was no line. Already there were disquieting reports of bullets coming from all directions and of men returning with wounds inflicted unmistakably by British bullets. If the Worcesters swept in firing as they went they would be bound to murder as many British soldiers as German.

The Worcesters, lined up on the open ground along the south-western edge of the wood between it and the wood they called Nonnebosschen, waited for Major Hankey to give the order. Then they went in with the bayonet. They went in running and they cheered as they ran to let the boys know they were coming. It would do no harm to let the Germans know it too.

For Cole and the boys of the machine-gun team it was a bizarre experience. As they plunged forward into the trees a phrase recalled from some blood-and-thunder tale of death and glory came uninvited into Jack Cole's mind and it stuck with him like a mantra throughout the fight.

Cpl. J. Cole, No. 12645, 2nd Bttn., The Worcestershire Regt., 2nd Division, B.E.F.

It was '*cold remorseless steel*'. Major Hankey led us in with his sword in his hand. There were hordes of these Germans. They were all fresh-faced boys! But they were tough youngsters. We were unshaven and we were haggard in comparison. We went into them stabbing. '*Cold remorseless steel.*' The heat soon went out of them.

Capt. H. F. Stacke, 2nd Bttn., The Worcestershire Regt., 2nd Division, B.E.F.

The struggle grew more and more desperate as reinforcements for each side forced their way through bushes and brambles into the fight. At one point a party of the Worcestershire charged cheering. The cheer echoed through the wood and was taken up all along the line. The pursuit continued for over half a mile. Then, as the wood began to thin and daylight showed between the trees, sharp bursts of fire from the edge of the open ground brought the advance to a stop. The cheering which had demoralised the enemy's infantry in the wood had also served to warn the German reserves on the far side, and on the edge of the wood the Battalion met a storm of shrapnel and machine-gun bullets. The companies took up the best position they could on the eastern edge of the wood and there they dug in.

By nightfall, every man who could still stand on his feet was standing on a line around the wood with rifle trained across the fields beyond. The machine-guns were there now, placed strategically at the corners, and now and again they fired a burst into the dark towards the German trenches, dangerously close. Behind them the sappers were coming up to strengthen the line, and in the hour before dawn the Germans attacked again.

Cpl. A. Letyford, 5th Field Company, Royal Engineers, 2nd Division, B.E.F.

At night we go forward to work. What awful sights in the wood! The dead are lying in groups everywhere. Our brigade had charged through here three times during the day. We have to man the trenches (or ditches!) while the enemy attacks.

The sappers were obliged to man the trenches because every man and every rifle, every shell and every gun, was needed to beat the enemy off. They were running short of them all. The first onslaught had fallen on the Wiltshires, and it had almost wiped them out. A hundred and seventy-two were left of the whole Battalion. Except for the Sergeant-Major who had led them out, and the Quartermaster who had not gone into the line, they had no NCOs left at all and not a single one of their officers had returned. Four hundred and fifty of the missing had been captured in the first surprise attack. The Warwicks had lost their colonel and three hundred men in the fight. The Worcesters had two hundred casualties.

Jack Cole had got through without a scratch. So had Alex Letyford.

There was no question of relief. For the moment there was no one to relieve them. So they stayed where they were, in hastily scratched-up platoons, taking orders from whoever chose to give them. The fighting had been so confused that hardly anyone was still with his own regiment, let alone with his own mates. Men of eleven separate battalions and from five different brigades lay out that night in the wood. The bodies of their comrades and their enemies lay so thickly entangled in the heavy undergrowth that runners and messengers making urgently for the line took a long, long time to reach it.

The Northumberland Hussars were pulled out into reserve. They trudged back a mile to fetch their tethered horses and clopped wearily down the Menin road, and the grooms came behind with a string of horses on leading-reins whose riders lay dead in the wood. It was well after midnight when they stopped to bivouac on the ridge at Hooge by the lake in the château grounds. They were bombarded all night, and weary troopers snoozing fitfully a little too near the verge leapt up cursing when shells plunged into the lake. They exploded harmlessly in the mud, but they threw up great columns of water that soaked them to the skin. Above the sound of the bombardment the accents of Northumberland rang loud and clear and blasphemous in the night.

Chapter 24

Next day, at least by comparison to the day before, it was quiet in Polygon Wood. Behind their line, the Germans were busy bringing up more guns. They were still shelling enthusiastically, and rifles crackled intermittently along the Front, but deep in the wood itself, among the trees that muffled the sound of the warring beyond, it was almost tranquil. The infantry attacks had tailed off and later the sorely pressed troops were relieved. The weather had changed too; and it was fine and mild for the end of October and the stray beams of sunlight glanced down through the tall pines. Where the fighting had been fiercest, stretcher parties scrunched and stumbled over broken twigs and fallen trees, hacking at the undergrowth, searching for the wounded and, where they could, retrieving the bodies of the dead. The 4th Guards Brigade moved up from Hooge and waited in the wood until nightfall would allow them to replace the shattered 5th in the open beyond. Some young officers found unlooked-for amusement that brought them a severe reprimand from their brigadier, the Earl of Cavan. There was a racecourse in the wood – or so they dubbed it. A few days earlier when they first came into the line the Guards Brigade had set up headquarters in a house on the outskirts of St-Jean. It had been the home of the Commandant of the Cavalry School at Ypres before he rode off with his pupils to join the Belgian army.*

Col. R. D. Whigham, GSO I, 2nd Division, B.E.F.

When I went back again to the Salient in February 1916 it was an appalling ruin – difficult to recognise as the pretty comfortable little villa that had sheltered us fifteen months previously. I well remember seeing on the wall of the Commandant's study the timetable of the lectures and exercises for August.

When we moved over to Polygon Wood we came upon a different type of country – heather and thick fir woods, not unlike Pyestock

---

* Later known to soldiers who served in the salient as Hasler House and used as an observation post.

Wood at Aldershot. Polygon Wood, for instance – by the way, I remember at that stage of the war we always spoke of this wood as Racecourse Wood – Polygon Wood was a large wood of young Scotch firs extending to within three or four hundred yards of the Menin road at Gheluvelt village. The so-called Polygon from which the wood took its name was just an elliptical-shaped cavalry schooling ground cut out of the centre of the wood. Why the school should have chosen such a curious spot for their training ground I was never able to find out. Many of the horses that did so well at the Olympia Show were trained on this course, and I remember when we first got there seeing all the well-known Olympia fences, triple bar, railway gate, stile etc. still in place. The sight of these fences was too much for some of our young officers, and in spite of the fact that there was a good deal of shelling going on and quite a number of shells were dropping into Polygon itself, a dozen or so of our young bloods were soon careering round the school and over the fences until they were sternly ordered by the Brigadier to stop.

Other sportsmen were also causing irritation and some bafflement too, for troops crossing the deeper reaches of the wood complained that they were being fired at and concluded that Germans left behind in the attack were lying low and potting at them with revolvers. Someone was certainly taking pot shots but it was not the Germans. Some British, sick of bully beef, were literally shooting for the pot in the hope of bagging a hare or two to augment their rations. Spent bullets, clearly British, gave the show away. The troops were reprimanded and told that this dangerous practice must cease and reminded that bullets were intended for the slaughter of Germans and under no circumstances for the slaughter of game.

But one marksman pulled off a double coup that brought him nothing but praise and admiration. He lay with his rifle trained along a ride and at intervals in the course of one satisfactory half hour succeeded in shooting four pheasants in addition to seven Germans as they dashed across. He crawled out after dark to fetch the pheasants back and diplomatically presented a brace to Battalion Headquarters. Mindful of the Earl of Cavan's strict injunction against the profligate expenditure of bullets, his company officer gave the Colonel to understand that the birds had been 'accidentally shot, Sir, while firing at the enemy', and did not omit to tell him the full extent of the bag. The verdict at Battalion HQ as they enjoyed this unexpected treat for dinner was that in the present circumstances and at a range of two hundred yards, seven hits out of eleven was not bad shooting and could hardly be described as a 'waste' of ammunition.

But the shortage of shells was a more serious problem. In the course of a difficult day, as he reshuffled his troops, throwing battalions in piecemeal to man the gaps and danger points, Sir John French had sent an urgent message to London. Supplies of ammunition were running dangerously low. They were expending ten times, twenty times, a hundred times more than the gloomiest pessimist had ever envisaged. After the last consignments of shells had been issued to the ammunition dumps only 150 shells per gun remained in France, and shipments from home were only topping this up by a derisory seven rounds per gun per day. Unless their fast-diminishing stocks could be replenished and built up, the infantry would very soon be fighting with no artillery to support them. French hardly needed to point out, he felt, what the consequence would be.

But someone in Whitehall, far from the scene of battle, lacked the imaginative powers of the Commander-in-Chief – or perhaps he spoiled his case by stating his opinion that the situation otherwise was 'favourable'. The result, in either case, was the same. The existing stocks of ammunition were checked, the Army's lavish use of shells noted with dismay, and a dusty answer was promptly despatched from the office of the Secretary of State for War. There were no reserves of shells. The supplies could not be stepped up. Economy must be exercised. And that was that.

The Germans were not subjected to the same restraints. They were not short of shells or aeroplanes or bombs. On 29 October, in preparation for a big attack, imagining that Ypres was full of British troops, six aeroplanes flew over Ypres and bombed it for the first time. There were few British troops in the city for they were all in the line, but Ypres was overflowing nonetheless. Its houses were packed with refugees; its hospitals were full of wounded and its long martyrdom was about to begin.

Maria van Assche (Mrs W. Blackmore)

When the fighting started in Langemarck we got scared again and we run away to Wieltje. That's near Ypres. We thought we'd be safe there. But the same night they started shelling there and we had to run again. We went to Ypres. Knocked on everybody's door, asked if we could have shelter, everybody said, 'We're full up.' There we are with the baby, we can't get in nowhere, and it's night. Finally we knock on one door, the woman opens the door, and lucky for my father she knew him, because the Van Assches were well known in Belgium. She said, 'Come in.' And we went in and we had to sleep on the floor on a blanket – all of us. That was our first night on a blanket.

So after a night there we went to a farm, to a friend of my auntie's, and we had to sleep in a barn in the straw and when you took your vest off in the morning you had all these louse, these little louse, on it. And it was terrible! So my father decided to go to Zillebeke. My uncle was in charge of Zillebeke Lake and in his house we thought we were safe again. We had to sleep eight in a bed, all children. My auntie couldn't keep us all inside, so we had to go out and it was all troops round there, plenty soldiers everywhere.

The first dead ones I ever saw was in Zillebeke and they was Englishmen. There was a cart come up, a farmer's cart, and it was full of bodies – you could see the boots, they were stiff – and they just took them down and put them all in this pit, and put lime on it – white stuff. That was the first time I saw dead ones.

The same day the first aeroplane come over. We young ones, we went along the road that goes to Ypres – you could hear the shells all the time, but they wasn't near so we went along there to see the soldiers. They had food, and sometimes they gave us a bit of cheese or chocolate. Then the soldiers said to us, 'there's an aeroplane on top' – and you know they were very loud – and shouted at us to get in the ditch. We got in this ditch and they tried to shoot this aeroplane down – the first aeroplane, just with their rifles. And I'll tell you what them aeroplanes did – that's the first bombs. They went over Ypres and the Boeterstraat – I remember the name, the Boeterstraat and the jeweller's shop – they throwed bombs on that one. The day after that we went to have a look at it. They was the first bombs.

Father Camille Delaere, Curé of the Church of St Jacques. Extract from his diary

There were many victims. Two children were killed in the rue de Thourout and near my presbytery a young girl (Valentine Dethoor) who was on her way to the wash-house had one leg blown off. It was lying some distance and her other leg was slashed to pieces. I ran to help and I found her lying in a lake of blood. While a French military doctor was trying to bandage her I tried to keep her old mother from seeing this horrible sight. They took the poor girl to the French aid post, but she breathed her last after a few moments.

That night the town was bombarded by guns for the first time. A shell fell on the Carmelite convent, another killed two children in the rue de Dixmude and wounded their mother, and other shells wounded many other people.

Every day after that the town was shelled.

Now the troops were ranged in a semi-circle round Ypres, and Ypres was the centre of the storm. But the events of the day had not been entirely unsatisfactory. The French and the British had attacked round the salient that now surrounded Ypres. They had not recaptured the high ground but they had taken back a little, a very little, of the ground that they had lost. And they were standing fast. It was a filthy night of pouring rain and all through the deluge Alex Letyford and the 5th Field Company sappers dug trenches for the Guards a little way beyond Polygon Wood across the fields of heavy clay in front of Gheluvelt. They were not much more than ditches and they were filling up with water as they dug. They had plenty of light to see by, for the Germans, still in possession of Reutel on the ridge above, were well aware that they were out there in the night and fired magnesium flares that bathed the land in light so strong that the sappers could almost count the raindrops falling in silver curtains against the glow, seeping into their clothing, trickling into streams at their feet. And all the time they dripped and cursed and laboured shells screeched past above their heads and whistled on to Ypres.

They were not the only engineers who had been labouring. On the line beyond the French troops, from Dixmude to the sea, the Belgian army had been swaying, staggering but miraculously resisting the Germans' efforts to push through. It was evident to all that they could not resist much longer. The night before, on the personal order of King Albert of the Belgians, engineers had succeeded in opening the long-disused lock gates at Nieuport. They had damned culverts, diverted ditches, and carefully planned the operation so that the land would flood precisely as required. Now the sea was creeping in, reaching further with every tide and swelling with the rain. Soon the waters would spread and wash across the land, flooding it from Nieuport all the way to Dixmude, mingling with the River Yser, with streams and ditches and canals to form an inland sea – a barrier so formidable that even the Kaiser's mighty army would flounder and drown if they tried to cross. The coastline to the north was now secure. And, on the landward side, it was now up to the British Army to bar the Kaiser's way at Ypres as he tried to break through to the sea. Or rather it was up to that part of the British Army that could be spared, and as the toll of casualties mounted, it was growing smaller all the time.

For Ypres was not the Army's sole concern. The line reached south for fifty miles and all along it the British and the Germans were locked in fearsome fighting, straining like Indian arm-wrestlers to gain ground and win the upper hand against the odds. Their casualties were frightful. There were no reserves. There was no possibility of detaching any troops to help to stem the Germans in the north. All who could be spared were there already, and there they must stand and there they must do their best. Ypres had now become the most important part of the Front. It was a great misfortune that it was also the weakest, but there was no help for it.

But the Commander-in-Chief still believed that his troops could take the offensive to regain the ridges and push the Germans back, and his orders for 30 October urged them to do so 'with vigour'. They had, after all, had some success. They were holding their own. They had even advanced in places. Again and again they had beaten off the enemy and inflicted such punishment on his troops that the attacks had cost him dear. It was not surprising that they had now tailed off. The fields were strewn with German dead. Their losses must by far outweigh his own. Surely they must soon crack.

General Sir Douglas Haig, in command of the First Corps, took a more practical view. He merely ordered his troops in the line to entrench themselves as strongly as they could, to continue to strengthen their positions, to send out strong reconnaissance patrols and to await further orders which would be issued in the morning *when the situation is clearer than it is at present*.

But neither the Commander-in-Chief, his corps commanders nor his Intelligence officers were aware of the card in the Kaiser's hand with which the Germans confidently expected to trump their plans. All night reports coming in from different quarters of the Front told of the sound of cavalry behind the enemy's line, of neighing horses and jingling harness and heavy wheels rumbling on cobbled roads. Digesting this information at Headquarters, the Staff did not feel any cause for alarm. The most likely explanation, they concluded optimistically, was that the enemy was retiring under cover of the night and that horse teams were galloping up to remove the guns.

They were a long way wide of the mark. The new German army had arrived and the German gun teams clattering on the roads behind their line were shunting two hundred and sixty heavy guns into position to support it. That night five additional infantry divisions marched up to the German line. They were fresh and fit and they were not to be compared with the brave and ignorant lads who had marched singing into battle days before. They were soldiers. As they paraded to march off, their company officers had read them a special Order of the Day.

. . . The breakthrough will be of decisive importance. We must, and will therefore, conquer, settle for ever with the centuries-long struggle, end the war, and strike the decisive blow against our most detested enemy. We will finish with the British, Indians, Canadians, Moroccans, and other trashy, feeble adversaries, who surrender in great numbers if they are attacked with vigour.★

The tone of the order was nicely calculated to sharpen the offensive spirit. To encourage them still further, each officer was authorised to inform his men that the Kaiser himself was on his way to the Front and would be there to greet them when they returned victorious. Marching to the line through the torrential rain that was misery for friend and foe alike, the German soldiers, like their commanders, were perfectly confident of delivering a knockout blow. Their first objectives were Zandvoorde and the Messines ridge.

The Household Brigade was at Zandvoorde and no doubt the Kaiser knew it, for he was not far away. He was at Crown Prince Rupprecht's headquarters, waiting, as he had waited earlier at Verdun, to witness the glorious break-through of his troops, to gloat over the humiliation of the British and those 'other trashy, feeble adversaries' – perhaps even to accept their surrender into his own imperial hands. Nothing would give him more exquisite pleasure. His aides had already been told to select a suitable residence near Ypres for the Emperor and his retinue. Dismissing certain noble houses, like the mansions at Hooge and Gheluvelt and Polderhoek which they had every reason to believe had been knocked about by their own shells, they had plumped for one on the doorstep of Ypres itself. Hollebeke Château – three miles to the south of Ypres. It was rather less than three miles west of the trenches where the Life Guards and the Royals were in the line at Zandvoorde.

The Household Brigade had close connections with the German Emperor. Many of their officers had met him on social occasions and some men of the Life Guards or the Royal Horse Guards, now face-to-face with the Kaiser's troops, had formed part of his escort on his visits to London, riding round his carriage as it clattered in state up the Mall. They had done so in the King's Coronation procession just three years previously, gorgeous in their plumed brass helmets and burnished breastplates, their high shining boots and immaculate breeches of finest white kid. The Kaiser, with his passion for elaborate uniforms, had been pleased to look on them with approval and sent a regal message of congratulation and thanks. He would have been hard put to it to recognise his glittering escort now, clad in grubby khaki smeared plentifully with mud. Conditions in the trenches at Zandvoorde were not conducive to spit and polish. It was hardly possible to keep clean. It was a full week since Charles Worsley had even managed

★ The Canadians were still in training and were not yet at the Front, but the Germans might have thought it possible that they were, since Intelligence would have known that the first Canadian contingent had arrived in the United Kingdom.

a shave and that, as he confessed ruefully when writing home, was 'all the washing I've had time for in the last ten days'.

Strictly speaking, Lord Worsley and his men should not have been in the trenches at all. Their own regiment, the Royal Horse Guards, had been relieved by the Life Guards after three arduous days and nights but Worsley and his machine-gunners had been left behind. There was no help for it. The Life Guards had a single machine-gun to cover a vulnerable section of the Front, for the other had jammed beyond redemption so Worsley and the machine-gun section of the Blues had stayed on to take its place. They knew that they were badly needed and it would not have been gentlemanly to complain, but they would not have been human had they not been disappointed. They were also weary and they were hungry too, since they had missed out on the meal prepared for the Blues when they left the line and the Life Guards had consumed their own rations before coming in. But mail had arrived and was waiting for the Blues when they trudged back to the transport lines at Klein Zillebeke and Lord Worsley's servant, Trooper Lockie, weary though he was from his own exertions in the trenches, had set off back to the line with the machine-gunners' share of it. There was a parcel from Worsley's mother with a welcome supply of chocolate and Worsley shared it out between his machine-gunners in lieu of supper. To cap it all, it poured with rain and blew a gale all night. Two days later, when the Blues returned to the line, the luckless machine-gunners were at least on the ration strength. When the Blues went out again at the end of their spell and the Life Guards came back, Worsley and his men were ordered once more to stay on in the trenches to support them. They had been in the trenches for six days and six nights.

They were terrible trenches, dug shallow, dug short and dug in the wrong place on the forward slope of the hill, clearly visible to the enemy, for the village of Zandvoorde standing high on a knoll above the plain could be seen for miles. The fact that they could also see the enemy was of little comfort to the troopers for it was plain to see that they were outnumbered and outgunned and that no one seemed to be doing much about it. Captain Lord Hugh Grosvenor sent an irritable message to Head-quarters: *There appears to be a considerable force of the enemy to my front and to my right front. They approach to within about seven hundred yards at night. Our shells have not been near them on this flank.* It was a new experience for the dashing cavalry to be parted from their horses, to be cowering in ditches, to be filthy, hungry and unshaven and, worst of all, to have lost the initiative and to feel that they were at the mercy of events. It was not their style and they did not care for it in the least. But they were all in the same boat, for the cavalry was stretched in a thin, frail line that stretched from Messines to Zandvoorde. It was not much of a bulwark, and they knew it. They knew too that the infantry stretched out on their left from Zandvoorde to Gheluvelt was also stretched to the limit.

The night of 29 October was Worsley's seventh consecutive night in the trenches at Zandvoorde. Next morning at dawn the Germans attacked.

The bombardment opened at six in the morning with all the might the Germans could muster, and it seemed that every gun was trained on Zandvoorde. There was no shelter and nothing to be done but to sit it out with teeth gritted, with ears ringing, with heads spinning, to bandage the wounded as best they could, and when the trenches blew in, to delve with bare hands to rescue the men engulfed in the reeking mud. Few British guns replied. For Worsley and his section the flying earth was almost worse than the explosions. They protected the machine-gun as best they could, hunched over it to shelter it from the showers of dirt and debris, and when the shelling stopped, in the stunning silence before the mass of German infantry moved forward, they hoisted it on to the remains of the parapet and began to fire.

The bombardment had lasted an hour and a half. The attack, when it came, was over in minutes.

The official report recorded with masterly understatement that '*the attack proved successful owing to greatly superior numbers*' and added baldly that '*the Regiment retired in good order*'.

Not quite all the Regiment had retired. In the pandemonium the order to withdraw never reached the slit trench where Hugh Grosvenor and his squadron and Charles Worsley with his gunners were spraying fire on the Germans, now at point-blank range. So they fought on, long after the others had left. Worsley kept his gun going until the end. The last man to leave looked back, he later said, and saw Worsley still standing, still firing at the enemy rushing towards the trench and only yards away. A moment later the gun stuttered and faltered to a stop. There was no one left to substantiate his story. No one was brought back wounded. No one was taken prisoner. No one was left alive to tell the tale. One whole squadron of Life Guards, and the best part of another, had disappeared as if they had never been. So had Worsley and his gunners.

By nine o'clock the Germans had captured the cavalry trenches and were working their way along the ridge past Zandvoorde village to attack the Royal Welch Fusiliers in their flank. By ten o'clock the Zandvoorde ridge was in German hands.* They sent up every available reserve to try

---

* The news that the 7th Cavalry Brigade had been pushed back at Zandvoorde, and with heavy losses, reached 1st Corps Headquarters at 8.30 in the morning, and it caused the Corps Commander Sir Douglas Haig great anxiety. In the midst of issuing orders to send forward what troops he had to retrieve the situation he perhaps spared a personal thought for Lord Worsley, who was married to his wife's younger sister.

to take it back and backed them up with every available gun. But far more guns were ranged against them. Battling through the fearsome shellfire, their progress was painful and slow. They were far too few and far too late to succeed in recapturing Zandvoorde and too late also to save the Royal Welch Fusiliers. The Battalion was annihilated, for only eighty-six survivors returned from a force that, three weeks earlier, had consisted of eleven hundred men. But the counter-attack at least ensured that the Germans got no further.

The Germans themselves had helped to save the situation for the British Army that day. Even where they had pressed the British back, the enemy's infantry had been slow to advance, and they seemed oddly reluctant to press home their advantage. The slaughter had by no means been one-sided. No one could pretend that the British gunners had inflicted much damage on the enemy, but the infantry had. They had been fighting now for ten full days (and most of them for as many nights) with little rest and not much food or comfort to sustain them. There was hardly a gunner, an infantryman or an officer whose eyes were not sunk and blackened by fatigue, whose clothing was not stiff with grime, who had not been soaked to the skin a dozen times, who had not slept standing up (if he had slept at all), who had not forgotten what it was like to have a square meal or a night's peaceful rest. But they had not forgotten how to shoot and how to fight. Time and again, all around the salient, the German infantry advanced in crowded ranks towards some pathetic trenchline that their shells had all but battered to oblivion, and time and again they walked into a hurricane of fire that tore their ranks apart. Time and again their lines bent and swayed and withered and time and again, even when they had penetrated the British line, the Germans stopped where they were and made no attempt to go further. As one officer remarked after one such breathless fight, 'The Germans seemed to have lost their spirit to advance and to have no zest for further casualties.' The troops had every reason to be thankful, but they were also astonished. In some sectors they estimated, at a rough guess, that they were outnumbered by four to one. In some parts of the line it was twice as many as that.

It was true that the Germans had been shaken by their losses, but there was another reason for their failure to push their victories home. They were not to know that the battalions facing up to them had been reduced to half, to a quarter, even to a tenth of their strength. They were not to know that the troops rushing out from the woods and thickets and spinneys to counter-attack were the last reserves of a force that was almost spent and that they were being shunted willy-nilly from pillar to post to 'putty up the Front' and to plug dangerous gaps where the situation was most critical. There were not enough of them to do more – there were hardly enough of them to do that – but the lavish scatter of woodland might easily have sheltered a hundred times as many and the Germans reasoned that it probably did. They also suspected that fresh troops were being rushed up all the time to swell their numbers, and it was logical reasoning, based less on lack of information than on their own experience. The Germans themselves were employing new reserve corps, ill-trained and inexperienced though they were, why then should the British not have brought their huge, much-vaunted Territorial Army to swell their force in France? In the light of such surmises they had every reason to be cautious.

The Territorials were certainly playing a vital part, though not in the role that the Germans were envisaging. It was the 7th Division that was holding them at bay and but for the Territorials there would have been no 7th Division at Ypres, and no 8th Division now hastily forming at home. They had come from every garrison of the Empire, from India, from Egypt, from Malta, from Africa, and Territorial battalions had sailed on the first tides of the war to replace them and release them for service at the Front where hard, experienced men were in short supply. Now that the 7th Division had been reduced to a remnant in the fighting around Ypres they were in shorter supply than ever.

To the cavalry, still clinging to parts of the long ridge that ran south of Ypres to Messines, it was all too clear from the day's fighting that the German cavalry with whom they had been skirmishing had been replaced by infantry, and strong forces of infantry at that, and they were backed by a fearsome arsenal of guns. They had taken a heavy toll of men dismounted in the line and of horses tethered at farms behind. The cavalry were so thinly spread that there was just a single rifle for every six yards of the Front. By some miracle they had held their line.

Zandvoorde had been lost, and so had Hollebeke, for the solitary company of Royal Dragoons who held the château grounds had been forced to draw back. Now they were digging a new line and the Germans, cautiously reconnoitring forward, found Hollebeke Château empty and deserted. Soon, if all went well, the Kaiser's Daimler would drive up to its gates and the Kaiser and his Staff would take possession. That night he dined at Courtrai, twenty miles away.

From the German point of view the results of that day's fighting had amounted to very little. Their gains at Ypres had been small and further north they had been forced to give up the attempt to cross the creeping floods that lay between them and the Belgian army. It had cost them dear in drowned and killed and wounded. But one thing had been gained. The troops who were no longer needed on the Yser could now be brought to Ypres and that night the Germans issued the order that would send them on their way. There were still more troops making for the battle. That morning British pilots flying over Courtrai had spotted five long troop trains standing in the station and seen a mass of soldiers, several thousand strong, moving towards the salient round Ypres.

Just before dusk on the ridge at Zandvoorde where No. 1 Company of the 1st Bavarian Jäger Battalion was waiting in reserve, out of sight of the British now dug in the valley, Oberleutnant Freiherr von Prankh went forward to inspect the captured trenches, and he made for the place where Charles Worsley and his section had kept firing their single gun. Von Prankh had watched it from a distance through binoculars until his own machine-guns, firing from the flank, had silenced it – or had knocked out the men who kept it going. He was curious to know. He stepped gingerly into the shallow trench, for it was full of dead men. The machine-gun had tumbled backwards on top of the gunners' bodies and the arm of the dead officer was trapped beneath the barrel. Von Prankh bent down to search the body and was astonished by what he found. His adversary of the morning was his own exact counterpart. Von Prankh himself was a cavalryman and a machine-gun officer and a member of the German nobility with the title of Freiherr. He was strangely moved by the coincidence. After a few moments he climbed out again, and walked back in the growing dusk across the slopes, picking his way between the sprawling bodies of the dead. Stretcher parties were still working in the carnage, retrieving the countless grey-clad corpses of German dead. There were also khaki uniforms strewn thick across the meadow. Eventually they too would be gathered in and buried in mass graves. There were too many and, as von Prankh well knew, time was too short to do more. He returned to his company, found Leutnant von Neubert and gave him certain personal instructions.

Platoon Leader Leutnant von Neubert, 3rd Platoon, No. 1 Company, 1st Bttn., Bavarian Jäger Regt.

He said that he had found the dead body of an English lord and he decided to have a grave made for this British officer. With several men of my company I fetched the body from the trenches, which were filled with dead enemy soldiers, and had a grave dug, in which we buried the body of the British officer. His effects, consisting of diaries, various papers and articles of some value (unless I am mistaken a golden engagement ring or wedding ring was among them) were handed to Oberleutnant von Prankh to send to the authorities and to inform the next of kin. What actually happened to these effects I am not able to say, and Oberleutnant von Prankh was killed himself a few days later.★

It was the eve of All Saints' Day, 31 October. All night, and all along the line the British Army was digging in, and it was digging for its life. For want of better tools, some Tommies dug with hayforks left in abandoned barns and, for want of better rations, gnawed as they worked on the turnips they unearthed as they gouged trenches across the fields. They were not especially appetising but they did at least assuage their thirst. The Germans were shelling the roads and precious little food or water or ammunition got through.

Early in the morning an interesting message was picked up by signallers listening in on the telephone wires. It was addressed to a German corps commander and it announced that the Kaiser would come to his battle headquarters at mid-morning and added that later in the day he proposed to motor on to Hollebeke. Battle headquarters was at Gheluwe, a mile or so east of Gheluvelt on the road to Menin, and it was on Gheluvelt that the Germans planned to launch the main thrust of the attack that would break the line. The village of Gheluvelt stood at the tip of the salient astride the Ypres to Menin road and once it was captured the road to Ypres would lie wide open and the way would be swept clear ahead to press on to the coast beyond.

★ Lord Worsley's effects never reached his family at home, but one curious relic did. Through diplomatic channels in Holland they received from the War Office in Berlin an accurate sketch map of the site of Worsley's grave. His body was found on the exact spot after the war and identified. The body was removed and is now buried in the Ypres Town Cemetery Extension, Plot 2, Row D, Grave 4. Nearby in the same cemetery is the body of HRH Prince Maurice of Battenberg, son of Queen Victoria's youngest daughter, who was killed not far away while serving with the King's Royal Rifle Corps. The plot of land where Lord Worsley's grave was found on Zandvoorde ridge was purchased by his widow and later the Household Division Memorial was erected on the site. None of the others who died that day was ever heard of again. No prisoners or wounded were reported. No bodies were ever recovered.

Chapter 25

In years to come, until another war arrived to blur the memory, the nation and the men who fought and survived called it Ypres Day and wore blue cornflowers in remembrance of those who had fought and died. To the Worcesters, the 31 October was, and always would be, Gheluvelt Day. It began in the wake of a nerve-racking night. The Germans had profited by the clear moonlight to shell the British trenches on the forward slope of the high ground east of Gheluvelt and their infantry not far away had been sniping at the British line off and on all night, to divert attention from the new assault forces massing round Menin across the plain. When the moon set and the sky clouded over in the early hours of the morning, they began to move up closer in the dark and with the first streaks of daylight they attacked. They came forward cheering. The German soldiers fully intended that this would be Kaiser's Day.

The terse message that reached the Worcesters a little later, as they waited in reserve a mile away, merely stated that the enemy's attack had failed. 'Repulsed with heavy losses' read the text; it might have added that the 'heavy losses' had not only been on the German side and that the attack had been repulsed by something like a miracle. But rifle drill and discipline had told again for the first of many times that day. If the Battle of Waterloo was judged by tradition to have been won on the playing fields of Eton, the Battle of Gheluvelt would be judged in the long run to have been won on the rifle range at Bisley. German officers reporting back spoke yet again of massed machine-guns, of strong entrenchments, of fortress-like redoubts, of large numbers of troops streaming forward to beat them back. This was nonsense in the light of the true facts.

Whole brigades were now reduced to the strength of single battalions and the five battalions in the line astride the Menin road at Gheluvelt numbered barely a thousand men. Men firing in pairs from shallow rifle pits, fifteen yards apart, represented trenchlines. Ditches hastily dug in the form of a square unprotected by so much as a strand of wire was a so-called 'fortress'. A dozen rifles firing in rapid unison were the 'massed machine-guns' that the Germans claimed had routed their attack, and across the fields on the far side of Polygon Wood the 2nd Worcesters were very nearly the last reserve of the British Army at Ypres.

The Worcesters had slept in the open. They were cold and dirty and damp and bedraggled, but miraculously boxes of bacon had come up and they had enjoyed a hot breakfast. They ate it to the sound of a bombardment more awesome than any they had yet heard in the war. The Germans,

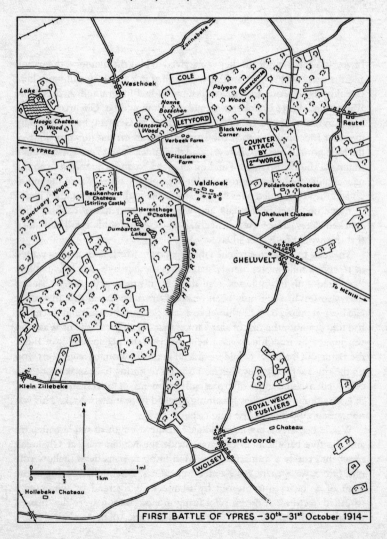

FIRST BATTLE OF YPRES — 30th–31st October 1914 —

switching their tactics to 'softening up the line', had now pulled back their infantry and trained their guns on the trenches about Gheluvelt. For the next two hours the bombardment thundered on without a break.

Fifty-three British batteries firing light shrapnel were of little use against a storm of high-explosive shells, fired by some three hundred batteries of heavy guns pounding the infantry and reaching out to pound the batteries firing to support them. The gunners did their best.

Gnr. C. B. Burrows, 104 Battery, 22nd Brigade, R.F.A., 7th Division, B.E.F.

Any sleep we had the night before we had standing up. We are stiff, exhausted. The Germans have been shelling since daybreak and about 10 o'clock they begin to shell our teams and we have to shift to another position. Hundreds of shells fall around us. A few drivers are wounded and we are lucky to get away. Heard our infantry are hard pressed. One driver and eight horses are killed. We take our teams back another half mile and we hardly get there before we have to go back at the trot. Our infantry are being pressed back and the enemy infantry are not far from our guns.

An arc of guns was ranged around the salient at Gheluvelt but the centre of the storm was on the Menin road. As the hours passed, as the road and the village quivered and danced and disintegrated about them, the troops gave way, crowding into trenches to the right and to the left to escape the pulverising bombardment, the deadly flying steel, the avalanche of earth and stone, the deafening noise, the numbing unremitting blast of the explosions, the trembling earth that threatened to engulf them. When the guns stopped, fresh waves of German infantry began to surge forward into the gap and fanned across the ground on either side. Raising their heads from their shattered trenches the men who had weathered the shelling levelled their rifles as they advanced and began to fire. Even with their number so diminished, even though the enemy was fresh and fighting fit, even though they outnumbered the ragged weary men of Gheluvelt by four or more to one, although few officers were left to rally or command them, they held the Germans off for the best part of an hour.

When it was clear that they could not hold on much longer the word went down to fetch the horses up to save the guns. The gunners at the transport lines had an almighty struggle to reach them.

Gnr. C. B. Burrows, 104 Battery, 22nd Brigade, R.F.A., 7th Division, B.E.F.

We pass through a perfect hail of shells up the Menin road. Awful time! It's a wonder we're not blown to bits! We pass the infantry in reserve digging trenches as fast as they can. We get to the guns at last. They are all ready to be removed. Our gunners are very cool. The German infantry are not far from them. We can see them coming over the hill. There are not many of our infantry left.

We get the guns out just as the enemy come over the hill in full view, and away we go. How we get out of it is a mystery. Shells are bursting all over the place. My off-horse is wounded and nearly drops down with exhaustion but we go on – we have to – along the Menin road. I never expected to get out of that alive. We go back about a mile and stop in a field. We lost an officer, 2 NCOs and one gunner in that affair and several drivers wounded. Even so we are lucky.

Six disabled guns were left behind. Here and there small pockets of men fought on until they were captured or annihilated. The remnants were pushed back. Gheluvelt village fell to the Germans and the road to Ypres was open.

Now the enemy's guns had lengthened their range and the bombardment was falling beyond the battle in the village, and the fields, the roads, the woods between Gheluvelt and Ypres leapt and quaked in the explosions. The men that Charlie Burrows saw on his dash back with the guns were not 'infantry in reserve'. They were the remnants of the men who had been pushed out of Gheluvelt, rallying in a hotch-potch of units half a mile down the road at Veldhoek. They were indeed 'digging trenches as fast as they could'. They were digging in for a last stand. A little way behind them, General Lomax who had commanded the 1st Division while there was still a 1st Division to command, and Brigadier-General Fitzclarence who commanded what was left of the 1st Guards Brigade, had a distinct feeling that it was perfectly likely to be the last stand of the British Army in Belgium.

But there were still the Worcesters waiting at the south-west corner of Polygon Wood. They were almost all that remained of the 2nd Division Reserve, and earlier in the morning General Monro had put them at General Lomax's disposal. Now that Lomax had sent in all that remained of his own reserves it was time to call on them, for he had seen for himself on his last dash to the line that German reinforcements were on the move, and on the march up the slopes to Gheluvelt.

Colonel Leach with the battered remains of his South Wales Borderers still held a foothold in the château grounds furthest from the village. They were clinging on. They had even counter-attacked from the further edge of the park and pushed the Germans slightly back. Gheluvelt Château stood in a hollow of pleasant parkland on the northern outskirts of the village on the edge of the fields and farmland that rippled across to Polygon Wood, separated from the village by a tree-lined sunken road. Some days earlier its owner, Monsieur Peerebone, had shuttered its many windows and departed in haste with his family leaving the house and his treasured collection of fine statuary to the mercies of the army and the war. Until the last attack it had been a useful refuge. The British Army had punctiliously respected his property – a little too punctiliously in the view of some famished Tommies who were not best pleased to find themselves placed smartly under arrest for helping themselves to produce from the deserted kitchen garden. Now the Borderers in the gardens stood among a litter of bodies, of abandoned weapons and equipment thrown aside. They had no inkling of what was happening, they were a fair way to being surrounded and for all they knew they were quite alone. The Germans had withdrawn to the village to wait for reinforcements. Despite the shells that flew above their heads as the British guns fired from their new positions, despite the shelling of German guns as they searched the Menin road beyond, a heavy threatening silence lay round the château itself as the Borderers hung on.

The Worcesters were preparing to attack. From Polygon Wood it was hard to see what was happening. The château on the low ground was hidden by a low ridge in the fields, but the burning church spire was clear to see and a cloud of black smoke above the village led the Worcesters towards their objective as they hastened across the fields, extended into line and advanced at a steady double. They advanced through a curtain of shrapnel, for the German artillery soon spotted them, and a hundred Worcesters fell dead or wounded before they reached the shelter of low ground. But there were enough of them left to throw back the Germans when they met them in the château grounds.

Major Hankey led C Company charging round the side of the shuttered house and they fought it out there on the lawn. The Germans were too astonished to put up much of a fight. The South Wales Borderers were, if anything, even more amazed. They had still been firing, now almost surrounded, when the Worcesters had charged up on their right. In the first lull, when it was clear that the Worcesters had the situation in hand, while the troops hunted the Germans crashing back through the hedgerows, Major Hankey sprinted across to find the Borderers' senior officer. Colonel Leach wrung him by the hand. 'Thank God you've come,' he said.

Lieutenant Slaughter had positioned the machine-gun near the sunken road and they were firing flat out to drive the Germans back and to discourage reinforcements from attempting to come forward.

Pte J. Cole, No. 12645, 2nd Bttn., The Worcestershire Regt.,
2nd Division, B.E.F.

They fled in a solid grey mass and we watched the boys winkling them out. Remorseless. It was slaughter. At one point in the sunken road we were firing the machine-gun, using dead bodies for cover, and there was a German lying there. He was wounded and he was begging us something. He unbuttoned his tunic and he took out a photograph of his wife and child and held it up – begging to be moved, maybe, from the line of fire, scared stiff. But we couldn't do nothing. Our lines weren't established and it was dangerous to hang around because the Germans were sweeping this sunken road with enfilade fire from Gheluvelt village. We linked up with the Welsh and had to send forward fighting patrols to clear them out of it – and we did it (apart from a few fanatics in a few pockets who held on and kept firing). We plugged the gap to Calais.

Two miles behind the battleline at Gheluvelt, the Generals and the fighting staffs of the 1st and 2nd Divisions were assembled at their head-quarters at Hooge Château beside the Menin road. It was lunchtime – or would have been in normal circumstances. But no Staff Officer today had the time or the heart to think of food, and the cooks who had prepared it, the mess waiters who had set out the linen and silver and filled the decanters on the sideboard, waited in vain in the dining room to serve the congealing meal to the officers who were too concerned and too busy discussing the situation to eat it. Half an hour earlier, General Lomax had returned and met General Monro at the doorway of his office. 'My line is broken.' He said it baldly, almost laconically. There was little else to be said.

At Corps Headquarters at the White Château a little way down the road at the foot of Hooge ridge, Sir Douglas Haig had received the same disconcerting news, and it confirmed his own worst fears for he had just returned from riding up the Menin road to judge the situation for himself. The road was congested with transport and ammunition wagons returning nose to tail, with walking wounded streaming back on either side, and although the field guns had moved back to new positions and were firing reassuringly some way ahead, heavy howitzers were rumbling past at the trot and they were making for Ypres. The enemy's heavy guns were searching now, shells exploded in the fields around and minute by minute the bombardment was hotting up. It had not required a soldier's eye to recognise the signs of retreat. When Haig returned to the White Château a Staff Officer met him at the door with the news that the line had gone. Haig himself had had a narrow escape. In his absence the heavy chandelier that hung above his table in the drawing room that was now his office had been brought down by concussion and the crystal splinters had flown in every direction. Crunching his way across the room, brushing aside the debris to clear a space, Haig sat down with his Staff Officers to decide what could be done and to issue his orders. There was not much that could be done, no options to consider, no reserves to draw on. The orders were quickly drawn up. The 7th Cavalry Brigade, although it could ill be spared, would go as fast as it could to Hooge and stand in line along the ridge. Behind this line, if the worst came to the worst, the troops would rally and would defend it, if they could, until the last. At half-past one this order was despatched to the Divisional Commanders at Hooge. They never received it.

All morning, knowing the German Emperor was in the vicinity, heavy guns had been shelling and aeroplanes had been bombing châteaux behind the German line in the hope of wiping out the Kaiser or at least his senior commander and their staffs. Now, by a dreadful irony, it was German shells on Hooge that wiped out the British Command at the most crucial moment of the battle. General Lomax was mortally wounded, seven senior officers were killed, General Monro was stunned and badly shaken.★

Just as the news of this latest catastrophe reached Haig at his headquarters a mile away, just as he had ordered his horse and was preparing to ride up to Hooge and take command himself, the Commander-in-Chief arrived in person and he arrived on foot because his car had been unable to make headway against the press of traffic along the congested Menin road. He slumped into a chair, pale with shock at the news of this fresh calamity. Later Sir John French freely admitted that it was the worst half-hour of his life. They discussed the possibilities. They discussed the practicalities of retreat. But this was not Mons. With Ypres at their backs and the River Yser beyond, with the men at the limit of fatigue and endurance, with bridges sparse and main roads few, with huge numbers of the enemy coming

★ Apart from Major-General Lomax, in command of the 1st Division, and General Monro, in command of the 2nd, the officers who were killed outright were Colonel F. W. Kerr and Major G. Paley (General Staff, 1st Division), Lieut. A. J. Percival and Captain R. Ommanney (General Staff, 2nd Division), Captain F. M. Chenevix-Trench (Brigade Major, Royal Artillery, 2nd Division) and Captain G. P. Sheddon of the 35th Heavy Battery. Captain R. Giffard, General Munro's ADC, was mortally wounded and four other officers seriously hurt. The dead are buried in the Ypres town cemetery near Captain Lord Worsley's grave.

up in hot pursuit, the chances of an orderly withdrawal were nil. There was nothing for it but to make a stand between Ypres and Messines – and there were not many men left to make it. The reserves had long ago been used up. Their only hope lay with the French. Deeply despondent, the Commander-in-Chief took his leave. He would go now, straight away, to see General Foch and he would beg for assistance. It was all the help he could offer and he himself had privately given up hope. As he hurried down the Menin road to find his car, Sir John French had little doubt 'that the last barrier between the Germans and the Channel seaboard was broken down'. The shelling had tailed off and, but for the clattering of transport wheels, it was quiet down the Menin road. This surely indicated that the German troops were moving forward.

Just as Sir John French reached the car which his driver had succeeded with difficulty in inching round to face back towards Ypres, he heard running footsteps and turned as his name was called. Haig's ADC, Lieutenant Straker, was pounding down the road, dodging round the wagons, elbowing through the straggling wounded, rushing to catch him up. Straker was flushed and breathless, but his face was jubilant. The Worcesters had counter-attacked. They had driven the Germans out of Gheluvelt. The enemy had fallen back, the troops had steadied, and the hole in the line was plugged.

Far ahead, where the remnants of the troops were rallying and the gunners were firing in their new positions, the good news had travelled fast.

Gnr. C. B. Burrows, 104 Battery, 22nd Brigade, R.F.A., 7th Division, B.E.F.

Hundreds of wounded pass by. We go into action in a field and shell the enemy heavily. Heard we had done good and have repulsed their attack. Stay there all night and keep up a heavy rate of fire. Heard that the enemy infantry were laying dead in heaps – also that we have lost heavy. Shall not forget this day in a hurry. 13th day of battle.

But this thirteenth day of battle was far from over and the enemy had not been content with pushing against the salient at Gheluvelt. The crescent of ridges round Ypres billowed into a single spur of high ground that swept south from Ypres to the village of Messines. They called it the Messines ridge and the enemy had been hammering it all day.

★

The yeomen of the Queen's Own Oxfordshire Hussars did not regard themselves as the scrapings from the bottom of the barrel. They were fully conscious that they owed their extended stay in France to the intervention of the Commander-in-Chief himself and they had not let him down. They had acquitted themselves well in various brushes with the German cavalry, they had performed their duties as Headquarters troops as smartly and efficiently as any regulars, they had turned out a personal bodyguard of which the King himself would not have been ashamed and, if anything, they looked on themselves unofficially as 'Sir John French's Own', rather than Sir John French's last resort. But there was no getting away from the fact that that was exactly what they were.

It was a long ride, a full thirty miles, from St-Omer to Bailleul and on across the Belgian border to the Front. They had set off in fine style, though the trail of farm wagons that constituted their transport and the convoy of private motor cars which the officers had no intention of leaving behind detracted somewhat from the military appearance of the squadrons of horsemen ahead. Rain, early in the evening, had not helped. By the time they arrived at their destination as dawn broke on 31 October, horses and men were stiff and cold and weary. For the last few miles the troopers had been falling asleep in the saddle, but now everyone was wide awake. The rain had gone off, the wind had dropped and touches of gold streaking the hazy horizon in the east promised a fine morning. But, as the Regiment collected and dismounted in the square of Neuve Eglise behind them, the officers looking eastwards through binoculars were not lost in admiration of the sunrise. They were gazing intently at the ridge across the valley and it was their first glimpse of a full-scale battle.

Between the Flemish dome of the church tower at Messines and the pointed spire of the church in Wytschaete village the ridge was wrapped in mist and rolling smoke. At half-past four that morning the Germans had attacked the ridge from Wytschaete to Messines. They had swarmed in from the east where a whole new army had moved up in the dark and thrown itself against the astounded cavalry and the scatter of infantry spread along the crest. They had held on by the skin of their teeth. They were still holding on to Messines, fighting behind barricades and from house to house; they were holding on along the spur where trenches were short and few and very far between; they were outnumbered by as many as six to one, and every man who could be found was being pushed into the fight. Listening from across the valley, the Oxfordshires could hear staccato rapping of machine-guns around Messines, and the boom of guns pounding the earth along the ridge as they waited to go forward into battle.

Pte. G. Huggins, No. 2178, D. Sqdn., 1st Troop, Queen's Own
Oxfordshire Hussars, B.E.F.

The thing is that with cavalry and yeomanry if they're going to fight
dismounted it doesn't matter how badly they need the men in the
line, you can't send everyone forward because so many have got to

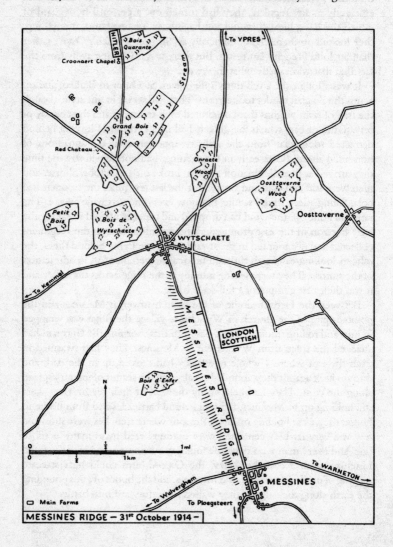

MESSINES RIDGE — 31st October 1914 —

stay behind to look after the horses. I was head horseman of our squadron then, so of course I was one of the ones who had to stay behind. They had to go up on to this ridge, so we rode up a certain distance and dismounted, and then some went forward on foot and the rest stayed behind, one man to every four horses. Well, we'd heard this gunfire all night as we came up – far off at first, like thunder rumbling, which we thought it *was* at first. Then it got louder and louder as we got near. Well they left us there, and I was standing under these trees just up from the foot of the ridge holding the horses and two shells came right close by – whistled past, and then a great boom and another boom as they exploded one after the other just behind us. Oh dear! My tummy seemed to come right up and go out of my ears. They were the first two shells I ever heard close by. And there's nothing you can do about it, you know! You've got these horses, so you can't take cover or get down anywhere. You just have to stand there and hold the horses – and of course *they* didn't like it any more than we did, but you just have to hold on to them and try and calm them down and hope for the best. And all the time, of course, you're wondering how the other fellows are getting on. You've no idea what's happening. You've just got to stay there.

The Oxfordshires who had gone forward had no more idea what was happening than the men left holding horses in the rear. Major Churchill had simply been sent forward with two squadrons, told to get on to the ridge, to choose a spot that was reasonably sheltered from shellfire and 'act as support to the cavalry'. They spent most of the day spread out across two fields sitting in a dry ditch while the fighting scorched above them.

Lce/Cpl. Edward Organ, No. 1745, A Sqdn., 1st Troop, Queen's Own Oxfordshire Hussars

We had no idea what was going on, but we could tell that things were pretty hot. You could see quite a distance where the ground fell away to the right of us into a kind of flat plain, and you could see farms and houses burning there, and there were shells falling all round us – really near. We were well down this ridge, sheltered you might say, but sometimes streams of bullets came zipping over our heads – like bees swarming. We were all nervous – well, frightened I suppose – and it's a funny thing, but when you get frightened someone starts a song and you all yell it out. It's a sort of bravado affair. So we lay there in that ditch with the shells falling round, and we were singing for all we were worth. We were singing 'Ragtime Cowboy Joe', and

I never hear that song but I think of us lying there and those guns banging away and those shells exploding. We got used to them before we got out of that lot, but I never knew a day of noise like that first time – I suppose because it *was* the first time. (It must have been worse later on in the war but it's that first time that always sticks in my mind.) After a while we were ordered to move (where to nobody knew!) and we went back and forwards from pillar to post all day. At night we were sent back into some trenches C Squadron had dug, and what a night *that* was. All round Messines you could see the flames where it was all on fire.

By morning Messines, or part of it, was still in British hands, but only just. So was the part of the ridge immediately left of the village. Beyond that the Germans were over the crest and, worse, they had moved into Wytschaete village and pushed the British out. No one had fought harder to defend it than the London Scottish. Like the Oxfordshire Hussars it had been their first time in the line; like the Oxfordshires they were Territorials – the first Territorial infantry battalion to have landed in France – and they had come as line-of-communication troops to supply the many needs and wants of the fighting army in the field. In everyday life these exiled Scots who happened to live or work in London had been bankers or clerks or civil servants, and many of them, even in the humble rank and file, held high positions in commerce or the professions. The London Scottish had been, in a sense, their club. They played rugby and football in teams that were the terror of the southern league, they held social events that ranged from a glittering Caledonian Ball and a traditional Burns Supper to informal socials and guest nights, where the London Scots whooped and skirled and reeled and swung the kilt as wildly as any Highlander in his native Scotland. Six weeks earlier they had whooped and skirled their way to France and since then they had been general dogsbodies.

They had acted as dockers, unloading ships and despatching supplies to the Army, as railwaymen, shunting trucks and engines round goods yards, as warders, escorting prisoners to the coast, as engineers, doing repairs and putting up telegraph poles, as labourers, heaving big guns, putting up huts, erecting tents and doing a thousand and one menial jobs that no one else had time to do. But they had supplied the Army with brain as well as brawn. A number of men who were accomplished linguists had been roped in as interpreters and on one illustrious occasion E Company had attained the dizzy heights of acting as bodyguard to the Commander-in-Chief, when he went to the Elysée Palace to visit the French President. The London Scottish had been in Paris before, and during the Battle of the Marne. There they had performed the role of policemen, rounding up

British stragglers who had drifted into the city, and they had thoroughly enjoyed the interest they attracted as they patrolled the city in all their kilted glory. Their duties had taken them as a matter of course into cafés and restaurants, picture palaces and other places of amusement, where they had cemented the Auld Alliance between France and Scotland by accepting a certain amount of strictly unofficial hospitality from admiring Parisians. They had enjoyed a pleasant stay. Nevertheless, like the Territorials of the Yeomanry, they had itched to get to the real war.

Yesterday their chance had come. Early in the morning, with Colonel Malcolm's rousing speech of encouragement ringing in their ears, fully conscious of the honour of being the first Territorial battalion of infantry to go into battle, the London Scottish had advanced with pipes playing and kilts swirling to uphold the honour of Scotland and the Territorials. Now they were straggling back in twos and threes, grim-faced and hollow-eyed from their ordeal.

Lce/Cpl. Edward Organ, No. 1745, A Sqdn., 1st Troop, Queen's Own Oxfordshire Hussars

They weren't an organised force at all. They'd been all split up because they'd been cut to pieces. The Germans mowed them down, and some said that only 25 per cent of them came back. Well, we saw them ourselves – there were only *handfuls* of them, and they certainly looked as if they'd been through the mill! They should never have been sent there. They were a Territorial regiment, never heard a shot fired before, and they were actually the first – because *we* were Yeomanry – they were actually the first Territorials in action in the war.

If the London Scottish had not succeeded in thwarting the enemy at Wytschaete it was not for want of trying, for they had fought like demons. They had also fought alone. Like those of the Oxfordshires, their orders were of the haziest and it was not remarkable that they had been misunderstood in the excitement and confusion. The London Scots had been shunted to and fro during the night, instructions were issued and then cancelled, and early in the morning, when they reached the ridge itself, they had to make a long detour, doubling back and forward to dodge the shelling to reach their position between Wytschaete and Messines. The latest of their orders was to 'reinforce the cavalry' and to attack with them 'if necessary'. From the steep slopes of the ridge it was difficult to see what was happening on the crest where the cavalry were holding a line along the road just beyond their view, but the ridge in front crackled with rapid fire. The cavalry were not attacking but to the London Scots, unpractised in warfare and green in judgement, it seemed as if they were. They were too impatient to be prudent, to dribble reinforcements forward in small inconspicuous groups, too charged with excitement, too anxious to get into the fight. They deployed for battle and they plunged forward like lions, keeping strict formation as they crossed the open slopes. Well before they reached the top of the ridge every gun was trained on them and firing.

Some reached the cavalry trenches. Some went well ahead of them and blazed at the German infantry regrouping beyond the ridge. One man in three was killed or wounded on the way and, within minutes, every other rifle jammed. The scattered survivors sheltering in shallow rifle-pits that passed for trenches (long ago abandoned by the cavalry) could have wept in sheer frustration. They were still there at nightfall when the moon came up, in groups of ten or twenty, widely separated. It was the night of Halloween, and by half-past ten when the Germans attacked it was almost as light as day. To the superstitious Scots the long lines of shadowy silhouettes coming towards them over the moon-blanched ridge looked like ghostly creatures of the night. Herbert de Hamel was taking his turn as look-out.

Pte. Herbert de Hamel, 14th Bttn., The London Regiment
(London Scottish) (T.F.)

Two of us stood side by side peering into the patches of moonlight and shadow, straining our eyes for the least movement. A terrific rattle of rifle and Maxim fire broke out and away in front of us a line of dim figures advanced. They were ghostlike in the moonlight. The CO told us to prepare to fire, but to wait for his command. He shouted out, 'Who are you?' There was no answer, so he shouted again and *again* there was no answer, so he sang out to us to open fire. We blazed away into them and I wondered why they lay down in twos and threes to fire back at us. Then it suddenly struck me that they were tumbling over.

They made no attempt to rush us, but they still advanced at a steady walk, falling as they came. Flashes spat out along their line. There was no sound – no shouts or cries, only the crackling of rifle shots. The bullets were cutting through the hedge in front of us and slapped into the bank behind us and all the while, as we tried to fire back, our new rifles jammed and stuck, it might be after one shot or after five shots. You dropped to the bottom of the trench and tugged and banged at the bolt to get it free. Then, as often as not, it would foul the next cartridge from the magazine and refuse to click home. And all the while the German line was advancing.

But after a while there were no more Germans walking towards us, though the heavy firing carried on in our near neighbourhood, and then there was a lull and we got our casualties back to the rear. At the time I thought this silence meant the attack had been repulsed. It was only later I found out that the British line had retired to a new position. But the message didn't get to the Scottish. There was still firing going on and we waited to see if anything else would happen. It did! It was the sound of cheering, and the CO shouted, 'We're charging! Get ready to join in!' There was a building on fire behind this trench and we could see the men running past, silhouetted against this blaze. But these men were advancing in the wrong direction! We could see their spiked helmets.

We jumped out of the trench and ran into a row of turnip tops to fire at them. Then somebody discovered that the Germans were coming up in a solid mass behind us, so we doubled back to hold the trench. The old proverb, 'more haste, less speed', seemed to hit me a bang in the ribs with a red-hot poker, and I was hit. The people we had fired on turned on us and started to advance, and a *third* lot was bearing down on us to enfilade us. The sergeant's rifle jammed permanently then. He took mine, but that had jammed too! So had most of the rest – and we were almost surrounded. There was a ring of fire round the trench and just one solid sound of bullets.

It was the fire that saved them, and a night breeze that shifted and enveloped the trench in thick smoke from a burning haystack. It clung there long enough for the men to slip away. Nine of them got back.

Of the seven hundred and fifty London Scots who had gone into the line more than three hundred were knocked out.* The Oxfordshire Hussars had been luckier, but the worst of their casualties were yet to come. So too was the worst of the crisis.

Not far from where the London Scots had made their first advance early in the morning, a young corporal in the German army was caught up in fierce fighting with the French close to Wytschaete village. Their attack had been repulsed, the Bavarians had been pushed back to Croonaert Wood, and the French guns had proved a match for the German. Shells were still crashing down, parts of the wood were on fire, the road and the fields beyond were littered with dead and wounded and a little distance along the road a wayside chapel was engulfed in flames. Captain Hoffman

---

* One of the survivors of the London Scottish who took part in the Battle of Messines Ridge was Ronald Colman who was to win fame and fortune in Hollywood as a film star.

lay wounded near the chapel and his corporal determined to bring him in. Even with smoke to give a certain amount of cover it was a risky business to crawl from the shelter of the wood into the open when any movement brought a volley of rifle fire from the watchful French infantry across the sloping fields, and the young German was awarded the Iron Cross in recognition of his bravery. Captain Hoffman died of his wounds, and in later life the corporal who had rescued him made no secret of the fact that he looked on his own miraculous preservation as a sign that great things were in store for him. A single bullet might have changed the course of history. His name was Adolf Hitler.

Captain Hoffman was one of some thousands of German casualties, killed or wounded or captured on what had been intended to be the Kaiser's Day.

Ypres Day had not saved the line but, for the moment, it had steadied it. Ground had been given up, but it had not been lost at bayonet point. The enemy now held most of the ridge and next day as the Oxfordshires prepared for an attack they saw long lines of British infantry streaming back down from Messines. But it was not a rout, and the enemy following on was shattered and dispersed by the fast-firing guns rushed up by the French. Messines had gone of course. So had Gheluvelt. But they had held out long enough to see to it that when the troops fell back it was to a position of their choosing – a position on which they could brace themselves to fight on and make sure that, if it were humanly possible to prevent it, the enemy would get no further.

The trouble was that Sir John French was no longer entirely sure that it *was* humanly possible with the slim resources that remained, and he was not alone. Major Jeffreys of the Grenadier Guards, finding himself alongside General Capper, offered his sympathy. 'I'm afraid the 7th Division has suffered badly, Sir.' 'Yes,' replied the General, and he gave a ghastly grin. 'I am now a curiosity – a divisional commander with no division left to command.'

Jeffreys made no reply. It was only a very slight exaggeration and, try as he might, he could think of nothing useful to say. He had precious few men left to command himself. And the battle was far from over.

Chapter 26

On Monday morning newsboys hawking papers on the streets of Britain did full-throated justice to two items of information, newly released by the Press Bureau, which appeared on their billboards in happy juxtaposition.

'*LONDON SCOTTISH IN ACTION!*' they yelled. '*EMDEN SUNK!*'

It gave rise to a joke that persisted for months. Question: *Who sank the* Emden? Answer: *The London Scottish.*

The German battlecruiser *Emden* had been sunk by the Australian navy, and it was Australia's first spectacular contribution to the war effort. Since the outbreak of war, the German navy had been marauding the seas in the Far East much as Germany's army had been marauding overland in the West. In the space of two days, the *Emden* had sunk five unarmed British merchant ships going about their lawful business off the coast of Bengal, she had shelled the oil storage tanks at Madras, she had coaled impudently within sight of the coast of Pondicherry, had gone on to capture six more merchantmen and sent four of them to the bottom. She had torpedoed a Russian and a French destroyer off the coast of Malaya. She had brought the eastern trade almost to a standstill and it was estimated that, in total, the *Emden* had cost the British Government not less than four million pounds. Meanwhile the British Navy scouring the ocean in search of her had not seen so much as a wisp of the *Emden*'s steam on the horizon.

Her captain, von Mueller, had become something of a hero for he had 'played the game' in what British public opinion regarded as a thoroughly sportsmanlike manner. In every case he had disembarked the crews before sinking their vessels. He had behaved with courtesy to civilian passengers and with particular gallantry to ladies. He had finally set all his prisoners free and allowed them to sail off packed into the *Katanga* (which he had thoughtfully refrained from sinking with this purpose in mind) and when they landed in India the passengers were loud in their praises of Captain von Mueller and the punctilious behaviour of the German navy which contrasted so markedly with the lamentable brutishness of the German army in Europe.

All this had been widely reported in the press and the exploits of the

Emden were hot news. They were also causing severe headaches at the Admiralty and at the War Office, anxiously awaiting supplies of hides from the Empire to supply boots and saddlery for the Army, jute for the manufacture of sandbags and large quantities of cotton and wool to make shirts and uniforms to clothe the new recruits. They were also awaiting the Empire's men. The first Indian contingent had set sail early in September and was already fighting at the Front. The first Canadian contingent was safely training in England. The first of the Australians were now on the high seas, sailing across the dangerous waters where the *Emden* lurked in wait. It was not surprising that the Admiralty was jumpy and that the departure of the convoy had been delayed until the escort of battleships and destroyers could be strengthened.

The convoy had sailed a week earlier from Sydney and the emotional send-off was the most thrilling experience of Ralph Langley's young life. Ralph was an apprentice steward on the White Star cargo-passenger ship *Afric* which had sailed for Australia towards the end of July.

Steward Ralph Langley (later C/1303 Rfn. H. R. Langley, 16th Bttn., King's Royal Rifle Corps)

We knew nothing about the war until we got to Cape Town because in those days wireless only had a range of about two hundred miles. It was two weeks to Cape Town and then another three to Australia and when we arrived they immediately collared us for a troopship and we had to wait there while they fitted the ship out – tore down bulkheads to make dormitories and so on. We took about fifteen hundred troops on board the *Afric*, and she wasn't a big ship. There were forty-two ships in our convoy, though of course that included our escort of destroyers, so you can imagine how many Aussie soldiers we were carrying. All these ships assembled in Sydney Harbour – and it was a most marvellous thing, because the place was packed with boats, little boats that had turned out to see us off, and up on the Heads of Sydney there were crowds and crowds of people waving and cheering.

There was terrific excitement! The soldiers on the troopships were packed on to the decks singing and shouting. All the ships sounded their sirens as we passed by the Heads and the little boats were whistling and hooting and the people on board were cheering and shouting *Good Luck* and *Bon Voyage* and calling out what they must do to the Kaiser and all that sort of thing. I was up on deck taking it all in, and one thing I'll never forget, there was a fellow on board (they said he was quite a well-known Australian baritone in civil life, though I never knew his name) and as we were coming out of Sydney Harbour he stood up near the prow of the ship and he sang 'Somewhere a Voice is Calling'. You could hear him all over the water. It was just getting dusk as we sailed and in Australia the sun goes down very quickly – it's dark in just a few minutes – and as we passed through the Heads a bugler from the camps up there stood and played the Last Post. And a hush fell. I was only a kid of sixteen then, but I've never forgotten it. It's a scene I shall never forget as long as I live.

The voyage was far from humdrum. Ralph and the other officers' stewards were soon on friendly terms with the Aussies who cultivated them assiduously, less for the pleasure of their society than for their ability to obtain bottles of whisky from the Officers' Mess. Within a week Ralph had made a useful profit on this lucrative sideline – and lost most of it again in his off-duty time playing nap or Crown and Anchor with the sociable Aussies on their mess deck.

It was an exceedingly crowded mess deck, for the *Afric* was a small ship, equipped in normal times to carry two hundred or so passengers, and most of the amenities enjoyed by her peacetime voyagers had been removed to make space for the troops. But she still had her printing press and she still produced a daily ship's newspaper which in honour of the Aussies was renamed the *Kangaroo*. Its existence was brief but glorious. Within a week it had scooped Fleet Street with a world-exclusive story; it was the first to print the news of the sinking of the *Emden*. It blazoned the story in no less than three headlines.

SENSATION AT SEA
THE *SYDNEY* ENGAGES THE *EMDEN*
EMDEN CAPTURED AND BEACHED

'The *Kangaroo*,' it crowed, 'is the first newspaper in the world to receive and publish this message which is of paramount interest to the shipping and commercial life of all nations.'

But, strictly speaking, by the time the *Kangaroo* appeared on the morning after the sinking, the news was stale, for not one of its readers did not know it already. They had seen HMS *Sydney* swing away from the convoy and race off rolling a trail of smoke behind her and, after a long pause filled with rumour and excitement, they saw HMS *Melbourne* and a small fast cruiser get up steam and disappear at such a speed that flames were flickering from their smoke stacks. They had heard how the *Sydney* had caught the *Emden* just fifty miles away at the Cocos Islands, and if they did not yet know all the details of the gun battle that followed they knew the only thing that mattered – the *Emden* had been sunk and it was the Aussies who had sunk her.

The *Kangaroo* followed up its scoop by printing an exultant paean of justifiable self-congratulation.

> *At rest at last, the* Emden*'s run her race.*
> *No more can she small harmless ships beguile.*
> *Complete her work of joining in the chase,*
> *Her battered hulk lies on the Cocos Isle.*
>
> *Australia's ships of war have gained the day*
> *And H M S* Sydney *takes the praise.*
> *Abuse of naval laws they now repay*
> *By laying low the ghost of recent days.*
>
> *The price of victory always must be paid*
> *So those who gave their lives die not in vain,*
> *Through centuries our Empire's name was made*
> *By those who died her freedom to attain.*
>
> *The pride we feel is echoed through the world*
> *Where'er by fame the* Emden*'s deeds are known,*
> *For o'er her grave our Empire's flag's unfurled,*
> *To mark the whirlwind where the wind she'd sown.*
>
> *Our Colonel was the first to spread the news,*
> *The first to greet the Commonwealth success,*
> *A happy moment for the Kangaroos*
> *By being first to send it through the Press.*
>
> *So we upon the* Afric *feel with pride*
> *That though the* Emden *has been lurking near,*
> *The watchful boys on whom we all relied*
> *Have held them true to all traditions dear.*

The news of the sinking of the *Emden*, welcome though it was, did little to mitigate the anxious news from Belgium. There were uplifting tales of the valiant stand of the Army 'near a town in Belgium' and the charge of the London Scottish shared the headlines with the *Emden* but, even to the man in the street trying to pierce the fog of censorship, the dreadful casualty lists, and the fact that the Territorials had been sent into the line at all, were evidence enough that matters at the Front were grave.

They were more than grave. They were critical.

Brigades were reduced to the strength of battalions. Battalions were down to the strength of companies and companies at full muster were little more than platoons. Now the units were so mixed up that it was almost meaningless to refer to corps or divisions and the maverick remnants of battalions that were collected and reorganised into single fighting units were described, even in official despatches, by the names of the officers who commanded them – Cavan's Force, Bulfin's Force, Fitzclarence's Brigade. As the toll of casualties mounted, Sir John French saw his army gradually melt away before his eyes – and there were few officers left to command what remained of it. The Royal West Kents had just four officers left – and they were all subalterns; the 1st Coldstream had two besides the Quartermaster; the Grenadiers, the Scots Guards, the Borderers and the Gordon Highlanders had five apiece. Battalions were now commanded by captains, and even in a few instances by lieutenants, in place of colonels.

And the men were tired – weakened by want of proper food, drained by the strain of the incessant fighting, without sleep, without rest, without relief or hope of respite from the shelling and the bullets and the battle that raged on along the line. In the circumstances they had performed miracles; they could hardly be expected to go on performing them indefinitely.

The Commander-in-Chief said as much in another message telegraphed to London and he also made it clear that the scarcity of ammunition was now acute. He could not make bricks without straw. He could not make war without men and guns and without ammunition for the men and guns to fire. The German push had only been repulsed by drawing heavily on the slim supply of shells in France, and even the stocks of rifle ammunition were going down fast. As for the rifles themselves, the complaints of the London Scottish had been amply borne out. On examination by the Ordnance Department, half of the Mark 1 Lee Metfords were found to be defective. In short, he needed reinforcements if the infantry were to carry on fighting, and shells if the guns were to carry on firing.

The Secretary of State for War sent a prompt reply. All he could offer in the way of reinforcements was to send eight selected battalions of Territorial infantry. All he could offer in the matter of ammunition was to suggest helplessly that the French should be asked for artillery assistance.

The French had already given assistance, and they had given it generously. Their fast-firing .75 guns had done much to thwart the German attacks or, where they had gained advantage, to discourage them from pressing it home. They had sent up their cavalry to help out at Messines and Wytschaete, and offered up their own reserves of infantry to assist the British in the line. But it was no longer possible to talk of reinforcing the line; all they could reasonably expect to do was to patch it up.

It was a mercy that, for the moment at least, the German attacks had abated. The fighting was still going on but the push appeared to be over. It was only a temporary lull.

★

Some days later, when he was relieved from the line, Corporal Adolf Hitler had the honour of receiving the Iron Cross from the hands of Kaiser Wilhelm himself as he travelled behind the line visiting his battle-weary troops. The Kaiser was by then on the point of departure and again he was leaving empty-handed, balked once more of a decisive victory. Although they had enjoyed some local success, although the Kaiser had sent his troops a message of fulsome congratulation, from the German point of view the results of the fighting had been deeply disappointing. Their gains had been small, they had been won at the price of huge casualties and they were no nearer breaking through to the coast than they had been in the week before their all-out effort. Time and again, even where they had succeeded by sheer weight of numbers, the inexperienced men of the German Reserve Corps had hesitated and held back in the face of counter-attacks, fearful that reserves who charged forward (like the Worcesters, like the London Scottish, like the fragmented reserves of scores of decimated battalions) were merely the forerunners of many more hiding and waiting in the shelter of the woods. The Kaiser was not pleased. Still less was Crown Prince Rupprecht who had longed to show him a victory. He addressed harsh words to his fighting commanders and railed at them for want of enterprise when they protested that the attacks in Flanders 'had cost the most dreadful sacrifices in blood, and very little had been achieved'.

But railing was no good. Neither, without stiffening, were the Reserve Corps. There was nothing for it but to bide their time, to bring up fresh troops – and this time the very best at their command – and when they arrived, to settle the matter once and for all.

The troops in the line hardly realised that the Germans were biding their time, nor did the people of Ypres. All round the salient the pressure was being kept up and while they awaited the arrival of reinforcements and the launch of the attack that would break the salient and win the war, the Germans concentrated all the fury of their powerful artillery on Ypres and on the flimsy circle of men who stood between them and the town. For soldiers and civilians alike the week that followed, Ypres Day was a week of mounting horrors.

Cpl. A. Letyford, 5th Field Company, Royal Engineers, 2nd Division, B.E.F.

1.11.14 We start to make barbed-wire fence, but the fire is too hot. The OC (Major North) is shot dead whilst giving directions for repairing entanglements between the trenches. The Colonel (Colonel

Boys) was severely wounded yesterday. During the morning we dig ourselves into the earth and in the afternoon prepare barbed wire which is erected at night. Very heavy fighting all day and we are surrounded by our own and French artillery. The noise is deafening. Some sappers wounded.

2.11.14 Cannot shift from our holes in the ground on account of rifle fire and get ready to move at a moment's notice. Late in the afternoon we prepare entanglements in the wood. At about 8 p.m. we go up to erect it. A moonlight night, and the Germans spot us. They open rapid fire and we have to run. Result – some casualties.

Father Camille Delaere, Curé of the Church of St Jacques. Extract from his diary

3.11.14 Today, 3rd November, the first shells fell on the hospital of Notre Dame causing terrible damage. Arthur Debos was mortally wounded. He died a few minutes after receiving extreme unction.

While I was looking after some French soldiers in the First Aid post which has been set up in the girls' school a huge shell fell nearby. The nurses were seized with terror. It fell in my own garden and made a huge hole, demolished a part of the cloister wall, felled or uprooted trees, blew the broken branches a great distance and broke the tiles of the vicarage and all round about. The people who were most frightened have already left the town. Those who stay are taking shelter in cellars or in the casemates of the ramparts.

Gnr. C. B. Burrows, 104 Battery, 22nd Brigade, R.F.A., 7th Division, B.E.F.

November 4th. 5.30 a.m. We are being shelled again heavily, mostly by light guns. We shelter in a wood. Weather is dull again. Heard that the 3rd Cavalry Division had made a charge on our left and captured 4 guns and also a Brigadier-General and about 50 prisoners, but that may only be a rumour, as I cannot imagine the cavalry charging the enemy when they are so strongly represented. The enemy attack very strongly towards dusk and we reply with every available gun and shell them heavily until about 10 p.m. Their attack failed. The infantry fire all the night. Plenty of shells coming over but no damage to us. Another stand up sleep in the rain! 16th day of Battle.

Cpl. A. Letyford, 5th Field Company, Royal Engineers, 2nd Division, B.E.F.

4.11.14 The terrible battle still continues. The French made bayonet charges yesterday. Unable to leave our holes until night. We dig trenches in pouring rain.

Father Camille Delaere, Curé of the Church of St Jacques. Extract from his diary

4.11.14 The shells cause many victims and the aid posts move back further from the Front. The exodus of inhabitants continues. The employees of the church, the clerk, the organist, the choir boys, have all gone. There is only one person left to serve Mass, and I have to make do with that.

   Since yesterday the wounded soldiers have been taken further away. Only wounded German prisoners are still at the hospital of Notre Dame. The great shells continue to rain down. A cow in a barn and a horse in its stable were killed at the farm of Nestor Boudry. Oscar Seghers was killed, also a woman. Many, many wounded. Many soldiers hit.

Gnr. C. B. Burrows, 104 Battery, 22nd Brigade, R.F.A., 7th Division, B.E.F.

November 5th. 5 a.m. After trying all night to get some sleep we are wet through – still pouring! Plenty of firing on our right but a bit quiet on our front. Our Battery starts firing at 9 a.m. Heard we expect to advance a little today. A big shell burst amongst us about 2 p.m. and we are again lucky. Only a trumpeter wounded (he was about 15 years old) and three drivers wounded and some horses hit. Heard that the Guards Brigade and the 3rd Cavalry Division are to counter-attack this afternoon about 4 p.m. Dozens of these heavy shells, which we call Jack Johnsons, burst all around us. Awful time! Never thought any of us would get out alive. 3 men and 6 horses killed. We managed to get away with this slight loss, but what a scramble! It was like being in hell. There are great holes in the ground made by the heavy shells. We go to another field but they spot us and shell again. We shift to yet another field. A bit better here, but they still send them over nearby all night and we have some narrow shaves. Try to get some sleep on some wet straw in a ditch. The hottest Guy Fawkes night I ever had! 17th Day of Battle.

Father Camille Delaere, Curé of the Church of St Jacques. Extract from his diary

5.11.14 The bombardment of the town starts up about 9 o'clock and never stops. There were many fresh victims. Joseph Notebaert, a good family man, had his hand cut off, his two elder children killed, the three others wounded.

Gnr. C. B. Burrows, 104 Battery, 22nd Brigade, R.F.A., 7th Division, B.E.F.

November 6th. 5 a.m. We take our guns to another position in a turnip field. Weather very misty. Enemy still find our wagon line and shell us heavily, but with only light shell. No damage. They shell Ypres all the afternoon with heavy shells. The carnage is awful. Dead men and horses everywhere and whole villages are wrecked by shell fire from the enemy. The roads have huge craters which make them almost impassable. We move to another position about 10 p.m. Another stand-up sleep. 18th Day of Battle.

Cpl. A. Letyford, 5th Field Company, Royal Engineers, 2nd Division, B.E.F.

6.11.14 A Germany battery gets in rear of us and gives us a hot time. Two sappers blown to pieces in the next dugout and Sergeant Blanche is killed. At night we man the trenches with the Connaught Rangers and stay all night, returning about 6.30 next morning.

Father Camille Delaere, Curé of the Church of St Jacques. Extract from his diary

6.11.14. Last night – what a terrible night. The choir of St Martin was damaged. Houses have tumbled down in all the streets. Today the bombardment has never stopped. People don't dare go into the streets. There are terrible sights everywhere. Towards 14.00 hours a huge shell fell in the cemetery of St Pierre and the vibration of the explosion broke all the windows in that part of town. The shells cause tremendous damage.

Cpl. A. Letyford, 5th Field Company, Royal Engineers, 2nd Division, B.E.F.

7.11.14 Off again at 7.30 to a wood nearer the trenches where we are shelled heavily and get more casualties. Return at 3 p.m. and at 5.30 go up with the Connaughts again and man the trenches all night returning at daybreak when the Worcesters relieved us.

Gnr. C. B. Burrows, 104 Battery, 22nd Brigade, R.F.A., 7th Division, B.E.F.

November 7th. Again being shelled about 5 a.m. Still misty. The infantry are very busy. Expect we soon will be also. The enemy attack strongly on our right. Horrible smell caused by dead men and horses which are lying everywhere. Ypres burning furiously – flames and smoke reach a great height. We expect a big attack soon. Heavy artillery duels all day and heavy fighting all night on our left. We are still being shelled. No damage. Another stand-up sleep by our horses. 19th Day of Battle.

Father Camille Delaere, Curé of the Church of St Jacques. Extract from his diary

7.11.14 This Saturday evening the sisters of the hospital Notre Dame left for Poperinghe taking their sick and wounded civilian patients who were in the English aid posts. Fifty-six wounded German soldiers were left in the care of four French soldier-priests.

The evening was quite terrifying. The incendiary shells mixed with shrapnel shells started fires all over the centre of the town and many of our loveliest buildings were destroyed. I went out under the falling shrapnel with my devoted vicar, Monsieur Leys, through the burning streets to see where we might be of use – black sky, intense heat, flames like red clouds thrown up by a storm – sublime among the horror – the flames leaping, the beams of the houses crashing down. More than once in the course of our journey through the streets the insupportable heat blistered our faces.

There was no water, no manpower to help to put the fires out and the shells went on whistling down. The very sky was on fire. The flames were leaping everywhere and our lovely buildings were turned into volcanoes. The corners of the rue du Temple and of the rue au Beurre are completely destroyed by fire. Many more at Leet, in the Grande Place, in the rue de Lille and the rue de Dixmude. A shell fell on the church of the Carmelite Fathers and another on the cathedral.

Gnr. C. B. Burrows, 104 Battery, 22nd Brigade, R.F.A., 7th Division, B.E.F.

November 8th. 5 a.m. Move to another position. They still shell and we have to move again at 9 a.m. The enemy attack strongly along our front. Our battery is shelling heavily and we get plenty back. They keep up the attack all night. 20th Day of Battle.

Father Camille Delaere, Curé of the Church of St Jacques. Extract from his diary

8.11.14. Sunday. The hurricane of shells continues. An enormous hole is torn out at the corner of the rue des Boudeurs. Two houses are collapsed, the bricks and even the paving stones thrown up in the air crash down on all the other houses round about. The exodus of inhabitants continues.

Gnr. C. B. Burrows, 104 Battery, 22nd Brigade, R.F.A., 7th Division, B.E.F.

November 9th. 5 a.m. We have orders to move at any moment as the enemy are attacking furiously. Our battery is very lucky. We have one gunner killed this morning. Weather still dull, cold and misty. Still fierce fighting. Heard that Ypres is being deserted by the inhabitants. Thousands of French infantry on the move at 2 p.m. Enemy redouble their attack and we catch it hot. We are again lucky and only have 1 driver wounded and a few horses killed. Pouring with rain and no rest all night. 21st Day of Battle.

Father Camille Delaere, Curé of the Church of St Jacques. Extract from his diary

9.11.14 For nine days now there has been shelling, for nine days people have been leaving. There is a tragic air about the town now. For two days now we have been without meat and without bread. Many, many houses have been completely destroyed by fire because of the absence of the fire brigade. There is looting all over the place. At the initiative of the Dean some devoted men form a committee to look after the well-being of the people who remain, first and foremost to try to feed the town, to try to save homes from destruction by fire and to prevent theft.

The force of the shells on the Place Van den Peereboom in front of the cathedral was so tremendous that the tramway rails were cut clean off and blown some distance away. An enormous hole appeared in the street, so big that you could hardly say where it ended. It covered at least fifty square metres. Four of the Sisters came back to Ypres to fetch some of their belongings. The wounded Germans were still there and they begged them not to leave them – so two of the Sisters stayed and two returned to Poperinghe.

Gnr. C. B. Burrows, 104 Battery, 2nd Brigade, R.F.A., 7th Division, B.E.F.

November 10th. Enemy still attack. A few shells drop near us. Fierce fighting on our right. They shell us heavily all afternoon, but they nearly all dropped short and caused us no damage.

Father Camille Delaere, Curé of the Church of St Jacques. Extract from his diary

10.11.14. Tuesday. A great calm fell. Shells were few and far between, but towards 10 o'clock this morning one did fall and lifted a part of the masonry of the new sacristy which is being constructed at my church. I ran with my faithful vicar, Monsieur Leys. We were in the church assessing the damage when suddenly there was another tremendous explosion. The church was instantly filled with a thick white cloud of plaster-dust so that we could not even see each other. I seized my vicar by the shoulder and pushed him to the ground. When the rumbling stopped we got up. There were six of us in the church.

The crashing of the shells, of wood, of stone blocks blown in every direction with a terrible force had virtually broken the building apart – holed, broken, destroyed – everything reduced to nothing! Of the six people who happened to be in the church not a single one was hurt. What a strange thing! A huge part of the apse has disappeared. The altar of St Sacremont and the high altar were buried in a mass of rubble.

Through a hole torn in the roof of the apse I saw that the roof beams had taken fire. Very soon an emergency fire brigade was organised – quite rudimentary – without ladders, without pumps and almost without water. Our efforts were crowned with some success and my church escaped being burned down. We spent a good part of the afternoon sifting through the rubble looking for the Blessed Host.

In the evening my vicar and I are in the little cellar of my bombarded vicarage. It is some days now since my servants left the town. We take our meals at the convent with the nuns and spend the nights in my little cellar.

The Carmelite Fathers, who are our confessors, have all gone from the town, so my vicar asked if he might make his confession to me (was this a presentiment?). Afterwards I made my own confession to him. When I had finished he spoke beautiful, comforting words, recommending me to resign myself to the Will of God in life and in death.

Gnr. C. B. Burrows, 104 Battery, 22nd Brigade, R.F.A., 7th Division, B.E.F.

10th November. Raining again. They attack again at dusk. It quietens down before midnight. 22nd Day of Battle.

Cpl. A. Letyford, 5th Field Company, Royal Engineers, 2nd Division, B.E.F.

10.11.14. The Section go out at night to blow up a house in No Man's Land, but are unable to get at it, the enemy having taken possession.

The Germans had every intention of taking possession of Ypres next day, and they had crept out as close as possible to the line to give themselves a head start. At midnight a hush fell around the salient and over the battered town below. Beneath its deserted streets, under the crumbling houses, people lay fearful and listening in dark cellars. There was nothing to hear but the occasional squeak of a rat and the whistling of the wind that rose in the early hours and tore through the debris of the ruined town, bringing down chimneys that swayed on a fragment of wall, wrenching at shutters that hung from a single nail. As Delaere and Leys knelt praying together and resigned themselves to the Will of God, and the soldiers keeping watch in the salient shivered, cursing the wind and the rain, the Kaiser's troops were bracing themselves for action in the morning. This time they were strengthened by reinforcements of picked troops. The Kaiser's élite 4th Division and the Kaiser's Guards were moving up for the final phase of the battle that would win the Kaiser's victory. Their orders were to '*drive back and crush the enemy*'.

At dawn the wind dropped and the rain went off. The morning was grey, misty and strangely quiet. With the dull fatigue of habit the gunners of 104 Battery roused before daylight and waited. Nothing happened. The cooks brewed up and doled out two dry biscuits to each man. Charlie Burrows reached for the stub of pencil in his tunic pocket and, as was now his habit, began the day by scribbling in his diary while he gulped the lukewarm tea.

Gnr. C. B. Burrows, 104 Battery, 22nd Brigade, R.F.A., 7th Division, B.E.F.

November 11th. 4.30 a.m. All quiet for once. Expect they are fed up attacking . . .

The bombardment began two hours later. By nine o'clock it had built up to a crescendo the like of which no living soldier had ever heard before. There was nothing to be done but to crouch in trenches, in ditches, in hollows, in any hole or cranny in the quaking earth that could offer the slightest shelter from the inferno of tumbling shells; to stomach it, to stick it out, to wait and to hope – but without much hope – that when the shelling stopped and the enemy came on they would be fit and ready to fight. Inevitably there were casualties, but there might have been many more. The Germans had ranged large numbers of their guns on a line immediately behind the British Front in order to prevent reserves from coming up to reinforce it. They had no idea that there were no reserves to speak of.★

★ The shelling did, however, discommode the Fighting Staffs whose headquarters were very close to the line. At Beukenhorst Château (later known to the troops as 'Stirling Castle') just down the Menin road, Brigadier-General Count Gleichen answered a polite knock on his bedroom door early in the morning and was startled to see his Brigade Major, naked but for a skimpy towel clutched round his middle, with his uniform over his arm. 'Do you mind if I finish dressing in here?' he asked. 'The blighters are shelling the bathroom.' The story of this admirable *sangfroid* was repeated with relish by Count Gleichen and in due course was immortalised in a *Punch* cartoon.

In front of Polygon Wood, across the fields between it and the Menin road almost every man was standing to, and all that stood behind them were the guns with a pitiful dole of shrapnel shells to back up the rifles of the infantry.

When the bombardment lifted and the enemy began to stream across the fields the gunners and the infantry began to shoot.

Just as they had been two months earlier at Mons the 4th Battalion, The Royal Fusiliers, were in the forefront of the fighting, standing directly in the enemy's path at the strongest point of their advance. They attacked along nine miles of Front – but it was on the Menin road that the line gave way.

Cpl. W. Holbrook, No. 13599, 4th Bttn., The Royal Fusiliers, 9th Brigade, 3rd Division, B.E.F.

They do silly things! We were on the right of the Menin road, and the Menin road itself was held by French Zouaves – the worst possible troops to stand shellfire. We had no trenches of course. The shelling was so near to you that you could feel the heat of these bursting shrapnel shells on your body as you were lying there, it was so close.

On the way up I'd seen a Guards NCO. We were resting on the side of the road, so I said, 'What's it like up there, Sarge?' – I didn't know how to pronounce the damn place! 'Boy,' he said, 'a dog couldn't live in it!' He was damn right about that.

We'd had a draft from England, two hundred men. We were about five hundred strong then. We had about thirty or so officers the night before. By nine a.m. on 11 November we had thirty-four men left. Not a single officer. Well, the Colonel got killed there; Colonel McMahon – he'd just been made a general then. We lost all our officers, except one, a fellow named O'Donnell. I didn't know where they'd gone. You see the few who were left occupied a front of four or five hundred yards and it's all thickets and bits of wood. I knew where I was facing but there wasn't a soul near me. They'd been killed and wounded, and we were driven back.

It was the Zouaves who had given way – but it was hardly their fault. They were one of two battalions lent by the French to Sir Douglas Haig and the previous evening they had asked urgently for the Zouaves to be returned. Haig had sent one battalion back, but he held on to the other to stiffen the line on the Menin road. The Zouaves were not the best troops he could obtain. They were the only ones. And Haig had no alternative, for here in front of Gheluvelt at the apex of the salient the line was thinner, weaker, shakier, than anywhere else along the Front. They had done their best to spread out such men as there were, and there they stood, some seven thousand strong, in twos and threes – if they were lucky in holes in the ground five yards or more apart, or, if they were less lucky, lying in the open behind a tree, a hump, a hillock. As the shells rained down, some eighteen thousand soldiers, the pick of the Kaiser's Army, were gathering and making ready to attack.

They poured down from Gheluvelt astride the Menin road, streamed across the fields towards the woods, dashed through the gap where the Zouaves had broken and the Royal Fusiliers had been forced back and, rearing grey out of the mist in the foggy aftermath of the bombardment, got round behind the Cameron Highlanders, before they even realised that the enemy was on the move. There were so few of the Camerons and so few officers to lead them into the fight that without regard for companies or platoons they had merely been split into two parts and placed along the line. They called each part a 'half-battalion' – but each comprised a hundred and sixty men. And all there were besides, to meet the Germans as they came, were two hundred Scots Guards, a company and a half of the Black Watch and, spread across the mile-long edge of Polygon Wood, 450 men of the 1st King's under six remaining officers. But they drove the Germans back.

As the wind got up and the mist cleared, the King's looked out from their battered ditch and the click of rifle bolts rattled along the line as they steadied to beat off a second attack. But the shapeless mass they saw stretching across the field was not a line of soldiers massing to advance. It was a line of heaped-up bodies and a mass of German dead.

No single German soldier had reached Polygon Wood. But they had gone to Nonnebosschen – Nun's Wood – the copse a stone's throw to their right. A little later, the powers-that-be, with one eye cast back in retrospect and one cast forward, with some imagination, to posterity, chose to name the fighting of that day the Battle of Nonnebosschen. It was here that the battle was won. It was here that the battle – and the war itself – was very nearly lost.

There is nothing behind Nonnebosschen. Only the few men who had been kept back in reserve, only the Headquarters' detachments, only the cooks and the signallers, the drivers, the transport men, the sappers, the quartermasters, the grooms, the walking wounded, the skrimshankers, the unfit. Only a row of guns – and most of them, having shortened to point-blank range, had fallen silent. They were silent because the gunners were out in front and they were shooting now with rifles to beat the Germans back. In the valley behind Nonnebosschen every man who could raise a rifle was firing, and he was firing rapid, reloading, and firing rapid again – and again – and again.

The enemy faltered, hesitated, and turned back.

And then the Tommies counter-attacked, charged into the wood and beat the Germans out. They beat them out as if they were beating pheasants and when they emerged from the further side, running much like pheasants from a covert, the King's ranged on the flank at Polygon Wood, and the remnants of the Camerons on their right, took aim and coolly picked them off.

It was the Ox and Bucks who charged through the wood. And on their left, Alex Letyford with the 5th Field Company, The Royal Engineers, charged across the open ground between Polygon Wood and Nonne-bosschen and helped to drive the Germans back.

The attack dwindled away. The Kaiser's Prussian Guards gave up.

It was the last serious attack of the First Battle of Ypres and there was one man at least who realised that the Germans had blundered. He was a wounded Prussian officer, picked up late in the afternoon by British stretcher bearers. The awful truth struck him as they carried him from the wood. He raised himself painfully on one elbow and looked at the line of guns, so close ahead. 'What is beyond there?' he asked. The reply came smartly back, 'Corps Headquarters'. 'God Almighty!' said the German officer. He slumped back on the stretcher. '*Gott Allemachtig!*' he said again. He realised, as no one else had done, that with one more infinitesimal effort the Germans would have won the day, and possibly the war.

It was truly a day to remember, and days later Corporal Matheson of the Camerons, writing home to his father in Nairn, was still full of it.

Cpl. G. Matheson, B Company, 1st Bttn., The Cameron Highlanders, B.E.F.

Well I think the Regiment has made a name for itself in this campaign. We have been in the most desperate fighting and gave a good account of ourselves. We had the Prussian Guards break through on our right somewhere. Well, first of all they shelled right along our trenches for two hours. It was pure hell, and we could do nothing – only keep under cover. As soon as a man showed himself over he went. Then there was a slight lull in the shellfire, and behold, when we looked round there were the Germans coming over the fields behind us. We got up and rushed into them, but they were too strong for us, so we had to retire into a wood behind our trenches. It was a race between them and us to get this wood – the Germans were also making for it, as our guns were behind the wood. However, we got to the guns first and when the Germans *did* come out of the wood, they got it, between rifle fire, shell and the bayonet. Not one of them got back to tell the tale. That saw off the Prussian Guards, but, to give them their due, they were brave men. They were all big men. I did not see a man that day less than 6 feet. After this was all over, we started to look for one another and D Company was missing; and I'm afraid they have been done in. Of course we can't say, as we did not get the trenches back when we were relieved the following day.

Cpl. A. Letyford, 5th Field Company, Royal Engineers, 2nd Division, B.E.F.

11.11.14. At nine we suddenly have to take up arms. The enemy has broken through! We man an old trench in the rear of the wood. The enemy approach and we begin to bowl them over. After a while we charge and drive them nearly back to their original position. Only about 110 of us in the charge against some hundreds of Prussian Guard. We suffered rather severely. The new OC (Major Jas. Collins) and Renny Tailour killed and Lt. Vibair wounded, leaving us with one officer. Many sappers were killed and a lot wounded. We get back to our bivvy at night very late, after the infantry have taken up position.

Cpl. George Matheson, B Company, 1st Bttn., The Cameron Highlanders, B.E.F.

We were complaining about the Aisne being bad, but it was a king to the fighting we have done since we came to Belgium. This is pure murder, not war. Major Craig Brown was left in the trenches, and after darkness he got away along with three men, and they say that the Germans were taking no prisoners that day, killing everybody. Now Captain Brodie's death was rather strange. He went through the wood after we had driven the Germans out and we think it must have been a wounded German lying beside where Brodie was that saw him off. At least the German did not last long after Brodie was found. From all accounts the wounded Germans lying about were firing on our chaps when they were collecting the wounded, so that shows what sort of crowd the Germans were!*

We have had some very trying experiences.

* Captain Ewan Brodie was the Laird of Lethen in Nairn. After the war a body was found in the place where he fell but it was not possible to identify it positively and it was buried as that of an unknown officer. However a private memorial was erected and still stands on the spot on the northern edge of Glencorse Wood.

Cpl. W. Holbrook, No. 13599, 4th Bttn., The Royal Fusiliers,
9th Brigade, 3rd Division, B.E.F.

After a while I came across some more of our fellows and one officer, Captain O'Donnell and about thirty men and one sergeant and the Sergeant-Major, Sergeant-Major Saville, and Sergeant Harris. Once we'd got together and were deciding what to do, a German officer came crawling through the bushes. When he saw us he said, 'I am wounded' – perfect English. He was wounded in his thigh. O'Donnell said to him, 'You shouldn't make these bloody attacks, then you wouldn't get wounded!' It gave us a laugh! Anyway we bandaged him up, waited on there and shortly afterwards O'Donnell got killed by a stray bullet, so we had no officers then. All you could hear was some firing going on, but I didn't know where the devil I was really. There was another fellow I knew there – name of Cainici, he was a London Italian, he was a real Cockney he was, I used to like him. Of course he was surprised to see me and I was surprised to see him. I says, 'Hello Cainy' and he says, 'Wotcher, Bill, how are you doing?' I said, 'Do you know where anyone else, is?' 'No,' he says, 'I haven't seen a soul!' While we was there they starting shelling pretty heavy with shrapnel shell and suddenly he shouted out in pain, 'Ooh,' he said, 'that's hot!' I always remember I was lying right next to him in this cover when this shell burst and it hit a sapling, and broke this sapling in half and he shouted out and grabbed his knee. I said, 'Have you got hit?' So I looked at it. The khaki was cut of course, so I tore it away and just a fraction inside his knee I could see a steel ball, steel shrapnel ball. So I said, 'I can see it, Cainy, shall I get it out?' So he said, 'If you like.' This is the solid truth, I got his jack-knife and dug round and got the knife under the ball and flicked it out. He got up and cleared off, dragging the leg behind him.

I thought, well I don't know, I've got to find a better place than this. So I crawled about and found a bit of a shell-hole for the night – it's November, it's getting a bit dark at four. Suddenly I heard these twigs break, somebody moving only about a foot or so from me. I looked down and I saw a German's head appear in a shell-hole just by me. They wore flat caps in those days. I'd got an entrenching tool handle, so just as I was going to get it out and make a dive for him I heard him groaning and I thought, Perhaps the poor devil's wounded. So I looked, and I'll never forget that fellow's eyes. He said, '*Wasser. Wasser.*' So I knew that was water, in fact that was about the only German word I knew. So I got my water bottle, held it to his lips and gave him some water. He was lying on his back and as I poured it into his mouth it was coming out of a hole in his side, blood and water. This is the honest truth, it was oozing out of a hole in his side. So we lay there a bit and he kept asking for water and every now and again I gave him some water. Then he said to me, '*Kleine Kinder.*' He'd got three – he held up three fingers. Well, he died, I suppose, about two o'clock in the morning. I covered him over with leaves and twigs, anything I could scoop up just there. I kept there till the morning, then I could hear where the firing was by then and I knew which direction I could go, so I crawled back.

Quarter-master Sergeant Gordon Fisher, 1st Bttn., The Hertfordshire Regt., B.E.F.

As soon as the Territorials arrived, we were rushed up in London general omnibuses to stop the gap in the line. It was the night of 11th November, midnight when we got to Ypres. The Cloth Hall was burning. There was flames coming out the top of it and it was all on fire. As we marched through, a French regiment was marching down on the other side of the road and and as soon as they heard a shell coming over they all dived into the gutter. I thought, Why are they doing that? – but I very soon learnt to do the same. My first reaction was, Doesn't it look pretty! Just like fireworks. It didn't occur to me that it was lethal. That was in the main square and the sky was lurid with these fires.

We marched through the town and up the Menin road to Hellfire Corner and I was told to wait there with half a dozen men with the tool-cart while the Battalion moved up light into the line.

There was a soldier there, wounded, resting on his way back. He was a Staffordshire, and when he looked at my shoulder strap he was amazed. He said, 'Good God! A Territorial?' I said, 'Yes, that's right.' 'Well,' he said, 'I don't care who you are. I've been seventeen days up the Front there and I don't care *who* comes out as long as they give us a hand.'

Sgt. Cecil Lancaster, 1st (London) Field Company, Royal Engineers (T.F.)

They sent us straight up to Ypres when we got to France, straight up into the line, and on the way in we passed my brother's regiment fell out on the side of the road. They'd just come out of an engagement

– a rough engagement by the look of them. I called over and I said, 'Are you the Ox and Bucks?' A fellow shouted, 'Yes.' So I said, 'Have you got a boy there, name of Freddie Lancaster?' He said, 'We did have, but we left him up there blown to smithereens.' I thought, Good God, my brother's gone. What will Mother say? (Because he *would* go in the Army, you know, and she never liked it.) Then another chap called out, 'What did you say the name was?' I said, 'Lancaster. My brother, Fred. A young chap, only nineteen.' He said, 'There he is, over there, laying in the ditch.' And there he was – asleep! Dirty, muddy, uniform all torn.

We kissed each other. I didn't know he was there, he didn't know *I* was there, me being a Territorial. I said, 'How are you getting on?' He said, 'We've had a rough'un, but we're all right.'

I had gold in my pocket, because I'd just got paid from work, so I gave him half a sovereign to treat himself and he gave me a twist of tobacco. It was all he had, because they didn't have nothing, only their rifles. They'd lost everything. There'd be thirty or forty of them I suppose, maybe fifty or sixty. No more. I said to him, 'Where's the rest of your mob then?' He said, 'There *isn't* no more. They've all copped it.'

Gnr. C. B. Burrows, 104 Battery, 22nd Brigade, R.F.A., 7th Division, B.E.F.

November 13th. We came out of action at 5.30 p.m. and things have calmed down a little. Heard we are going to a rest camp to be overhauled and to get our strength made up. We need it very much and are not sorry to get away from the Ypres sector. We march down the Menin road and pass by Ypres which is still being shelled. March 7 miles on, stop at a farm, sleep in a barn. The best sleep for a month. 25th and last day of battle in which we lost our Major, Captain, two section officers, Sergeant Major, two sergeants and about 20 NCOs and gunners, besides 20 drivers and about 50 horses, also our trumpeter. A very dear price to pay, but that I suppose is war. I count myself very lucky.

Cpl. George Mattheson, B Coy, 1st Bttn, The Queen's Own Cameron Highlanders, B.E.F.

We are now in billets 20 miles behind Ypres in a small village. It was a sorry-looking battalion that came back for our first rest since we came out here. We are in the 1st Guards Brigade, as you know, so that we do not get much rest in that brigade. Well, you may know that out of the 1,100 officers and men that came out at the start we have Major Yeadon and about 80 men left.

I believe you have plenty soldiers at home. Well, we could do with a few here. That is all that is needed here.

The battle was all but finished. Winter was setting in. The Germans continued to make desultory attacks, but 11 November had seen the end of the serious fighting. It was exactly ninety-nine days since the war had begun and four years to the day before it would be over. Long before then Ypres was reduced to rubble – but in a sense the city survived. The Germans never took it. The salient held. The line stood.

Hard battles lay ahead, but they would be fought by other men. The Old Army was finished. The battles of Mons, Le Cateau, the Marne, the Aisne and Ypres had already passed into history – and most of the men who had fought them were dead and gone.

Part Five
Epitaph

The gallant old 'Contemptibles'! There isn't much remains of them,
So full of fun and fitness, and a-singing in their pride;
For some are cold as clabber and the corby picks the brains of them,
And some are back in Blighty, and a-wishing they had died.

Robert Service

Chapter 27

It was clear now that the war would not be won by Christmas when Britain had so confidently expected to be celebrating victory – but it was not immediately obvious that an era had ended. The cut and thrust of old-style warfare, the beguiling panoply of flashing swords, the glittering lances, of flying pennants, the sound of drums and bugles, the hammer of hooves, the dash and glory of the charge – all these were not entirely dead, but they had begun their dying. So too had feudal concepts of service and duty, for so long bred in the bone.

By the end of 1914, the Army had suffered 90 per cent casualties. Of course, they were not all dead. There were many, like Private Godley who defended the bridge at Mons, like the Gordons left behind at Le Cateau, who were captured and marched off to long imprisonment in Germany. Many of the wounded recovered, like Rory Macleod, and in due course returned to the war. And there was a nucleus of surviving officers and men to help turn a happy-go-lucky mob of civilians into soldiers and to form the backbone of the citizens' armies when eventually they took the field. But the Regulars were finished as a single fighting force.

Debrett's *Peerage* did not appear as it usually did in early spring; so many sons of the aristocracy were dead, so many baronets, and lords, and knights, so many heirs to great lands and titles had been killed, that it took the editors many months to revise the entries of almost every blue-blooded family in the United Kingdom. The Grosvenors, the Worsleys, the Desboroughs, Gordon-Lennoxes, Crichtons, Dawnays, Fitzclarences, Cecils and Cholmeleys, Manners and Wellesleys – the list went on and on. When it finally did appear, the 1915 edition of Debrett made very sorry reading.

The Smiths, the Browns, the Robinsons, the Jones and the Atkins had suffered too. But their losses, though they shocked the Empire, appeared merely as statistics. Killed 8,631. Missing 40,342. Wounded 37,264. By the end of the year the casualties, including officers, amounted to ninety thousand men.

The heady days were not quite over, but henceforth it would be a different kind of war. The thin line of troops was settling down for the winter, strengthening the line, burrowing like animals into the earth. There, much like animals, they would live or they would die, in the miseries and dangers of the trenches. All that was over by Christmas was the first wild wave of illusion. A grim awareness began to dawn that this war would be won by grit and not by glory.

Bibliography
Author's Note
Index

Bibliography

Military Operations, France and Belgium, 1914, Vol. 1, by Brigadier-General Sir James E. Edmonds (Macmillan, 1923).

Military Operations France and Belgium, 1914, Vol. 2, by Brigadier-General Sir James E. Edmonds (Macmillan, 1925).

History of the Great War. Transportation on the Western Front, compiled by Col. A. M. Henniker, CBE, RE Retd. (H. M. Stationery Office, 1937).

The Oxfordshire Hussars in the Great War (1914–1918), by Adrian Keith-Falconer (John Murray, 1927).

The History of the Second Division, 1914–1918, Vol. 1, 1914–1916, by Everard Wyrall (Thomas Nelson, 1921).

The History of the XII Royal Lancers, by P. F. Stewart, -MC (Oxford University Press, 1950).

The Coldstream Guards, 1914–1918, by Sir John Ross of Bladensburgh, KCB, KCVO (Oxford University Press).

The Record of the Coldstream Guards, 1650–1918 (Regimental Headquarters, 1923).

History of the Northumberland (Hussars) Yeomanry, 1819–1923, by Howard Pease, MA (Constable, 1924).

The Worcestershire Regiment in the Great War, by Captain H. FitzM. Stacke (Privately published, 1928).

The History of the Rifle Brigade in the War of 1914–1918, Vol. I, August 1914–December 1916, by Reginald Berkeley, MC (The Rifle Brigade Club, 1927).

The Royal Regiment of Artillery at Le Cateau, by Major A. F. Becke (Royal Artillery Institution, 1919).

Gunners at War, by Shelford Bidwell (Arms and Armour Press, 1970).

'Fifteen Rounds a Minute': The Grenadiers at War, 1914, by J. M. Craster (Macmillan, 1976).

War in the Air: The History of the Royal Flying Corps, Vols. 1 and 2.

The Supreme Command, 1914–1918. Vol. I, by Lord Hankey (George Allen & Unwin, 1961).

The World Crisis, 1911–1914, by Winston S. Churchill. (Thornton Butterworth, 1923).

My War Memories, 1914–1918, by General Ludendorff (Hutchinson).

1914, by Field Marshal Viscount French of Ypres (Constable, 1919).

Experiences of a Dug-Out, 1914–1918, by Major-General Sir C. E. Callwell, KCB (Constable, 1920).

The Marne – and After, by A. Corbett-Smith (Cassell, 1917).

The Night of August 3–4, 1914, at the Belgian Foreign Office, by Baron Alfred de Bassompierre (Hodder & Stoughton, 1916).

Milestones to the Silver Jubilee, edited by H. C. Dent (Halcyon Book Co., 1935).

The Retreat from Mons, by A. Corbett-Smith (Cassell, 1916).

From Mons to Loos, by Major H. A. Stewart, DSO (Wm. Blackwood, 1917).

From Private to Field Marshal, by Sir William Robertson (Constable, 1921)

Students Under Arms, by Alexander Rule, MC, MA (Aberdeen, The University Press, 1934).

Brodick Arran and the Great War, by James C. Inglis (Oliver and Boyd, 1919).

Bermondsey's 'Bit' in the Great War, by Henry Fuller Morriss (The Clifton Publishing House and Richard J. James).

A Hilltop on the Marne: Correspondence of Mildred Aldrich (Constable, 1915).

On the Edge of the War Zone: Correspondence of Mildred Aldrich (Constable, 1921).

Charles Sackville Pelham, Lord Worsley, by his father (Privately published, October 1924).

King Edward VII, by Christopher Hibbert (Allen Lane, 1976).

King George V, by Kenneth Rose (Weidenfeld and Nicolson, 1983).

The Last Kaiser, by Tyler Whittle (William Heinemann, 1977).

From Hell to the Himalayas, by Col. C. F. Hodgson (King and Wilks, 1983).

Liaison 1914, by Brigadier-General E. L. Spears (William Heinemann, 1930).

A History of Europe, by H. A. L. Fisher (Edward Arnold, 1949).

Twentieth-Century Germany: From Bismarck to Brandt, by A. J. Ryder (Macmillan, 1973).

The Phantom Brigade, by A. P. G. Vivian (Ernest Benn, 1930).

The History of the Great European War, Vol. 1., by W. Stanley Macbean Knight (Caxton Publishing Co.).

O Beloved Kids. Rudyard Kipling's Letters to His Children, edited by Elliot L. Gilbert (Weidenfeld & Nicolson, 1983).

A Record of the Year's Work, by Lt.-Col. R. B. Crosse (Privately printed, (1953).

Forty Days in 1914, by Maj.-Gen. Sir. F. Maurice (Constable, 1921).

My Four Years in Germany, by James W. Gerard (Hodder & Stoughton, 1917).

I Was There, Vol. I., edited by Sir John Hammerton (The Amalgamated Press, 1914–1915).

Twenty Years After: The Battlefields of 1914–18 Then and Now, Vol. I. edited by Maj.-Gen. Sir Ernest Swinton, KBE, CB, (George Newnes, 1936).

The First Casualty, by Philip Knightley (André Deutsch, 1975).

On the Path of Adventure, by Julius Price (John Lane, 1919).

Alarms and Excursions, by Sir Tom Bridges (Longmans Green & Co., 1938).

Unwilling Passenger, by Arthur Osborn (Faber & Faber, 1926).

The Pageant of the Years, by Sir Philip Gibbs (Wm. Heineman, 1946).

The Press and the General Staff, by Neville Lytton (W. Collins, 1920).

The History of The Times, Vol. 4.

The War Illustrated, Vols 1, 2 & 3. edited by A. J. Hammerton (The Amalgamated Press, 1915).

Little Folks Annual, 1915.

German Atrocities, An Official Investigation, by J. J. Morgan (Fisher Unwin, 1916).

Oorlogsdagboeken over Ieper (1914–1915), by Genootschap Voor Geschiedenis (Brugge, 1974).

Van Den Grooten Oorlog, edited by Elfnovembergroep (Volsboek).

La vie quotidienne de Bapaume dans la première guerre mondiale, by Gaston Degardin (unpublished papers).

Le Temps des Guerres, 1914–1939, by Gerard Boutet (Editions Denoël, 1981).

Author's Note

I should like to acknowledge my debt to the following people without whose much-appreciated assistance this book would not be possible.

Private J. W. Alderson,
Grenadier Guards.
Corporal F. T. Akers,
2nd Battalion, Oxfordshire
and Buckinghamshire Light
Infantry.
Private C. D. Ashby,
4th Battalion, Duke of
Cambridge's Own (Middlesex
Regiment).
Private G. Ashurst,
1st Battalion, The Lancashire
Fusiliers.
Lieutenant F. G. A. Arkwright,
11th (Prince Albert's Own)
Hussars, 1st Cavalry Brigade.
Able Seaman W. J. Austin, RN.
L/Corporal S. F. Bailey,
1st Battalion, The Life
Guards.
Trooper G. O. Barson,
Household Battalion, 2nd
Battalion, The Life Guards.
Trooper Percy Batchelor,
D Squadron, Queen's Own
Oxfordshire Hussars.
Lance-Sergeant J. L. Bouch,
1st Battalion, Coldstream
Guards.
Private H. R. Brown,
2nd Battalion, Royal Marine
Light Infantry.
Private F. Burbeck,
2nd Battalion, Oxfordshire
and Buckinghamshire Light
Infantry.
Private H. J. Berry,
Duke of Wellington's
Regiment.
Sergeant T. Berry,
1st Battalion, The Rifle
Brigade.
Able Seaman J. S. Bentham,

Benbow Battalion, 1st RN
Brigade.
Mrs W. Blackmore
(Maria Van Assche).
Gunner C. B. Burrows,
104 Battery, 22nd Brigade,
R.F.A., 7th Division.
Major D. Bonar,
2nd Battalion, Highland Light
Infantry, 2nd Division.
Rifleman W. Barnard,
The Rifle Brigade.
Sergeant R. Berry, DCM,
1st Battalion, The Rifle
Brigade.
Bombardier B. Bloye,
116 Heavy Battery, Royal
Garrison Artillery.
Signaller G. W. Brown, MBE
(1962), 1st Battalion,
Honourable Artillery
Company.
Captain C. J. D. Church,
1st Battalion, The King's Own
Scottish Borderers.
Rifleman H. W. Cozens, MM,
1st Battalion, Queen's
Westminster Rifles.
Signaller J. Currie,
Royal Field Artillery.
Mrs E. Churchman
(Eva Leach).
Private J. Cole,
2nd Battalion, The
Worcestershire Regiment.
Private H. V. Day,
4th Royal Fusiliers.
Sergeant R. Dickson, MM,
3rd Battalion, Grenadier
Guards.
L/Corporal W. Ellett,
Leicestershire Regiment.
L/Corporal G. England,

3rd Battalion, Grenadier
Guards.
Private A. W. Fenn,
2nd Battalion, The Suffolk
Regiment.
Driver J. J. Field,
1st East Anglian Brigade
Territorials, Royal Field
Artillery.
Quartermaster-Sergeant
Gordon Fisher,
1st Battalion, The
Hertfordshire Regiment.
Private A. B. Foster,
Queen's Own Oxfordshire
Hussars.
Private S. R. Fraser,
The Honourable Artillery
Company.
L/Corporal C. Frost, MM,
1st Battalion, The
Leicestershire Regiment.
Lieutenant E. C. Foulsham,
1st Battalion, Suffolk
Regiment.
Rifleman E. Gale,
1st Battalion, The Rifle
Brigade.
Trooper C. A. Garratt,
1st Derbyshire Yeomanry.
Private W. J. Green,
The London Regiment.
Petty Officer H. Hart,
R.N.A.S.
Captain A. W. Hawes, MC,
Honourable Artillery
Company.
Able Seaman J. Haynes,
Anson Battalion, Royal Naval
Division.
Private F. A. Hill,
Gloucestershire Regiment.
A/Corporal J. Howard,

2nd Battalion, The Rifle
Brigade.

2nd Lieutenant C. F. Hodgson,
122 Battery, XXVIII
Brigade, Royal Field
Artillery.

Corporal W. Holbrook,
No. 13599, 4th Battalion,
Royal Fusiliers.

Private G. Huggins,
D Squadron, 1st Troop,
Queen's Own Oxfordshire
Hussars.

Bugler H. Johnson,
2nd Battalion, Lancashire
Fusiliers.

Private E. C. Kimber,
2nd Battalion, Grenadier
Guards.

Sergeant G. W. Kimble,
Queen's Own Oxfordshire
Hussars.

Captain J. Kirkwood,
Seaforth Highlanders.

Sapper C. Lancaster,
1st London Field Company,
Royal Engineers.

Private E. Lloyd,
1st Battalion, Worcestershire
Regiment.

Private W. Lockey,
1st Battalion, Sherwood
Foresters.

Rifleman H. R. Langley,
16th Battalion, King's Royal
Rifle Corps.

Corporal A. Letyford,
5th Field Company, Royal
Engineers.

E/A John A. Macdonald,
Royal Naval Division.

Private J. Makin,
Royal Marine Light Infantry.

Gunner Maltby, MM,
Royal Field Artillery.

Sub-Lieutenant W. Marlow,
MC,
Howe Battalion, Royal Naval
Division.

Gunner D. N. Meneaud-
Lissenburg,
Royal Horse Artillery.

Sergeant G. W. Maxwell,
2nd Battalion,
Northamptonshire Regiment.

Lieutenant L. J. Miles,
1st Battalion, Essex Regiment.

Private W. Minds,
2nd Battalion, East Lancashire
Regiment.

Private G. E. F. Morgan,

Honourable Artillery
Company.

Corporal E. Moss,
3rd Battalion, Grenadier
Guards.

Trooper F. W. Miller,
1st Battalion, The
Hertfordshire Regiment.

Driver W. Maltby,
3rd Battalion,
Northumberland Fusiliers.

Lieutenant R. A. Macleod,
80th Battery, R. F. A., XV
Brigade, 5th Division.

General Sir G. Macmillan, CB,
KCVO, MC,
Seaforth Highlanders
(Captain).

Sergeant Henry Mann,
Queen's Royal West Surrey
Regiment.

Corporal W. Mann,
Royal Field Artillery.

Sergeant N. Mackechnie,
14th London Regiment
(London Scottish).

Corporal J. H. Marks,
1/1st Battalion, Warwickshire
Regiment.

Corporal G. Matheson,
B Company, 1st Battalion,
The Cameron Highlanders.

Private H. Mellor,
2nd Battalion, The
Manchester Regiment.

Trumpeter J. Naylor,
3rd Division, Royal Field
Artillery.

Lieut-Colonel J. W. Naylor,
Royal Field Artillery.

Major-General Sir R. Neville,
KCMG, CBE,
Royal Marines.

Private F. G. North,
1st Battalion, Lincolnshire
Regiment.

Private Stewart Oncken,
14 London Regiment
(London Scottish).

Sergeant R. E. Owens,
1st Battalion, Royal Welsh
Fusiliers.

Able Seaman B. J. Pearman,
Royal Navy.

Lieutenant B. B. Rackham, MC
and Bar,
Hawke Battalion, Royal Naval
Division.

Corporal G. E. Rippon,
2nd Battalion, King's Own
Yorkshire Light Infantry.

Major C. A. A. Robertson,
1st Battalion, Scots Guards
(Lieut.).

Private W. G. Reynolds,
4th Battalion, Duke of
Cambridge's Own (Middlesex
Regiment).

Wing-Commander W. H. N.
Shakespeare, OBE, MC, AFC,
Royal Flying Corps.

Major R. Smart, MC,
1st Battalion, Worcestershire
Regiment.

Lieut.-General Sir A. Smith,
DSO, MC, Croix de Guerre,
Coldstream Guards.

Sergeant A. Spinks,
Worcestershire Regiment.

Sergeant H. J. Staff,
Essex Regiment.

Private F. Stephens,
1st Battalion, Border
Regiment.

Private R. E. Sutton,
The Rifle Brigade.

Cpl. A. E. Somerset,
3rd Battalion, Grenadier
Guards.

Private C. S. Stevens,
1st Battalion, The
Leicestershire Regiment.

Private J. Simpson,
2nd Battalion, Grenadier
Guards.

Sergeant J. Skuce,
2nd Battalion, Irish Guards.

Bandsman H. V. Shawyer,
1st Battalion, The Rifle
Brigade.

Private E. Slaytor,
3rd Battalion, The Coldstream
Guards.

L/Corporal Edward Organ,
A Squadron, 1st Troop,
Queen's Own Oxfordshire
Hussars.

Guardsman S. L. Perry,
3rd Battalion, Grenadier
Guards.

Rifleman J. A. Pincombe,
1st Battalion, Queen's
Westminster Rifles.

Sergeant H. Smith,
R.A.M.C., attached to 1st
Battalion, King's Own
Yorkshire Light Infantry.

Chaplain E. V. Tanner, MC and
Bar,
2nd Battalion, Worcestershire
Regiment.

Lieutenant F. W. C. Thomas,

2nd Battalion, Suffolk
Regiment.
Sergeant E. E. Turner, MM,
1st Battalion, Queen's Royal
West Surrey Regiment.
Corporal J. Wallace,
Oxfordshire &
Buckinghamshire Light
Infantry.
Trooper H. P. Ward,
Queen's Own Oxfordshire
Hussars.
Sergeant W. Ward, MM,

2nd Battalion, Grenadier
Guards.
Private A. E. West,
Duke of Cambridge's Own
(Middlesex Regiment).
Corporal D. Whittaker,
1st Battalion, King's Royal
Rifle Corps.
Private C. A. Wilson, MM,
1st Battalion, Grenadier
Guards.
Maj.-General D. Wimberley,
CB, SO, MC,

The Queen's Own Cameron
Highlanders.
L/Sergeant G. E. Winterbourne,
1st Battalion, Queen's
Westminster Rifles.
Private J. H. Worker,
1st Battalion, Scots Guards.
Sergeant G. S. W. Yarnall,
14th London Regiment, The
London Scottish.
Captain H. J. Young,
1st Battalion, The Essex
Regiment.

Index